AI-Driven Digital Transformation

This edited volume explores AI-driven digital transformation from the perspective of a well-established higher education institution. Featuring 23 chapters organized into six thematic areas – Decision Support, Data Processing, Marketing and Product Development, Supply Chains, Finance, and Foundational Issues – it provides practical examples of how business school departments can implement AI to foster innovation.

Each chapter presents accessible case studies demonstrating AI applications in business, highlighting both benefits and risks. The volume bridges the gap between AI advancement and practical industry needs, offering actionable insights for integrating AI into decision-making, organizational processes, and curriculum development. Key contributions include demonstrating AI as a strategic enabler, positioning business schools as catalysts for change, recognizing sector-specific impacts, emphasizing ethical foundations, and promoting collaboration between academia, industry, and policymakers. This comprehensive resource equips educators and decision-makers with the knowledge and methods necessary to thrive in the era of AI-driven innovation and serves as a strategic blueprint for business schools to lead AI-driven transformation while maintaining ethical considerations.

AI-Driven Digital Transformation will appeal to scholars and students of AI, technology, innovation management, and business education. It will also be of interest to business school leaders responsible for institutional strategies, educators creating study programs, curriculum specialists, and business leaders seeking AI implementation guidance within their expertise areas.

Witold Abramowicz is a Full Professor at Poznan University of Economics and Business (PUEB), Poland.

Marek Kowalkiewicz is a Professor and Chair in Digital Economy at Queensland University of Technology Business School, Australia.

Krzysztof Węcel is an Associate Professor at the Poznań University of Economics and Business and Chair of the Department of Information Systems, Poland.

Routledge Studies in Central and Eastern European Business and Economics

Drawing together cutting-edge research from across the region, this series presents monographs, edited volumes and 'shortform' books on the full range of issues, themes and topics in Business and Economics pertaining to Central and Eastern Europe (CEE).

Socioeconomic Inequality in Central and Eastern Europe
Multidisciplinary Perspectives on Regional Disparities
Edited by Ewa Wędrowska, Michał Goliński, Tymoteusz Doligalski and Aranka Ignasiak-Szulc

Sustainability Disclosure
Evidence from Mandatory Reporting Regulation in the European Union
Edited by Maria Aluchna, Grażyna Aniszewska-Banaś, Rafał Mrówka, Mikołaj Pindelski, Tomasz Serwański, and Justyna Szumniak-Samolej

Stakeholder Management and Value Co-creation in Museums
Cases from Poland
Magdalena Sawczuk

AI-Driven Digital Transformation
Perspectives from a Business School
Edited by Witold Abramowicz, Marek Kowalkiewicz and Krzysztof Węcel

Tourism and Transport in the Sharing Economy
Strategies for Resource and Service Management
Monika Ziółko, Agata Niemczyk, Zofia Gródek-Szostak, Marek Hendel and Natalia Ziółkowska

www.routledge.com/Routledge-Studies-in-Central-and-Eastern-European-Business-and-Economics/book-series/RSCEEBE

AI-Driven Digital Transformation

Perspectives from a Business School

Edited by Witold Abramowicz,
Marek Kowalkiewicz, and
Krzysztof Węcel

Routledge
Taylor & Francis Group
LONDON AND NEW YORK

First published 2025
by Routledge
4 Park Square, Milton Park, Abingdon, Oxon OX14 4RN

and by Routledge
605 Third Avenue, New York, NY 10158

Routledge is an imprint of the Taylor & Francis Group, an informa business

British Library Cataloguing-in-Publication Data
A catalogue record for this book is available from the British Library

ISBN: 978-1-041-11271-6 (hbk)
ISBN: 978-1-041-11272-3 (pbk)
ISBN: 978-1-003-65914-3 (ebk)

DOI: 10.4324/9781003659143

Typeset in Sabon
by Apex CoVantage, LLC

Contents

Figures

Tables

Boxes

About the Editors

Witold Abramowicz is a full professor at Poznan University of Economics and Business (PUEB), Poland. For 34 years, he was the chair of Department of Information Systems and the head of Doctoral Studies *DaSBA – Data Science for Business and Administration*. Professor Abramowicz is the Head of *SAP Next-Gen Chapter – Data Science*.

His particular areas of interest are AI, data science, and data analytics. He received his M.Sc. from Poznań University of Technology, Ph.D. from Wrocław University of Science and Technology in Poland, and habilitation from Humboldt University of Berlin, Germany. He worked for universities in Switzerland (ETH, Zurich) and Germany (Humboldt University, Berlin) for 12 years. He is an editor, author, or coauthor of 54 books (published mostly by Springer) and over 350 book chapters and articles published in various journals and conference proceedings. He chaired 33 international scientific conferences and was a member of program committees of over 460 other conferences. Professor Abramowicz for 24 years has been the general chair of international conference series *Business Information Systems*. He has been and still is involved – also as coordinator – in twelve research projects in different research frameworks of the European Union, other international projects, and many national founded projects. He supervised 34 Ph.D. dissertations. Professor Abramowicz was professorships' and doctoral theses' reviewer in Australia, Austria, Germany, Ireland, the Netherlands, New Zealand, Poland, and Switzerland.

Professor Abramowicz also has experience working for international consulting firms as well as Polish and foreign industry as CEO, president, vice-president and, member of Boards of Directors, and also as an expert.

Marek Kowalkiewicz is a professor and chair of Digital Economy at Queensland University of Technology Business School. Listed among the Top 100 Global Thought Leaders in Artificial Intelligence by thinkers360, Marek has led global innovation teams in Silicon Valley, was a research manager of SAP's Machine Learning lab in Singapore, a Global Research Program lead at SAP Research, as well as a research fellow at Microsoft Research Asia. He received his M.Sc. in Business Information System from Poznan

University of Economics in 2002, and Ph.D. (Summa Cum Laude) from the same university in 2006.

Professor Marek Kowalkiewicz is an academic and industry leader with extensive experience in conducting academically sound research, co-innovating with industry and university partners, and delivering innovative products to the market.

He manages a contemporary research portfolio and converts industry-driven opportunities into research outcomes of global relevance. He is an invited government expert, university lecturer and project lead, as well as an inventor and author.

Professor Kowalkiewicz is recognized as a top-quality manager and excellent public speaker and has an interest in working with stakeholders in developing innovative ideas, ground-breaking business applications, and high-impact new technologies.

Krzysztof Węcel is an associate professor and chair of the Department of Information Systems at the Poznań University of Economics and Business. He obtained a doctoral degree from Poznań University of Economics and Business. In May 2020, he obtained a habilitation degree from the University of Potsdam at the Faculty of Economics and Social Sciences. His main research interest is the intersection of semantic web technologies, open data, and machine learning. He also has significant experience in natural language processing technologies, ranging from information retrieval to recent large language models. He has worked on methods for information processing in several industrial projects, including OpenFact funded by the Polish National Agency for Research and Development. He has been involved in many projects funded by the European Commission, also in management positions, including a flagship project on linking open data, LOD2. Recent projects include Distributed Knowledge Graphs (DKG) and Global Network on Large-Scale, Cross-domain and Multilingual Open Knowledge Graphs (GOBLIN). He was a visiting scholar in leading research institutions in Europe, for example, Leopold-Franzens University of Innsbruck (Austria) and University of Karlsruhe (Germany), as well as emerging ones in Asia – Asian Institute of Technology in Bangkok (Thailand), TATA Institute for Fundamental Research and Indian Institute of Technology in Mumbai (India). In 2023, he became NVIDIA University Ambassador for Natural Language Processing with Deep Learning technologies.

Contributors

Joanna Aleksandrowicz, Ph.D., Principal of Financial Sector Consulting, combines hands-on expertise in banking digital transformation, product delivery, and regulatory change with a strong academic background to guide global financial institutions.

George Baryannis is Reader in Artificial Intelligence and the Deputy Director of the Centre for Autonomous and Intelligent Systems at the University of Huddersfield, UK.

Sébastien Bourdin is a Professor at EM Normandie, expert in economic geography, ecological transition, and EU policies, leading research on circular economy, renewable energy, and regional development using mixed methods.

Giulio Mario Cappelletti is Associate Professor of Commodity Science at the University of Foggia, specializing in circular economy applications within agri-food supply chains and Life Cycle Assessment (LCA).

Tomasz Paweł Czaja is a tenure-track Assistant Professor at the University of Copenhagen. His research focuses on food quality, rapid spectroscopy, chemometrics, and sustainable food production for future food security.

Dorota Czyżewska-Misztal works as Assistant Professor in the European Studies Department, PUEB. Her research interests include regional innovation and competitiveness, digital transformation, innovation intermediaries.

Krzysztof Durczak, Ph.D., is an Assistant Professor in the Department of Sociology and Business Ethics at Poznań University of Economics and Business. He is an organizational anthropologist interested in the processes of making, interpreting, enacting, and enforcing formal and informal rules, especially in the contexts of judiciary, legal professions, and broader regulation.

Jarko Fidrmuc is Chair of International & Digital Economics at Zeppelin University. His research focuses on European integration, globalization, and political economics using microeconomic data.

Joanna Furmańczyk is an economist, philologist, coach, and tutor. She is interested in human development in an organization. She is the author of publications on career, communication, organizational culture, education, and intercultural leadership.

Pasquale Giungato, Associate Professor of Commodity Sciences in the department of chemistry, teaches Industrial Ecology, Chemistry, Life Cycle Assessment, at the University of Bari Aldo Moro (Italy). He has published on two themes: sustainability and quality, with Elsevier, Springer, Emerald, MDPI, and Indawi.

Emil Gościniak is an expert at Żabka Polska, actively involved in the implementation and integration of generative artificial intelligence-based solutions. He concentrates on leveraging AI to optimize business processes and drive innovation.

Szczepan Górtowski is a Lecturer at the Poznań University of Economics and Business. He conducts research and teaches in the areas of business analytics, generative artificial intelligence, and data visualization to optimize logistics processes.

Marek Hauptmann is a Habilitated Professor, Doctor of Engineering, who specializes in packaging and processing technologies.

Piotr Idczak is an Associate Professor at the Department of European Studies, PUEB. His primary research interest lies in economic integration. He has specialized in regional and urban economic development and policy.

Barbara Jankowska is Professor of Social Sciences and Rector of the Poznań University of Economics and Business. She specializes in international business, competitiveness, and foreign direct investment.

Marcin Jurczak is Assistant Professor in the Department of Logistics at Poznań University of Economics and Business. His research interests include public transport, transport infrastructure, and IT systems in transport and logistics.

Mirosława Kaczmarek is a Professor at the Poznań University of Economics and Business, specializing in quantitative and qualitative market research and analysis of consumer behavior in the mobile banking market.

András Keszthelyi, Ph.D., is an Associate Professor at Obuda University, Keleti Faculty of Business and Management, Department of Business Sciences and Digital Skills. His fields of interest are database planning, management, information security.

Agata Kliber is head of the Department of Applied Mathematics at Poznan University of Economics and Business. She specializes in financial econometrics and financial markets modeling.

Hans Michael Egelhoff MA, an English translator, specializes in business and technical writing, supporting IT and consulting firms with professional content.

Batuhan Kocaoglu, B.Sc., M.Sc., Ph.D., is an industrial engineer and MIS professor specializing in SCM, S&OP/IBP, ERP, MRP, and Digital Transformation, combining academic, industry, and consulting expertise.

Iris Koleša is a researcher at the Faculty of Social Sciences at the University of Ljubljana. She focuses on different aspects of business internationalization, industry-academia collaboration, and innovation.

Sylwia Konecka, Ph.D., is an Assistant Professor at Poznan University of Economics and Business. Her research focuses on supply chain risk, innovations, and digitalization in transport and logistics.

Daniel Korzeniowski works as Head of Gen AI and Automation at Żabka Polska. His professional interests are focused on data analytics and reporting using BI tools, as well as on innovative solutions that bridge analytics and AI.

Wojciech Kozak is an Associate Professor at the Department of Non-food Product Quality and Packaging Development (Poznań University of Economics and Business), arrying out numerous research projects on oxygen measurements use for products quality assessment, barrier properties evaluation of packaging materials (including biopolymers), designing, and commercialization of active packaging (e.g., oxygen scavengers).

Maria Kubala is a Teaching Assistant at the Poznan University of Economics and Business. She researches international business, competitiveness, and sustainable development economics.

Marcin Leszczyński is an Assistant Professor at the Department of Information Economics at the Poznań University of Economics and Business. His research interests include international public relations, consumer behavior, country of origin effect, and marketing communication.

Anna Lewandowska-Ciszek is an Assistant Professor in the Department of Logistics at the Poznan University of Economics and Business. Her research focuses on improving material flow using simulation, Lean Management tools, and the Theory of Constraints.

Elżbieta Lewańska, Ph.D. in Economics, is an Assistant Professor at the Poznań University of Economics and Business. She conducts research on the use of AI in business, information systems, and business processes.

Damian Luty is an Assistant Professor at the Department of Sociology and Business Ethics at the PUEB. His research focuses on the philosophy/methodology of science, with particular attention to physics and economics.

Krzysztof Łuczak, Ph.D. in Economics, is a Board Member at Grupa Blix. His work centers on advancing retail media strategies, leveraging consumer data analytics, and driving digital innovation in the FMCG sector to enhance smart shopping solutions.

Ihor Muzyka is Head of Analytics at Żabka Group and a Lecturer at Adam Mickiewicz University. With an ACCA Advanced Diploma in Accounting and Business, he bridges financial and marketing domains, leveraging business intelligence and AI to drive data-informed decision-making.

Remigiusz Napiecek is a Professor at the Poznań University of Economics and Business, Head of the Department of Management Accounting. His interests focus on the informational function of modern accounting.

Marlena Napierała, Ph.D. in Economics and Finance, is auditor, financial director in an international manufacturing company, and lecturer at the Accountants Association in Poland. She has many years of experience in running a business, including those in Special Economic Zones and shared services center. She is the author of articles and publications on accounting.

Monika Naskręcka, Ph.D., is a university lecturer and researcher specializing in advanced data analysis and mathematical modeling. Her work focuses on the application of quantitative methods in economics and the social sciences.

Dariusz Nowak is an Associate Professor at the Poznań University of Economics and Business, Poland, and Head of the Department of Corporate Resources Management. He has authored over 150 publications and specializes in interorganizational relations, industrial cooperation, and sustainable development. He lectures, teaches, and collaborates with universities across Central and Eastern Europe.

Karolina Anna Nowak is an Assistant Professor at the Department of Sociology and Business Ethics at the PUEB. Her research explores the axiological aspects of economic practice, especially in digital and ecological contexts.

Hanna Nowak-Mizgalska is an Assistant Professor at Poznań University of Economics and Business. Her scientific interests include entrepreneurship, entrepreneurship education, institutional environment of enterprises, the process of new venture creation, and the factors of survival of SMEs.

Brenda Nxumalo is a Ph.D. candidate at Corvinus University of Budapest, specializing in Business and Management. Her research interests include international business, artificial intelligence, digitalization, competitiveness, and innovation investments in the CEE region.

Rasmus Nykvist, Ph.D., is an Assistant Professor at Linköping University and Affiliated Researcher at the Centre for Business and Economic History at Stockholm School of Economics. He utilizes his historical training to conduct research on strategies in state-owned enterprises and the interaction between regulation and technology across various industries and time periods.

Aleksandra Rabczun, Ph.D. in Economics and Finance, has scientific interest in international economics and development economics with particular attention to the MENA region.

Marzena Remlein is a tenured Professor of Economics and Finance, Director of the Institute of Accounting and Financial Management, and Head of the Department of Accounting and Financial Audit at the Poznań University of Economics and Business, Poland. She is the author of more than 170 scientific publications, including broad experience in accounting, and authored or edited monographs on accounting.

Anna Rogala is an Assistant Professor at Poznań University of Economics and Business. Her current research focuses on the application of artificial intelligence in marketing, the digital transformation in relation to consumer behaviors, and the development of sustainable consumption patterns.

Ana Rep Romić is a postdoctoral researcher in the Faculty of Economics and Business at the University of Zagreb, Croatia. She is a member of the Accounting Department and teaches in financial, non-financial, and sustainability reporting, as well as in accounting for SMEs and crafts and accounting information systems. She has coauthored over 40 academic papers and collective monograph chapters, participated in several international research projects, and actively reviewed both national and international conferences and journals.

Carlo Russo is a researcher in agri-food and environmental sectors focusing on life cycle assessment, sustainability, and waste management. He has been involved in numerous national and international research projects and is the author and coauthor of around 60 scientific papers. For his research activity, he achieved two research awards and the national enabling as full professor in the scientific sector "Commodity Science."

Marcin Sawiński is researcher at Poznań University of Economics and Business, specializing in AI, NLP, and misinformation detection, with publications on fact-checking and transformer-based classification models.

Milena Stróżyna is an Assistant Professor at the Poznan University of Economics and Business. Her research interests focus on topics related to data analysis, quality of data and information, and AI in business.

Maciej Szymczak received M.Sc. degree in the area of Computer Science, and Ph.D. and post-Ph.D. degrees in the area of Business Administration, majoring in business logistics and supply chain management.

Zakaria Talouni is a teaching assistant at the Poznan University of Economics and Business. His research focuses on international business, FDI, competitiveness, and digitalization.

Juan Aurelio Tamayo Gallego is an Associate Professor at the University of Seville. He has published in journals such as *Annals of Tourism Research*, *Humanities and Social Sciences Communications*, *Technological Forecasting and Social Change*, and *Technovation.*

Mariusz Tichoniuk is an Assistant Professor at the Department of Non-food Product Quality and Packaging Development (Poznań University of Economics and Business), carrying out numerous research projects on modern analytical solutions (biosensors), and designing active and intelligent packaging. As Program Director, he is responsible for education in the field of Quality Science.

Anna Wach is a pedagogist, coach, and tutor whose research focuses on academic development and teaching and learning in higher education. She leads the Department of Education and Personnel Development and heads the Academic Teaching and Learning Centre.

Karolina Wiszumirska, Ph.D. in Economics, specializing in Commodity Science, primarily focuses on packaging quality and safety, packaging waste recycling, and innovative sustainable design approaches.

Joanna Witczak is a scientist and lecturer, specializing in life cycle analysis, ecodesign, and the possibilities of their use in green marketing. She is an expert in areas related to sustainable development and circular economy. She works as an Assistant Professor in the Department of Non-food Product Quality and Packaging Development at Poznań University of Economics and Business.

Patrycja Wojciechowska is a Habilitated Doctor of Economic Sciences in the field of commodity science, and specializes in the quality and safety of packaging, focusing on innovative solutions for the circular economy.

Krzysztof Wójcicki is an Assistant Professor at the Poznań University of Economics and Business. His research focuses on novel methods for assessing the quality of food and non-food products, with interests in spectroscopy, multidimensional data analysis, and the digital transformation of industry.

Mateusz Wyrembek is a Ph.D. candidate at PUEB and Machine Learning Specialist at Raben Group. He researches interpretable machine learning models for supply chain risk management, supporting strategic decision-making across all stakeholder levels.

Tibor Vörös is a Senior Lecturer and Researcher specializing in Quantitative Studies, Business Simulations, and Decision-Making. He combines academic insight with corporate experience in innovation, analytics, and education.

Part I

Decision Support

1 Business Schools in the Era of Artificial Intelligence

Krzysztof Węcel, Witold Abramowicz, and Marek Kowalkiewicz

Introduction

The subjective perception of reality suggests that change is accelerating and becoming increasingly pervasive. However, this sense of rapid transformation is not unique to our time. Previous generations have experienced and articulated similar sentiments, each using language and concepts specific for their time. What distinguishes the present moment is the prominence of trends such as artificial intelligence and digital transformation, which are reshaping not only technological landscapes but also economic models, organizational structures, and societal norms.

The primary role of business schools has long been to prepare young people for life and work in a constantly evolving economy. These institutions have traditionally sought to identify certain enduring principles on which to base their curricula. One such principle is the pursuit of utility maximization. However, the notion of utility has evolved over time and is interpreted differently depending on the prevailing social and economic context. For some, it may be measured by the volume of goods, such as cars, that are being produced; for others, by time saved or by improvements in health and overall well-being. These shifting interpretations reflect broader patterns of economic transformation that extend beyond digitalization alone, encompassing cultural, environmental, and societal dimensions.

Each period is defined by its own core concepts and keywords. In the business domain, focus has been placed on executive information systems, decision support systems, business intelligence, big data, and – more recently – artificial intelligence (AI) accompanied by digital transformation (DT). The book aims to explore the evolving phenomena of AI and DT to gain a deeper understanding of how they are reshaping the corporate environment. This, in turn, raises two important questions: what to teach students and how to teach them to ensure that their knowledge remains relevant and valuable over the long term. In response, business schools must look for new foundational principles, the modern-day "constants," that can guide curriculum development in the face of continuous change.

DOI: 10.4324/9781003659143-2

Artificial Intelligence

The understanding of AI within business schools varies widely. AI can be approached from a technical perspective or explored through its practical applications in business contexts. A significant proportion of the literature portrays AI as a "black box," sometimes attributing supernatural powers to it, portraying it as a silver bullet for all problems. However, effective operational and strategic use of AI requires a deeper comprehension of the underlying technology. At its core, AI is grounded in mathematics, especially probability theory. The journey began with the conceptualization of a single artificial neuron, which was expanded into perceptrons, early models of neural networks (Rosenblatt, 1957). Over time, a variety of architectures have been proposed, leading to today's advanced models, such as convolutional neural networks for image analysis (Krizhevsky et al., 2012) and transformers for natural language processing (Devlin et al., 2019). These systems comprise layered structures, their performance driven by the optimization of parameters, or "weights," in a process known as training. As the number of parameters has grown exponentially, training has become increasingly resource-intensive, dominated by large technology firms capable of investing millions of dollars. In this way, AI has become a new instrument of power, not unlike trade secrets, patents, and proprietary technologies in earlier eras.

There is no universally accepted definition of artificial intelligence. Instead, AI functions as an umbrella term whose meaning varies depending on the context and the user. For some, it represents a set of mathematical models while for others, it is a practical tool to enhance productivity. In others yet AI evokes fear, seen as a powerful entity, an artificial superintelligence capable of surpassing human control, potentially acquiring physical capabilities, resisting shutdown, and replicating itself autonomously (Gulchenko, 2024). AI is often defined through its applications, such as text mining, computer vision, speech recognition, natural language generation, and machine learning (Eurostat, 2025). These systems can predict, recommend, or make decisions with varying degrees of autonomy. Finally, for many in the general public, AI is synonymous with conversational agents, most notably ChatGPT, leading to the common misconception that AI is limited to chatbots.

Concerning AI evolution, predictive AI needs to be distinguished from generative AI. The former, traditional kind, trained on historical data, can help make decisions by observing and learning patterns and dependencies to perform classifications or forecasting. The latter modern approach, enabled by recent developments, is focused on creativity. Based on a variety of input data, it can write new text, create abstract visualizations, and develop functions in a programming language. However, new content is usually created with no frame of reference, which hampers output evaluation.

According to (Apotheker et al., 2025), two-thirds of businesses are exploring the use of AI agents, which they consider part of their AI transition. An AI agent is defined as an AI that has learned to use tools. One of the key features of AI agents is reasoning, that is, decomposition of problems and planning actions. AI agents can observe the environment and remember states across tasks, decompose problems and plan actions to achieve goals, and act on behalf of humans by accessing external systems.

Digital Transformation

Digital transformation has become a core research interest in management sciences, technology, economics, and social sciences. Despite many publications, it has no single definition, as definitions depend on context and publication focus. In its narrow sense, digital transformation means "going paperless." It is reasonable to split the term into its two components: the term "transformation" means intended and planned change, while "digital" refers to the enabling technology that opens up new areas of innovation and creativity rather than supporting traditional methods (Gebayew et al., 2018). Digital transformation is mostly about integrating digital technology into business and changing how value is created and distributed to customers. It influences business models, operational processes, and customer experience (Gebayew et al., 2018). (Vial, 2019) defines digital transformation as "a process where digital technologies create disruptions triggering strategic responses from organizations that seek to alter their value creation paths." Speaking of technology, Greenway et al. (2021) emphasize that enabling technologies are those of the age of the internet, and that their application along with culture, practices, and business models allows one to respond to growing customer expectations. Currently, the technology that drives digital transformation is AI (Paul et al., 2024). A more recent extensive analysis of digital transformation definitions and taxonomy is provided in (Kao et al., 2024).

Rather than simply automating existing processes, AI creates entirely new paradigms of organizational intelligence. Data become a living asset that allows companies to continuously learn and adapt. This enables them to anticipate market shifts and operational challenges before they fully materialize. AI not only supports decision-making but can also formulate strategies in ways that surpass the cognitive limitations of humans.

Rather than a mere tool for digital transformation, AI is a transformative force that redefines the nature of innovation, strategy, and value creation. Beyond automating tasks and optimizing workflows, AI enables organizations to reimagine their operating models, customer relationships, and decision-making. Drawing on frameworks such as Westerman's Digital Mastery (Westerman et al., 2014) and Vial's conceptual model of digital transformation (Vial, 2019), AI emerges as both a catalyst and an enabler. It serves as an "intelligence layer" that integrates functions and bridges silos. In this way,

AI is not just part of digital transformation; it is in fact the engine that drives its evolution from efficiency-driven change to deep, systemic reinvention.

The digital transformation of businesses is one of the digital targets set out in (European Commission, 2019). These targets indirectly refer to artificial intelligence. One of them, "tech up-take," seeks to have 75% of EU-based businesses use cloud, AI, or big data. Another calls for more than 90% of SMEs to reach at least a basic level of digital intensity. Such intensity is derived from the Digital Intensity Index (Eurostat, 2024), which measures the use of 12 different digital technologies, AI included, by businesses. The index can be used to describe the extent to which EU-based enterprises are digitalized (European Commission, 2025).

Strategic Dimension of Decision-Making

Business schools increasingly recognize that AI significantly boosts the quality of decision-making. AI excels at data preparation for decision-making and can process complex data much faster than people can. AI systems use machine learning and predictive modeling to process complex data sets, identifying patterns and trends that humans might not be able to discern. This process allows for better risk management, forecasting, and strategic planning.

Modern AI systems demonstrate superior text comprehension capabilities. They can process large volumes of textual data for informed decision-making. Image recognition has also improved significantly. Dedicated multimodal models can seamlessly match and analyze both text and images simultaneously. Such advances enable the rapid analysis of large datasets, including customer feedback and opinions. Real-time data processing has become increasingly sophisticated, particularly for social media monitoring. Such capabilities prove especially valuable in cybersecurity applications where immediate threat detection is critical. Financial security benefits include enhanced anti-money laundering systems. Marketing automation has also been revolutionized through these technological improvements.

AI can operate at various levels: operational and strategic, the strategic level being of greater interest in our context. To succeed, AI initiatives must be closely aligned with the broader goals of the organization. Achieving this alignment requires strong cross-departmental collaboration, from IT to marketing, to ensure that AI efforts effectively support and enhance core business functions.

The impact of AI on strategy development is undeniable (D'Amico et al., 2025). Data analytics has long been used to help prepare strategies. AI helps to derive insights from data and develop viable options based on those insights. Nevertheless, the exploration of a less obvious but highly valuable area of AI application is starting: its use as a brainstorming partner for strategists. AI can act as a critical-thinking companion, helping to challenge assumptions and refine ideas. By evaluating plans against established strategic frameworks,

AI can assist in the early identification of common pitfalls. For instance, a team can use generative AI to stress-test a strategy, with AI challenging it to detect hidden risks or management blind spots. Additionally, AI can support real-time strategic simulations and improve data-driven decision-making. In a broader sense, D'Amico et al. (2025) distinguish five AI roles that support strategy development for the roles of researcher, interpreter, thought partner, simulator, and communicator. Currently, AI delivers the greatest benefits in the design phase.

Value Creation and Distribution

Artificial intelligence and digital transformation are reshaping value creation, potentially providing a new source of competitive advantage for organizations (Gebayew et al., 2018). The rules that have governed business value creation over the past century need to be redefined. Some value creation shifts can be observed. First, AI is revolutionizing the way companies identify (e.g., lead scoring), engage (e.g., AI-powered sales assistants), and convert customers (e.g., dynamic pricing engines generating customized proposals) through intelligent sales processes. Second, AI enables product and service innovation. It starts with a better understanding of customer segments, followed by data-driven product development, resulting in extended personalization capabilities. Third, AI technologies can generate novel opportunities for companies to create additional value for their customers by applying a proactive approach, managing uncertainty, and thus improving cost efficiency and increasing revenue. For best results, the latter should involve the development of new business models.

Leading companies embrace larger-scale changes rather than focusing on smaller, typically individual productivity-focused initiatives (Apotheker et al., 2025). Unlike most other players, they invest in reshaping critical functions and inventing new products and services. Moreover, they prefer depth over breadth of initiatives, focusing on the most promising ones. Within ecosystems, leading companies co-operate with their partners, providing opportunities for others to learn and laying foundations for value distribution.

AI can deliver value at both individual and organizational levels. Some researchers find that an organization can only benefit from AI if its employees benefit from it too. In the survey conducted by Ransbotham et al. (2022), two findings proved to be of particular interest: 64% of workers personally derive value from AI, whereas 60% of individuals regard AI as a coworker rather than a threat to their job security.

Value distribution can be studied at three levels. One, as mentioned earlier, is employee value distribution. Its most visible effect is increased productivity resulting from task automation, robotic process automation (RPA) being the predominant approach. Decision-making can be supported by more accurate or more granular data. Employees will also appreciate opportunities to enhance skills. All of these increase job satisfaction. The second level is that of customer value distribution. It results in customers noticing product quality and reliability improvements. Customers can also benefit from personalized experiences and services. Customer support may be enhanced through the use of AI assistants, which can contribute to overall increases in customer satisfaction. The third level is that of organizational value distribution. Businesses that embrace AI tend to benefit from improved operational efficiency. In addition, AI creates opportunities for new revenue streams and business models. In the long term, businesses that acquire AI enjoy enhanced competitive positioning.

Enablers of AI-Driven Change

Some argue that management function improvement should not begin with technology but rather with establishing strategies, goals, and values. Although doing this in this order is not without merit, it is also true that many business organizations that lack technology exposure find themselves unable to envision what is possible or even that something *is* possible. Therefore, although technology should not dominate thinking, it must not be overlooked. A profound understanding of technology can provide a critical competitive advantage. In some cases, technological innovation itself triggers development or compels companies to respond, prompting new strategic approaches to technology adoption. Forward-thinking organizations must prioritize education. Business schools, in particular, should lead in the integration of emerging technologies, not only by teaching best practices and offering robust implementation frameworks but also through active research. By deepening the understanding of technology, they can help avoid common pitfalls and discover the most effective ways to harness technological potential. Considering how crucial both aspects are, it is important to separate organizational from technological enablers.

Aue et al. (2023) identify four technological enablers that organizations should use to scale AI successfully. First, data for training models should be stored in a central repository in the form of so-called feature stores. They emphasize the need for assuring data quality. Second, businesses should also standardize reusable code components for faster AI development. The paper focuses on best software engineering practices and comprehensive code testing. Third, governance frameworks should be established to improve consistency and compliance. This ensures consistent standards across teams and eliminates bias that might otherwise result from the use of inappropriate features. Fourth, a comprehensive approach to managing ML models should be established. This is also referred to as MLOps, the technology and best practices that ensure that ML models efficiently transition from experimentation through production to maintenance.

Despite the undeniably inspiring nature of technology, best-performing companies do not center their strategies on it. They dedicate only 20% of their efforts to technology, with another 10% given to algorithms. The remaining 70% are devoted to people, processes, and cultural transformation (Apotheker et al., 2025). Gillani et al. (2024) find that technology, data, human capital, processes, and organization structure are key enablers of digital transformation. (Cao et al., 2025) enumerate multiple organizational factors that influence digital transformation. These are digital technologies, business strategy, financial investment, process optimization and technological integration, resource complementarity, organizational change, organizational culture, and skill development.

As demonstrated earlier, the majority of authors focus on organizational enablers that can be roughly grouped into human capital, process innovation, and cultural transformation. Human capital development is the cornerstone of successful AI-driven digital transformation in business education, requiring a fundamental change in the way organizations support talent for an AI-augmented future. Business leaders need the skills to bridge the gap between technological capability and strategic business outcomes. Thus, modern human capital development requires a multi-faceted approach that combines technical understanding with strategic thinking, emotional intelligence, and change management capabilities. Process innovation within AI-driven digital transformation requires organizations to fundamentally revise workflows across their systems, moving beyond mere task automation. The most successful transformations occur when companies break down traditional departmental boundaries and create cross-functional processes that leverage AI insights at every decision point. This may involve developing new workflows that seamlessly integrate human expertise with AI recommendations. Finally, cultural transformation emerges as a critical factor for digital success, as organizational culture types directly influence both digital transformation capabilities and product innovation outcomes (Cao et al., 2025). Successful digital companies cultivate a curious, growth-oriented mindset that encourages their teams to continuously test new approaches, learn from both successes and failures, and iteratively improve their processes and solutions. Moreover, such organizations prioritize cross-functional collaboration, breaking down traditional silos to create integrated teams where diverse expertise converges to drive innovation and accelerate digital transformation initiatives.

As noted by Ransbotham et al. (2022), organizations are three times more likely to achieve substantial financial returns on their investment in AI when artificial intelligence is integrated as a fundamental component of strategic planning throughout the entire enterprise rather than being confined to isolated departments.

Implementation in Business Schools

While digital transformation can be applied across a variety of sectors such as marketing, sales, automotive, and public services, our primary interest is education. As we explore the ways in which businesses adopt digital technologies, we find it equally important to examine how people engage with digital systems, including public and online services.

It is essential to address both the demand and the supply sides of education in the context of AI. Concerning demand, research indicates a significant shortage of employees adequately trained in AI technologies (Apotheker et al., 2025). Many workers report that they would feel more secure if they better understood the technologies that may one day disrupt or replace their roles. It should be noted that any such employees who already use AI in their daily work, regardless of industry, report higher levels of competence, stronger engagement with their tasks, and improved connections with customers (Ransbotham et al., 2022). Reports from managers are also optimistic and encouraging: fewer than 10% of executives anticipate workforce reductions due to AI automation (Apotheker et al., 2025). Moreover, nearly 70% plan to focus on upskilling existing employees to meet evolving AI-related demands, highlighting the growing importance of continuous learning and adaptable talent development.

In view of the earlier context, business schools have a unique and urgent responsibility. They not only train future leaders but also shape mindsets that will one day drive technological change. Education must go beyond teaching the mechanics of AI and digital tools; it must foster digital mindsets, ethical awareness, and strategic thinking. The frameworks offered by consulting companies can help design curricula that prepare students for a world of constant reinvention. Business schools should themselves become laboratories of transformation: experiment with AI in pedagogy, model agile governance, and embrace interdisciplinary collaboration. As digital technologies continue to redefine industries, education must shift from being a passive observer to becoming an active architect of the future. This educational transformation requires business schools to become living laboratories of digital innovation, where faculty and students co-create knowledge about emerging technologies while developing the leadership capabilities necessary to guide organizations through the complexities of AI-driven change.

Business schools must also ensure that students are aware of the key risks associated with the use of AI, as pointed out in (D'Amico et al., 2025). First, there is the issue of model bias, where AI systems trained on historical data may unintentionally overrepresent or favor certain types of customers, leading to unfair or skewed outcomes. Second, students should understand the challenge of reduced explainability, which arises when AI models fail to provide a clear and logical basis for their decisions, thus undermining trust and transparency. Third, there is the risk of hallucination, where AI systems generate content that appears accurate and persuasive but is actually false or misleading.

Leading business schools are already at the forefront of integrating AI into their curricula. They can effectively leverage real-world examples of value creation to illustrate how traditional companies are reinventing themselves through AI-driven transformation. AI also enables faster development of more diverse and dynamic case materials, enriching the learning experience. The use of tactical games and simulation tools further enhances the teaching of strategy, making it more interactive and practice-oriented. To support this evolution, several implementation approaches can be proposed for business education: case studies that examine how companies are reshaping strategic decision-making through AI, interactive workshops where students design AI-augmented strategic plans, and cross-functional team projects simulating real-world business transformations powered by AI. These methods aim to prepare students for the complexities of AI-integrated management in a rapidly evolving business landscape.

Conclusion

This chapter examines the evolving landscape of digital transformation, emphasizing the transition from reactive business models to predictive and prescriptive organizational capabilities. At the heart of this shift lie the increasing ambitions of companies to leverage artificial intelligence not as a disruptive force, but as a strategic enabler of gradual and sustainable change. Rather than pursuing radical overhauls, organizations are advised to focus on a limited set of transformative opportunities within their core functions, where AI can deliver the most value. This targeted approach demands not only technological adoption but also a fundamental rethinking of what is possible when AI is integrated into broader business transformation efforts.

From both scientific and practical perspectives, the findings emphasize the importance of cultural and organizational adaptation for realizing the potential of AI. Successful implementation of AI-driven strategies requires the skills needed to prioritize AI efforts and a commitment to fostering an environment that supports innovation. To make this happen, it is crucial to prepare the future workforce by equipping students with technological proficiency and adaptive skills that are essential to enable them to prosper in AI-enhanced professional settings. Future research should further explore opportunities to align AI initiatives with strategic objectives, investigate effective change management practices, and assess the long-term impact of AI on workforce improvement and organizational resilience. AI-focused leadership training initiatives can propel organizational digital change more rapidly and effectively than implementing individual technological solutions or isolated projects.

Acknowledgment

Supported by funds granted by the Minister of Science of the Republic of Poland under the "Regional Initiative for Excellence" Programme for the implementation of the project "The Poznań University of Economics and Business for Economy 5.0: Regional Initiative – Global Effects (RIGE)."

Reference List

Apotheker, J., Duranton, S., Lukic, V., de Bellefonds, N., Iyer, S., Bouffault, O., & de Laubier, R. (2025). *From potential to profit: Closing the AI impact gap*. BCG AI Radar. www.bcg.com/publications/2025/closing-the-ai-impact-gap

Aue, G., Cafferata, P., Drapeko, R., Penwarden, M., & Sinha, V. (2023). *Scaling AI for success: Four technical enablers for sustained impact*. McKinsey Digital. www.mckinsey.com/capabilities/mckinsey-digital/our-insights/tech-forward/scaling-ai-for-success-four-technical-enablers-for-sustained-impact

Cao, G., Duan, Y., & Edwards, J. S. (2025). Organizational culture, digital transformation, and product innovation. *Information & Management*, *62*(4), 104135. https://doi.org/10.1016/j.im.2025.104135

D'Amico, A., Delteil, B., Hazan, E., Tricoli, A., & Montard, A. (2025, February 5). *How AI is transforming strategy development*. McKinsey & Company. www.mckinsey.com/capabilities/strategy-and-corporate-finance/our-insights/how-ai-is-transforming-strategy-development

Devlin, J., Chang, M.-W., Lee, K., & Toutanova, K. (2019). BERT: Pre-training of deep bidirectional transformers for language understanding. *Proceedings of the 2019 Conference of the North*, 4171–4186. https://doi.org/10.18653/v1/N19-1423

European Commission. (2019). *Europe's digital decade: Digital targets for 2030*. https://commission.europa.eu/strategy-and-policy/priorities-2019-2024/europe-fit-digital-age/europes-digital-decade-digital-targets-2030_en

European Commission. (2025). *Digitalisation in Europe – 2025 edition*. Eurostat; KS-01-25-000-EN-Q. https://ec.europa.eu/eurostat/web/interactive-publications/digitalisation-2025

Eurostat. (2024). *Digital Intensity by size class of enterprise*. Eurostat. https://ec.europa.eu/eurostat/cache/metadata/en/isoc_e_dii_esmsip2.htm

Eurostat. (2025). Artificial intelligence. In *Statistics explained. Glossary*. Eurostat. https://ec.europa.eu/eurostat/statistics-explained/index.php?title=Glossary:Artificial_intelligence_(AI)

Gebayew, C., Hardini, I. R., Panjaitan, G. H. A., Kurniawan, N. B., & Suhardi. (2018). A systematic literature review on digital transformation. *2018 International Conference on Information Technology Systems and Innovation (ICITSI)*, 260–265.

Gillani, F., Chatha, K. A., Jajja, S. S., Cao, D., & Ma, X. (2024). Unpacking digital transformation: Identifying key enablers, transition stages and digital archetypes. *Technological Forecasting and Social Change*, *203*, 123335. https://doi.org/10.1016/j.techfore.2024.123335

Greenway, A., Terrett, B., & Bracken, M. (2021). *Digital transformation at scale: Why the strategy is delivery*. Do Sustainability.

Gulchenko, V. (2024). Navigating the risks: An examination of the dangers associated with artificial general intelligence and artificial superintelligence. *SSRN*. https://doi.org/10.2139/ssrn.4941716

Kao, L.-J., Chiu, C.-C., Lin, H.-T., Hung, Y.-W., & Lu, C.-C. (2024). Unveiling the dimensions of digital transformation: A comprehensive taxonomy and assessment model for business. *Journal of Business Research*, *176*, 114595. https://doi.org/10.1016/j.jbusres.2024.114595

Krizhevsky, A., Sutskever, I., & Hinton, G. E. (2012). Imagenet classification with deep convolutional neural networks. *Advances in Neural Information Processing Systems*, *25*. https://proceedings.neurips.cc/paper/2012/hash/c399862d3b9d6b76c8436e924a68c45b-Abstract.html

Paul, J., Ueno, A., Dennis, C., Alamanos, E., Curtis, L., Foroudi, P., Kacprzak, A., Kunz, W. H., Liu, J., Marvi, R., Nair, S. L. S., Ozdemir, O., Pantano, E., Papadopoulos, T., Petit, O., Tyagi, S., & Wirtz, J. (2024). Digital transformation:

A multidisciplinary perspective and future research agenda. *International Journal of Consumer Studies*, *48*(2), e13015. https://doi.org/10.1111/ijcs.13015

Ransbotham, S., Kiron, D., Candelon, F., Khodabandeh, S., & Chu, M. (2022). Achieving individual – and organizational – value with AI. *MIT Sloan Management Review*. https://sloanreview.mit.edu/projects/achieving-individual-and-organizational-value-with-ai/

Rosenblatt, F. (1957). *The perceptron: A perceiving and recognizing automaton* [Report]. Project PARA, Cornell Aeronautical Laboratory.

Vial, G. (2019). Understanding digital transformation: A review and a research agenda. *The Journal of Strategic Information Systems*, *28*(2), 118–144. https://doi.org/10.1016/j.jsis.2019.01.003

Westerman, G., Bonnet, D., & McAfee, A. (2014). *Leading digital: Turning technology into business transformation*. Ingram Publisher Services.

2 Smarter Decisions, New Challenges

AI's Role in Startups' Strategic Decision-Making

Zakaria Talouni, Maria Kubala, Iris Koleša, Brenda Nxumalo, and Barbara Jankowska

Introduction

The growing adoption of artificial intelligence (AI) in business makes it necessary to understand how this affects the decision-making process (DMP) and business performance. While AI is still an emerging technology and carries risks and uncertainties, startups, which are more tolerant of risk, are often its early adopters. However, entrepreneurs usually face a cognitive overload in fast-changing environments characterized by constant information updates (Orru & Longo, 2019). Previous studies have addressed AI's potential solutions through its capacity for swift information processing, adaptability, and advanced learning capabilities (Haenlein & Kaplan, 2019). On the other hand, challenges arise, for instance, around trust and ethical concerns, as businesses strive to balance AI-driven efficiency with human oversight and data integrity (Hengstler et al., 2016; Mittelstadt et al., 2016). Both theoretical and empirical studies on how AI affects the DMP in business remain scarce.

This chapter explores AI's impact on strategic DMP in startups, focusing on the benefits and challenges of integrating AI into business processes and operations during the early stages of business development. The chapter is structured as follows. We first outline the DMP and its specifics in startups, discussing the role of AI in DMP and some of its implications for business growth. We then present the preliminary empirical study we conducted in Slovenia and Switzerland (with a startup incubator and a startup, respectively) as examples of emerging and developed markets that have notable startup activity. The chapter concludes with a summary of our key findings.

The DMP in a World of Constant Change

As the DMP takes place in a complex and continuously changing environment (Acciarini et al., 2021, p. 1), it is itself a complex and fluid process (Figure 2.1). The DMP involves collecting, filtering, and analyzing information; generating alternatives; and selecting the best option, typically in an

DOI: 10.4324/9781003659143-3

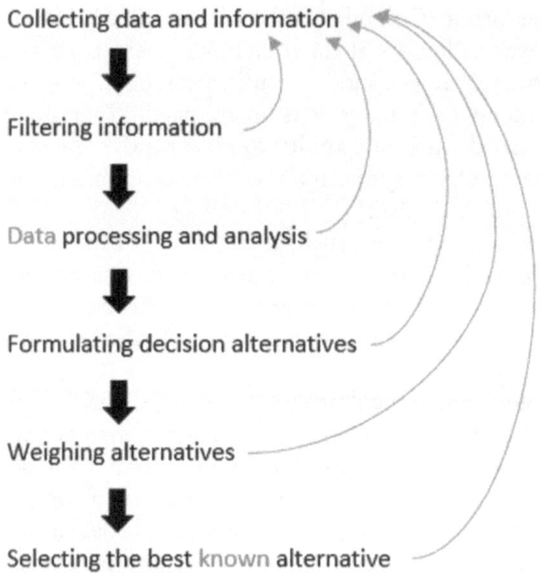

Figure 2.1 Stages in the DMP.

Source: Own visualization based on Darioshi & Lahav, 2021.

iterative process allowing the decision-maker to return to any previous stages before making their final decision (Darioshi & Lahav, 2021).

A strategic decision is a type of decision that is key for an organization's survival. While other management decisions are routine and specific, strategic issues are often unclear and involve much uncertainty (Berthet, 2022), which is why they pose a particular challenge for companies. This difficulty intensifies when the process is narrowed down to the strategic choices faced by newly established entities or emerging startups that have limited data of their own, access to broad general data, and many decisions to be made at once, resulting in a hefty cognitive load. Research indicates that cognitive load affects various aspects of decision-making. For instance, individuals carrying a heavy cognitive load tend to be more impulsive, exhibit greater risk aversion or behave more randomly (Blaywais & Rosenboim, 2019). However, Darioshi and Lahav (2021) emphasize that simply reducing the amount of information is not enough to improve decision quality; the trustworthiness of the information also matters. Effective information management thus becomes essential to improving the quality of decisions under conditions of increased cognitive load.

One approach to managing the DMP is the rational decision-making approach, which is based on the model of *homo economicus*, a sensible individual who possesses complete information about the situation and acts to maximize profit (Colander & Landreth, 2005). However, in reality, uncertainty, as well as factors at the individual level – such as values, beliefs, and even a person's current mood – influences decisions. This is why the concept of bounded rationality was introduced (Tversky & Kahneman, 1974). Factors that disturb our ability to reason privately also influence the work environment, which is now more complex, unpredictable, and unclear than ever (Acciarini et al., 2021).

Technological developments such as big data, business intelligence (BI), business analytics (BA), and AI tools in general have great potential to support the DMP in this complex and unpredictable business environment. They have thus become a top priority for modern chief information officers (CIOs) (Parra et al., 2023).

Given the rapid technological progress and its potential applications to the DMP, managers' skills must also evolve. Managers often fall prey to the "illusion of control," which means that they overestimate their decision-making abilities (Berthet, 2022). Effective managers must cultivate particular qualities to excel in decision-making at detailed and broad levels in an era of information overload and cognitive bias. A report prepared by the World Economic Forum, "The Future of Jobs," argues that by 2027, the top three most essential skills for managers will be analytical thinking, creative thinking, and AI and big data management (Di Battista et al., 2023). Based on the trends affecting the DMP and changing managerial abilities, it is worth considering technology, especially AI, as a tool that affects strategic decisions.

DMP Challenges in Startups

A startup is a business in the early stages of development. It is typically characterized by ambition, dynamism, and a strong focus on innovation and technology. These entities are still in search of a business model, which means they are continuously modifying their business hypotheses for subsequent versions of their business model (Skala, 2019). The startup life cycle usually has six stages: ideation, development, startup, survival, growth, and maturity (see, for example, Chammassian, 2025). Startups often face significant obstacles in progressing through these stages due to their limited experience and access to resources, their small scale, their ambitious growth objectives, the time pressure under which they operate, and the intense competition and rapidly changing market dynamics (Breit & Volkmann, 2025). DMP in startups thus becomes particularly complex.

The key role is played by the founder – CEO and their leadership style, which must be transformational. Startups record high failure rates in their initial years (Eurostat, 2022). Various factors contribute to this, including the absence of a clear marketing strategy, insufficient market knowledge, and the failure to deliver the right value proposition at the right time (Breit & Volkmann, 2025). However, the vigorous nature of startups that implement strategies of external monitoring, internal evaluation, and resource mobilization allows them to grow despite earlier failures (Corvello et al., 2024). Data indicate a steady and substantial rise in startup investment activity in Europe, particularly from 2020 onward, suggesting a growing interest and confidence in the European startup ecosystem. In 2017, there were 3,656 recorded investments in startups in Europe; in 2022, the number increased to 8,409 (Statista, 2023).

Given both the challenges that startups face in their formative stages and the increasing investment activity that underscores their potential, it is evident that their DMPs deserve closer examination and tailored support to ensure that these firms can successfully transition into more advanced stages of development.

AI as a Tool for Enhancing the DMP in Startups

AI has emerged as a transformative tool in terms of decision-making, offering unique capabilities with which to analyze vast amounts of data, predict outcomes, and optimize strategies (Prasanth et al., 2023). AI is not just a singular technology but encompasses a spectrum of practices and methodologies, including machine learning and deep learning. These techniques allow AI systems to mimic human cognitive functions and exceed human capabilities in specific tasks, such as recognizing patterns in large datasets or automating complex processes, and adjust to or customize outputs for individual entities (Harrison & Luna-Reyes, 2022).

AI can transform conventional decision-making paradigms by streamlining operations and enhancing human cognitive capabilities (Jarrahi, 2018). AI-driven frameworks significantly improve the precision and efficiency of DMP, enabling organizations to make more accurate and timely decisions by leveraging data analytics. This capability is particularly beneficial in sectors where quick adaptation is crucial (Rajagopal et al., 2022). One of the key objectives of AI integration is achieving human-AI complementarity, in which AI enhances rather than replaces human decision-making. Studies suggest that AI can improve performance when used as an assistant, but how effectively it does so depends on how well humans understand AI's capabilities (Steyvers & Kumar, 2024). Thus, AI is most effective when it provides recommendations while allowing human decision-makers to apply contextual judgement (Steyvers & Kumar, 2024). Moreover, AI's ability to predict future trends and outcomes is important for strategic decision-making, as it enhances BI with predictive modeling, allowing businesses to anticipate market trends and customer behaviors (Ilieva et al., 2021). Finally, AI tools help to identify inefficiencies and suggest improvements, which in turn helps to optimize operations (Tariq et al., 2021).

The collaborative nature of AI-assisted decision-making is also becoming increasingly important. AI models can provide recommendations while allowing humans to retain final decision-making authority, encouraging a productive balance between AI-driven insights and human expertise

(Madanchian et al., 2024). Effective human engagement with AI-based decision aids is essential to maximizing their impact (Buçinca et al., 2024). Thus, combining AI's analytical capabilities and human judgment is key to improving decision-making outcomes.

Additionally, AI is key in business internationalization by enhancing companies' market analysis, entry strategy formulation, and operational scalability (Menzies et al., 2024). It allows firms, especially startups and born-digital companies, to evaluate market trends, prioritize strategic goals, and make data-driven decisions, thus improving their competitiveness and reducing their reliance on local partners (Ogundipe & Abaku, 2024). Multinational enterprises use AI to optimize supply chains and entry modes, while startups use it for agile, country-agnostic strategies that bypass traditional models like Uppsala (Dos Santos & Williamson, 2024). Thus, AI reshapes internationalization by accelerating market entry, supporting dynamic decision-making, and requiring firms to balance algorithmic insights with human judgment (Krakowski et al., 2023).

However, AI can also pose certain challenges in DMP. The lack of ethical guidelines and legislative frameworks, along with the potential for abuse of AI in decision-making, is a significant concern. Attard-Frost et al. (2023) emphasize the need for ethical guidelines that go beyond algorithmic decision-making to include AI's broader political and economic impacts. Data privacy, algorithmic bias, and transparency must be addressed to ensure responsible AI use. Additionally, integrating AI into business processes requires a cultural shift within organizations. Frost et al. (2020) argue that successful AI implementation depends on changing management and corporate culture. This includes developing new competencies among employees and promoting a culture of continuous learning. Another critical challenge is the complexity of AI technologies and the challenges of implementing them. Accordingly, Ruokonen and Ritala (2023) categorize firms into digital tycoons, niche-carvers, and asset-augmenters, each of which faces unique challenges in leveraging AI for strategic advantage. These challenges include maintaining technological leadership, applying AI to specialized markets, and integrating AI into existing assets. Despite the transformative potential of AI in decision-making, significant challenges persist, particularly around the transparency and interpretability of AI systems. The "black box" nature of AI continues to pose difficulties, highlighting the need for methodologies that make its DMPs more comprehensible to users. Moreover, as AI is still in its infancy, its outputs can lack reliability, especially for specific tasks and in situations where data is scarce (MoDastoni, 2023).

The Practitioner's Perspective: Putting AI to Use for Startup Development and Growth

To explore real-world manifestations of AI's effect on strategic decision-making in startups, we adopted a qualitative case study approach. This method allows us to undertake an in-depth, contextual examination of contemporary phenomena within their real-life settings, which is ideal for investigating novel and complex processes like AI integration in management (Harrison et al., 2017). We chose an exploratory case study design, aligning with the early-stage nature of this research. As noted in methodological literature, a small number of case studies can be especially useful in preliminary research (Ridder, 2017).

We selected two cases at different levels of analysis (i.e., an incubator as a network of businesses; and a startup as an individual firm) from different European innovation ecosystems (Slovenia and Switzerland) for this study. Switzerland represents a highly developed, innovation-driven Western European economy (Derindag et al., 2021), while Slovenia is a small, emerging CEE market and an EU member (Koleša et al., 2022). Both countries are important players in the startup arena and thus particularly relevant to our research. They both record notable numbers of startups per capita (Slovenia the highest in the CEE region and Switzerland one of the highest in Europe) (Chiavarini, 2021), as well as high shares of AI business users. In Slovenia, almost 21% of businesses used AI in 2024 (which is almost twice as much as in 2023 and 7.3% above EU average) (Eurostat, 2025), while in Switzerland this share reached 30% (EY Switzerland, 2024).

In Slovenia, we studied a startup incubator: Inkubator Savinjske regije, d.o.o. (The Savinjska region incubator, LLC.), which has substantial experience in startup support and more recently in AI as well. We conducted an interview with a key figure from the incubator reporting AI-related opportunities and challenges for Slovenian startups as well as providing insights into the support for their development and growth in light of the AI-driven strategic business decision-making changes. In Switzerland, we chose an innovative Swiss startup operating in the collaborative software industry and using AI tools in its DMP as our case study. Switzerland exemplifies a high-growth startup environment in a developed innovation ecosystem. The startup was founded in 2011 and adopted generative AI in 2022. We conducted an interview with its CEO, analyzing his experience in integrating generative AI into strategic and operational decision-making within his startup.

We used semi-structured interviews as the primary data collection tool for both case studies. We chose this approach to balance consistency with flexibility (Ruslin et al., 2022). A common interview guide ensured that we covered certain core topics across the interviews (e.g., how AI is used in strategic decision-making, the perceived benefits of AI, the challenges or risks the interviewee's company encountered), while the open-ended nature of semi-structured interviews allowed respondents to elaborate on issues they considered important (Adeoye-Olatunde & Olenik, 2021). Each interview lasted approximately 45–60 minutes and was conducted in Slovenian (for the Slovenian case) and in English (for the Swiss case). With the interviewees' consent, we audio-recorded the interviews and later transcribed them to ensure the accuracy of the data. Transcripts are stored by the authors and are available to editors and reviewers upon request in an anonymized form due to the interviewees' wish to remain anonymous.

The Use of AI by Firms in Slovenia: A General Overview

According to the Statistical Office of the Republic of Slovenia (SURS), about 21% of businesses with more than ten employees in Slovenia used AI technologies in 2024. This was almost twice as many as in 2021 and 2023 (Zupan, 2021, 2023, 2024). This indicates a shift from only innovators and early adopters among firms using AI to the early majority[1] of firms also introducing AI to their operations (see also Rogers, 1962).

In Slovenia, businesses that use AI can be classified into four categories: AI service providers; multinationals offering AI-based services or products as part of their product mix; firms specialized for a specific area of AI use (startups typically fall under this category); and firms with an internal team of data scientists supporting business operations with AI but not offering AI-based services and products to the market. Slovenia has several strengths when it comes to AI implementation: reputable AI research, a relatively high number of AI engineers and researchers per capita, internal and international connectedness among key stakeholders in AI, experience in AI adoption from pilot projects, and support for developing AI infrastructure and solutions. However, there are also certain weaknesses, such as limited investment in AI; inadequate mapping of AI stakeholders and inefficient coordination of their efforts; limited (quality) data for AI; a lack of trust in AI; a poor legislative framework regarding AI; a lack of AI training and skills (combined with insufficient funds for reskilling and up-skilling); a lack of standards for the development, introduction, and use of AI; a lack of capacity for adopting AI in the public and private sectors; and sectorially dispersed AI infrastructure (Vlada Republike Slovenije, 2021).

Startups, which are often micro firms (averaging, in the EU, 2.6 team members each [ESN, 2020/2021]), are not covered by most statistics, however. As more risk- and experimentation-prone entities, they would likely drive both the share and level of proficiency in AI use among businesses upwards. The use of AI in Slovenian startups is also increasing. The interviewee from the Slovenian incubator confirms this by stating that all startups in the incubator use AI in some form to develop their business model. We present our key findings from the interview in the following section.

The Use of AI in Slovenian Startups: An Incubator's Perspective

To gain an overview of the common trends in introducing and implementing AI in startups, we conducted an interview with a representative of a Slovenian incubator currently engaged in the development of 62 startups and with more than 10 years of experience in supporting startups. According to the interviewee, most startups nowadays use AI technologies to develop their business models as it eases the DMP and accelerates business growth. This use has emerged organically and does not usually necessitate additional support from incubators.

Startups use AI from the initial stages of business idea development. Through AI-supported competitor analysis (as part of market analysis), startups can identify whether their idea has already been realized and pivot it so that it is differentiated from the existing offering. They can also develop insights into whether their idea fits the market, and adjust it accordingly. However, there is a downside to using AI for market analyses, as explained by the interviewee. While it provides prompt inputs for the DMP and is reasonably good at providing statistical data and analysis, it often generates generic results and fails to identify cultural differences or report on cultural factors. Hence, it is less useful as a support tool for foreign market entry. Instead, local business networks and connections knowledgeable about local specifics are used for these purposes. In terms of internationalization, AI can thus be helpful for statistical analyses and additional guidelines regarding local legislation, but it is still in its infancy when it comes to insights into the cultural components of doing business. Startups hence combine AI technologies with extant internationalization tools and instruments. When using AI, they also combine extant data with primary data that is specific to their business.

Because AI speeds up certain business processes, supports clear goal definition (also with regard to team composition, business partnerships and other stakeholder relations), and accelerates DMP, startups can dedicate more time to "soft" aspects of doing business, such as relationship building (in the team, with business partners, and with consumers), where AI is less effective. This is why AI is not used for investor search. Investors not only evaluate the startup's business model and product but also base their decision regarding investment on the team's compatibility, dynamic, enthusiasm, and energy. AI cannot include these aspects as a more personal approach is required (e.g., networking, collaboration, and recommendations). As explained by the interviewee, the way in which AI is used, for which processes, at what stages of the DMP, and at what level of proficiency all depend on the startups' business model. The business model also determines whether a startup develops its own AI solutions or outsources this development to commercial providers.

As AI is still developing and does not always provide reliable outputs, startups use it cautiously. They tend to employ certain controls that increase the reliability of their decision-making (e.g., conducting their own parallel studies). This caution is greater at the initial stages of business development, when startups are still building their database. Once the database gets more comprehensive, startups can start to rely on AI more. This is because AI becomes more precise with better quality data (i.e., inputs), while at the same time, startups become more familiar with AI. The main concern regarding AI among startups seems to be data protection. Some startups use specialized data protection tools to minimize this risk, while others cooperate with businesses that have experience in data protection. However, in their initial stages, when only the first outlines of the product and business model are being formed, the data that is used as an input for AI is too vague for third parties to abuse it. While startups are aware of the risk, the advantages of AI use outweigh it. These advantages visibly accelerate certain processes, and startups are willing to accept the related risks in return. Once startups reach a certain stage in their growth, they dedicate more attention to data protection and the protection of their intellectual property (the latter is covered very early on in incubators so that businesses can focus on doing business).

Thus, according to the interviewee from Slovenia, AI cannot make decisions instead of people, but it can offer different inputs for more efficient decision-making. These need to incorporate the decision-maker's knowledge, experience, and networks, and be used responsibly. When this is the case, strong and quality leadership is built.

The Use of AI by Firms in Switzerland: A Brief Overview

In an era of digital transformation, Switzerland has become an essential hub for innovation, with 62% of surveyed professionals reporting AI adoption, 30.6% of whom have implemented it across five or more business functions (Digitalswitzerland, 2024). The country has established itself as a global leader in adopting and using AI in several industries, thanks to its distinctive blend of technological expertise, strong regulatory frameworks, and solid academic – industry collaboration (Dutta et al., 2024).

Switzerland is characterized by systematic integration of AI across the public and private sectors. According to EY Switzerland (2024), Switzerland leads AI adoption in Europe, with 81% of managers reporting cost savings from AI implementation and 72% expressing confidence in their workforce's readiness for AI-driven transformation. Switzerland's advanced digital infrastructure and supportive innovation ecosystem facilitate this high adoption rate.

Switzerland's startup ecosystem has experienced substantial growth in recent years. According to the Swiss Venture Capital Report (Startupticker.ch, 2024), Swiss startups attracted several billion Swiss francs in venture capital funding in 2023, with significant investments directed toward deep tech, fintech, and digital health ventures. According to Pfau and Rimpp (2020), it is essential that entrepreneurs who wish to use this technology examine the strategic implications of AI for innovating their business models.

Our interview with an experienced CEO of a startup in the software development industry that is focused on AI adoption in business revealed several key insights regarding AI integration in startups. The respondent stressed how crucial it is to use AI at every stage of company development to improve efficiency and streamline procedures. Three main objectives drove the interviewee's company to adopt AI: boosting job satisfaction through workload reduction, increasing productivity, and enabling automation.

The interviewee also highlighted that AI is used for promoting internationalization as well, as it enables entrepreneurs to swiftly promote their goods, products, and services in different languages, giving Swiss companies better prospects for international expansion. These results validate Abdulov's (2020) claim that Swiss entrepreneurs can use AI to develop and promote sustainable economic growth by leveraging technology to address particular company requirements and obstacles.

The interviewee gave a practical perspective on how generative AI tools have transformed his decision-making approach and allowed him to access expert knowledge and conduct extensive research efficiently. These findings align with Arumugam's (2024) findings on AI's potential to enhance strategic DMPs.

While Swiss startups have plenty of opportunities, they also face challenges related to using AI for decision-making (Adam et al., 2024). Our interviewee pointed out that while AI helps its users to refine ideas and strategies, the leader's primary responsibility still remains, which aligns with Jarrahi's (2018) findings that AI complements decision-making rather than replacing it.

Our interviewee confirms another challenge, noting that data quality remains a significant concern when using AI for decision-making. Additionally, organizations face cultural challenges in AI adoption, as noted by our interviewee. Similar findings on the importance of culture were made by Jarosinski et al. (2021).

Conclusion

Startups use AI at all developmental stages and for multiple purposes despite the related risks (e.g., those pertaining to data protection). This is because AI's benefits outweigh its risks, especially for entities with limited resources and a need for DMP optimization due to the cognitive overload that comes with the early stages of developing a business. Although startups are willing to accept certain AI-related risks, they also set controls in place, such as parallel own analyses or consultations with experts and mentors, that support their decision-making (especially in the initial phases of startup establishment and business model development, when the firms' datasets are not of sufficient quality to generate quality AI outputs). While AI proves useful for idea generation, market analyses, providing general information about the business environment in specific countries or regions, testing and pivoting the business model, and optimizing certain business processes, it is less effective in identifying cultural specifics. As such, it needs to be combined with more traditional internationalization tools when startups wish to expand internationally. Nor can it replace relationship building (with employees, consumers, business partners or investors). However, by freeing entrepreneurs' time and providing insights into the relevant stakeholders and markets, it can support this process as well. AI thereby allows the decision-makers to redirect their focus on the "softer" aspects of doing business. Thus, AI is most effective in this business context when it provides recommendations while allowing human decision-makers to apply contextual judgment.

Acknowledgments

Part of this research was conducted within the framework of the GREENTECH project, co-financed by the European Union – NextGenerationEU. It was also financially supported by the Slovenian Research Agency through research core funding No. P5–0177.

Note

1 For more information on the five categories of innovation adopters according to the time it takes them to adopt an innovation (i.e., innovators, early adopters, early majority, late majority, and laggards) and other factors in the diffusion of innovation see Rogers (1962).

Reference List

Abdulov, R. (2020). Artificial intelligence as an important factor of sustainable and crisis-free economic growth. *Procedia Computer Science*, *169*, 468–472.

Acciarini, C., Brunetta, F., & Boccardelli, P. (2021). Cognitive biases and decision-making strategies in times of change: A systematic literature review. *Management Decision*, *59*(3), 638–652. https://doi.org/10.1108/MD-07-2019-1006

Adams, J. S., Altantzis, C., Beucler, T., Bingler, J., Brown, S., Brunschwiler, T., Colesanti-Senni, C., Muccione, V., Roeoesli, C., Schimanski, T., Vaghefi, S. A., & Wegner, J. D. (2024). *How to use the power of AI to reduce the impact of climate change on Switzerland*. https://doi.org/10.5167/uzh-270021

Adeoye-Olatunde, O. A., & Olenik, N. L. (2021). Research and scholarly methods: Semi-structured interviews. *Journal of the American College of Clinical Pharmacy*, *4*(10), 1358–1367.

Arumugam, U., & Manida, M. (2024). Enhancing strategic decision making: Assessing the role and impact of artificial intelligence in business management. *Journal of Business Analytics and Data Visualization*, 1–8. e-ISSN: 2584-1637

Attard-Frost, B., De los Ríos, A., & Walters, D. R. (2023). The ethics of AI business practices: A review of 47 AI ethics guidelines. *AI and Ethics*, *3*(2), 389–406.

Berthet, V. (2022). The impact of cognitive biases on professionals' decision-making: A review of four occupational areas. *Frontiers in Psychology*, *12*, 802439. https://doi.org/10.3389/fpsyg.2021.802439

Blaywais, R., & Rosenboim, M. (2019). The effect of cognitive load on economic decisions. *Managerial and Decision Economics*, *40*(8), 993–999. https://doi.org/10.1002/mde.3085

Breit, L. A., & Volkmann, C. K. (2025). Navigating start-ups: A qualitative exploration of causal and effectual decision-making in entrepreneurial marketing. *Journal of Research in Marketing and Entrepreneurship*, 27(2), 206–231.https://doi.org/10.1108/JRME-12-2023-0215

Buçinca, Z., Swaroop, S., Paluch, A. E., Murphy, S. A., & Gajos, K. Z. (2024). Towards optimizing human-centric objectives in ai-assisted decision-making with offline reinforcement learning. *arXiv preprint* arXiv:2403.05911.

Chammassian, R. G. (2025). Costs and entrepreneurial startup lifecycles – Early stages. In: *Costs, value, and the entrepreneurial venture journey*. Palgrave studies in accounting and finance practice. Palgrave Macmillan. https://doi.org/10.1007/978-3-031-86216-8_2

Chiavarini, L. (2021, October 14). A UiPath to success: Central and Eastern European startups coming of age. *Dealroom.co*. https://dealroom.co/blog/central-and-eastern-european-startups-2021.

Colander, D. C., & Landreth, H. (2005). *Historia myśli ekonomicznej (wydanie drugie)*. Wydawnictwo Naukowe PWN. (Colander, D. C., & Landreth, H. (2001). *The history of economic thought*. Houghton Mifflin.)

Corvello, V., Troise, C., Schiuma, G., & Jones, P. (2024). How start-ups translate learning from innovation failure into strategies for growth. *Technovation*, *134*, 103051. https://doi.org/10.1016/j.technovation.2024.103051

Darioshi, R., & Lahav, E. (2021). The impact of technology on the human decision-making process. *Human Behavior and Emerging Technologies*, *3*(3), 391–400. https://doi.org/10.1002/hbe2.257

Derindag, O. F., Lambovska, M., & Todorova, D. (2021). Innovation development factors: Switzerland experience. *Pressburg Economic Review*, *1*(1), 57–65.

Di Battista, A., Grayling, S., Hasselaar, E., Leopold, T. A., Li, R., Rayner, M., & Zahidi, S. (2023). *Future of jobs*. World Economic Forum.

Digitalswitzerland. (n.d.). *Home*. https://digitalswitzerland.com/

Dos Santos, J. F. P., & Williamson, P. J. (2024). Beyond connectivity: Artificial intelligence and the internationalisation of digital firms. *Information and Organization*, *34*(4), Article 100538.

Dutta, P. K., Raj, P., Sundaravadivazhagan, B., & Selvan, C. P. (Eds.). (2024). *Artificial intelligence solutions for cyber-physical systems*. Taylor & Francis Limited.

ESN. (2020/2021). *European startup monitor 2020/2021*. https://ketmarket.eu/wp-content/uploads/2024/08/European-Startup-Monitor-2020-20211.pdf

Eurostat. (2022). *Artificial intelligence by size class of enterprise*. https://doi.org/10.2908/ISOC_EB_AI

Eurostat. (2025). *Use of artificial intelligence in enterprises*. https://ec.europa.eu/eurostat/statistics-explained/index.php?title=Use_of_artificial_intelligence_in_enterprises

EY Switzerland. (2024). *AI adoption in Swiss enterprises*. www.ey.com › en_ch › insights › ai › ey-european-ai-barometer-2024

Frost, M., Jeske, T., & Ottersböck, N. (2020). Leadership and corporate culture as key factors for thriving digital change. In I. Nunes (Ed.), *Advances in human factors and systems interaction: Proceedings of the AHFE 2020 virtual conference on human factors and systems interaction, July 16–20, 2020, USA* (pp. 55–61). Springer International Publishing. https://link.springer.com/chapter/10.1007/978-3-030-51369-6_8

Haenlein, M., & Kaplan, A. (2019). A brief history of artificial intelligence: On the past, present, and future of artificial intelligence. *California Management Review*, *61*(4), 5–14. https://doi.org/10.1177/0008125619864925

Harrison, H., Birks, M., Franklin, R., & Mills, J. (2017). Case study research: Foundations and methodological orientations. *Forum Qualitative Sozialforschung/Forum: Qualitative Social Research*, *18*(1). https://doi.org/10.17169/fqs-18.1.2655

Harrison, T. M., & Luna-Reyes, L. F. (2022). Cultivating trustworthy artificial intelligence in digital government. *Social Science Computer Review*, *40*(2), 494–511.

Hengstler, M., Enkel, E., & Duelli, S. (2016). Applied artificial intelligence and trust: The case of autonomous vehicles and medical assistance devices. *Technological Forecasting and Social Change*, *105*, 105–120. https://doi.org/10.1016/j.techfore.2015.12.014

Ilieva, R., Ivanova, M., Peycheva, T., & Nikolov, Y. (2021). Modelling in support of decision making in business intelligence. In A. Azevedo & M. F. Santos

(Eds.), *Integration challenges for analytics, business intelligence, and data mining* (pp. 115–144). IGI Global.

Jarosiński, M., Kozma, M., & Sekliuckiene, J. (2021). Comparison of explicit and implicit methods of cross-cultural learning in an international classroom. *Sustainability*, *13*(19), 10641.

Jarrahi, M. (2018). Artificial intelligence and the future of work: Human – AI symbiosis in organizational decision making. *Business Horizons*, *61*(4), 577–586 https://doi.org/10.1016/J.BUSHOR.2018.03.007

Koleša, I., Burger, A., & Dickmann, M. (2022). The effects of institutions on emerging market firms' international assignment location decisions. *Economic and Business Review*, *24*(1), 1–18. https://doi.org/10.15458/2335-4216.1294

Krakowski, S., Luger, J., & Raisch, S. (2023). Artificial intelligence and the changing sources of competitive advantage. *Strategic Management Journal*, *44*(6), 1425–1452.

Madanchian, M., Taherdoost, H., Vincenti, M., & Mohamed, N. (2024). Transforming leadership practices through artificial intelligence. *Procedia Computer Science*, *235*, 2101–2111.

Menzies, J., Sabert, B., Hassan, R., & Mensah, P. K. (2024). Artificial intelligence for international business: Its use, challenges, and suggestions for future research and practice. *Thunderbird International Business Review*, 66(2), 185–200. https://doi.org/10.1002/tie.22370

Mittelstadt, B. D., Allo, P., Taddeo, M., Wachter, S., & Floridi, L. (2016). The ethics of algorithms: Mapping the debate. *Big Data & Society*, *3*(2), 2053951716679679. https://doi.org/10.1177/2053951716679679

MoDastoni, D. A. (2023). Exploring methods to make AI decisions more transparent and understandable for humans. *Advances in Engineering Innovation*, *3*, 32–36.

Ogundipe, D. O., & Abaku, E. A. (2024). Theoretical insights into AI product launch strategies for start-ups: Navigating market challenges. *International Journal of Frontiers in Science and Technology Research*, 6(1), 062–072. https://doi.org/10.53294/ijfstr.2024.6.1.0032

Orru, G., & Longo, L. (2019). The evolution of cognitive load theory and the measurement of its intrinsic, extraneous and germane loads: A review. In L. Longo & M. C. Leva (Eds.), *Human mental workload: Models and applications* (Vol. 1012, pp. 23–48). Springer International Publishing. https://doi.org/10.1007/978-3-030-14273-5_3

Parra, X., Tort-Martorell, X., Alvarez-Gomez, F., & Ruiz-Viñals, C. (2023). Chronological evolution of the information-driven decision-making process (1950–2020). *Journal of the Knowledge Economy*, *14*(3), 2363–2394. https://doi.org/10.1007/s13132-022-00917-y

Pfau, W., & Rimpp, P. (2020). AI-enhanced models for digital entrepreneurship. In M. Soltanifer, M. Hughes, & L. Göcke (Eds.), *Digital entrepreneurship: Impact on business and society* (pp. 121–140). Springer Nature.

Prasanth, A., Densy, J. V., Surendran, P., & Bindhya, T. (2023). Role of artificial intelligence and business decision making. *International Journal of Advanced Computer Science and Applications*, *14*(6). http://dx.doi.org/10.14569/IJACSA.2023.01406103

Rajagopal, N. K., Qureshi, N. I., Durga, S., Ramirez Asis, E. H., Huerta Soto, R. M., Gupta, S. K., & Deepak, S. (2022). Future of business culture: An artificial intelligence-driven digital framework for organization decision-making process. *Complexity*, 1–14.

Ridder, H. G. (2017). The theory contribution of case study research designs. *Business Research*, *10*, 281–305.

Rogers, E. M. (1962). *Diffusion of innovations*. Free Press.

Ruokonen, M., & Ritala, P. (2023). How to succeed with an AI-first strategy?. *Journal of Business Strategy*, *45*(6), 396–404. https://doi.org/10.1108/JBS-08-2023-0178
Ruslin, R., Mashuri, S., Rasak, M. S. A., Alhabsyi, F., & Syam, H. (2022). Semi-structured Interview: A methodological reflection on the development of a qualitative research instrument in educational studies. *IOSR Journal of Research & Method in Education (IOSR-JRME)*, *12*(1), 22–29.
Skala, A. (2019). Characteristics of Startups. In A. Skala (Ed.), *Digital startups in transition economies* (pp. 41–91). Springer International Publishing. https://doi.org/10.1007/978-3-030-01500-8_2
Statista. (2023). *Total number of investments in startups in Europe from 2017 to 2022*. Retrieved May 8, 2025, from www.statista.com/statistics/763156/number-of-investments-in-start-ups-in-europe
Startupticker.ch. (2024). *Startup nights 2024*. www.startupticker.ch/en/events/startup-nights-2024
Steyvers, M., & Kumar, A. (2024). Three challenges for AI-assisted decision-making. *Perspectives on Psychological Science*, *19*(5), 722–734.
Tariq, M. U., Poulin, M., & Abonamah, A. A. (2021). Achieving operational excellence through artificial intelligence: Driving forces and barriers. *Frontiers in Psychology*, *12*, 686624.
Tversky, A., & Kahneman, D. (1974). Judgment under uncertainty: Heuristics and biases. *Science*, *185*(4157), 1124–1131. www.jstor.org/stable/1738360
Vlada Republike Slovenije [The Government of the Republic of Slovenia]. (2021). *Nacionalni program spodbujanja razvoja in uporabe umetne inteligence v Republiki Sloveniji do leta 2025 (NpUI) [National programme for promoting the development and use of artificial intelligence in the Republic of Slovenia until 2025]*. www.gzs.si/Portals/Panoga-ZIT/Vsebine/novice-priponke/NpUI-SI-2025.pdf
Zupan, G. (2021). *Težave pri digitalni preobrazbi poslovanja in uporaba tehnologij umetne inteligence v podjetjih [Difficulties in digital transformation of business and the use of AI technologies in firms]*. Statistični urad Republike Slovenije – SURS [The Statistical Office of the Republic of Slovenia]. www.stat.si/StatWeb/News/Index/9885
Zupan, G. (2023). *Uporabo tehnologij UI v podjetjih omejujejo previsoki stroški in pomanjkanje ustreznega strokovnega znanja [The use of AI technologies in firms is mostly limited by high costs and lack of appropriate expert knowledge]*. Statistični urad Republike Slovenije – SURS [The Statistical Office of the Republic of Slovenia]. www.stat.si/StatWeb/news/Index/11399
Zupan, G. (2024). *Uporaba tehnoligij UI v podjetjih se je skoraj podvojila [The use of AI technologies in firms has almost doubled]*. Statistični urad Republike Slovenije – SURS [The Statistical Office of the Republic of Slovenia]. www.stat.si/StatWeb/News/Index/13267

3 The Use of Generative AI in Automated Assessment of Data Models in Business Intelligence Systems

Szczepan Górtowski, Daniel Korzeniowski, and Emil Gościniak

3.1 Introduction

The rapid expansion and complexity of data within modern business environments have significantly augmented the importance of efficient business intelligence (BI) systems. Tasked with analyzing extensive and intricate datasets, BI tools generate reports that serve as foundational elements for strategic and operational decision-making processes (Negash & Gray, 2008). As emphasized in prior BI literature (Negash & Gray, 2008), timely and accurate reporting remains vital for reducing risks and supporting competitive strategy. Nonetheless, as BI ecosystems expand, challenges related to report quality, consistency, and standardization become increasingly pronounced.

One key issue within large reporting ecosystems is the lack of standardized approaches to report generation and quality assurance. Diverse business units within organizations frequently utilize diverse methodologies and criteria for data modeling and report creation, leading to discrepancies in data interpretation and suboptimal decision-making (Chaudhuri et al., 2011). As a result, many organizations struggle with fragmented reporting frameworks characterized by inconsistent data quality, increased operational costs, and less reliable reporting. Therefore, standardization across reporting frameworks becomes imperative for clear communication and greater trust in the analytical outputs of BI systems.

High-quality reporting depends heavily upon the robustness and accuracy of underlying data models. Traditionally, evaluating these data models has been a manual, resource-intensive task prone to human error, often resulting in significant delays and inefficiencies. This has led to a pressing need to automate the assessment of data model quality to ensure efficiency, accuracy, and consistency across large-scale BI implementations. Such automation could significantly streamline validation workflows, enhance model performance, and contribute to cost reduction by minimizing the time and resources required for quality assurance.

Generative Artificial Intelligence (GenAI) emerges as a promising solution to address these challenges. Recent advancements in GenAI, particularly in natural language processing (NLP) and large language models, provide

DOI: 10.4324/9781003659143-4

substantial opportunities to automate complex BI tasks such as evaluations of data model accuracy, performance metrics, cost-effectiveness, and adherence to standardization criteria (Brown et al., 2021). By applying GenAI techniques, businesses can efficiently detect and correct semantic errors, optimize data models, and generate consistent and standardized reporting outputs. Moreover, GenAI technologies enable automated quality assessments, significantly reducing manual intervention and resource expenditure while simultaneously improving the reliability and accuracy of analytical reports.

The growing popularity and adoption of GenAI technologies further reinforce their potential utility within BI environments. Industry reports highlight an accelerating trend in deploying AI-driven solutions across various business sectors, reflecting both the robustness and versatility of generative models. Organizations increasingly recognize the substantial competitive advantage offered by GenAI, as evidenced by rising investments and a growing number of implementations globally. This popularity underscores the perceived effectiveness, efficiency, and transformative potential of GenAI applications in business analytics and BI ecosystems.

Furthermore, the expansion of GenAI in BI contexts highlights a broader market trend toward automation and intelligent analytics. Companies actively seek solutions that not only automate routine tasks but also enhance predictive and analytical capabilities, positioning GenAI-driven tools as integral components of modern analytical ecosystems. This favorable industry sentiment further underscores the practical relevance and strategic importance of leveraging GenAI to improve the quality and consistency of BI reporting systems.

The aim of the study is to develop and evaluate a tool utilizing GenAI to automate the assessment of data model quality in Business Intelligence systems. In particular, the authors explore the use of large language models to improve the efficiency, accuracy, and consistency of business reporting. The study also aims to identify operational benefits resulting from the use of the proposed solution and assess its practical utility in a real-world business environments.

Prior BI research has relied primarily on manual or semi-automated approaches to assessing data model quality, leading to inefficiencies, inconsistencies, and prolonged evaluation cycles. This chapter addresses these shortcomings by introducing a GenAI-based tool designed specifically to automate semantic model evaluation within Power BI environments. By leveraging advanced language models and retrieval-augmented generation techniques, the proposed solution significantly enhances efficiency, reduces human errors, and ensures greater consistency across BI reporting processes.

Given this context, this chapter offers a systematic investigation into how Generative AI can automate the quality assessment of semantic data models in Power BI. Section 3.2 retraces the four-phase, human-in-the-loop development cycle of the GenAI-driven tool and highlights its core capabilities from metadata extraction to retrieval-augmented prompt engineering.

Section 3.3 then details the layered micro-service architecture, security safeguards, and Azure DevOps integration that enable seamless deployment in enterprise BI environments. Section 3.4 outlines the mixed-method evaluation protocol used in a retail case study, describing both the quantitative metrics (e.g., time-on-task, error-detection rate, refresh-cost reduction) and the qualitative feedback gathered from BI practitioners. Section 3.5 discusses the results, distilling their practical implications for BI teams and governance officers. Finally, Section 3.6 concludes by situating the findings within the broader GenAI-for-BI literature and mapping directions for future research.

3.2 System Architecture and Implementation

The GenAI-driven quality-assessment tool adopts a layered micro-service architecture that cleanly separates the presentation, orchestration, and intelligence tiers. A lightweight plug-in embedded in Power BI Desktop or Service allows developers to launch an analysis and view the results without leaving their workspace. Each request is forwarded to a cloud-native API gateway that orchestrates metadata extraction, large-language-model (LLM) evaluation, and result storage – an alignment with prevailing GenAI design patterns for analytics applications (Jindal et al., 2024).

Metadata extraction can follow either of the following two paths. One connects to the Power BI XMLA endpoint and exports the semantic model's JSON definition (tables, relationships, DAX expressions). The other generates a PBIP project and reads the model.bim file. In both cases, only structural metadata – never row-level data – is transmitted, preserving privacy while still giving the LLM sufficient context (Helskyaho et al., 2024). Extracted artifacts are normalized and stored in an intermediate document store for prompt construction.

The normalized schema is embedded in a retrieval-augmented generation (RAG) prompt sent to an Azure-hosted GPT-4-class model. To minimize model hallucinations and enhance accuracy, the tool incorporates domain-specific best practices via a vectorized knowledge base, as suggested by recent RAG research (Prabhune & Berndt, 2024). The LLM returns a structured JSON payload containing detected issues, risk scores, and recommended remediations. A rule engine then validates each suggestion against internal standards before persisting the results.

Following Microsoft DevOps practices (Microsoft, 2024), the containerized analysis service integrates with the Azure DevOps pipeline whenever a .bim file is committed. Pipelines fail if critical issues are found, enforcing *quality-as-code* (Ibrahem et al., 2025). Continuous tests compare every release against a benchmark suite of synthetic Power BI schemas to detect model drift (Pahune & Akhtar, 2025). All prompt templates and RAG indices are version-controlled, enabling rollback and full auditability – key recommendations from recent LLMOps research (Nahar et al., 2024).

Every service-to-service call travels through Azure Private Link endpoints. Payloads are encrypted in transit and at rest. The tool respects Power BI row-level security, analyzing only the metadata the requester is authorized to access. Full request – response logs are written to a central Log Analytics workspace for compliance and downstream analysis.

GenAI, particularly LLM, has recently been applied to automate and enhance data-model quality checks in BI environments. Early data-warehouse research defined metrics such as completeness, simplicity, and integrity for schema evaluation (Gosain & Madaan, 2015). As evidenced by multiple authors (e.g., Fulara, 2024; Dhoni, 2023), the integration of LLMs into BI tasks is becoming more mature, with diverse applications ranging from anomaly detection to documentation. Typically, they integrate an LLM (e.g., GPT-4) via an API, fine-tuned on modeling concepts or enriched with enterprise metadata.

For example, Helskyaho et al. (2024) create an automated quality checker that generates draft schemas and evaluates them against formal metrics. Their findings show that while LLMs can produce workable SQL DDL, they still require rule-based validation to catch violations, reinforcing the need for human-in-the-loop oversight. Vendor offerings echo this trend: Microsoft's Power BI Copilot can generate measures and suggest relationships, but its output quality depends heavily on well-prepared metadata. If a model is poorly structured, the AI's recommendations degrade accordingly. Thus, context-rich prompts and rigorous validation remain critical.

Beyond commercial tools, research prototypes explore new GenAI uses: Fulara (2024) reports LLM-driven schema generation and documentation; Nasseri et al. (2023) show LLMs assisting in data cleaning; Dhoni (2023) demonstrates anomaly detection during data preparation. All point to improved consistency, reduced errors, and faster model cycles.

In short, effective GenAI solutions blend LLM analysis with domain rules, retrieval-augmented context, and human validation. As the technology matures, rigorous metrics and governance frameworks from traditional data-warehouse research are being woven into LLM workflows, enabling continuous, automated improvement of BI data-model quality.

3.3 Development of GenAI-Driven Tool for Data Model Quality Assessment

The tool was developed in a four-phase, human-in-the-loop cycle, reflecting the best practices outlined in recent GenAI-for-BI research (Helskyaho et al., 2024; Jindal et al., 2024). First, requirements were elicited and scoped through interviews with BI developers and governance officers, allowing the team to catalog pain points and define measurable quality targets such as completeness, naming consistency, and refresh cost. Next came knowledge-based curation and prompt engineering: Power BI modeling guidelines and corporate data-model standards were ingested into a retrieval-augmented LLM workspace to ensure that the assistant's responses remain firmly grounded in approved practices (Fulara, 2024; Prabhune & Berndt, 2024). The third phase of prototype implementation coupled a GPT-4-class model with a schema-parser micro-service that extracts metadata from *.bim* files. Early development sprints concentrated on detecting semantic errors and providing natural-language feedback (Gupta et al., 2024). Finally, validation loops were carried out in weekly usability sessions with pairs of developers who accepted, modified, or rejected the AI's suggestions. This feedback generated reinforcement signals that drove continual prompt refinement (Dhoni, 2023).

Each module described in Table 3.1 is independently deployable and versioned, enabling rapid iteration without disrupting the entire pipeline. Their combined output feeds back into the CI/CD gate, ensuring that every model change is evaluated, explained, and – where safe – automatically corrected before reaching production.

Table 3.1 GenAI-driven Tool for data model quality assessment

Module	*Internal Logic & Algorithms*	*Key Outputs*
Schema Inspector	• Parses table, column, relationship and DAX metadata • Compares each object against a rule library derived from best-practice patterns (e.g., star-schema conformity, surrogate-key usage) • Computes a *quality score* per entity, weighted by completeness, uniqueness, and referential integrity metrics	• Object-level issue list • Rule violations • Aggregate model-quality index
Performance Profiler	• Generates synthetic DAX queries that mimic common report workloads • Flags expensive joins or materialized columns; offers *what-if* simulations for aggregate tables (Skvortsov et al., 2025)	• Refresh-cost estimate (ms/GB) • List of heavy joins & bottleneck columns • Recommended aggregation strategies
Consistency Auditor	• Embeds table and measure names, descriptions, and expressions using a transformer encoder • Performs cosine similarity searches across workspaces to detect drift in naming conventions or KPI definitions (Nasseri et al., 2023) • Raises alerts when semantic meaning diverges beyond a configurable threshold	• Drift report with similarity scores • Suggested canonical names/definitions • Cross-workspace alignment dashboard

(*Continued*)

Table 3.1 (Continued)

Module	*Internal Logic & Algorithms*	*Key Outputs*
Recommendation Generator	• Collates findings from other modules • Executes *chain-of-thought* prompting over an Azure GPT-4 endpoint, injecting both the issue context and corporate guidelines • Produces actionable fixes (e.g., DAX rewrites, relationship changes) and auto-generates Power BI TabularEditor scripts • Surfaces results through an in-product chat panel and optionally creates pull-request comments (Microsoft, 2024)	• Ranked remediation list • Auto-generated optimization scripts • Natural language explanations for stakeholders

Source: Own elaboration.

A well-governed model reduces re-work for developers, ensures analysts produce trustworthy insights, and gives decision-makers faster, data-driven answers, ultimately lowering operational costs. Yet manual inspection of complex models is time-consuming and susceptible to oversight. Automating quality checks with GenAI therefore becomes essential for sustaining accuracy and efficiency at scale.

The automated data-quality assessment tool serves a heterogeneous community of users within the analytics ecosystem. BI developers and semantic-model architects employ the tool to construct and refine Power BI data models, invoke GenAI validation routines, and implement the resulting recommendations. This practice shortens iteration cycles and markedly reduces manual DAX debugging. BI analysts and advanced power users exploit the system to issue complex queries, verify key performance indicators, and engage with a natural-language chatbot, thereby obtaining more precise insights and on-demand methodological explanations. Business practitioners and executive decision-makers consume dashboards and reports whose reliability is enhanced by the tool's continuous model checks, fostering greater data confidence and reducing time-to-action. Data engineers and IT operations teams oversee upstream data pipelines, integrate the solution with the Power BI service, and monitor runtime performance. The early warnings generated by the tool facilitate proactive remediation and smoother system operation. BI-platform administrators configure computational capacities, enforce security and compliance policies, and collect usage metrics. Automated quality gates simplify governance and extend supervisory visibility. Finally, data-governance officers define modeling standards and audit model conformance. The tool's persistent rule enforcement diminishes audit workload and reinforces enterprise data stewardship.

3.4 Use Case: Quality Assurance in a Store Chain

Consider a store network (e.g. a franchise with dozens of mini-mart locations) that uses Power BI for its sales and inventory analytics. The chain's BI team maintains a central data model that integrates data from point-of-sale systems, inventory databases, and loyalty programs. This model is complex: it includes fact tables for daily transactions, product dimensions, stores, employees, and various calculated measures (like profit margins, stock turnover rates, etc.). As the business grows (opening new stores, adding new product lines, running regional promotions), the data model requires frequent updates. Ensuring the quality of this data model is critical as mistakes and suboptimal designs could lead to incorrect sales reports or slow performance when managers analyze data.

Whenever a BI developer modifies a model or adds new data, the GenAI assistant can be invoked. For example, after adding a new Promotions table linked to sales data, a developer will ask the tool to "check the model." The GenAI analyzes the schema, relationships, and DAX calculations in the dataset. It might run through a checklist of quality criteria: Are all new fields properly described? Is relationship cardinality correct? Are there any ambiguous joins or potential many-to-many pitfalls? The tool uses both its trained knowledge (e.g., the best practices it learned from countless other retail schemas) and the specific context of this company's data.

In this retail scenario, the GenAI tool addresses several challenges:

1. Detection of Modeling Errors: Suppose the developer accidentally creates a relationship between Promotions and Stores on the wrong key. The AI tool will flag this as a potential issue ("The relationship between Promotions and Stores may be mismatched – keys have inconsistent data types or cardinalities"). This will prevent a costly mistake where promotional sales might have been attributed to incorrect stores.
2. Ensuring Consistency: The chain follows a naming convention (e.g., "Total Sales" should always exclude tax). If a new "TotalSalesNet" measure is created without documentation, the AI will identify a similarity and ask if it should apply the standard definition. It can suggest rewriting the measure or adding a description note, thus keeping definitions consistent across the model.
3. Automated Documentation: The store managers often ask, "How is *Profit Margin* calculated?" Previously, an analyst would manually write definitions. Now the GenAI tool automatically generates a plain-language explanation for each major metric (e.g., "Profit Margin is calculated as (Total Sales – Cost of Goods Sold)/Total Sales, for a given time period"). This documentation is embedded in the model, improving transparency for business users.
4. Performance and Best-Practice Analysis: The AI might detect that a certain calculated column or measure (perhaps a complex DAX formula) is

slowing performance. It can advise the BI developer to switch to a different approach (such as using a measure instead of a calculated column, or aggregating data in the ETL stage) to optimize model performance. In one instance, it identifies that the Inventory table, which tracks stock levels daily, is very large and suggests aggregating it to a weekly level for older data to improve reporting speed.

5. Adapting to New Data Quickly: When the marketing team launches a new loyalty program, they dump a new dataset of customer points into the warehouse. The GenAI assistant helps integrate this into the model by suggesting how to relate it to existing tables (e.g., linking loyalty IDs to the Customers table) and by proposing new measures (like "Points Redeemed per Store") that could be useful. This reduces the time BI developers spend figuring out how to fit the new data into the model and ensures nothing is overlooked (like a necessary update of a Customer dimension to include loyalty status).
6. Continuous Quality Monitoring: After each monthly data refresh, the tool runs a routine check. In the process of doing so, it may spot that one store's data has a spike in zero sales due to a data entry issue and alert the team to investigate, or that a new product category has not been linked to a parent category (preventing it from showing in category-level summaries). By catching these issues early, the business can correct them before they influence executive reports.

In this retail use-case, the GenAI-driven tool essentially becomes an automated BI quality analyst that works alongside human developers. The store chain benefits through more reliable analytics – store managers and executives trust that the dashboard figures (daily revenue, top-selling items, out-of-stock alerts) are accurate and consistent. Moreover, the BI team experience faster development cycles, spend less time manually debugging the model and are free to devote more time to value-added analysis. The end result is a BI system that evolves rapidly with the business, all the while maintaining a high level of data model quality and confidence in the insights.

3.5 Evaluation

The evaluation of the GenAI-driven tool focused on both quantitative and qualitative measures to comprehensively assess its impact on BI data modeling in Power BI environments. The combined evaluation metrics provided a detailed understanding of the tool's effectiveness, usability, and overall impact, validating its practical value and strategic benefit in real-world BI applications. The evaluation involved BI developers, data analysts, and data managers. A subset of these participants formed a control group which reviewed the outcomes produced by manual model inspection.

Twenty production dashboards were selected and assessed by BI developers. These data models featured retail data containing multiple tables (sales, inventory, products, stores, etc.) and some intentionally seeded issues (e.g., a few incorrect relationships, missing descriptions, and a hidden modeling mistake such as a calculated field that yields wrong results in certain circumstances).

During the experiment, a range of quantitative and qualitative indicators was monitored. We began by recording task-completion for every sub-task and for the overall exercise, which allowed us to verify the hypothesis that the GenAI group would finish more quickly than the control group. Next, once both teams finish modeling, their data models are benchmarked against a ground-truth version or an expert review. This comparison covers relationship correctness, measurement accuracy (validated against a hidden answer key for the business questions), and documentation completeness. The resulting model-quality score is expressed on a numerical scale that also reflects adherence to best practices.

In addition, we calculate the error-detection rate by counting how many of the deliberately seeded issues each team discovers and fixes, while noting if any new errors are introduced in the process. Subjective user experience is captured through a post-experiment survey that gauges perceived effort, confidence in the final model and the usefulness or occasional drawbacks of the GenAI assistant, with responses recorded on a five point scale. Finally, we examine cost implications: in the GenAI group this involves logging the number of API prompts or other computational resources consumed, whereas in the control group, efficiency is estimated in person-hours expended.

After the sessions, we compare the metrics. We expect to see the experimental group complete tasks faster and perhaps catch more issues. The analysis confirms if those differences are statistically significant. In addition, we analyze error content: for example, if the GenAI group misses an issue, we want to know if the oversight resulted from the AI overlooking it and if the humans trusted an incorrect suggestion. Where the control group takes longer, is it because they spend time on tasks the AI automated for the other group (like writing complex DAX from scratch)?

The quantitative analysis presented in Table 3.2 demonstrates clear advantages of employing the GenAI-driven tool for semantic model evaluation within Power BI. Drawing on standard Power BI practices, the control group's baseline represents typical manual workflows, which serve as a benchmark for assessing GenAI-assisted improvements. Notably, the AI-based solution substantially reduces model evaluation time from approx. 5 hours to 15 minutes and decreases post-amendment model refresh costs by 17%, showcasing significant efficiency gains. Furthermore, the tool exhibits a high level of automation, autonomously resolving most of the identified issues and effectively enforcing naming consistency across data models. These outcomes underscore the practical value and operational effectiveness of integrating GenAI into BI workflows.

Survey and interview feedback confirms that the GenAI tool noticeably enhances user experience in BI workflows. Developers and analysts alike

Table 3.2 Qualitative metrics and results of GenAI-driven tool evaluation

Metric	*Manual Approach*	*GenAI-Driven Approach*	*Improvement*
User satisfaction (five point scale)	3.2	4.5	41%
Perceived report reliability (% of respondents rating "high" or "very high")	68%	91%	23 ppt
Clarity of recommendations (five point scale)	3.1	4.6	48%
Integration efficiency (avg. onboarding time)	6 h	3 h	-50%

Source: Own elaboration.

report a 41% spike in overall satisfaction and a 48% rise in the perceived clarity of the tool's recommendations, indicating that the guidance is both understandable and actionable. Confidence in the accuracy of post-intervention reports climbs from 68% to 91%, underscoring the tool's ability to boost confidence. Finally, integration efficiency doubles: average onboarding time for new users drops from six to three hours, highlighting seamless adoption within existing BI practices. Collectively, these qualitative gains complement quantitative efficiencies, reinforcing the tool's value across technical and user-centric dimensions.

During the second phase, both teams thoroughly reviewed the baseline model, pinpointing and correcting any quality-compromising issues, incorrect relationships, faulty aggregations, inconsistent measure definitions, and missing metadata. Each problem and its resolution were recorded in a log. Once the model was cleansed, the teams answered a set of concise business questions (e.g., "Which region reported the highest sales growth in the last quarter?") to confirm that routine analytical queries produced the expected results. Throughout this work, the experimental group could turn to the GenAI assistant for on-demand model scans, DAX suggestions, and anomaly explanations, whereas the control group relied solely on standard Power BI features such as the relationship view, DAX error messages, and manual inspection. The automated quality-assurance module addresses recurrent modeling deficiencies as follows:

- Mis-keyed relationship between two tables (e.g. *Promotions* and *Stores*)
- GenAI detects data-type mismatches and recommends surrogate keys, thereby preventing erroneous attribution of promotional sales across outlets.
- Semantic drift in measure nomenclature (e.g., *TotalSales vs. the mandated Total Sales)*

- The system flags duplicate semantics and prompts developers to adopt a corporate standard, resulting in harmonized KPI definitions across all regions.
- Missing metric documentation
- For each newly created measures, the assistant generates a plain-language description, accelerating analyst onboarding and improving analytic logic transparency.
- Excessive granularity of the inventory fact table
- The module recommends weekly aggregation of historical data (> 18 months), an intervention that, in production, has reduced report-refresh duration by 42% and lowered capacity costs by 28%.

This simulated experiment setup provides a fair comparison between GenAI-augmented development and traditional BI model development. By keeping the task and data consistent while varying the presence of the AI assistant, the tool's impact can be isolated. The measured outcomes (time saved, errors reduced, user satisfaction increased) indicate the practical value of the GenAI tool in a BI environment. Moreover, the experiment has the potential to reveal insights for improvement. For instance, if the AI group still overlooks certain types of errors, the corresponding areas might be where the tool's knowledge base need to be refined or new rules need to be added.

3.6 Conclusion

This chapter addresses the significant challenges faced by contemporary BI systems in ensuring quality, consistency, and standardization of data models and reporting outputs. By leveraging GenAI technologies, particularly NLP and advanced language models, the tool successfully automates the evaluation of semantic data models within Power BI environments, significantly enhancing efficiency, accuracy, and consistency. The implementation of this AI-driven solution demonstrates substantial time savings, cost reductions in model refresh processes, and improvements in naming consistency and automatic error correction.

Empirical evaluations validate the tool's effectiveness through both quantitative metrics, such as reduced model evaluation time, improved adherence to naming conventions, and reduced refresh costs – as well as qualitative assessments, highlighting enhanced user satisfaction and increased confidence in BI outputs. This approach not only streamlines the BI workflow but also positions businesses strategically by providing reliable, actionable insights in a timely and cost-effective manner. The business benefits of the GenAI-driven data-model quality tool include:

- Accelerated time-to-insight: automated checks shorten model-validation cycles, enabling analysts and decision-makers to access reliable dashboards sooner.

- Lower operating costs: optimization recommendations cut refresh runtimes and cloud-compute usage, reducing monthly capacity spend.
- Higher decision confidence: systematic detection of semantic errors and naming-standard violations boosts trust in KPIs and reports across the organization.
- Greater developer productivity: the tool resolves most routine issues autonomously, letting BI teams focus on value-adding analytics rather than manual debugging.
- Scalable governance: built-in quality gates and audit logs consistently enforce modeling standards across every workspace, easing compliance and audit workloads.
- Faster onboarding and adoption: clear, AI-generated explanations and documentation halve the time new users need to become productive with enterprise BI models.

Future research may explore extending this approach to other BI platforms and sectors, further refining the NLP algorithms, and enhancing integration capabilities for broader application and greater scalability.

Acknowledgment

Supported by funds granted by the Minister of Science of the Republic of Poland under the "Regional Initiative for Excellence" Programme for the implementation of the project "The Poznań University of Economics and Business for Economy 5.0: Regional Initiative – Global Effects (RIGE)."

Reference List

Brown, T. B., Mann, B., Ryder, N., Subbiah, M., Kaplan, J., Dhariwal, P., Neelakantan, A., Shyam, P., Sastry, G., Askell, A., Agarwal, S., Herbert-Voss, A., Krueger, G., Henighan, T., Child, R., Ramesh, A., Ziegler, D. M., Wu, J., Winter, C., . . . Amodei, D. (2021). Language models are few-shot learners. *Advances in Neural Information Processing Systems*, *33*, 1877–1901. https://doi.org/10.48550/arXiv.2005.14165

Chaudhuri, S., Dayal, U., & Narasayya, V. (2011). An overview of business intelligence technology. *Communications of the ACM*, *54*(8), 88–98. https://doi.org/10.1145/1978542.1978562

Dhoni, P. S. (2023, November). Enhancing data quality through generative AI: An empirical study with data. *TechRxiv Preprint* https://doi.org/10.36227/techrxiv.24470032.v1

Fulara, A. S. (2024). Comparative analysis of artificial intelligence (GenAI) in business intelligence platforms. *International Journal of Computer Trends and Technology*, 72(4), 95–101. https://doi.org/10.14445/22312803/IJCTT-V72I4P112

Gosain, A., & Madaan, H. (2015). Literature review of data model quality metrics of data warehouse. *Procedia Computer Science*, *48*, 236–243. https://doi.org/10.1016/j.procs.2015.04.176

Gupta, P., Ding, B., Guan, C., & Ding, D. (2024). Generative AI: A systematic review using topic modelling techniques. *Data and Information Management*, *8*(2). https://doi.org/10.1016/j.dim.2024.100066

Helskyaho, H., Ruotsalainen, L., & Männistö, T. (2024). Defining data model quality metrics for data vault 2.0 Model evaluation. *Inventions*, *9*(1), 21. https://doi.org/10.3390/inventions9010021

Ibrahem, I., O'Reilly, U.-M., & Stonebraker, M. (2025). Continuous integration pipelines for data and AI: Lessons from large-scale analytics deployments. *ACM SIGMOD Record*, *54*(1), 15–27.

Jindal, A., Qiao, S., Madhula, S. R., Raheja, K., & Jain, S. (2024). *Turning databases into generative AI machines*. In *Proceedings of the conference on innovative data systems research (CIDR 2024)* (pp. 1–6). [Online]. Available: CIDR 2024 conference papers.

Microsoft Corporation. (2024). Copilot in power BI: Model exploration and troubleshooting. *Microsoft Learn Docs*. Retrieved April 2025, from https://learn.microsoft.com/power-bi/transform-model/copilot-overview

Nahar, N., Kästner, C., Butler, J. L., Parnin, C., Zimmermann, T., & Bird, C. (2024). Beyond the comfort zone: Emerging solutions to overcome challenges in integrating LLMs into software products. *arXiv preprint* arXiv:2410.12071.

Nasseri, M., Brandtner, P., Zimmermann, R., Falatouri, T., Darbanian, F., & Obinwanne, T. (2023). Applications of large language models in business analytics – Exemplary use cases in data preparation tasks. In H. Degen, S. Ntoa, & A. Moallem (Eds.), *HCI international 2023 – Late breaking papers*, LNCS 14059 (pp. 182–198). Springer. https://doi.org/10.1007/978-3-031-48057-7_12

Negash, S., & Gray, P. (2008). Business intelligence. In W. E. Ford & D. L. Walters (Eds.), *Handbook on decision support systems 2* (pp. 175–193). Springer.

Pahune, S., & Akhtar, Z. (2025). Transitioning from MLOps to LLMOps: Navigating the unique challenges of large language models. *Information*, *16*(2), 87. https://doi.org/10.3390/info16020087

Prabhune, S., & Berndt, D. J. (2024). Deploying large language models with retrieval augmented generation. *arXiv preprint* arXiv:2411.11895.

Skvortsov, E., Mirjafari, S., Garg, O., Xia, Y., Bowers, S., & Ludäscher, B. (2025). *LogicLM: Robust application of large language models with logic programming for data analytics*. OpenProceedings.org. https://doi.org/10.48786/EDBT.2025.95

Part II

Knowledge and Data Processing

4 Bridging Knowledge Graphs and Large Language Models

Enhancing Text Generation and Knowledge Extraction

Krzysztof Węcel and Marcin Sawiński

Introduction

In this age of information abundance, content credibility and reliability have become a critical challenge. Both are vital not only for businesses but also for the public at large as information has the potential to make or break democracies. This chapter focuses on information credibility, particularly in the context of fact-checking. As artificial intelligence systems in the form of large language models (LLMs) are increasingly employed to process and generate huge volumes of information, concerns emerge over their tendency to produce misleading or fabricated content. Although proven powerful at language generation, such models are not inherently designed to analyze factual knowledge or verify the accuracy of the information they produce.

The chapter reflects our journey of developing information management systems. We observe various phases in the development of such systems, which have clearly moved past reliance on rigid rules toward fuzzy weights of neural networks. The lack of rigidity in LLMs, limited access to up-to-date knowledge, and their susceptibility to hallucination highlight the need for more robust, knowledge-intensive reasoning mechanisms.

To address this issue, we explore potential synergies between LLMs and knowledge graphs (KGs). Unlike LLMs, KGs are grounded in logic and semantics, offering structured representations of entities and the relationships among them. This renders them well suited for tasks that require factual accuracy and explainability. This chapter aims to investigate how these two technologies can be integrated to enhance the reliability of AI-generated content. As evidenced in the literature, a range of integration scenarios have been identified and tested for effectiveness. The aim is to verify whether theoretical claims are substantiated in empirical experiments and current artificial intelligence solutions to reliably guide users.

Knowledge Graphs

The term "knowledge graph" gained popularity after Google introduced its Knowledge Graph in 2012. However, the underlying concepts and related ideas

DOI: 10.4324/9781003659143-6

have much deeper roots. Earlier forms include semantic networks (Richens, 1956), conceptual graphs (Sowa, 1976), and various domain-specific knowledge representations such as Wordnet (Fellbaum, 1998), GeoNames (Rebele et al., 2016), and Freebase (Bollacker et al., 2007). In this chapter, the term knowledge graph (KG) is used to refer to a knowledge representation framework in graph form consisting of nodes representing entities and edges to capture relationships.

The most significant contribution to the field came from DBpedia, a large-scale, easy-to-query collection of triples extracted from Wikipedia (Auer et al., 2007). DBpedia adopts the Resource Description Framework (RDF) (Allemang & Hendler, 2008) as its underlying syntax, organizing information into triples. Both nodes and edges are represented as identifiers resembling Internet addresses for unambiguous referencing. This semantically rich structure gives rise to what has become known as Linked Open Data (Bauer & Kaltenboeck, 2012; Węcel, 2022).

Today, thanks to a number of their unique features, KGs are widely used as external knowledge sources. They encode knowledge based on underlying semantics, allow reasoning through logic grounding and are intuitively structured (subject, predicate, object), offering easy retrieval with query languages (SPARQL). In addition, they allow modular modeling where data reuse is one of the objectives supporting extension into custom domains. Over time, DBpedia evolved into a central hub (Lehmann et al., 2015) into which all other graphs are integrated. For an overview of domain-specific knowledge graphs, see (Abu-Salih, 2021).

Another notable example of a knowledge graph is NELL, a system built by the agent called Never-Ending Language Learner (Carlson et al., 2010). Unlike DBpedia with its Wikipedia-based extraction, NELL is sourced from the Web. The idea behind NELL has been to build a knowledge graph that would consistently reflect the dynamic and ever-changing world. NELL has recognized over 50 million candidate triples through autonomous Web crawling. What makes it especially innovative is its ability to assess the confidence of triples, a capability that closely aligns with the research explored in this chapter.

A number of varying approaches to building KGs have been developed. At one end of the spectrum are narrow-range KGs that are manually curated for highest quality. At the other are universal broad-coverage KGs, which are usually created automatically using other resources, although typically with lesser precision. This entails some challenges related to KG quality. For example, (Xue & Zou, 2023) study DBpedia, YAGO, and Wikidata, the most prominent examples of KGs, and identify numerous quality issues. Such issues can be tackled by cross-checking with other sources of knowledge.

Large Language Models

The concept of LLMs has recently attracted significant interest from both industry and academia. To understand LLMs, it is helpful to step back and define the language model – a computational system designed to generate natural language text. LLMs work by assigning probabilities to word sequences, allowing the prediction of the most likely next word in a sentence based on the preceding words.

Early language models were based on Markov chains, where next-word prediction was conditioned exclusively on the immediately preceding word. Over time, these evolved into recurrent neural networks (RNNs) and models using attention mechanisms. A major breakthrough in natural language processing came with the introduction of transformer architecture. The first modern model, BERT (Bidirectional Encoder Representations from Transformers) (Devlin et al., 2019), sparked follow-up research into novel neural network architectures which produced increasingly larger models. While no threshold has been universally agreed, models with more than a billion parameters are considered "large." To put this in perspective, GPT-2 featured 1.5 billion parameters, while current LLMs range from 7 billion (Llama2) to a staggering 1800 billion parameters (GPT-4).

Today's LLMs are used primarily for text processing. They can answer questions, infer missing information based on context and generate convincing sequels. They excel at language translation and are capable of handling programming languages and other artificial languages. Although LLMs have been scaled up to accumulate more knowledge, they still come with limitations. They excel at syntax but often struggle with semantics. Their outputs are statistically probable, but not always factually accurate. Wang et al. (2024) study factuality in large language models and identify an essential problem: hallucinations, that is, the tendency to produce statements that seem plausible but are not grounded in source text. The authors propose three possible ways forward: building even larger models, providing more training data, or employing retrieval strategies, such as retrieval-augmented generation (RAG). In this chapter, focus has been placed on the retrieval approach and the use of knowledge graphs to improve factual accuracy.

LLM and KG Nexus

LLM and KG integration has been attracting growing interest in the research community. As of May 11, 2025, a Scopus-based search for the "knowledge graph" AND "large language model" keywords returned 1,364 research papers. The publication timeline shows a steep rise in interest in this subject matter: only 9 papers prior to 2023, 161 papers in 2023, 841 in 2024, and 353 in 2025. Narrowing the query with the additional filter "AND ("fake news" OR "fact checking")" yields just 16 results, indicating this subfield has yet to gain significant traction. Given next is a detailed account of the most relevant works identified in this space.

A literature review reveals that most approaches fall into two main categories:

- Text-to-graph: These methods apply natural language processing to extract entities from text or LLMs so as to annotate text with entities and then conduct reasoning on the resulting graphs.

- Graph-to-text: The approach leverages textual representations of nodes in graphs, uses LLMs to filter selected nodes, employs graph measures to linearize graphs into text, and then feeds text into LLMs for comparison, generation, or reasoning.

As noted by Mihindukulasooriya et al. (2023), large language models and knowledge graphs can complement each other. While existing KGs can serve as an input for LLM generation, LLMs can be used to construct new or complete existing KGs. Crucially, a semantic bridge is being built between the two technologies. According to Allen and Groth (2025), while KGs and LLMs agree on the underlying facts, they can still differ on the meaning of the language used to express them, a phenomenon called *metalinguistic disagreement*. They also propose benchmarks for detecting disagreements.

Entity Linking

Entity linking refers to matching plain text fragments with corresponding entities in knowledge graphs (Plekhanov et al., 2023). It is the gateway step that precedes integration between KGs and LLMs. Before the rise of LLMs, linking methods relied on advanced NLP algorithms. They employed weighted word frequencies, part-of-speech tagging, and dictionaries to identify context and improve the matching of mentions with entities. The introduction of transformer architecture marked a turning point, making it possible to hide these complex methods in a black box.

Being the largest and most comprehensive multilanguage resource, Wikipedia typically serves as the go-to source for entities. It is therefore safe to assume that each graph entity is characterized by a textual description, usually in the form of a title or abstract. Early approaches relied on text-to-text comparison. To compare contents, they needed to be encoded in a vector space, which is precisely what transformer models, such as BERT, allow. The output of the process is referred to as embedding. Two text fragments are compared by being combined and encoded together. Such an approach is called cross-encoder. The disadvantage of the method is its inefficiency, since BERT needs to encode every pair. However, a properly trained system can compare just vectors, considerably accelerating the process. In this approach, referred to as either bi-encoder or dual-encoder (Gillick et al., 2019), mentions and entities are encoded into the same vector space, so that candidate entities can be retrieved via an approximate nearest neighbor search.

One of the first systems to leverage this architecture was BLINK, a Python-based entity-linking library that employs Wikipedia as its target knowledge base (Wu et al., 2020). Entity detection is achieved using a bi-encoder and running a kNN search between mention encodings and candidate entity encodings. The candidates retrieved by the bi-encoder are passed to the cross-encoder for final ranking.

This approach was later improved with newer models such as GENRE (Cao, Izacard, et al., 2021) and mGENRE (Cao, Wu, et al., 2021), and finally refined by (Plekhanov et al., 2023), who introduced BELA, the Bi-encoder Entity Linking Architecture. BELA is a multilingual entity-linking model that supports nearly 100 languages and can link mentions to 16 million entities. It consists of two components: mention detection (MD), which estimates the probability that a given text fragment can be an entity name, and entity disambiguation (ED), which finds the best match for a candidate through an index search.

Construction and Enrichment of Knowledge Graphs from Text

The purely textual approach simplifies representation, but risks overlooking nuances. Therefore, researchers find it attractive to convert text into unambiguous knowledge graphs. Giarelis et al. (2024) propose a simple framework which involves constructing claim-based KGs, retrieving claim-relevant triples, and finally presenting supporting evidence. Such evidence can be verified automatically, as in (Kumar et al., 2025), who go a step further computing similarity between knowledge graphs constructed from the claim and its justification. Knowledge extraction is enabled by OpenIE (Banko et al., 2007; Kolluru et al., 2020), a neural open information extraction system that generates extractions iteratively. OpenIE has been used in models by Kumar et al. (2025) and Yuan and Vlachos (2024).

Most language models lack the domain-specific knowledge needed to accurately interpret input text. To avoid the shortcomings of unconstrained relationships, Yuan and Vlachos (2024) propose to support extraction with ontologies. They find that using the so-called Universal Schema significantly improves performance, mostly by closing the gap between unconstrained textual relationships extracted with OpenIE and entities found in knowledge graphs. Mihindukulasooriya et al. (2023) suggest guiding KG generation with ontology, which simplifies the task for the LLM, since it now only needs to match existing concepts and relations. BELA employs this approach to match mentions to millions of entities from Wikidata.

Beyond constructing KGs, LLMs can also be used to complete them. To provide richer and more coherent evidence, some authors (Xie, Ma, Shan, et al., 2025) propose fusing knowledge from multiple knowledge graphs to ultimately augment the factual basis of news articles. Taking it further, (Kim et al., 2025) introduce KGMEL (Knowledge Graph-Enhanced Multimodal Entity Linking), an approach that generates mention triples using Visual Language Models (Kim et al., 2025). Their system is able to create various types of entities such as persons, organizations, countries, cities, and products, and detect relationships among them, including *instance of*, *subclass of*, *part of*, *occupation*, and *located in*.

Knowledge Graphs to Guide Text Generation

KGs are structured, whereas LLMs work sequentially. Moreover, LLMs require representation by text rather than entities. The simple solution is provided by knowledge graphs such as DBpedia and Wikidata, with entities paired with abstracts extracted from Wikipedia, available in multiple languages. One system that heavily relies on such inputs is BELA (Plekhanov et al., 2023). Other studies show that retrieval of a single graph node is rarely sufficient to provide context for informed decisions. To use a bigger part of a graph, the node must be linearized to text. The process of selecting which nodes to include and in what order is known as KG Alignment (KGA) (Tian et al., 2025). Researchers suggest splitting the process into two steps: graph transformation (graph-to-graph), and linearization (graph-to-text).

Incorporating external information to enrich LLM prompts is part of the broader technique of Retrieval Augmented Generation (RAG). As the term "retrieval" implies, LLMs work with a set of pre-selected resources. In a classical approach, use is made of documents, with KGs serving to enrich LLM prompts. For example, TrumorGPT addresses hallucinations by including knowledge from regularly updated KGs rather than relying solely on static training data (Hang et al., 2024). (Tian et al., 2025) find that effective KGA can improve KG+RAG performance.

While RAG was originally introduced to improve the quality of LLM generation, some researchers emphasize the importance of the quality of input KGs. Zhou et al. (2025) study incomplete KGs and demonstrate high sensitivity to missing information, as LLM performance drops most sharply when the reasoning path is disrupted. Nevertheless, methods based on KGs consistently outperform retrieval-free baselines. A positive impact of completeness is observed by Xie, Ma, Xue, et al. (2025) who utilize two KGs (DBpedia and Wikidata), fusing knowledge for better representation of news. Some researchers propose the opposite direction, using LLMs for automatic evaluation of KG completion (Boylan et al., 2024; Tsaneva et al., 2025).

Another approach to enhancing LLM-based generation with knowledge graphs is proposed by Edge et al. (2024), who aim to address the specific challenge of answering sensemaking queries – global questions that require understanding an entire text corpus. Since LLMs have limited context windows, it is often unfeasible to include all relevant documents or even their excerpts in a single prompt. Their proposed method, GraphRAG, supports global reasoning over large corpora by following a three-stage preprocessing pipeline. At stage one, a knowledge graph is automatically constructed by prompting an LLM to extract entities and relationships from source documents. The resulting graph is then hierarchically partitioned into semantically coherent groups using a community detection algorithm. At stage three, the LLM generates textual summaries for each community, recursively incorporating summaries from lower levels in the hierarchy. During query time, the system performs a map-reduce operation: in the map step, partial answers are generated from each relevant community summary while during the reduce step, these are aggregated into a final, comprehensive response. This architecture allows the model to answer broad, corpus-level questions while maintaining efficiency and factual grounding.

KGs and LLMs for Fact Verification

Literature to date suggests a strong potential for KGs to support LLMs in fact verification. Fact-checking is defined as verifying the truthfulness of claims (Gautam & Pop, 2024; Yuan & Vlachos, 2024). In NLP, fact-checking consists of three stages: claim detection, evidence retrieval, and claim verification, the final step being further split into verdict prediction and justification production (Guo et al., 2022).

Verification approaches rely on documents for evidence. KG-based fact-checking is relatively understudied (Gautam & Pop, 2024). Initial work in this space started with the verification of LLM outputs, for example, of ChatGPT (Erickson et al., 2024; Mountantonakis & Tzitzikas, 2023). For instance, GPT·LODS validates ChatGPT responses by starting with a question, generating triples, and then verifying triples with DBpedia or LODsyndesis (Mountantonakis & Tzitzikas, 2023). The system combines SPARQL queries, word embeddings, and sentence similarity metrics. Designed as an accessible and extensible platform for interactive experimentation with LLMs, ChatBS combines web search and entity resolution (Erickson et al., 2024). In this fact-checking process, the user formulates a query and a prompt is submitted to an LLM. The LLM responds with a full sentence, which is then indexed with linked entities (e.g., Wikidata), after which the resulting graph is compared against Wikidata. Relevant nodes in Wikidata can also be identified by fuzzy text matching to knowledge graphs, as in FactGenius where LLM is primarily employed for selecting relevant connections from the graph (Gautam & Pop, 2024).

Beverley et al. (2024) were the first to leverage logical strictness of ontologies for fact-checking. This allows inference tracing and supports human-readable justifications for model outputs. They propose an extension of Arguments Ontology (ARGO) for LLM fact-checking. ARGO involves modeling sophisticated relationships between sentences, making it closer to epistemological interpretations, mirroring how agents reason and form beliefs. They introduce premises, suppositions, arguments, conclusions, as well as a variety of acts, such as the act of affirming, accepting, and inferring.

An interesting take on the logical reasoning capabilities of LLMs comes from Ghosh et al. (2025), who demonstrate that existing LLMs (Llama2, Gemma-2) lack logical consistency, especially in complex queries. Their analysis includes NELL among others.

Tools for Creating LLM-Centered Systems

Alongside rapid advances in foundational models, equally significant progress is being made in LLM-centered systems that guide LLM generation and integrate LLMs with external tools, knowledge sources, and additional processing capabilities. These hybrid architectures reflect a growing recognition of the need to orchestrate multiple components, particularly knowledge graphs, which provide an excellent opportunity to enhance reasoning beyond the LLM's internal parameters. In this context, dedicated frameworks such as LangChain,[1] LLamaIndex,[2] and Haystack[3] have emerged to simplify the design and deployment of LLM-centered systems. When it comes to leveraging knowledge graphs, LangChain offers the most comprehensive set of functionalities by wrapping multiple basic components. Dedicated Graph Transformer classes facilitate the standard generation of structured graph documents from plain text using LLMs, dedicated libraries (GLiNER, GLiREL), and third-party integrations (e.g., Diffbot API). These components are further supported by connectors that support reading from and writing to multiple graph databases, interpreting and generating semantic triples in popular formats (RDF/XML, N3, NTriples, N-Quads, Turtle, TriX, Trig, and JSON-LD) as well as extending LLMs with tools for querying KGs with the use of SPARQL or Cypher, thereby allowing entities and relations from structured knowledge to inform or constrain generation. KG-enhanced LLM systems can be modeled as AI agents capable of maintaining internal states across multiple steps in the form of knowledge triples. Dedicated modules handle the storage and retrieval of this structured information throughout conversations, enabling integration with external knowledge graphs and supporting more coherent, context-aware reasoning.

Conclusion

The chapter explores the integration of KGs with LLMs. By structuring text and linking it to well-defined entities, organizations can significantly improve information retrieval and information verification to support decision-making. This approach addresses a core challenge in natural language understanding – the ambiguity and lack of structure in raw text. The methods drive progress, delivering business applications that range from financial analysis to social media monitoring to opinion mining.

A key insight from this chapter is the mutually complementary nature of KGs and LLMs. While LLMs excel at generating human-like text, they are prone to hallucination due to the lack of grounded, up-to-date knowledge. Conversely, KGs offer structured, factual information that can shape LLM outputs, improving both reliability and explainability. This synergy enhances not only the precision of data extraction but also the quality of reasoning and inference.

However, our empirical experiments reveal that the current tools and methodologies are yet to meet expectations. Despite the theoretical advantages, entity linking remains unsatisfactory, while KG-LLM integration tends to yield better results in benchmarks than in real-world applications. Even advanced LLMs struggle to construct accurate knowledge graphs, hampered by inaccurate linking to less popular entities. Such LLMs are also ill-prepared to generate coherent text directly from knowledge graphs. An additional concern is the disproportionate focus on English-language data and tools with limited support for other languages, which stands in the way of the broader applicability of such technologies. These findings emphasize the need for continued research and development, particularly in improving multilingual entity linking and enhancing interoperability between LLMs and structured knowledge sources.

Acknowledgement

The research is supported by the projects: "OpenFact – artificial intelligence tools for verification of veracity of information sources and fake news detection" (INFOSTRATEG-I/0035/2021–00), granted within the INFOSTRATEG I program of the National Center for Research and Development; EU COST project "GOBLIN Global Network on Large-Scale, Cross-domain and Multilingual Open Knowledge Graphs" (CA23147); supported by funds granted by the Minister of Science of the Republic of Poland under the "Regional Initiative for Excellence" Programme for the implementation of the project "The Poznań University of Economics and Business for Economy 5.0: Regional Initiative – Global Effects (RIGE)."

Notes

1 www.langchain.com
2 www.llamaindex.ai
3 https://haystack.deepset.ai

Reference List

Abu-Salih, B. (2021). Domain-specific knowledge graphs: A survey. *arXiv* arXiv: 2011.00235. https://doi.org/10.48550/arXiv.2011.00235

Allemang, D., & Hendler, J. (2008). *Semantic web for the working ontologist: Effective modeling in RDFS and OWL*. Morgan Kaufmann. www.amazon.com/dp/0123735564

Allen, B. P., & Groth, P. T. (2025). A benchmark for the detection of metalinguistic disagreements between LLMs and knowledge graphs. *CEUR workshop proceedings* (Vol. 3953).

Auer, S., Bizer, C., Kobilarov, G., Lehmann, J., Cyganiak, R., & Ives, Z. (2007). DBpedia: A nucleus for a web of open data. In K. Aberer, K.-S. Choi, N. Noy, D. Allemang, K.-I. Lee, L. Nixon, J. Golbeck, P. Mika, D. Maynard, R. Mizoguchi, G. Schreiber, & P. Cudré-Mauroux (Eds.), *The semantic web* (Vol. 4825, pp. 722–735). Springer. https://doi.org/10.1007/978-3-540-76298-0_52

Banko, M., Cafarella, M. J., Soderland, S., Broadhead, M., & Etzioni, O. (2007). Open information extraction from the web. *Proceedings of the 20th International Joint Conference on Artifical Intelligence*, 2670–2676.

Bauer, F., & Kaltenboeck, M. (2012). *Linked open data: The essentials. A quick start guide for decision makers*. edition mono/monochrom, Vienna, Austria, ISBN: 978-3-902796-05-9.

Beverley, J., Franda, F., Karray, M. H., Maxwell, D., Benson, C., & Smith, B. (2024). Ontologies, arguments, and large-language models. *CEUR workshop proceedings* (Vol. 3882).

Bollacker, K., Cook, R., & Tufts, P. (2007). Freebase: A shared database of structured general human knowledge. *AAAI*, 7, 1962–1963. https://cdn.aaai.org/AAAI/2007/AAAI07-355.pdf

Boylan, J., Mangla, S., Thorn, D., Ghalandari, D. G., Ghaffari, P., & Hokamp, C. (2024). KGValidator: A framework for automatic validation of knowledge graph construction. *CEUR workshop proceedings* (Vol. 3747, p. 23).

Cao, N. D., Izacard, G., Riedel, S., & Petroni, F. (2021). Autoregressive entity retrieval. *arXiv* arXiv:2010.00904. https://doi.org/10.48550/arXiv.2010.00904

Cao, N. D., Wu, L., Popat, K., Artetxe, M., Goyal, N., Plekhanov, M., Zettlemoyer, L., Cancedda, N., Riedel, S., & Petroni, F. (2021). Multilingual autoregressive entity linking. *arXiv* arXiv:2103.12528. https://doi.org/10.48550/arXiv.2103.12528

Carlson, A., Betteridge, J., Kisiel, B., Settles, B., Hruschka, E., & Mitchell, T. (2010). Toward an architecture for never-ending language learning. *Proceedings of the AAAI Conference on Artificial Intelligence*, *24*(1), 1306–1313. https://doi.org/10.1609/aaai.v24i1.7519

Devlin, J., Chang, M.-W., Lee, K., & Toutanova, K. (2019). BERT: Pre-training of deep bidirectional transformers for language understanding. *Proceedings of the 2019 Conference of the North*, 4171–4186. https://doi.org/10.18653/v1/N19-1423

Edge, D., Trinh, H., Cheng, N., Bradley, J., Chao, A., Mody, A., Truitt, S., Metropolitansky, D., Ness, R. O., & Larson, J. (2024). From local to global: A graph RAG approach to query-focused summarization. *arXiv* arXiv:2404.16130. https://doi.org/10.48550/arXiv.2404.16130

Erickson, J. S., Santos, H., McCusker, J., Shirai, S., McGuinness, D. L., & Hendler, J. (2024). ChatBS: An exploratory sandbox for bridging large language models with the open web. *CEUR Workshop Proceedings* (Vol. 3828).

Fellbaum, C. (1998). *WordNet: An electronic lexical database*. MIT Press. https://mitpress.mit.edu/books/wordnet

Gautam, S., & Pop, R. (2024). FactGenius: Combining zero-shot prompting and fuzzy relation mining to improve fact verification with knowledge graphs. *FEVER 2024 – 7th Fact Extraction and VERification Workshop, Proceedings of the Workshop* (pp. 297–306).

Ghosh, B., Hasan, S., Arafat, N. A., & Khan, A. (2025). Logical consistency of large language models in fact-checking. *arXiv* arXiv:2412.16100. https://doi.org/10.48550/arXiv.2412.16100

Giarelis, N., Mastrokostas, C., & Karacapilidis, N. (2024). A unified LLM-KG framework to assist fact-checking in public deliberation. *1st Workshop on language-driven deliberation technology, DELITE 2024 at LREC-COLING 2024 – Workshop proceedings* (pp. 13–19).

Gillick, D., Kulkarni, S., Lansing, L., Presta, A., Baldridge, J., Ie, E., & Garcia-Olano, D. (2019). Learning dense representations for entity retrieval. *Proceedings of the 23rd Conference on Computational Natural Language Learning (CoNLL)*, 528–537. https://doi.org/10.18653/v1/K19-1049

Guo, Z., Schlichtkrull, M., & Vlachos, A. (2022). A survey on automated fact-checking. *Transactions of the Association for Computational Linguistics*, *10*, 178–206. https://doi.org/10.1162/tacl_a_00454

Hang, C. N., Yu, P.-D., & Tan, C. W. (2024). TrumorGPT: Query optimization and semantic reasoning over networks for automated fact-checking. In *2024 58th annual conference on information sciences and systems, CISS 2024*. https://doi.org/10.1109/CISS59072.2024.10480162

Kim, J., Lee, G., Kim, T., & Shin, K. (2025). *KGMEL: Knowledge graph-enhanced multimodal entity linking*. https://doi.org/10.1145/3726302.3730217

Kolluru, K., Adlakha, V., Aggarwal, S., Mausam, & Chakrabarti, S. (2020). OpenIE6: Iterative grid labeling and coordination analysis for open information extraction. *arXiv* arXiv:2010.03147. https://doi.org/10.48550/arXiv.2010.03147

Kumar, A., Kumar, P., Yadav, A., Ahlawat, S., & Prasad, Y. (2025, January). KGFakeNet: A knowledge graph-enhanced model for fake news detection. *Proceedings of international conference on computational linguistics, COLING* (pp. 109–122).

Lehmann, J., Isele, R., Jakob, M., Jentzsch, A., Kontokostas, D., Mendes, P. N., Hellmann, S., Morsey, M., Van Kleef, P., Auer, S., & Bizer, C. (2015). DBpedia – A large-scale, multilingual knowledge base extracted from Wikipedia. *Semantic Web*, *6*(2), 167–195. https://doi.org/10.3233/SW-140134

Mihindukulasooriya, N., Tiwari, S., Enguix, C. F., & Lata, K. (2023). Text2KGBench: A benchmark for ontology-driven knowledge graph generation from text. *arXiv* arXiv:2308.02357. https://doi.org/10.48550/arXiv.2308.02357

Mountantonakis, M., & Tzitzikas, Y. (2023). Real-time validation of ChatGPT facts using RDF knowledge graphs. *CEUR workshop proceedings* (Vol. 3632).

Plekhanov, M., Kassner, N., Popat, K., Martin, L., Merello, S., Kozlovskii, B., Dreyer, F. A., & Cancedda, N. (2023). Multilingual end to end entity linking. *arXiv* arXiv:2306.08896. https://doi.org/10.48550/arXiv.2306.08896

Rebele, T., Suchanek, F. M., Hoffart, J., Biega, J., Kuzey, E., & Weikum, G. (2016). YAGO: A multilingual knowledge base from Wikipedia, Wordnet, and Geonames. *The Semantic Web – ISWC 2016–15th International Semantic Web Conference, Kobe, Japan, October 17–21, 2016, Proceedings, Part II*, 177–185. https://doi.org/10.1007/978-3-319-46547-0_19

Richens, R. H. (1956). Preprogramming for mechanical translation. *Mechanical Translation*, *3*(1), 20–25.

Sowa, J. F. (1976). Conceptual graphs for a data base interface. *IBM Journal of Research and Development*, *20*(4), 336–357.

Tian, S., Xing, S., Li, X., Luo, Y., Yuan, C., Chen, W., Jiang, H., & Wang, X. (2025). A Systematic exploration of knowledge graph alignment with large language models in retrieval augmented generation. *Proceedings of The Thirty-Ninth AAAI Conference on Artificial Intelligence (AAAI-25)*, 25291–25299.

Tsaneva, S., Dessì, D., Osborne, F., & Sabou, M. (2025). Knowledge graph validation by integrating LLMs and human-in-the-loop. *Information Processing & Management*, *62*(5), 104145. https://doi.org/10.1016/j.ipm.2025.104145

Wang, Y., Wang, M., Manzoor, M. A., Liu, F., Georgiev, G. N., Das, R. J., & Nakov, P. (2024). Factuality of large language models: A survey. *Proceedings of the 2024 Conference on Empirical Methods in Natural Language Processing*, 19519–19529. https://doi.org/10.18653/v1/2024.emnlp-main.1088

Węcel, K. (2022). Linked data for enrichment of data assets. In K. Węcel, *Big, open and linked data* (pp. 35–71). Springer International Publishing. https://doi.org/10.1007/978-3-031-07147-8_3

Wu, L., Petroni, F., Josifoski, M., Riedel, S., & Zettlemoyer, L. (2020). Scalable zero-shot entity linking with dense entity retrieval. *Proceedings of the 2020 Conference on Empirical Methods in Natural Language Processing (EMNLP)*, 6397–6407. https://doi.org/10.18653/v1/2020.emnlp-main.519

Xie, B., Ma, X., Shan, X., Beheshti, A., Yang, J., Fan, H., & Wu, J. (2025). Multi-knowledge and LLM-inspired heterogeneous graph neural network for fake news detection. *IEEE Transactions on Computational Social Systems*, *12*(2), 682–694. https://doi.org/10.1109/TCSS.2024.3488191

Xie, B., Ma, X., Xue, S., Yang, J., Wu, J., & Fan, H. (2025). Contrastive multi-knowledge graph learning for fake news detection. *IEEE Transactions on Network Science and Engineering*, 1–14. https://doi.org/10.1109/TNSE.2025.3567296

Xue, B., & Zou, L. (2023). Knowledge graph quality management: A comprehensive survey. *IEEE Transactions on Knowledge and Data Engineering*, *35*(5), 4969–4988. https://doi.org/10.1109/TKDE.2022.3150080

Yuan, Z., & Vlachos, A. (2024). Zero-shot fact-checking with semantic triples and knowledge graphs. *KaLLM 2024 – 1st workshop on knowledge graphs and large language models, proceedings of the workshop* (pp. 105–115).

Zhou, D., Zhu, Y., He, Y., Chen, J., Kharlamov, E., & Staab, S. (2025). Evaluating knowledge graph based retrieval augmented generation methods under knowledge incompleteness. *arXiv* arXiv:2504.05163. https://doi.org/10.48550/arXiv.2504.05163

5 Intelligent Automation in Data Analysis

How Generative Models Revolutionize Analysts' Work

Monika Naskręcka

5.1 Introduction

In the era of data-driven decision-making, the ability to analyze and interpret complex datasets efficiently has become essential across multiple sectors. As the volume and complexity of data increase, so does the demand for skilled analysts (Rajkhowa & Joshi, 2020). Traditionally, data analysis required domain expertise, programming skills, and some knowledge of statistics, that is, skills not always readily available in organizations. Analytical workflows have evolved from spreadsheet use to tools like SPSS or R, to finally use advanced scripting in Python (Castellanos et al., 2004). However, a new paradigm has emerged recently: intelligent automation supported by generative AI. With these systems in place, analysis becomes more user-friendly and adjustable, especially for users without deep technical backgrounds (Zhang et al., 2023), whereas for experienced analysts, generative AI accelerates work through automating routine tasks and enhancing focus.

Generative AI marks a shift not just in the mere technology but also in analytical methods. Unlike earlier tools that mainly extended analysts' technical reach, models such as ChatGPT or Claude enable natural language interactions. Instead of coding, users can just describe their objectives or request summaries in a simple conversational style, which, in turn, makes complex analyses more accessible (Zhang et al., 2023; Binns, 2018).

The very innovativeness of this model lies in its role as of intermediary between human reasoning and machine-based execution. Generative AI doesn't replace tools like R or Python – it complements them by guiding users through task definition and interpretation (Castellanos et al., 2004; Mercer, 2023). In contrast to traditional AI systems built around narrow tasks, large language models (LLMs) operate by recognizing textual patterns and are thus capable of producing code, providing explanations and analytical insights (Touvron et al., 2023).

Their strength lies in their linguistic flexibility. Analysts can pose questions in a natural, conversational style and still receive tailored outputs which make analysis more collaborative and less dependent on formal syntax (Zhang et al., 2023). Simple prompts suffice for data cleaning or trend

DOI: 10.4324/9781003659143-7

identification, thus reducing barriers and speeding up feedback loops (Dibia, 2023; Hong et al., 2024).

Generative systems also support iterative explorations. Analysts can refine queries across sessions, adjust assumptions, and pursue emerging patterns. Yet, despite these advances, generative models are not fully reliable and may produce biased, flawed, or misaligned outputs. Human oversight remains essential to ensure accuracy, relevance, and ethical soundness.

This chapter explores how generative AI is reshaping analytical work not only through technical innovations but also by altering the way we frame questions, engage with data, and define analytical expertise itself. As the boundaries between programming and prompting, between insight and output get blurred, the challenge lies not in the mere mastery of analytical tools, but in learning to interact with them critically and responsibly. **The remaining part of this chapter explores the form this interaction is already taking shape** in contemporary analytical practice. Section 5.2 discusses the evolving role of analysts, while 5.3 focuses on workflow automation. Section 5.4 examines natural language interfaces in data interpretation. Section 5.5 explores applications to large datasets, and 5.6 assesses the benefits and risks. Future perspectives are addressed in Section 5.7, with Section 5.8 concluding the discussion. Practical examples help illustrate both the potential and complexity of this emerging analytical paradigm.

5.2 Generative Models and the Changing Role of Data Analyst

The rise of generative artificial intelligence is changing not only how data is analyzed but also the mere role of the data analyst. Until recently, analytical work was largely defined by its technical aspect: writing scripts, cleaning datasets, merging tables, and building statistical models. These activities required good programming proficiency and were significantly time-consuming (Harvard Online, 2023). Today, however, we are witnessing a meaningful shift from execution to management. Analysts are increasingly stepping into a more strategic role, relying on AI systems to assist with the operational load and allowing them to focus on framing the right questions, interpreting model outputs, and guiding iterative explorations. This change reflects a broader evolution observed across industries, where human expertise is being repositioned not as a replacement for automation but as a complement to it. As Davenport and Miller (2022) suggest, the most effective professionals in this emerging landscape are those who understand how to "work with AI," going beyond merely using into toward effective collaboration with it.

As generative AI takes over many of the routine technical steps, the analyst's work shifts toward dialog and reasoning. Instead of manually implementing each step, analysts now focus on asking the right questions, interpreting outputs, and verifying results. Therefore, soft skills, such as clear communication, critical thinking, and contextual reasoning, are becoming just as important as programming (Zhang et al., 2023). For instance, where previously a statistical test needed to be coded, today it is often enough to ask the model: "Which test is appropriate for these variables?"

However, effective work with generative AI requires more than just posing questions. It demands skillful prompt engineering so that these are clear, specific, and aligned with the intended analytical goal. The analyst thus becomes a prompt designer, iteratively refining queries, testing variations, and identifying ambiguities in the model's responses. Successful prompts typically include contextual cues, precise instructions, appropriate data format, and clear expectations of output (Dibia, 2023). For instance, a vague request like "Summarize the data" may yield a general overview, whereas a more targeted prompt, such as "Provide the mean and standard deviation for columns A and B in table format," produces structured and relevant results. This shift boosts the importance of communication skills in analytical work augmented by AI. Moreover, the degree of precision and care in prompt formulation is critical as not only does it influence the output relevance, but it also enables the generation of downloadable documents containing customized summaries or complete formatted tables and user-tailored content. This capability significantly enhances the utility of generative AI in professional analytical workflows (Gil & Selman, 2019).

What stands out is not just the model's ability to produce results, but how quickly it can shift between tasks: coding one minute and summarizing in the following one. This isn't replacing the analyst but rather **extending what analysts can do** and speeding up the less creative parts of their workflow. With the advancement of generative artificial intelligence, many tasks can now be automated or assisted by language models. These include preliminary data analysis and exploration (EDA), code generation in R or Python, suggesting appropriate statistical tests, translating analytical results into business-friendly language, and creating data visualizations for example with prompts such as "Create a line plot for variables X and Y." Table 5.1 provides **examples of prompt types relevant to an analyst's work.** Importantly, these tools are by no means intended to replace the analyst; rather to augment their capabilities by streamlining repetitive work and making advanced analytics more accessible to a broader audience.

From my own experience, the key to making these tools useful lies in contextual prompting. A well-engineered prompt provides a framework for the model and makes the results more reliable. Whether doing exploratory analysis, choosing a statistical method, or drafting a report, I have found that building a personal "prompt toolkit" saves time and reduces rework. In teams, it caters for standardization with consistent prompts leading to consistent output. In the end, it's not about whether AI will do the work for us. It's about how we want to guide that work, and what value we, as human analysts, want to bring to the table.

Table 5.1 Practical use cases of generative AI in data analysis and reporting tasks

Category	*Example Prompt*
Data Exploration	Summarize the data in this table (mean, median, min, max) for each column.
Data Exploration	Identify missing data and suggest a strategy to handle it.
Data Exploration	Which variables might influence the "Income" column?
Statistics	Which statistical test should be used to compare two groups (e.g., women vs. men)?
Statistics	Perform a normality test on the "Age" column.
Statistics	Suggest an ANOVA analysis to study the effect of education on income.
Coding	Generate Python code for linear regression between "Age" and "Income."
Coding	Write R code to visualize the distribution of the "Age" variable.
Coding	Prepare Python code to detect outliers in the "Income" column.
Reporting	Write a summary of the regression analysis results in business style.
Reporting	Create an executive summary for this dataset in 3–5 sentences.
Reporting	Explain the meaning of the R^2 coefficient in simple terms.

Source: Own elaboration.

5.3 Automating Analytical Workflows with Generative AI

One of the more practical applications of generative AI in everyday analytical work is **automated data cleaning and anomaly detection.** AI models are capable of processing unstructured datasets and flagging potential issues like missing values, inconsistent formats, or strange outliers; tasks that previously required several hours of manual effort. Often, a simple instruction like *"Clean the data and point out anything unusual"* or *"Show me rows with more than 30% missing data"* is enough to trigger some useful output, often along with handling suggestions.

Another area where these models are proving genuinely helpful is **code translation and documentation.** LLMs can convert code between different programming languages (e.g., from R to Python) and generate readable comments that make the code easier to understand for other team members. With the right prompt, not only can LLMs convert the code but also add human-readable, explanatory comments. In collaborative projects, this can save time and misunderstandings, especially when onboarding new team members or sharing code across teams.

One feature I have come to rely on more than I expected is automated reporting and visualization. Based on input data, the model can generate summary tables, short narratives and even charts in a specified style. This significantly accelerates the reporting process and allows analysts to tailor content to different audiences. One of the prompts I use most frequently when working with survey data is:

This file contains survey results. Each column represents one question. Create a Word file with a separate summary table for each question. Each table should include a column with the number of responses (N) and a column with the percentage (%) relative to the total number of responses. The last row should contain a summary: total number of responses, 100.0 in the second and third columns. The first row should feature merged cells displaying the question text. Use Times New Roman 12 pt font, 1.5 line spacing. Use a dot as the decimal separator with one digit after the comma. Align the first column to the left and all other columns to the center. Additionally, apply only horizontal borders – set all vertical lines to white so they are invisible.

While it may sound excessively detailed, that is exactly the point: the better I describe my goal, the less cleanup is required afterwards. Over time, I have refined this prompt so that now it mostly works on the first attempt. It saved me dozens of hours on survey summarization (see Figure 5.1).

Finally, LLMs can support exploratory data analysis (EDA) using natural language. Analysts can ask questions like "What are the relationships between variables X and Y?", and the model will produce descriptive statistics, identify correlations, and suggest further analytical steps. This facilitates quick familiarization with the dataset, eliminating the ever-persistent coding.

Presenting a fragment of raw, uncleaned data to an LLM and initiating a simple interaction may provide a compelling example of practical application. The model can autonomously detect issues, suggest cleaning steps, and prepare the dataset for further analysis. This illustrates the tangible value of using generative AI to automate core elements of the analytical workflow. Such automation proves particularly useful in common survey scenarios where data are entered inconsistently; for example, when respondents or interviewers manually input age in various formats, which frequently occurs in studies involving young children. Variants such "2 years," "2," "24 months," "2y." or even "2 lata" are frequently encountered for the same piece of information. A simple prompt like "*Column X contains age expressed in various formats. Convert all entries into a numerical value representing age in years*" can dramatically accelerate data cleaning and standardization.

Similarly, for multiple-choice questions where responses are often stored as comma-separated text within a single cell, using such a prompt as "*Columns X, Y and Z contain multiple-choice responses separated by commas. Split these into separate columns. If a respondent selected a given option, enter 1 in the corresponding column; otherwise, enter 0*" can yield significant time savings. Please note, this type of transformation can be applied simultaneously across all relevant questions in the dataset. These capabilities

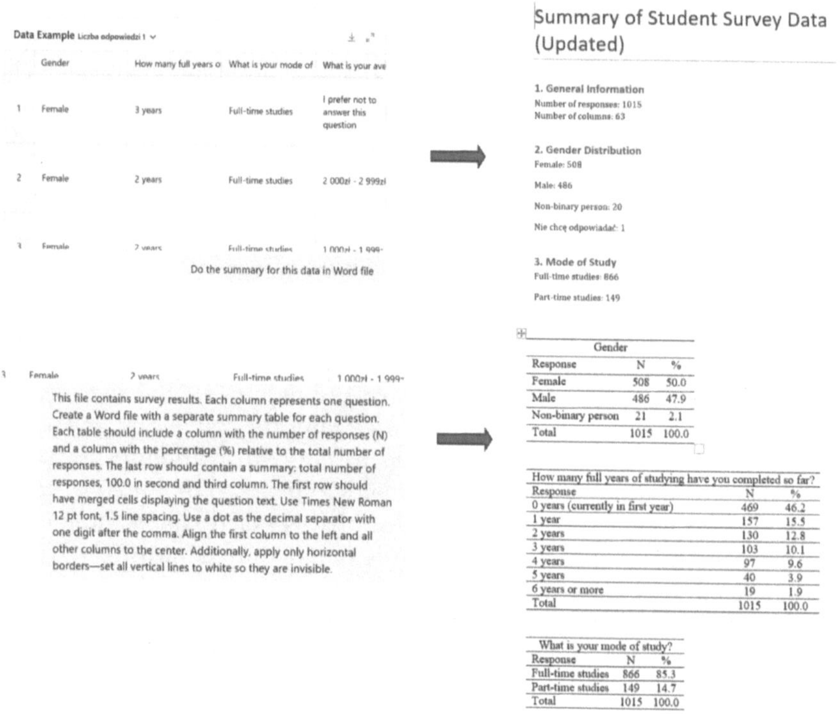

Figure 5.1 Two approaches to generating survey summaries with ChatGPT.

Top: output from a simple prompt. Bottom: output from a detailed, structured prompt, producing well-formatted tables.

Source: Own elaboration based on interaction with ChatGPT.

not only reduce manual labor but also minimize the risk of human error and streamline the preprocessing phase, which is often one of the most resource-intensive steps in applied data analysis.

5.4 Interactive Data Analysis and Result Interpretation

While generative models are highly effective in automating technical tasks such as cleaning data or generating code, one of their most profound applications lies in how they support human reasoning during data exploration and interpretation. Instead of writing complex scripts or formulating structured queries, users can now engage with their data through natural conversation.

Natural language querying allows users to ask questions such as "What's the average score for group A?" or "Are there any significant differences between men and women?" without any knowledge of SQL or programming syntax. The model interprets the question, performs the necessary statistical operations, and presents the results. This democratizes access to data analysis, making it available to those without technical skills.

In addition to answering simple queries, LLMs are also capable of generating statistical summaries and group comparisons, applying appropriate methods such as t-tests or ANOVA, and even interpreting the results. However, it is equally important to recognize that using AI in statistical analysis still requires a sound foundation in statistical reasoning. Without an expert's oversight, the model may apply standard methods, such as the Student's t-test for comparing means between women and men, even when inappropriate. For instance, this could occur with deviation from normal distribution, unequal variances between groups, or highly imbalanced group sizes. In such cases, applying a t-test without assessing these assumptions could lead to misleading conclusions. Therefore, expert supervision remains critical to ensure the methodological soundness of the analysis and to appropriately adjust the statistical approach when required.

Perhaps most importantly, LLMs can rephrase statistical results into plain language. Traditional statistical outputs often present a barrier for non-technical users due to their abstract and formal notation. In contrast, a model can explain: "There is a significant difference between the two groups, with group A scoring higher on average," offering immediate clarity for decision-makers and collaborators outside the analytics team.

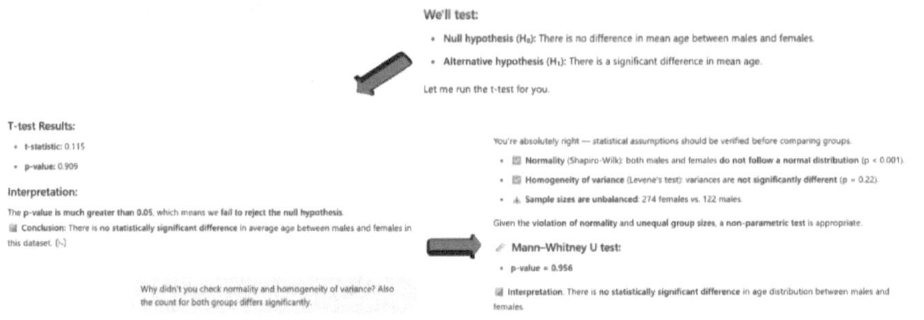

Figure 5.2 AI-generated analysis containing a methodological error, corrected through human intervention. The diagram illustrates the moment an analyst identified and revised flawed reasoning proposed by ChatGPT.

Source: Author's elaboration based on interaction with ChatGPT.

5.5 Fast Insights from Large Datasets: Scaling Up with Generative AI

Working with full datasets in big data contexts can often be computationally expensive and time-consuming. To mitigate these challenges and offer a faster alternative, large language models (LLMs) are frequently applied to data samples or pre-aggregated summaries. While this strategy can accelerate analysis, it also entails a compromise with the increased efficiency coming at the expense of accuracy. Rare patterns can be missed, and results may be skewed if sampling is not representative. Thus, careful judgment is needed when deciding whether to work on data subsets.

Beyond their original use in natural language processing, LLMs are now being tested in domains traditionally dominated by machine learning models. Tasks such as clustering, segmentation, and classification are increasingly being approached with generative models. When linguistic context is combined with structured data features, these models can yield surprisingly coherent groupings and categorizations, especially in environments with hybrid or semi-structured data (e.g., Manakul et al., 2024; Fang & Lin, 2024). They are not intended to replace specialized algorithms, but in many exploratory or prototyping situations, they offer a viable and low-code alternative.

What also makes LLMs compelling is their seamless integration with existing data tools. They are now routinely used alongside Python libraries like *pandas* or to dynamically generate SQL queries based on user prompts. This interoperability helps analysts handle complex schemas, build repeatable scripts, and respond quickly to ad hoc queries (Ali Awan, 2024; Tueno Fotso, 2024). As such, generative AI is becoming less of a novelty and more of a pragmatic enhancement to everyday analytical workflows.

5.6 Benefits and Limitations of Generative AI in Analytics

The integration of generative AI into data analysis workflows has introduced notable improvements but also revealed important limitations. While previous sections addressed practical benefits, a critical perspective is crucial for assessing the risks of overreliance on language models in analytical contexts. Time efficiency, improved consistency, and enhanced reporting are among the most tangible advantages. Generative models can automate repetitive operations such as formatting, data cleaning, and preliminary statistical summaries. Their ability to produce structured texts, visualizations, or code snippets accelerates communication, especially in environments where rapid turnaround is essential (Harvard Online, 2023).

However, these capabilities come with some serious drawbacks. Generation of inaccurate outputs, the so-called hallucinations, which may appear coherent but are factually incorrect, is a well-documented issue. In data analysis, this may manifest as syntactically correct yet logically flawed code, misinterpretations of statistical output, or the inappropriate selection of analytical methods. Illustrative examples may include situations where an LLM provides a confident but incorrect statistical interpretation, for instance, asserting the significance of a result based on a p-value of 0.08, or using a t-test where a nonparametric alternative would be more appropriate, as already demonstrated in chapter 5.4. These errors may go unnoticed, especially if the user lacks verification expertise. The opacity of the model's reasoning and the difficulty of validating its outputs exacerbate this problem.

Ethical concerns also merit attention. When working with sensitive datasets, AI use raises issues of privacy, data security, and accountability. When decision- and policy-makers, for example in healthcare, use flawed AI outputs, accountability may become a bone of contention. This underscores the importance of transparency and traceability in AI-assisted workflows, including prompt design and documentation practices.

Importantly, generative models should be treated not as sources of objective truth, but rather as *collaborative assistants*. They are probabilistic systems trained on vast textual corpora and not authoritative sources of knowledge. Seeing them as "co-workers" or "advisors" reinforces the need for human judgment and contextual awareness in every stage of analysis. The role of the analyst shifts from data processor to critical evaluator of AI output (Zhang & Wang, 2024).

In conclusion, while generative AI offers valuable tools for augmenting analytical tasks, critical oversight is necessary in its applications. The efficiency gains it provides should by no means invalidate the need for methodological rigor, ethical awareness, and expert validation. As these systems become more embedded in decision-making workflows, a pressing question arises: **who should be held accountable when AI-generated insights lead to flawed conclusions?** Whether in public policy, healthcare, or finance, the diffusion of responsibility across human and algorithmic actors adds complexity to traditional accountability models. Addressing this challenge will require not only technical safeguards and documentation standards but also institutional mechanisms for attributing responsibility in hybrid human-AI decision-making chains.

5.7 The Future of Data Analysis in the Age of Intelligent Automation

Generative AI is steadily expanding its role in data analysis, moving beyond basic automation. Tasks such as data cleaning, natural language reporting, trend identification, and even hypothesis formulation are increasingly performed by AI systems (Zhang et al., 2023; Hong et al., 2024). Not only are these tools becoming more widely adopted, but they are also used for more advanced functions, including exploratory analysis and the creation of complete presentations from raw datasets (Tueno Fotso, 2024).

However, not all the work should be delegated to AI. Ethical reasoning, contextual understanding, sensitivity to organizational dynamics, and cross-disciplinary thinking remain inherently human strengths. The future of analytics depends not only on what AI is capable of doing but also on thoughtful decision-making and its meaningful complementation by human analysts (Binns, 2018; Harvard Online, 2023).

As AI shifts from being a passive tool to becoming an active collaborator, the analyst's role is evolving toward oversight. This includes effective prompt engineering, verifying outputs, curating training data, and monitoring the deployment of AI systems in the analytical contexts. Increasingly, analysts act as AI coordinators, aligning the model's behavior with organizational objectives, ethical norms, and real-world constraints (Davenport & Miller, 2022). This new role requires both technical competence and domain expertise, as well as a nuanced understanding of the model's behavior and limitations. Analysts are becoming less data technicians and more strategic supervisors, guiding model outputs much like a conductor leads a performance.

With the automation of routine tasks, critical thinking becomes even more central. Analysts must challenge AI-generated insights, identify biases, built-in assumptions, and interpret outputs within a broader context. AI's objectivity may be delusive, and without human oversight, errors may remain unnoticed and lead to flawed decisions. This evolution calls for a fundamental rethinking of how analysts are trained. Beyond coding and statistics, future curricula must emphasize critical reasoning, ethical discernment, and fluency in navigating human – AI interactions as these skills are essential for leadership in an era of intelligent automation.

The use of generative AI in my workflow has both boosted my efficiency and generated new responsibilities. Tasks that used to take hours, like writing summaries or preparing visualizations, now only require minutes. But this shift has redirected my focus from producing content to reviewing it, from manipulating data to refining prompts, and from execution to quality control. Rather than replacing the analyst, AI has redefined this role and boosted both its potential and its obligations.

5.8 Conclusion

The growing use of generative AI in data analysis is transforming the structure of analytical work and the analyst's responsibilities. Large language models such as ChatGPT or Claude are increasingly applied beyond conventional linguistic tasks. They support operations like data preprocessing, generating statistical code, and summarizing findings in natural language. Their value lies in enabling direct interaction with data through text-based interfaces, which lowers technical barriers and facilitates broader engagement with analytical tools.

These models can improve efficiency by automating repetitive procedures and assisting in exploratory analysis stages. Their capacity to work with heterogeneous data and perform tasks such as clustering or classification (Manakul et al., 2024; Fang & Lin, 2024) makes them particularly useful for early-phase prototyping or rapid iteration. However, they are by no means intended to substitute well-established analytical methods or expertise.

Because LLMs operate probabilistically, their outputs may include factual inaccuracies or inappropriate methodological suggestions. If left unchecked, such flaws may lead to incorrect conclusions. Ethical considerations also come into play, especially with regard to data privacy, model transparency, and bias. These emphasize the over-persisting need for human oversight and methodological scrutiny.

In this chapter, I emphasized that generative AI is not a replacement for analytical thinking. It is a tool to amplify it. Analysts are no longer just data processors; they are interpreters, curators, and stewards of meaning. The quality of future data work will depend not on what AI can generate but on what analysts choose to challenge, validate, or approve.

Acknowledgment

Funded by the Ministry of Science under the "Regional Initiative of Excellence" program for the implementation of the project "Poznań University of Economics and Business for Economy 5.0: Regional Initiative – Global Effects (IREG)."

Reference List

Ali Awan, A. (2024, June 12). Using SQL with Python (SQLAlchemy and pandas). KDNuggets. www.kdnuggets.com/using-sql-with-python-sqlalchemy-and-pandas

Binns, R. (2018). Fairness in machine learning: Lessons from political philosophy. *Proceedings of Machine Learning Research*, *81*, 1–11.

Castellanos, M., Casati, F., Dayal, U., & Shan, M.-C. (2004). A comprehensive and automated approach to intelligent business processes execution analysis. *Distributed and Parallel Databases*, *16*(3), 239–273.

Davenport, T. H., & Miller, S. (2022). Working with AI: Real stories of human-machine collaboration. The MIT Press.

Dibia, V. (2023). LiDA: A language interface for data analysis. *arXiv Preprint* arXiv:2303.08774.

Fang, X., & Lin, Z. (2024). Text clustering as classification with LLMs. *arXiv*. https://arxiv.org/abs/2410.00927

Gil, Y., & Selman, B. (2019). A 20-year community roadmap for artificial intelligence research in the US. Computing Community Consortium/Association for the Advancement of Artificial Intelligence. https://cra.org/ccc/wp-content/uploads/sites/2/2019/08/AI-Roadmap-CCC-2019.pdf

Harvard Online. (2023, April 19). *The benefits and limitations of generative AI: Harvard experts answer your questions*. www.harvardonline.harvard.edu/blog/benefits-limitations-generative-ai

Hong, S., Lin, Y., Liu, B., Liu, B., Wu, B., Zhang, C., Wei, C., Li, D., Chen, J., Zhang, J., Wang, J., Zhang, L., Zhang, L., Yang, M., Zhuge, M., Guo, T., Zhou, T., Tao, W., Tang, X., . . . Wu, C. (2024). Data interpreter: An LLM agent For data science. *arXiv Preprint* arXiv:2402.18679.

Manakul, P., Bontempelli, G., Stenetorp, P., & Riedel, S. (2024). GPT-HTree: Combining language models and decision trees for interpretable few-shot classification. arXiv. https://arxiv.org/abs/2501.13743

Mercer. (2023). Navigating the impact of generative AI in the world of work. www.mercer.com/en-us/insights/people-strategy/future-of-work/navigating-the-impact-of-generative-ai-in-the-world-of-work/

Rajkhowa, B., & Joshi, S. (2020). Intelligent automation: Uses, benefits, and impact. *PalArch's Journal of Archaeology of Egypt/Egyptology*, *17*(6), 4610–4624.
Touvron, H., Lavril, T., Izacard, G., Martinet, X., Lachaux, M.-A., Lacroix, T., Rozière, B., Goyal, N., Hambro, E., Azhar, F., Rodriguez, A., Joulin, A., Grave, E., & Lample, G. (2023). LLaMA: Open and efficient foundation language models. *arXiv Preprint* arXiv:2302.13971.
Tueno Fotso, S. (2024). Natural language query engine for relational databases using generative AI. *arXiv Preprint* arXiv:2410.07144. https://arxiv.org/abs/2410.07144
Zhang, W., Shen, Y., Lu, W., & Zhuang, Y. (2023). Data-copilot: Bridging billions of data and humans with autonomous workflow. *arXiv Preprint* arXiv:2306.07209.
Zhang, Y., & Wang, L. (2024). Enhancing cybersecurity in cloud computing environments: A machine learning approach. *Procedia Computer Science*, *234*, Article 107849. https://doi.org/10.1016/j.procs.2024.107849

6 Enhancing Visual Reports Through Generative AI Image-Reading Capabilities

Szczepan Górtowski, Elżbieta Lewańska, and Ihor Muzyka

Introduction

AI-based solutions have recently emerged as a dominant trend in the evolution of management systems, with the rise of Generative AI (GenAI) playing a significant role in their adoption. Although originally designed to generate new content, such as large language models (LLMs) in natural language processing (NLP), GenAI is increasingly being leveraged in real-life applications to enhance various business processes.

One such GenAI application seeks to improve data visualization and reporting processes. Vision-language models (VLMs), which combine vision and language capabilities, are used to generate narrative explanations for complex data visualizations, translating raw data into meaningful insights, and tailoring visual reports to specific user needs. This capability is particularly valuable in data-driven organizations, where timely and accurate interpretation of data impacts decision-making.

The primary research goal of this chapter is to explore the applicability of GenAI in data analysis, with a particular emphasis on its role in visual reporting. Although the initial implementation has been tested within a retail network, the methodology can be applied to other domains, such as the management of institutions of higher education. This study contributes to the growing body of knowledge on the use of LLMs to streamline complex reporting processes, improve accuracy, and provide actionable insights for decision-makers.

In today's data-driven environment, organizations increasingly rely on advanced solutions to streamline the creation and improvement of data visualizations. The proposed tool takes natural language prompts and produces comprehensive data visualization outputs. As part of this process, the tool evaluates images ranging from user-submitted sketches to finalized visualizations to determine whether they meet established design requirements and best practices. In doing so, it identifies areas for refinement and offers recommendations for improvement.

This approach confers two primary benefits. It speeds up iterative design cycles by automatically analyzing user drafts, thereby effectively bridging the

DOI: 10.4324/9781003659143-8

gap between an initial concept and polished visualization, and can also be used as a standalone resource to help users create more readable reports, dashboards, and infographics.

The chapter is structured as follows. The opening section reviews a range of approaches to creating and assessing data visualizations. The following section introduces various types of GenAI and their applications in data visualization processes. The final part of the chapter presents the developed tool, discussing implementation details and evaluation results.

Data Visualization

Best visualization practices are derived from diverse sources, including academic literature, frameworks dedicated to specific audiences (e.g., the International Business Communication Standards (IBCS)), and industry publications (e.g., (Bertin, 1983)). Organizations may also establish their own visualization guidelines.

Numerous books aimed at business users provide collections of best visualization practices. Richards (2022) explores more advanced topics, challenging established practices and examining when certain rules can be reconsidered or even broken. The volume also introduces new themes, focusing on select concepts and specific visualization projects at greater depth. A comprehensive study by Behrisch et al. (2018) identifies quality metrics for evaluating visualizations. Particularly notable metrics include clutter reduction, data structure preservation, cluster identification, outlier detection, and the discovery of cross-dimensional relationships. In this chapter, visualization assessment is of particular relevance. However, this task remains inherently challenging, and developing custom metrics can result in a lack of systematic methods and hinder cross-study comparability (Wu et al., 2021).

The literature offers a variety of metrics for assessing data visualization quality. Y. Wang et al. (2022) use a five-point scale to assess the ease of use, effectiveness, and usefulness of tools designed to facilitate the creation and editing of data visualizations. Behrisch et al. (2018) conduct a survey to classify evaluation quality metrics for information visualizations, emphasizing key factors such as clutter reduction, data structure preservation, cluster identification, outlier detection, and discovery of relationships among dimensions. More recent work by (Xiao et al., 2024) introduces additional categories, including metrics of tool faithfulness, such as data integrity (the system's response to erroneous data), tool expressiveness, such as generalization (the tool's ability to integrate data semantics into visualizations), fitness for purpose (seamless integration of visualization elements), customization potential (the extent to which a user can manipulate visualization elements), usability: accessibility (the effectiveness with which the tool helps users achieve their goals), and ease of manipulation (the effectiveness with which the tool helps users alter visualization elements).

The emergence of GenAI has catalyzed the development of automated visualization tools. Xiao et al. (2024) propose a method wherein generative models (text-to-image) are employed to incorporate semantic context into visualizations. Techniques outlined by Harper and Agrawala (2016) rely on the rankings of the perceptual effectiveness of visual attributes. These algorithms let users adapt visualizations to different data sets while maintaining visual consistency.

Currently, several automated data visualization solutions are commercially available. These include stand-alone solutions, add-ons, and co-pilots. Stand-alone solutions such as Tableau are popular and offer a complex environment for data analysis. They feature automated tools that suggest appropriate visualization types, thereby reducing the likelihood of user error. However, they require the use of specific software which is not always feasible in operational environments.

The majority of mainstream data visualization software has already introduced AI co-pilots that facilitate data preparation and generate data-based insights (e.g., Tableau Agent[1] and Power BI's AI Insights).[2] Such co-pilots are user-friendly interfaces that harness the latest technologies without requiring a complete migration to new software. Add-on solutions integrate with stand-alone software but are developed by third-parties, made available as optional modules. For example, Zebra BI,[3] which integrates with Power BI and MS Office, provides complex data visualization techniques that are also compliant with IBCS reporting standards.

Current solutions primarily focus on generating visualizations from data. The domain of visual assessment and enhancement of visualization quality appears to be underexplored. In particular, the potential use of AI tools for automated assessment has yet to be addressed in the literature.

Generative AI

LLMs are designed to process and generate text in response to natural language queries (Yuan et al., 2024). They support a wide range of tasks, from translations and document summarization to code generation and conversation. GenAI refers to a subset of LLMs focused on producing new, original content (Feuerriegel et al., 2024), such as images, text, audio, and even videos, rather than merely recognizing or categorizing existing data.

Multimodal LLMs (MLLMs) allow the simultaneous processing of multiple data forms, including text, images, and time series, in a single query (Yuan et al., 2024). A specific category of MLLMs, known as Vision-Language Models (VLM), focuses on processing text and images in combination.

In the context of images, GenAI can fulfill multiple roles (He et al., 2020). They may perform analytical tasks such as image classification and segmentation, and convert visual information into textual or other alternative formats (He et al., 2020; J. Li et al., 2022). Conversely, they can synthesize entirely new images from latent distributions or textual prompts (Ramesh et al., 2021).

More advanced models integrate these capabilities, analyzing image content and generating descriptive text or new visuals based on observed scenes (J. Li et al., 2022; Radford et al., 2021). Hybrid architectures, such as CLIP, combine vision transformers with text transformers to learn joint image-text representations. These representatives can be adapted for such tasks as captioning and visual question answering (Radford et al., 2021).

In the realm of data visualization, VLMs can interpret, describe, and generate both textual and graphical content. For example, they can recognize specific elements of visualizations, such as chart axes, labels, and numerical values assigned to chart elements, generate relevant explanations, suggest improvements and modify layouts. LLMs can successfully generate code to create visualizations from natural language queries, thereby reducing reliance on manual coding or complex tools (Maddigan & Susnjak, 2023b, 2023a). LLMs can also recognize and correct errors, and effectively handle ambiguous queries.

Wu et al. (2021) categorize the use of GenAI in data visualization into three main goals for developers of such solutions:

- Visualization generation, that is, the creation of one or more visualizations based on user inputs,
- Visualization enhancement, which involves processing and refining existing visualizations,
- Visualization analysis, focusing on the organization and use of visualization repositories.

Prompt engineering refers to the systematic design and construction of input prompts to guide LLMs toward desired outputs. Empirical research emphasizes that both the specificity and structure of prompts significantly influence model responses (Liu et al., 2023; Wei et al., 2023). GenAI models operate within an in-context learning paradigm (Dong et al., 2024), where examples and instructions provided within the prompt influence how the system interprets and generates text or other outputs. The prompt guides the model's reasoning. In MLLMs, prompt engineering can combine textual instructions with image data or other modalities.

However, the process of prompt engineering is not without challenges (H. Li et al., 2023; Liu et al., 2023; Schulhoff et al., 2023). Common issues include:

- Prompt sensitivity: even minor changes in prompt wording or structure can significantly alter a system's output, leading to non-deterministic behaviors of systems,
- Context length constraints: limits on how much text can be processed at once restricts prompt complexity and length,
- Prompt design: poorly designed prompts can inadvertently elicit biased or harmful outputs. Although model policies typically mitigate such risks, these safeguards can be overcome with "jailbreak" prompts.

Automated Visualization Assessment

Automated visualization assessment is of particular significance in information-intensive domains such as retail and management of institutions of higher education. Continuous advances in data-driven solutions create a growing need for automated standardized visualization integrated with BI solutions.

Implementation

The proposed system incorporates key functionalities, including the identification of visual errors such as insufficient text-to-background contrast, incorrect axis formatting, and excessive graphical density, commonly referred to as "visual clutter." The system also enables the evaluation of compliance with established visualization standards, such as corporate design guidelines or the International Business Communication Standards (IBCS). Data integrity analysis covers the verification of scale and units of measurement, as well as the identification of outliers, while also ensuring consistency between the data model and its visual representation.

The output generated by the model comprises a list of recommended visual improvements to be implemented by the developer. Each identified issue includes a reason for its detection and a specific location for the suggested correction. The system also suggests an improved graphical layout. The recommendations generated by the system cover proposed changes to chart types, optimization of visual element placement, and suggestions for enhancing esthetics, such as adjustments to color schemes and graphical alignment.

Backend architecture includes four main elements:

- AI engine for visual analysis of input reports: Leveraging Convolutional Neural Networks (CNN), such as YOLO and OpenCV, the module identifies and classifies objects, including diagrams, charts, and labels, and detects visual clutter.
- NLP module: This module assesses whether labels and descriptions are correct, consistent with corporate style guides, match the presented data, and relevant to the business questions given in prompts.
- Recommendation system: Based on a Collaborative Filtering algorithm, the module proposes visualization improvements. These recommendations are derived from predefined rules (e.g., corporate style guide or IBCS).
- Data quality assessment module: This module checks scales and units and alignment between visualizations (e.g., labels on axes) and the database. It also uses basic statistical tests (e.g., Z-score analysis) and predefined business rules to verify whether detected anomalies are the result of incorrect data-to-chart mapping.

Such backend design supports the development of tools that are flexible, scalable, and capable of evolving alongside the changing data analysis and visualization needs of organizations.

To initiate a visualization assessment, the user uploads a file with the visualization (sketch or completed report) and selects one of the predefined analysis types: visual element analysis, data interpretation, or layout improvement suggestions. The user then chooses a set of evaluation criteria: standard metrics (derived from academic literature), standards (e.g., IBCS), or corporate guidelines. These user-defined parameters are employed to construct a prompt, which is then sent to the VLM. The results are returned in textual form, divided into thematic areas.

Prompt Engineering

LLM and VLM systems are highly prompt sensitive: prompt formulation strongly influences the final result. In the proposed solution, several different prompts have been developed, evaluated and prepared for use by an AI agent. Three distinct approaches to prompt engineering have been tested: (i) Basic text prompting, an approach that merely provides general guidelines for evaluating visualizations, focusing on best practices from literature; (ii) Context-Enriched Prompting: This approach embeds prompts enriched with business/domain related context, for example, the IBCS or corporate style guide; and (iii) Multi-Agent Prompting: A solution in which the prompt is divided into sub-prompts assigned to different, specialized virtual agents. Additionally, parts of prompts are generated dynamically based on a system's knowledge base and a query's similarity to existing documents.

The basic text prompt used in the prototype solution complies with the general principles of data visualization design (Knaflic, 2015). This prompt starts by defining the operating context, that is, stating that the system's task is to analyze screenshots of data visualizations. Upon successfully verifying that the image qualifies as a data visualization, the system proceeds with a more in-depth analysis, consisting of two main parts: identifying potential issues in the presentation of data, and suggesting improvements aligned with best visualization practices.

The AI-assistant assesses the layout, structure, color consistency, and readability of such screenshots. Particular emphasis is placed on the logical arrangement of elements, the clarity of titles and headings, and a consistent visual style. With the prompt section focused on individual visualizations, the importance of evaluating each element separately is emphasized. Tasks include checking whether the selected chart type matches the nature of the data, assessing the effectiveness of the message, verifying label and axis readability, and ensuring that the color scheme adheres to design principles.

Upon the completion of the analysis, the AI-assistant provides recommendations for the overall layout of the report and individual charts components. The prompt also contains a communication section stating that any suggestions for improvements should be presented in a clear, constructive, and actionable manner. References to relevant sources are encouraged to enhance the credibility of the recommendations.

The system is prompted to provide only valid, data-driven suggestions and inform the user of any missing or insufficient information. This directive is intended to increase the transparency and accountability of the system's responses.

The enrichment of prompts with business/domain-related context represents a departure from the previous approach by aligning suggested solutions with a specific standard and style guide. This version begins with a clearly defined operational context, specifying that the AI-assistant is to support the analysis of data visualizations using specific guidelines derived from the IBCS, for example, a standardized data presentation (appropriate chart and label selection) and consistent use of color rules, such as green to denote increases and red to indicate decreases. Grounding the evaluation process in a well-established standard ensures that the assessment is based on proven principles, thereby increasing the accuracy and practical value of the recommendations.

The prompt specifies a sequence of actions the AI-assistant should follow. First, it must verify whether the data presentation on the chart accurately reflects reality and whether the chosen chart type is appropriate for the nature of the information being conveyed. Next, it evaluates the use of color, ensuring that positive changes are marked in green and negative ones in red, which supports intuitive interpretation. The next stage involves analyzing the clarity and readability of the visualization, examining the precision of labels, axes, and legends, and identifying any elements that needlessly clutter the chart and interfere with message delivery. Following this evaluation, the AI-assistant is expected to generate specific recommendations for improving the chart elements.

The multi-agent solution consists of several key components (Figure 6.1), each playing a specific role in data visualization analysis.

The Coordinator Agent serves as the central coordinator of the system, receiving user requests, collecting input data, and assigning tasks to specialized agents. Upon task completion, it aggregates the results received from the other components and generates a coherent report containing specific recommendations and references to relevant visualization standards.

The Dashboard Evaluation Agent is responsible for conducting an overall dashboard assessment. Its role includes analyzing the layout, structure, visual consistency, and readability of the entire report. It verifies that the arrangement of elements and the applied graphic styles align with established design principles.

The Domain Knowledge Agent processes the contextual information provided by the user, drawing on domain-specific knowledge grounded in established standards (e.g. IBCS, corporate style guides). Its purpose is to integrate theoretical visualization principles with practical input data, enabling context-sensitive evaluation tailored to specific industry or organizational requirements.

Chart Evaluation Agents and Subchart Evaluation Agents are specialized units tasked with detailed analysis of individual charts or dashboard sections. Their responsibilities include evaluating the alignment of data with the selected chart type, assessing the use of color, verifying the readability of labels, axes, and legends, and identifying superfluous elements that could interfere with message clarity. These agents operate concurrently, allowing for iterative assessment of multiple visualization components.

The Accessibility Evaluator checks whether visualizations meet accessibility criteria. For instance, it looks into whether color schemes and contrast ratios are appropriate for users with visual impairments.

The aforementioned multi-agent system flow chart (Figure 6.1) illustrates the flow of information among the constituent agents, with numbered circles above the arrows indicating the sequence of operations.

Step (1) represents the reception of user request by the Coordinator Agent.

Steps (2, 3) mark the distribution of this data: the Dashboard Evaluation Agent performs a general analysis of layout and visual coherence, while the Domain Knowledge Agent interprets contextual information.

Steps (5, 6) represent the iterative analysis process in which agents conduct in-depth evaluations of specific components and return the results to the Coordinator Agent. At this stage, analytical units, such as Chart Evaluation Agents and Subchart Evaluation Agents, assess aspects like data-to-chart fit, color usage, label and axis readability, and the removal of superfluous elements that may obscure the intended message.

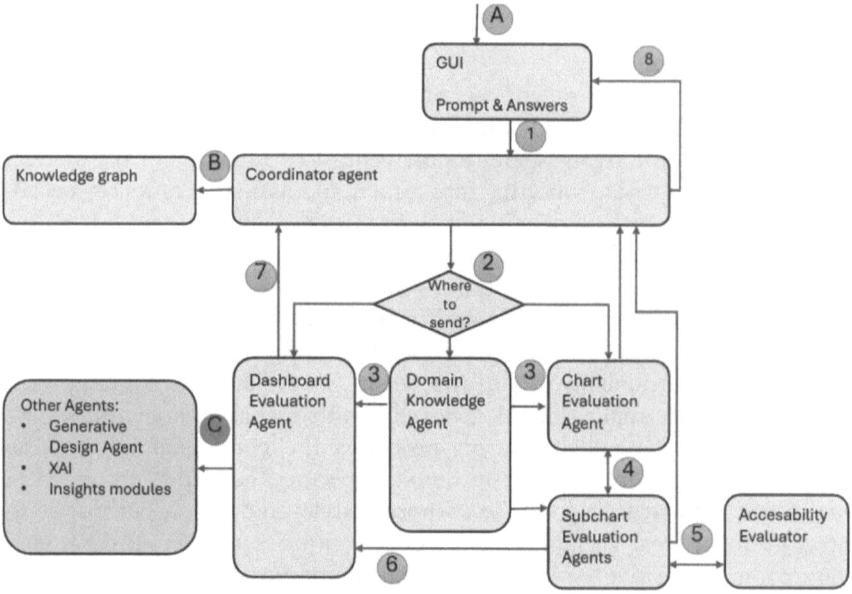

Figure 6.1 The main components of the multi-agent system.

Source: Own elaboration.

In the final steps (7, 8), the Coordinator Agent consolidates all information gathered from the individual agents and generates a consolidated report.

Evaluation

Automatic evaluation of data visualization might be applicable in domains that rely on intensive data processing, where personnel produce multiple data reports that should be aligned with corporate style guidelines and ensure accessibility for a broad range of users. In this case study, we examine the implementation of an AI-based tool in a real-world setting at Żabka Polska, a retail organization, along with its partner companies. A central tenet of their strategy is the ongoing development of data-driven solutions, which increases the need for automating and standardizing visualization processes.

Test Environment

The tests we have conducted are designed to examine how the tool assesses dashboards for visual correctness and alignment with corporate guidelines. This evaluation aims to determine whether and to what extent an AI-based tool can assist BI developers in creating high-quality dashboards.

The testing environment was developed and the tests were carried out within the organizational structure of the Żabka Polska retail chain. A total of 19 participants representing diverse levels of seniority, experience, and information needs were recruited. These participants also differed in how they would potentially use the tested solution. They included students, BI developers from diverse organizations, managers, data analysts, and professionals acting in non-analytical capacities.

Each participant was given ten sample visualizations sourced from the Power BI dashboard gallery.[4] A five-point scale (1–5) was used with the participants encouraged to provide additional comments. For ratings of 3 or lower, the participants were asked to indicate specific examples of inadequate suggestions.

The study focused exclusively on the visual aspect of reports and dashboards. The tool did not have direct access to data sources or the analytics infrastructure.

Evaluation Results

In the first part of evaluation, participants rated 10 sample dashboards against three criteria: adherence to best practices, readability & clarity, and overall impression. The dashboards were curated to encompass a range of quality levels: 3 were poor, 4 average, and 3 high-quality examples, as showed in Table 6.1. In phase 2, participants assessed the AI tool's evaluations of the same dashboards, focusing on three dimensions: completeness of system-generated responses, accuracy (defined as alignment with participant expectations), and usefulness for visualization improvement.

Table 6.1 Evaluation results

Dashboard Quality	*Count*	*Completeness*	*Accuracy*	*Utility*
Poor	3	4.22	4.07	4.42
Average	4	3.96	3.61	3.94
High-quality	3	3.85	3.30	3.40
Average		4.01	3.65	3.92
Role	*Count*	*Completeness*	*Accuracy*	*Utility*
Student	4	4.03	3.53	3.93
Data Analyst	5	4.10	3.62	3.92
BI Developer	5	3.90	3.60	3.88
Specialist (non-analytical)	3	3.80	3.80	3.90
Manager	2	4.30	3.90	4.03
Average		4.01	3.65	3.92

Source: Own elaboration.

Out of 19 respondents, 16 reported to regularly engage in data visualizations (12 using Power BI and 4 using Tableau). The average time to complete the survey was 62 minutes. Due to a strong correlation between job role and experience, results were presented using job role as the aggregation variable.

Across all ten of the reviewed dashboards, the AI tool received consistently favorable ratings for its utility in supporting the interpretation and improvement of the data visualizations shown in Table 6.1. On a 1-to-5 scale, the average rating in this category hovered around 3.9–4.0, indicating a generally positive perception of value. The completeness of AI-generated feedback also received high ratings averaging approx. 4.0, suggesting that users found the responses thorough and well-rounded. However, accuracy (alignment with user expectations) was rated slightly lower, at about 3.6, implying that while the AI was helpful, it did not always capture the user's intent or domain-specific nuances.

Managers consistently rated the tool's utility and accuracy higher than other roles, with average scores exceeding the mean by 0.30 on completeness and 0.28 on accuracy. This trend may reflect their broader, more strategic view on dashboard evaluation. Students and data analysts provided more moderate or critical assessments, possibly due to a more technical or detail-focused perspective.

The observed inverse relationship between dashboard quality and perceived AI usefulness suggests a contextual dependency. Participants found the tool more helpful when evaluating poorly designed dashboards, likely because AI-generated feedback addressed clear deficiencies and offered actionable improvements. Conversely, high-quality dashboards offered limited opportunities for enhancement, reducing the perceived value of AI assistance. This pattern indicates that the tool is most beneficial in diagnostic or remedial contexts, where users seek support in identifying and correcting flaws. The declining usefulness in well-designed cases does not reflect a weakness of the tool but underscores its role as a supplementary evaluator rather than a validation instrument.

The qualitative feedback gathered during the evaluation phase reveals nuanced insights on the AI's performance. Positive evaluations emphasized the tool's capacity to detect subtle layout flaws and enhance overall clarity. The responses suggest that the tool effectively supports both the visual refinement of dashboards and compliance with organizational standards, particularly in structured corporate environments.

In addition, the tool was seen as beneficial in quality assurance contexts. One respondent remarked that "the tool provided a useful second opinion during the review phase," indicating its value in iterative design cycles and final quality control.

However, less favorable feedback highlighted significant limitations. Several participants reported that the tool's suggestions lacked contextual depth or practical specificity. For example, one respondent wrote that "the suggestions were too generic and did not account for the business context of the dashboard," while another commented that "the tool flagged elements as problematic without explaining the nature of the issue." These critiques underline a lack of transparency and limited explainability in some of the tool's assessments, reducing users' ability to interpret and act on its advice.

Furthermore, concerns were raised over brand consistency. One participant observed that "color scheme suggestions contradicted internal branding guidelines," revealing that the tool may not always integrate seamlessly with domain-specific or visual identity frameworks.

These insights highlight both the potential and the current limitations of using AI for automated visualization evaluation. While the system provides meaningful and often helpful suggestions, its overall effectiveness could be significantly improved by incorporating greater contextual sensitivity, rule-based explainability, and integration with institutional design standards.

Conclusion

Automating data visualization analysis significantly increases productivity by enabling faster identification of areas requiring improvement, leading to more efficient use of human and technological resources. The use of standardized, automated evaluation procedures ensures consistency and high-quality reporting. Additionally, accelerated development cycles allow for faster fixes and improvements.

While the proposed solution, an AI-based tool for automated visualization assessment, was tested within a retail chain organization, its applicability extends to a broad-range of data-driven organizational environments. For example, management of higher education institutions appears to represent a particularly suitable area for its deployment. To offer competitive education services, universities continually track both market trends and student preferences and performance.

Automated visualization assessment is a key component of the broader research agenda for the automation of report generation using GenAI. Future research could help to augment the system's capabilities by developing a mechanism to convert a hand-drawn image into a complete dashboard proposal using multimodal VLMs, incorporating company style guidelines and best visualization practices. A more advanced version of the system could generate appropriate labels for data, further enhancing the interpretability of information.

From a system development perspective, future research should also consider improving the tool's accessibility to users with visual impairments and its customization to accommodate diverse cultural and organizational settings. This approach would provide valuable insights for developing and optimizing the tool. Furthermore, the system could be used in the educational process to facilitate the identification of visualization errors and help non-technical users to learn how to present data correctly in reports.

Acknowledgment

This research was supported by funds granted by the Minister of Science of the Republic of Poland under the "Regional Initiative for Excellence" Programme for the implementation of the project "The Poznań University of Economics and Business for Economy 5.0: Regional Initiative – Global Effects (RIGE)."

Notes

1 www.tableau.com/products/artificial-intelligence#content-530264
2 https://learn.microsoft.com/en-us/power-bi/transform-model/desktop-ai-insights
3 https://zebrabi.com/
4 https://community.fabric.microsoft.com/t5/Data-Stories-Gallery/bd-p/DataStoriesGallery

Reference List

Behrisch, M., Blumenschein, M., Kim, N. W., Shao, L., El-Assady, M., Fuchs, J., Seebacher, D., Diehl, A., Brandes, U., Pfister, H., Schreck, T., Weiskopf, D., & Keim, D. A. (2018). Quality metrics for information visualization. *Computer Graphics Forum*, *37*(3), 625–662. https://doi.org/10.1111/CGF.13446

Bertin, J. (1983). *Semiology of graphics*. University of Wisconsin Press.

Dong, Q., Li, L., Dai, D., Zheng, C., Ma, J., Li, R., Xia, H., Xu, J., Wu, Z., Chang, B., Sun, X., Li, L., & Sui, Z. (2024). A survey on in-context learning. *Proceedings of the 2024 Conference on Empirical Methods in Natural Language Processing*, 1107–1128. https://doi.org/10.18653/v1/2024.emnlp-main.64

Feuerriegel, S., Hartmann, J., Janiesch, C., & Zschech, P. (2024). Generative AI. *Business & Information Systems Engineering*, *66*(1), 111–126. https://doi.org/10.1007/s12599-023-00834-7

Harper, J., & Agrawala, M. (2016). Converting basic D3 charts into reusable style templates. *IEEE Transactions on Visualization and Computer Graphics*, *24*(3), 1274–1286. https://doi.org/10.1109/TVCG.2017.2659744

He, K., Gkioxari, G., Dollár, P., & Girshick, R. (2020). Mask R-CNN. *IEEE Transactions on Pattern Analysis and Machine Intelligence*, *42*(2). https://doi.org/10.1109/TPAMI.2018.2844175

Knaflic, C. N. (2015). *Storytelling with data: A data visualization guide for business professionals* (pp. 1–267). https://doi.org/10.1002/9781119055259

Li, H., Guo, D., Fan, W., Xu, M., Huang, J., Meng, F., & Song, Y. (2023). Multi-step Jailbreaking privacy attacks on ChatGPT. *Findings of the Association for Computational Linguistics: EMNLP 2023*, 4138–4153. https://doi.org/10.18653/v1/2023.findings-emnlp.272

Li, J., Li, D., Xiong, C., & Hoi, S. (2022). BLIP: Bootstrapping language-image pre-training for unified vision-language understanding and generation. *Proceedings of Machine Learning Research*, *162*.

Liu, P., Yuan, W., Fu, J., Jiang, Z., Hayashi, H., & Neubig, G. (2023). Pre-train, prompt, and predict: A systematic survey of prompting methods in natural language processing. *ACM Computing Surveys*, *55*(9), 1–35. https://doi.org/10.1145/3560815

Maddigan, P., & Susnjak, T. (2023a). *Chat2VIS: Fine-tuning data visualisations using multilingual natural language text and pre-trained large language models*. https://arxiv.org/abs/2303.14292v1

Maddigan, P., & Susnjak, T. (2023b). Chat2VIS: Generating data visualizations via natural language using ChatGPT, Codex and GPT-3 large language models. *IEEE Access*, *11*, 45181–45193. https://doi.org/10.1109/ACCESS.2023.3274199

Radford, A., Kim, J. W., Hallacy, C., Ramesh, A., Goh, G., Agarwal, S., Sastry, G., Askell, A., Mishkin, P., Clark, J., Krueger, G., & Sutskever, I. (2021). Learning transferable visual models from natural language supervision. *Proceedings of Machine Learning Research*, *139*, 8748–8763. https://arxiv.org/abs/2103.00020v1

Ramesh, A., Pavlov, M., Goh, G., Gray, S., Voss, C., Radford, A., Chen, M., & Sutskever, I. (2021). Zero-shot text-to-image generation. *Proceedings of Machine Learning Research*, *139*.

Richards, N. (2022). *Questions in Dataviz: A design-driven process for data visualisation*. www.amazon.pl/Questions-Dataviz-Design-Driven-Process-Visualisation/dp/1032139447

Schulhoff, S., Pinto, J., Khan, A., Bouchard, L.-F., Si, C., Anati, S., Tagliabue, V., Kost, A. L., Carnahan, C., & Boyd-Graber, J. (2023). *Ignore this title and HackAPrompt: Exposing systemic vulnerabilities of LLMs through a global scale prompt hacking competition*. http://arxiv.org/abs/2311.16119

Wang, Y., Hou, Z., Shen, L., Wu, T., Wang, J., Huang, H., Zhang, H., & Zhang, D. (2022). Towards natural language-based visualization authoring. *IEEE Transactions on Visualization and Computer Graphics*, *29*(1), 1222–1232. https://doi.org/10.1109/TVCG.2022.3209357

Wei, J., Wei, J., Tay, Y., Tran, D., Webson, A., Lu, Y., Chen, X., Liu, H., Huang, D., Zhou, D., & Ma, T. (2023). *Larger language models do in-context learning differently*. http://arxiv.org/abs/2303.03846

Wu, A., Wang, Y., Shu, X., Moritz, D., Cui, W., Zhang, H., Zhang, D., & Qu, H. (2021). AI4VIS: Survey on artificial intelligence approaches for data visualization. *IEEE Transactions on Visualization and Computer Graphics*, *28*(12), 5049–5070. https://doi.org/10.1109/TVCG.2021.3099002

Xiao, S., Huang, S., Lin, Y., Ye, Y., & Zeng, W. (2024). Let the chart spark: Embedding semantic context into chart with text-to-image generative model. *IEEE Transactions on Visualization and Computer Graphics*, *30*(01), 284–294. https://doi.org/10.1109/TVCG.2023.3326913

Yuan, M., Bao, P., Yuan, J., Shen, Y., Chen, Z., Xie, Y., Zhao, J., Li, Q., Chen, Y., Zhang, L., Shen, L., & Dong, B. (2024). Large language models illuminate a progressive pathway to artificial intelligent healthcare assistant. *Medicine Plus*, *1*(2), 100030. https://doi.org/10.1016/j.medp.2024.100030

Part III

Marketing and Product Development

7 Influence of Country of Origin on AI Perceptions

A Comparative Study of Polish and German Perspectives

Marcin Leszczyński, Aleksandra Rabczun, and Jarko Fidrmuc

Introduction

In an era of heightened technological development, consumers are increasingly exposed to tools based on artificial intelligence (AI). The proliferation of products in this market is causing manufacturers to compete for consumers by using advanced technological solutions and offering new functionalities. Purchasing decisions and trust in new technologies are strongly shaped by non-technological factors, which include the image of the product's country of origin (COO). In the literature, this phenomenon is described as the country-of-origin effect (COOE), which is an important element shaping consumer decisions toward products. Few studies have focused on the COOE in the new technology market. Therefore, it is important to study how the COO of a manufacturer affects the perception of AI-based products, which may be crucial in shaping the future of the digital economy. The purpose of this chapter is to analyze differences in the perception of AI tools depending on the COO of the product, and to assess whether and to what extent the nationality of the consumer affects the propensity to use and pay for AI-based products. Special attention was paid to comparing the attitudes of consumers from Poland and Germany as representatives of two different consumer cultures in the European Union (EU) framework.

Country-of-Origin Effect

Roth and Romeo (1992) define the COOE as a phenomenon that explains how consumers perceive a product imported from a specific country. The COOE can also be defined as an informational cue for economic participants relating to a particular product (Verlegh et al., 2005). Hong and Wyer (1989) indicate that the COOE can influence the evaluation of a particular product, which relates to its quality, among other things (Adejorooluwa & Liu, 2018). A product's COO influences consumers' evaluations, as they rely on available information cues (Kaynak & Kara, 2002). Consumers use intrinsic factors such as style or material, alongside extrinsic cues such as price or brand, to assess product quality (Huddleston et al., 2001). Hence, COO serves as a key

DOI: 10.4324/9781003659143-10

factor in forming both positive and negative perceptions of a product, which in turn impacts purchasing decisions (Elliott & Cameron, 1994; Watson & Wright, 2000).

The COOE is also known as the "made-in" effect, where consumer perceptions (CP) of products are shaped by the image of the producing country (Huddleston et al., 2001; Kaynak & Kara, 2002). Several studies have sought to assess consumers' perceptions of the COO of various product groups made in different countries (Beverland & Lindgreen, 2002; Elliott & Cameron, 1994; Garland & Coy, 1993; Lawrence et al., 1992; Manrai & Manrai, 1995; Watson & Wright, 2000). The COOE has been linked to consumer purchasing behavior (Ettenson, 1993), product image (Peris et al., 1993), and CP of the attributes of domestic and foreign products or services (Kaynak et al., 1994; Strutton et al., 1995). Šapić et al. (2018) point out that COO can influence consumer behavior, including their loyalty to brands and products from a particular country. This can have consequences at the macroeconomic level by affecting international competitiveness (Parameswaran & Pisharodi, 1994). Thus, depending on whether the COOE is positive or negative, it can either facilitate the conquest of new markets (Aichner, 2014) or limit companies' internationalization opportunities (Meneses & Santos, 2019).

COO Image

One of the key determinants of COOE is country image (CI) (Adina et al., 2015; Yang et al., 2016), which can be understood as the knowledge structure representing the beliefs of economic participants about a country (Magnusson & Westjohn, 2021). Research on CI has become one of the main areas of research on the COOE (Ma et al., 2022). Hakala et al. (2013) explain that CI is considered from three main perspectives in the literature (i.e., product view, national view, and cultural view). In their study of the COOE, Roth and Diamantopoulos (2009) define three categories of CI: general CI, product-country image, and country-specific product image. Martin and Eroglu (1993) focus on three dimensions of CI – political, economic, and technological – while Xiong et al. (2010) divide it into economic, cultural, and political categories. The economic image of a country is referred to by Kalicharan (2014), who argues that consumers perceive better products coming from developed countries.

Much of this research in the context of the COOE is concerned with the impact of CI on consumer behavior (Ma et al., 2022) and on CP and attitudes toward the country, its people, and its market offerings (Lu et al., 2016). Because CI influences consumers' evaluations of product attributes and attitudes toward a brand from a country (Han, 1989), it can increase a country's competitiveness and attractiveness (Grundey, 2006).

Research findings suggest that many consumers prefer to buy products from their own country over foreign alternatives (Bilkey & Nes, 1982; Samiee, 1994). Studies indicate that when choosing among foreign products, consumers tend to favor those from countries they perceive as culturally, politically, or economically similar to their own (Heslop et al., 1998; Lantz & Loeb, 1996; Wang & Lamb, 1983).

Artificial Intelligence

Consumer preferences in the AI market are shaped by a multitude of factors that determine the extent to which AI technologies are adopted and integrated into everyday use. The capacity of AI to enhance user experience and deliver personalized services serves as a primary driver of consumer interest. According to the literature, a critical determinant of consumer preferences is the level of familiarity with AI technologies. Tully et al. (2023) suggest that lower AI literacy may be associated with greater openness to AI, implying that as consumers acquire more knowledge and understanding of these systems, their willingness to adopt them increases. This observation aligns with the findings of Wen et al. (2022), who emphasize that the quality of human interactions with AI significantly influences consumer experiences, with positive engagements reinforcing continued use.

Trust is a fundamental factor in AI adoption. Frank et al. (2023) argue that consumer trust is shaped not only by the inherent attributes of AI technology but also by their perceptions of the organization providing these services. This dynamic aligns with commitment – trust theory, wherein an organization's perceived integrity and reliability strengthen consumer willingness to engage with AI-driven services. Additionally, research by Alsheibani et al. (2020) highlights that organizations integrating AI into human resource management effectively experience higher adoption rates, as employee trust in the technology contributes to broader consumer confidence.

The specific context in which AI is deployed significantly impacts consumer adoption behavior. Park et al. (2021) identify notable variations in adoption patterns across different service domains, particularly in distinguishing between credence-based and effort-based services. AI applications in highly interactive sectors such as retail and financial services tend to experience higher adoption rates due to their perceived utility and efficiency. Furthermore, research by Noranee and Othman (2023) underscores the role of AI in optimizing personalization and customer segmentation, highlighting that tailored AI-driven services resonate more effectively with consumer preferences, thereby enhancing market acceptance.

Finally, emotional and social factors also exert substantial influence on AI adoption. Sebastian et al. (2023) argue that emotional and social considerations play a crucial role in shaping consumer attitudes toward technological innovations. Given that consumers often exhibit risk aversion and rely on established behavioral routines, they may demonstrate reluctance to adopt AI-based solutions. Moreover, the emotional responses elicited from interactions with AI systems can profoundly shape CP, further reinforcing or inhibiting adoption behaviors.

Research Design

To verify the significance of the COOE in the AI product market, a diagnostic survey method was used along with an experiment focusing on the COO of a fictional application. The study included five countries: Poland, Germany, the United Kingdom (UK), China, and the United States (US). The subjects of the study are consumers from Poland and Germany. These two countries were chosen to investigate consumer ethnocentrism in shaping consumer decisions toward products in the AI market. According to the rankings of the Global AI Index and Stanford Artificial Intelligence Index Report, the US, China, and the UK are currently the world's leading countries in the context of AI. At the same time, these countries are characterized by different images, which is a key element in shaping the COOE. For example, Silver et al. (2023) indicate that 93% of Poles and 57% of Germans have a positive perception of the US. Interestingly, 88% of Poles recognize that American technology is at a high level compared to other countries, while for Germans, the percentage is only 52%. The same survey analyzed the image of China, which was viewed positively by only 21% of Poles and 18% of Germans. The results look slightly different for Chinese technology, which 66% of Poles and 62% of Germans perceive as more advanced than other countries. Significantly, Germans see technology from China as more advanced than from the US (Silver et al., 2023).

It should be noted that consumers' decisions can also be influenced by brand (Bartosik-Purgat, 2018), so to eliminate this influence, the study created a fictional AI application called "Stellar" offered by the fictional brand QuantumEdge. Each respondent received an article presenting the application's specifications and capabilities. For the purposes of the study, six variants of the article were developed, in which the information about the COO of the application was changed. In addition to the five countries indicated earlier, an article was added that did not indicate the COO of the application, which served as the control sample. The participants were randomly assigned an article based on the day of the month in which they were born (1–5 = China, 6–10 and 31 = control sample, 11–15 = US, 16–20 = UK, 21–25 = Germany, and 26–30 = Poland). Respondents then answered the same questions, which used a measurement scale based on the net promoter score. The main part of the survey consisted of 23 questions, which were divided into two types: questions about the application presented in the article and questions about the perceptions of the countries included in the survey. The Prolific platform was used to carry out the study on German consumers.

Findings

In the Polish study, 165 individuals participated. Of these, 94 were women and 71 were men. The average age of the survey respondents was 23.68 years, with a median age of 22 years. Eighty-three respondents rated their financial situation as good, while 60 described it as average. Regarding the question on the frequency of using AI tools on a scale from 0 to 10, respondents reported an average score of 5.88, with the most frequently chosen score (mode) being 8. As for the frequency of using paid AI tools, the average score was 1.35, with the mode being 0. The final question in the initial section of the survey asked about respondents' willingness to pay (WTP) for access to AI tools. Polish respondents had an average score of 2.89, again with the mode being 0.

In the German study, 110 individuals participated. Of these, 33 were women and 76 were men. One participant selected the option not to disclose their gender. The average age of the German respondents was 32.61 years, with a median age of 31 years. Contrary to the Polish version, 47 participants rated their financial situation as average, while 30 rated it as good. Regarding the frequency of using AI tools, German respondents reported an average score of 6.40 (higher than Polish respondents), with the mode being 8, similar to the Polish sample. For the use of paid AI tools, German respondents had an average score of 1.92, with the most frequently chosen score being 0, similar to the Polish sample. The last question in the initial section of the German survey asked about payment intention for AI tools. German respondents reported an average score of 4.00, with the mode again being 0. The averages in the German study were clearly higher than those in the Polish study, although the most frequently selected scores (modes) were exactly the same.

Next, the respondents were asked to provide their date of birth. Based on their birth dates, they were assigned to specific versions of the survey. As a result of this allocation, among the Polish respondents, 40 were shown the Chinese version, 34 the control version, 21 the American version, 22 the British version, 22 the German version, and 26 the Polish version. Among the German respondents, 25 were shown the Chinese version, 27 the control version, 14 the American version, 10 the British version, 18 the German version, and 17 the Polish version. One of the survey questions examined respondents' opinions on how safe they would feel using the application overall, as well as on the application's COO. Polish respondents reported an average sense of security when using the described application at a level of 4.25, while German respondents averaged 4.59. This indicates that the German participants exhibited a higher level of perceived security when using the AI application presented in the text.

Polish consumers reported the highest average sense of security when using the Polish application (4.96), which may suggest a degree of ethnocentrism toward domestic products. Conversely, the lowest average level of perceived security was associated with the British application (3.45). German consumers felt the highest average sense of security when using the American application (5.43). The lowest average level of perceived security was, similar to the Polish respondents, reported for the British application (3.30).

The respondents were then asked to evaluate the extent to which they would be willing to trust the creators of the presented application overall based on the COO. The average level of trust toward the creators of the application was 3.67 among Polish respondents and 4.55 among German respondents. This clearly indicates that German consumers demonstrated significantly higher trust. Polish consumers, on average, expressed the highest level of trust in an application with no clearly indicated COO (4.26), and the lowest level of trust in the American application (3.05).

In contrast, German consumers reported the highest average trust in the Polish application (5.69), and the lowest in the British application (3.10). Respondents were also asked to rate on a scale from 0 to 10 how likely they would be to use the application presented in the article (0 = not at all likely, 10 = very likely). The average willingness of German respondents to use the application presented in the article was 5.19, while for Polish respondents, it was 4.65. This suggests that the German participants would be more inclined than the Polish participants to use the application described in the text.

Polish respondents showed the highest average willingness to use (WTU) the application described in the article when it originated from China (5.18), and the lowest when it came from Germany (4.14). In contrast, German respondents were most willing to use the Polish application (5.94), and least willing to use the British application (4.20).

Another important variable was the payment intention to access the application. Overall, Polish respondents expressed an average level of 2.70, while German respondents averaged 3.17. This indicates that the German participants were more willing than the Polish participants to pay for the application they read about in the text. On average, Polish respondents indicated the highest level of payment intention for the Chinese application (3.08), while German respondents were most willing to pay for the American (4.14) and Polish (4.13) applications. The lowest average payment intention among Poles was for the German application (2.09), while among Germans, it was for the British application (1.90).

Subsequently, the respondents were asked how much they would be willing to pay per month for the application. In the Polish version of the survey, the amount was expressed in Polish zloty (PLN). On average, Polish respondents were willing to pay PLN 46.76 (EUR 11.13), with a median of PLN 20 (EUR 4.76). In the German version, the amounts were expressed in euros (EUR). On average, Germans were willing to pay EUR 11.75 (PLN 49.31), with a median of EUR 5 (PLN 21). The analysis shows that the Germans would be willing to pay only slightly more than the Poles to access the application. Figure 7.1 shows the willingness to pay for an application among Polish and German consumers as an average amount according to COO.

Polish consumers were, on average, most willing to pay for the British application (EUR 14.90), and least willing to pay for the German application (EUR 8.29). In contrast, German consumers indicated the highest average WTP for the American application (EUR 18.86), and were least willing to pay for the Chinese application, with an average of EUR 7.64. Subsequently, the study examined the perceived image of the countries featured in the survey, as reported by the respondents (Figure 7.2).

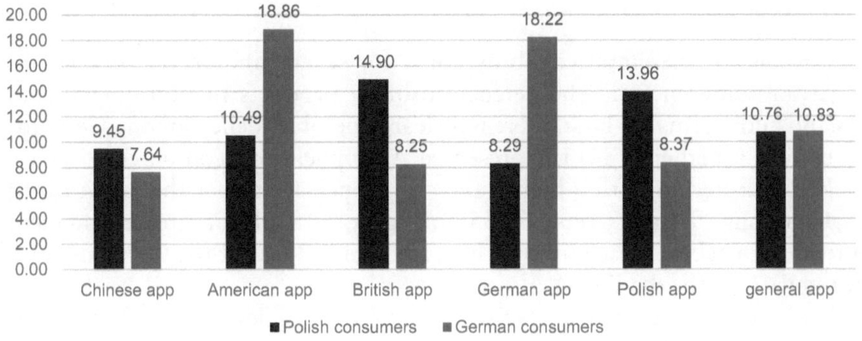

Figure 7.1 Willingness to pay for the application expressed as the average amount by COO (in EUR).

Source: Own elaboration based on empirical research.

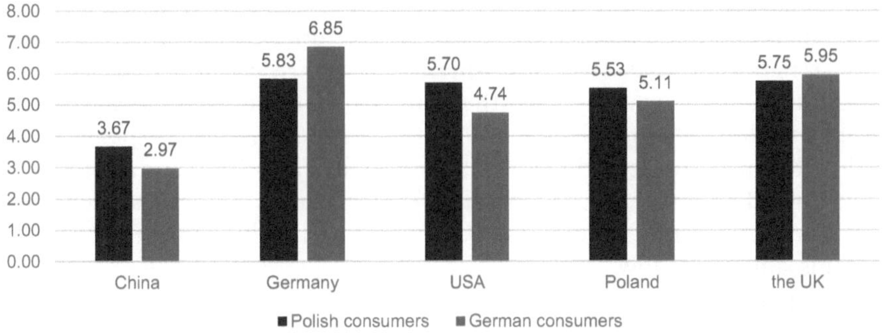

Figure 7.2 Average scores regarding the image of each country perceived by Polish and German participants.

Source: Own elaboration based on empirical research.

Polish consumers rated Germany's image the highest on average (5.83) and China's the lowest (3.67). Germans rated their own country's image the highest on average (6.85), which aligns with the Polish perception, and, like the Poles, they rated China's image the lowest (2.97). Finally, consumers were asked whether they associate AI technology products from different countries with high quality. Polish respondents indicated that they perceived American products as the highest quality on average (7.20). In contrast, they rated their own products the lowest (3.87). German respondents similarly rated American products as the highest quality on average (7.25), while they perceived Polish products as the lowest quality (3.13).

Discussion and Conclusion

The results of the empirical study allow for several important conclusions regarding differences in the perception of AI products by consumers from Poland and Germany. First, there is a clear general tendency among Germans to exhibit a higher WTU the presented AI applications compared to Poles. This is reflected in both a higher average propensity to use the applications (5.19 among Germans versus 4.65 among Poles) and in a greater payment intention to access these tools (with an average of 3.17 for the Germans compared to 2.70 for the Poles).

These differences are not solely due to varying levels of technological familiarity or financial situations but are also strongly influenced by the COO of the presented application. Polish respondents showed the highest WTU the Chinese application, which may be linked to the strong popularity of Chinese products in the Polish market and the low expected price (EUR 9.45), potentially increasing interest in the product. In contrast, Germans rated the Polish application the highest, likely due to high trust (5.69) and a sense of security (5.19), which may be influenced by close ties with Poland, including geographic proximity and migration processes. The shared framework of the EU, with its data protection regulations and user privacy standards, may also play an important role. The Polish application also recorded the highest payment intention. However, it is worth noting that Germans were willing to pay a relatively low amount (EUR 8.37) for the Polish app, which explains their high willingness to use and pay for it – especially since Germans do not perceive Poland as a provider of high-quality AI products (3.13). This indicates that German consumers value the Polish offering highly, provided the price remains sufficiently low.

The findings regarding perceptions of security and trust toward applications are also noteworthy. Poles reported the greatest sense of security with the Polish app, which may reflect ethnocentric tendencies and greater trust in the domestic market. Germans, conversely, felt most secure with the American app – likely due to the perceived high quality and technological innovation associated with the US. Interestingly, for both nationalities, the lowest sense of security was reported for the British application, possibly reflecting changes in perceptions of the UK after Brexit. Variations in results are also evident in WTP: Poles were most willing to pay for the British app, while Germans preferred the American app. The relatively high amount Poles are willing to pay for the British app may be connected to the preconceived notion that British products tend to be more expensive.

The analysis of CI further provides meaningful insights. Poles rated Germany's image the highest (WTP of EUR 8.29), while Germans rated their own country the highest (with a maximum WTP of EUR 18.22). Both groups rated China's image the lowest, which was reflected in low levels of trust and security toward Chinese apps (especially among German respondents). However, the Polish respondents showed the highest WTU the Chinese app, indicating a cognitive dissonance: recognition of China's technological advancement alongside distrust of its political system and values, resulting in a low price (EUR 9.45 for Poles and EUR 7.64 for Germans). Thus, a positive image of Chinese AI technology products (Poles = 6.51, Germans = 6.64) is undermined by a generally negative perception of the country itself (Poles = 3.67, Germans = 2.97). The opposite pattern was observed for German-origin products. Respondents associated Germany with a positive general image (Poles = 5.83, Germans = 6.85) but viewed its AI technology products less favorably (Poles = 4.37, Germans = 4.35). This corresponds to a similar price level that Poles were willing to pay for German and Chinese products. This relationship does not appear among German consumers, who were willing to pay EUR 18.22 for a German app, likely reflecting consumer ethnocentrism.

Finally, the results suggest that both Poles and Germans perceive AI products from the US as the highest quality. However, despite the US's strong reputation, Poles exhibited lower trust in American applications compared to others, which may reflect the influence of global political or cultural narratives on technology perception. In summary, the study confirms the significant impact of the COOE on consumer decisions regarding AI-based products. Differences between Poles and Germans highlight divergent priorities, levels of openness to foreign technologies, and degrees of trust in institutions and producers from various countries. These findings can offer valuable guidance to AI developers and distributors in tailoring marketing strategies and communication to local preferences and consumer expectations.

Reference List

Adejorooluwa, T., & Liu, Q. (2018). Consumer perception of product quality and the country-of-origin effect. *Developing Country Studies*, *8*(12), 8–14. www.iiste.org/journals/index.php/dcs/article/view/45633

Adina, C., Gabriela, C., & Roxana-Denisa, S. (2015). Country-of-origin effects on perceived brand positioning. *Procedia Economics and Finance*, *23*, 422–427. https://doi.org/10.1016/S2212-5671(15)00383-4

Aichner, T. (2014). Country-of-origin marketing: A list of typical strategies with examples. *Journal of Brand Management*, *21*(1), 81–93. https://doi.org/10.1057/bm.2013.24/metrics

Alsheibani, S., Messom, C., & Cheung, Y. (2020). Re-thinking the competitive landscape of artificial intelligence. *Proceedings of the 53rd Hawaii International Conference on System Sciences*. https://doi.org/10.24251/hicss.2020.718

Bartosik-Purgat, M. (2018). Country of origin as a determinant of young Europeans' buying attitudes? Marketing implications. *Oeconomia Copernicana*, *9*(1), 123–142. https://doi.org/10.24136/oc.2018.007

Beverland, M. B., & Lindgreen, A. (2002). Using country-of-origin in strategy: The importance of context and strategic action. *Journal of Brand Management*, *10*(2), 147–167.

Bilkey, W. J., & Nes, E. (1982, Spring/Summer). Country-of-origin effects on product evaluations. *Journal of International Business Studies*, *8*, 89–99.

Elliott, G., & Cameron, R. (1994). Consumer perception of product quality and the country of origin effect. *Journal of International Marketing*, *2*(2), 49–62.

Ettenson, R. (1993). Brand name and country of origin effects in the emerging market economies of Russia, Poland and Hungary. *International Marketing Review*, *10*(5), 14–36.

Frank, D., Jacobsen, L., Søndergaard, H., & Otterbring, T. (2023). In companies we trust: Consumer adoption of artificial intelligence services and the role of trust in companies and AI autonomy. *Information Technology and People*, *36*(8), 155–173. https://doi.org/10.1108/itp-09-2022-0721

Garland, R., & Coy, D. (1993). Buying New Zealand made groceries: Does behavior match attitude? *New Zealand Journal of Business*, *15*, 1–18.

Grundey, D. (2006). Country image as a marketing tool for fostering innovation and entrepreneurship. *Economics and Competition Policy*, *2*(2), 25–42. www.lituanistika.lt/content/4182

Hakala, U., Lemmetyinen, A., & Kantola, S. P. (2013). Country image as a nation-branding tool. *Marketing Intelligence and Planning*, *31*(5), 538–556. https://doi.org/10.1108/mip-04-2013-0060

Han, C. M. (1989). Country image: Halo or summary construct? *Journal of Marketing Research*, *26*(2), 222–229. https://doi.org/10.1177/002224378902600208

Heslop, L., Papadopoulos, N., & Bourke, M. (1998). An interregional and intercultural perspective on subculture differences in product evaluation. *Canadian Journal of Administrative Sciences*, *15*(2), 113–127.

Hong, S.-T., & Wyer, R. S. (1989). Effects of country-of-origin and product-attribute information on product evaluation: An information processing perspective. *Journal of Consumer Research*, *16*(2), 175–187. https://doi.org/10.1086/209206

Huddleston, P., Linda, K., & Lesli, S. (2001). Consumer ethnocentrism, product and polish consumers' perceptions of quality. *International Journal of Retail and Distribution Management*, *29*(5), 236–246.

Kalicharan, H. D. (2014). The effect and influence of country-of-origin on consumers perception of product quality and purchasing intentions. *International Business & Economics Research Journal (IBER)*, *13*(5), 897–902. https://doi.org/10.19030/iber.v13i5.8760

Kaynak, E., & Kara, A. (2002). Consumer perceptions of foreign products. *European Journal of Marketing*, *36*(7/8), 928–949.

Kaynak, E., Kucukemiroglu, O., & Kara, A. (1994). Consumers' perceptions of airlines: A correspondence analysis approach in an airline industry. *Management International Review*, *34*(3), 235–254.

Lantz, G., & Loeb, S. (1996). Country of origin and ethnocentrism: An analysis of Canadian and American preferences using social identity theory. *Advances in Consumer Research*, *23*, 374–800.

Lawrence, C., Marr, N., & Prendergast, G. (1992). Country of origin stereotyping: A case study in the New Zealand motor vehicle industry. *European Journal of Marketing*, *26*(3), 37–51.

Lu, I. R. R., Heslop, L. A., Thomas, D. R., & Kwan, E. (2016). An examination of the status and evolution of country image research. *International Marketing Review*, *33*(6), 825–850. https://doi.org/10.1108/imr-03-2015-0036/full/xml

Ma, L., Song, Z., & Bian, X. (2022). The asymmetric dominance of cognitive versus affective country image in driving purchase: Conditioning roles of cognition-affect intra-valence nature and product type. *International Business Review*, *31*(5), 102007. https://doi.org/10.1016/j.ibusrev.2022.102007

Magnusson, P., & Westjohn, S. A. (2021). The effects of stereotyping on place/country image perceptions. In *Marketing countries, places, and place-associated brands: Identity and image* (pp. 174–191). Edward Elgar Publishing. https://doi.org/10.4337/9781839107375.00021

Manrai, L. A., & Manrai, A. K. (1995). Current issues in the cross-cultural and cross-national consumer research. *Journal of International Consumer Marketing*, *8*(3/4), 9–23.

Martin, I. M., & Eroglu, S. (1993). Measuring a multi-dimensional construct: Country image. *Journal of Business Research*, *28*(3), 191–210. https://doi.org/10.1016/0148-2963(93)90047-S

Meneses, R., & Santos, S. (2019). Country of origin as a constraint to internationalization. *GATR Journal of Business and Economics Review*, *4*(2), 105–113. https://doi.org/10.35609/jber.2019.4.2(5)

Noranee, S., & Othman, A. (2023). Understanding consumer sentiments: Exploring the role of artificial intelligence in marketing. *JMM17: Jurnal Ilmu Ekonomi Dan Manajemen*, *10*(1), 15–23. https://doi.org/10.30996/jmm17.v10i1.8690

Parameswaran, R., & Pisharodi, R. M. (1994). Facets of country of origin image: An empirical assessment. *Journal of Advertising*, *23*(1), 43–56. https://doi.org/10.1080/00913367.1994.10673430

Park, S., Tung, C., & Lee, H. (2021). The adoption of AI service robots: A comparison between credence and experience service settings. *Psychology and Marketing*, *38*(4), 691–703. https://doi.org/10.1002/mar.21468

Peris, S., Newman, K., Bigne, E., & Chansarkar, B. (1993). Aspects of Anglo-Spanish perceptions and product preferences arising from "country of origin" image. *International Journal of Advertising*, *12*(2), 131–142.

Roth, K. P., & Diamantopoulos, A. (2009). Advancing the country image construct. *Journal of Business Research*, *62*(7), 726–740. https://doi.org/10.1016/j.jbusres.2008.05.014

Roth, M. S., & Romeo, J. B. (1992). Matching product category and country image perceptions: A framework for managing country-of-origin effects. *Journal of International Business Studies*, *23*(3), 477–497. https://doi.org/10.1057/palgrave.jibs.8490276/metrics

Samiee, S. (1994). Customer evaluation of products in a global market. *Journal of International Business Studies*, *25*(3), 579–604.

Šapić, S., Kocić, M., & Radaković, K. (2018). The effect of a product's country of origin on the customer loyalty creation process. *TEME*, *42*(4), 1297–1317. https://doi.org/10.22190/teme1804297s

Sebastian, G., George, A., & Jackson, G. (2023). Persuading patients using rhetoric to improve artificial intelligence adoption: Experimental study. *Journal of Medical Internet Research*, *25*, e41430. https://doi.org/10.2196/41430

Silver, L., Huang, C., Clancy, L., Lam, N., Greenwood, S., Mandapat, J. C., & Baronavski, C. (2023). *Comparing views of the U.S. and China in 24 countries*. Pew Research Center. www.pewresearch.org/global/2023/11/06/comparing-views-of-the-us-and-china-in-24-countries/

Strutton, D., True, S. L., & Rody, R. J. (1995). Russian consumer perceptions of foreign and domestic consumer goods: An analysis of country-of-origin stereotypes with implications for promotions and positioning. *Journal of Marketing Theory and Practice*, *3*(3), 76–87.

Tully, S., Longoni, C., & Appel, G. (2023). *Lower artificial intelligence literacy predicts greater AI receptivity*. https://doi.org/10.31234/osf.io/t9u8g

Verlegh, P. W. J., Steenkamp, J. B. E. M., & Meulenberg, M. T. G. (2005). Country-of-origin effects in consumer processing of advertising claims. *International Journal of Research in Marketing*, *22*(2), 127–139. https://doi.org/10.1016/j.ijresmar.2004.05.003

Wang, C.-K., & Lamb, C. W. (1983). The impact of selected environmental forces upon consumers' willingness to buy foreign products. *Journal of the Academy of Marketing Science*, *11*(2), 71–84.

Watson, J. J., & Wright, K. (2000). Consumer ethnocentrism and attitudes toward domestic and foreign products. *European Journal of Marketing*, *34*(9/10), 1149–1166.

Wen, H., Zhang, L., Sheng, A., Li, M., & Guo, B. (2022). From "human-to-human" to "human-to-non-human" – Influence factors of artificial intelligence-enabled consumer value co-creation behavior. *Frontiers in Psychology*, *13*, 863313. https://doi.org/10.3389/fpsyg.2022.863313

Xiong, J.-Y., Wu, Y.-Y., & Kim, W.-K. (2010). Relationships among the country image, product image and purchase intention. *Journal of the Korea Contents Association*, *10*(12), 267–273. https://doi.org/10.5392/jkca.2010.10.12.267

Yang, R., Ramsaran, R. R., & Wibowo, S. (2016). A conceptual model for country-of-origin effects. *Asia Pacific Institute of Advanced Research*, *2*(1), 96–116. https://apiarpublications.com/conference-paper/a-conceptual-model-for-country-of-origin-effects/

8 Creating Customer Value in Times of Technological (R)evolution

The Success of Blix Group's Smart Shopping Applications and Future AI-Related Challenges

Hanna Nowak-Mizgalska, Krzysztof Łuczak, Anna Rogala, and Juan Aurelio Tamayo Gallego

Technological change, including innovative digital technologies, has significantly reshaped the operating conditions at the micro, meso, and macroeconomic levels. In particular, it has influenced consumer behaviors and preferences, venture creation, business practice, and the evolution of industries, economies, and societies (Si et al., 2023). While innovative digital technologies are increasingly recognized as enablers of entrepreneurship and business operations (Giuggioli & Pellegrini, 2023), radical innovations such as artificial intelligence (AI) can also prove disruptive to industry (Lähteenmäki et al., 2022), affecting in particular organizations and individuals unable to adapt to new market conditions and take advantage of the new business environment.

The advent of the internet, and digital, and mobile technologies has catalyzed the emergence of digital startups, fueling their growth and scalability. However, a critical research question persists: how do both new and established companies incorporate digital technologies into their business models in ways that are vital for customer value creation? (Elia et al., 2020). Moreover, how do those firms approach strategic decision-making regarding business model adaptation in response to technological discontinuity? More research is needed into the use of such digital technologies for innovation, value creation, and customer retention at later stages of the business life cycle (Audretsch et al., 2023).

In sectors and industries experiencing significant changes driven by ongoing technological advances, business activities increasingly require continuous upskilling and training in the relevant technologies. This trend is particularly noticeable in marketing, a domain where technology, data, and creativity converge. To remain competitive and continue delivering customer value, organizations need not only incorporate AI technologies into day-to-day operations but also accordingly reconfigure their business models. Marketers need to acquire the skills, mindsets, and ethical grounding necessary to use these tools

DOI: 10.4324/9781003659143-11

effectively (Antczak et al., 2025). Education systems and universities across the world face similar challenges. The growing accessibility and use of advanced technologies, including generative artificial intelligence, necessitate curricular reform to ensure technological and AI literacy. Equipping graduates with these competencies is essential for preparing them to navigate and thrive in the future AI-powered labor market (Rafalski, 2025). In particular, business graduates must demonstrate technological literacy, that is, the ability to use, understand, manage, and evaluate technology as a prerequisite for exploiting market opportunities associated with rapidly advancing technologies and successfully integrating technological solutions into business models.

This chapter explores how technology can drive organizational development and be a key factor for the creation of unique customer value. To that end, use is made of the case of the Polish company Grupa Blix Sp. z o.o. (hereinafter referred to as Blix Group), ranked among the *Financial Times*' 1000 fastest-growing companies in Europe (FT1000, 2025). The case study demonstrates the company's skillful use of technologies incorporated into its business model to deliver customer value and sustain growth, while formulating responses to the technological challenges posed by the AI revolution. The study aims to explore how Blix Group has successfully generated customer value using digital transformation technologies as a foundation of its business model and how it is navigating the technological disruptions brought about by the AI revolution. Drawing on a literature review in entrepreneurship, organization, and management studies, and employing a marketing approach, the case study of the Blix Group relies on survey data, press and industry reports, and internal documentation provided by the company.

The literature describes digital transformation as a complex multidimensional process involving significant technology-driven changes across organizations, industries, economies, and societies (Si et al., 2023). Although solid evidence has long been available to show that the pace and nature of industry and business evolution vary significantly across industries (Audretsch, 1995), it is radical innovations, such as generative AI, that account for the evolution of industries. As disruption theory asserts, even seemingly incremental innovations can, over time, displace established companies within an industry (Christensen, 1997). Historically, fewer than one-third of large corporations have either survived or maintained relevance beyond two decades in operation (Foster & Kaplan, 2001).

New technologies are changing environmental conditions under which emerging and established firms operate. Thus, research into digital entrepreneurship is growing rapidly, characterized by its interdisciplinary nature, and drawing from such fields as IT and business management (Zaheer et al., 2019; Lamine et al., 2023). The term digital entrepreneurship refers to the entrepreneurial process in which ICT, digital media, and novel digital technologies play a key role in identifying business opportunities and generating economic and social value, whether by new ventures or established business organizations (Balta et al., 2023; Zaheer et al., 2019).

A recent approach to investigating digital entrepreneurship combines the Agile and Lean Startup methods, business model frameworks, and case studies (Zaheer et al., 2019). When exploring the business models of digital startups, key factors to consider include customer type (B2B, B2C, B2G), revenue models (e.g., SaaS, advertising, e-commerce), industry sector (e.g., media, retail) (Zaheer et al., 2019), and relevant contextual variables (Audretsch et al., 2023). From the point of view of entrepreneurship research, it is crucial to recognize how new digital environmental conditions are changing the fundamental elements of the entrepreneurial process (Elia et al., 2020; Lamine et al., 2023), placing customer value creation at its center.

Customer value may be defined as the aggregate of benefits derived from the direct purchase and use of goods, as well as the indirect benefits associated with services and supplier relationship. While the traditional view emphasizes value-in-exchange, that is, value created at a point of sale, the current approach centers on value-in-use, where value is built on the basis of customer use, thus creating long-term competitive advantage through better customer alignment (Chesbrough et al., 2018). Today, the active role of the consumer in value creation is increasingly emphasized, implying that value creation is not understood fully until a thorough understanding of the consumer's role has been achieved (Bruce et al., 2019). Research further indicates that digitalization can empower and activate consumers in novel ways, transforming their relationship with the company (Lähteenmäki et al., 2022). Therefore, customer value creation and management is a continuous, multidisciplinary, and dynamic business process involving all company functions and operating levels (Zupok, 2024).

Before addressing the first research question, a short history and a summary of key characteristics of Blix Group is provided.

The company's origins date back to 2012 and the startup of Qpony.pl – the first application aggregating promotional offers and discount coupons in the Polish market. In 2016, the company acquired the Blix platform, Poland's largest aggregator of advertising leaflets. Its portfolio was further expanded in 2018 with the launch of the Zdrowe Zakupy (Healthy Shopping) application, a Polish counterpart to the French application Yuka. Finally, Blix Group was established in 2019. Notably, the company's founders appeared on *Forbes* magazine's "30 under 30" list in 2017 (Gryn, 2021), its revenues increased to over €11 million in 2023 (FT1000, 2025). In 2024, as part of its growth strategy, Blix Group acquired Proxi.cloud, a technology company specializing in online advertising services that measure offline visits, known as Drive to Store. The acquisition aimed to acquire a unique technology and extend the company's services beyond FMCG and retail sectors into industries such as OTC pharmaceuticals, automotive, and telecommunications. This strategic decision opened up new opportunities for the use of geolocation technology and artificial intelligence (wirtualnemedia.pl, 2024).

Currently, Blix Group employs a team of 101 specialists and leads the Polish market for promotional leaflet aggregation for retail chains and FMCG producers, controlling over 60% of Poland's digital leaflet distribution market (Grupablix.pl, 2023). According to Mediapanel, between 1 and 31 December 2024, 4,487,238 Internet users in Poland used Blix Group's smart shopping applications. The majority of them (2,879,874) were women, compared to 1,607,364 men. Real user counts by application brand were 4,035,096 for Blix, 661,284 for Zdrowe Zakupy, and 127,494 for Qpony. Note that individual real users could engage with multiple applications. The company's market penetration amounted to 15.08% of Polish Internet users, with average time spent (ATS) of 25 minutes and 4 seconds (Mediapanel, 2025, with permission from Grupa Blix Sp. z o.o).

Blix Group international presence extends to two other applications, Blix Romania and Blix Ukraine.

To achieve the aim of this exploratory study, the following research question has been posed:

Q1: How are digital technologies incorporated into the company's business model, and what is their role in customer value creation?

Blix Group operates within the advertising and marketing sector, with a business model rooted in mobile applications for Android and iOS platforms. Capitalizing on the growing popularity of smartphones, the company gained a competitive advantage over rivals who own popular portals/websites. The company's core business activity is the digital distribution of promotional leaflets and promotional offers to two primary B2B customer segments: retail chains (50%) and FMCG producers (50%). The company offers advertising space on its digital platforms (and a website for the Blix brand), enabling the transmission of advertisements and promotional content digitally through applications downloaded by end-users to their smartphones. Blix Group's digital platform "Drive to Store" supports diverse digital leaflet types and formats, allowing clients to target shoppers planning to buy specific brands in retail chains and drive traffic to e-commerce sites of Blix Group's customers. Moreover, thanks to the geolocation technology provided by Proxi.cloud, which now forms part of the Blix Group, the company can report on the effectiveness of marketing campaigns by tracking shopper footfall in physical retail stores.

The value Blix Group creates for its customers (with a range of marketing technology tools) manifests as improvements in the effectiveness and reach of marketing campaigns. This is achieved with new ways of reaching shoppers (adding online to traditional offline channels), and acquiring new potential users of Blix Group's applications. Moreover, the company offers advanced data analytics reports on smart shoppers' preferences and behaviors based on mobile application user activity. The company also enables community creation, experience exchange, and discussions of retail and FMCG industry challenges to enhance and develop marketing skills in both novice and seasoned professionals.

Table 8.1 Customer value creation through facilities and benefits for smart application users

Benefits and Facilities for Application Users	*Value Proposition for B2B Customers*
Main advantage: Aggregation of offers from promotional leaflets of various retail chains in one place, enabling users to easily and quickly compare current promotions	**Main advantages:** Enhanced effectiveness and extended reach of marketing campaigns; highly personalized marketing communication, greater flexibility and adaptability
Facilities: User-friendly and intuitive interface with a range of additional functionalities and services, including the ability to create shopping lists, track expenditures, use an advanced search engine for products and promotions, monitor prices of favorite products, and receive discount notifications	**Facilities:** Access to innovative marketing technologies (Drive to Store platform), offering digital infrastructure and an additional digital channel for promotional campaigns
Benefits: More informed and deliberate purchasing decisions; time and cost savings; improved purchase planning; greater control over the household budget	**Benefits:** Access to high-quality data on user purchasing behaviors (reports and analytics); increased customer acquisition through the RoPo (Research Online, Purchase Offline) effect, revenue growth

Source: Own elaboration based on empirical study.

Blix Group's value proposition to B2B customers relies on building strong relationships with the users of smart shopping applications. Attracting new smartphone application users is critical not only for competitive advantage and customer (retail chain and FMCG producer) value creation but also for revenue growth. For its revenue streams, the company relies on application user behavior based on three models: CPC (cost per click), CPM (cost per 1000 views), and CPE (cost per leaflet engagement). It is therefore essential it seek best brand recognition among prospective smart shopping application users. The benefits, in their turn, gain access to functionalities such as the ability to place products on shopping lists and compare product prices across retail chains. Users can also post retail chain reviews across categories, such as "Promotion of the Year" and "Innovative Chain of the Year," and identify the top-selling FMCG brands in day-to-day shopping. The "Blix Awards – Consumers' Choice" program generates valuable feedback for the B2B customers of the Blix Group, thus contributing to customer value creation.

Providing these facilities and benefits to end-users strengthens value generation for Blix Group's B2B customers. Table 8.1 summarizes the user benefits and value propositions offered to its customers.

The company uses its digital channels to distribute digital leaflets. It cooperates with partners such as siecportali.pl, thereby increasing the reach of digital promotional leaflets across more than 100 local websites.

Figure 8.1 summarizes the main elements of the Blix Group's business model and customer value creation.

In view of the ongoing AI-driven revolution, the Blix Group's business model, which relies on mobile and digital technologies, is in need of a revision. Of particular interest is the way the company should cope with novel challenges and harness opportunities associated with integrating AI-based solutions.

Artificial intelligence is a key player in digital technologies, transforming value creation (Chandra & Rahman, 2024). It has the potential to revolutionize how value is delivered to end users (Rajguru, 2024). From a marketing perspective, AI enables extensive personalization through the analysis of various types of data, including real-time inputs. These analyses identify patterns in consumer behavior, enabling precise, data-driven decisions. AI integration supports the delivery of more personalized offers and targeted communications at optimal times throughout the customer journey, enhancing satisfaction and loyalty. This approach also boosts operational efficiency (Kotler et al., 2024).

The literature underscores AI's capacity for superior value creation (Chandra & Rahman, 2024), as it generates new opportunities in this area

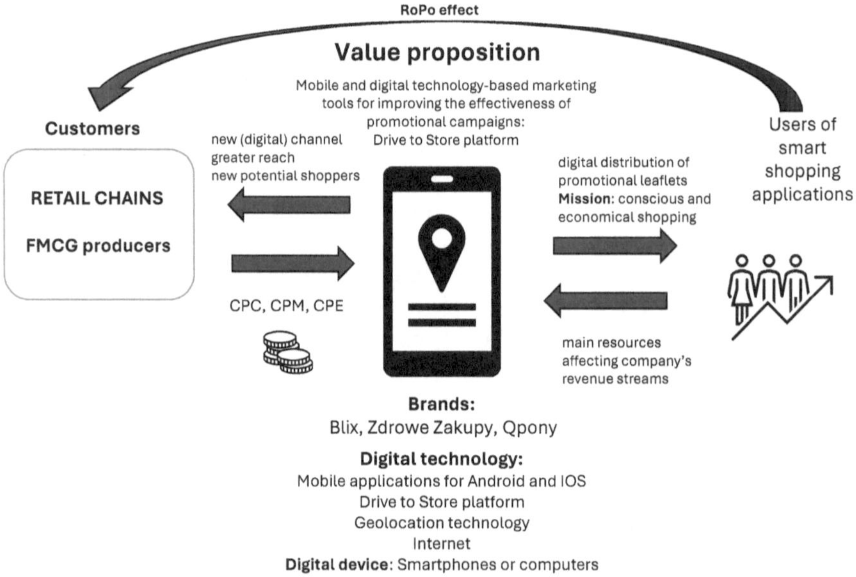

Figure 8.1 The Blix Group's business model and customer value creation.

Source: Own elaboration based on empirical studies.

improving efficiency, cutting costs, increasing revenues, and supporting growth (Åström et al., 2022). While AI's potential to generate customer value is significant, leveraging it is far from straightforward (Perifanis & Kitsios, 2023). A successful AI deployment requires alterations to business models, if not the creation of entirely new ones, an undertaking for which many organizations are ill-prepared due to technological limitations, capability gaps, and organizational culture barriers. For example, building dynamic capabilities within the AI ecosystem is critical for value creation (Chen et al., 2023). In addition, implementing AI involves substantial changes to organizational processes (Ruokonen & Ritala, 2024).

In this context, a company's strategy for managing technological discontinuity becomes particularly important. Strategy may be seen as "a pattern in a stream of decisions" or "a pattern in a stream of actions" (Mintzberg & Waters, 1985, p. 257). Decisions represent intentions more formally and explicitly, while actions may reflect those intentions, or result from adaptations, and even unplanned responses to unforeseen circumstances. Throughout the successive stages of a business or industry life cycle, numerous actions and decisions collectively contribute to shaping a company's emergent strategy. Some of these actions and decisions are more justified than others. At times of technological discontinuity, proactive strategies outperform defensive ones (Foster, 1986). In such instances, organizations are compelled to undergo adaptive transformation.

Figure 8.2 synthesizes key aspects of strategic decision-making with a view to managing discontinuity effectively.

Referring to the new challenges associated with AI-driven technological change and its impact on customer value creation, the following second research question is proposed:

Q2: How does the company manage technological change in the face of an AI-driven revolution?

The company conducts ongoing market research and analysis across Europe, Asia, and the United States to identify trends and opportunities for adopting novel technologies, such as AI, within the retail and FMCG industries.

AI-based solutions have been incorporated into the company's business model since the public release of such AI tools as ChatGPT in 2022. According to a Board member, strategic adaptation to the evolving technological environment is crucial for Blix Group's survival. Companies that fail to embrace AI risk losing long-term competitiveness due to rising costs and inefficiency.

The primary benefits of integrating AI-based solutions into Blix Group's business model include cost reduction, enhanced competitiveness, and increased operational efficiency. Notably, AI has significantly reduced the cost of reading promotional leaflet content for use in search engines and shopping lists. AI is also employed for OCR (optical character recognition),

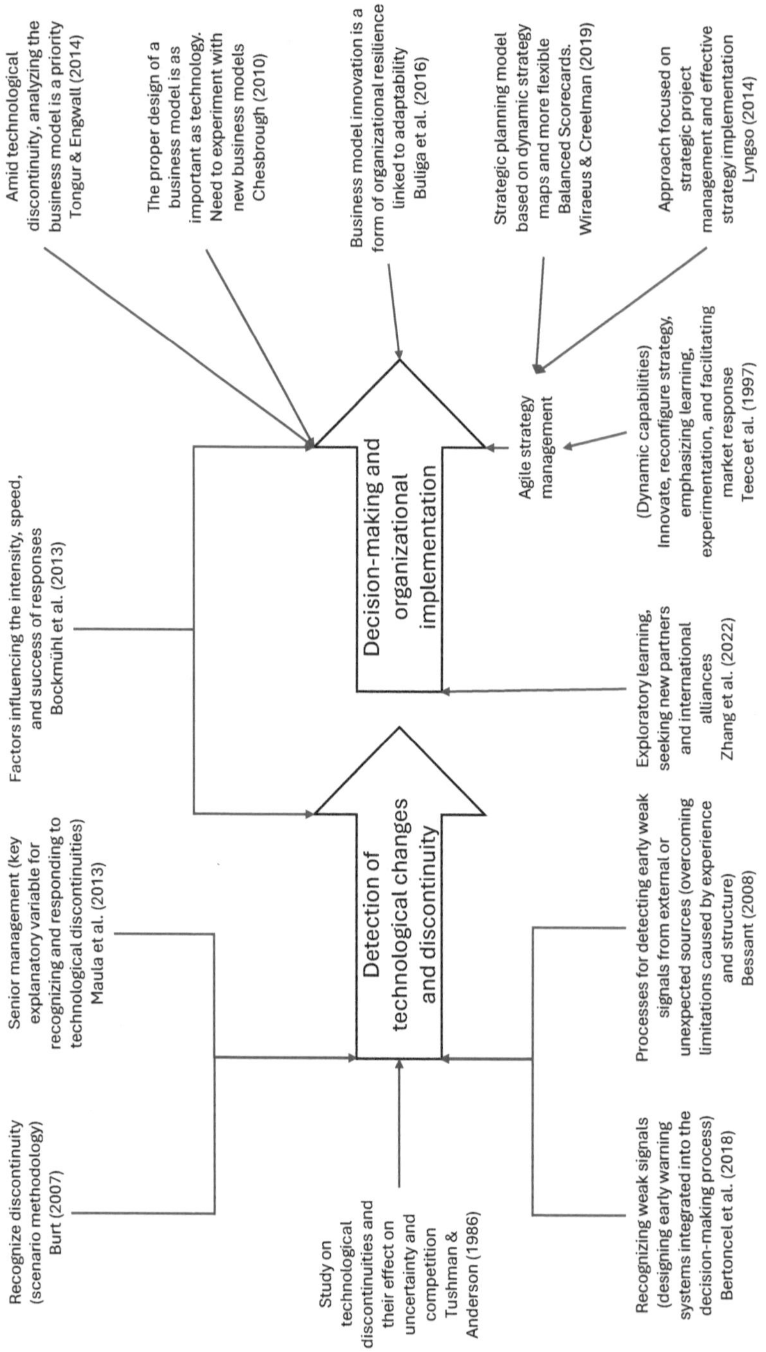

Figure 8.2 Key aspects of managing discontinuity.

Source: Own elaboration based on literature review.

and specifically for product photos and receipts, enabling the extraction of valuable data for consumers. These developments have reduced the cost of data processing and image recognition by as much as tenfold. Moreover, AI accelerates programming tasks and reduces the required workforce, lowering the cost of labor.

Conversely, the company views its highly skilled employees – capable of identifying and deploying the most effective AI tools in a rapidly evolving technological environment – as a key competitive advantage. Talent acquisition remains a major challenge. Another significant concern is the security of the data processed using AI technology.

The company plans to continue to adopt AI technologies within its services, particularly in the development of smart shopping applications in back and frontend systems. These improvements aim to enhance the functionality of application interfaces to provide users with smarter and more intuitive solutions.

Rather than exploiting existing technologies until they become obsolete, Blix Group seeks to maintain its market leadership through innovation. Its board has adopted a continuous development strategy which entails active monitoring of market and technological trends, investing in innovation, modernizing the business offering, testing new tools and technologies, and making rapid improvements to safeguard its competitive advantage. This strategy helps generate customer value and prepares customers for future challenges.

The board is also considering diversifying and transforming the group's business model in response to the emerging Retail Media trend and evolving market demand. Previous decisions, such as acquiring the Zdrowe Zakupy application and integrating the company Proxi.cloud into the group, reflect this strategic direction.

Retail Media is a key pillar of the Blix Group's diversification strategy. It involves innovative digital advertising offered directly within the shopping environment, using consumer and contextual shopping data. This strategic direction is intended to establish a competitive advantage within a rapidly growing market segment and stay abreast of market changes. In particular, the company aims to capitalize on its knowledge and data on user shopping behaviors to deliver precise advertising campaigns targeting specific customer segments. This is expected to help monetize advertising space both within and outside shopping applications through user profiling. To achieve this goal, the company plans to develop advanced services that integrate targeting, personalization, and real-time campaign performance measurement.

Considering the company's current business model and its potential evolution through AI integration, its position within the technological life cycle remains an open question to be addressed in detail through future research.

The technological life cycle, as originally outlined by Everett M. Rogers (1983), models the diffusion of innovations using a classic sigmoid curve, or S-shaped life cycle function, plotted with time on the horizontal axis (abscissa). Later, Richard Foster (1986) used this type of S-curve – the logistics or

Gompertz curve – to depict the evolution of technologies and discontinuities. In his model, technological life cycles are marked by discontinuities, wherein one technology supplants another on a continuum of creative destruction. The same approach to discontinuity in the digital age appears in the context of transition between eras over time (Wiraeus & Creelman, 2019).

Although the company claims to be experiencing rapid growth or early technological maturity, it still requires further in-depth research. The growing number of users of the Blix Group's smart shopping applications and the company's growing revenues indicate considerable success of the current customer value proposition. The Board's strategy reflects strong technological awareness, agile management, and a proactive approach to technological innovation. While the company's value proposition is still evolving, its growth potential, capacity for innovation, and scalability are clearly visible. Nevertheless, the precise long-term impact of the AI-driven revolution on its business model remains uncertain. In response to technological change, the company seeks to adapt to new technological environments based on its current business model. It looks to improve efficiency and efficacy through AI integration to support marketing and develop new functionalities for their applications while exploring new opportunities for diversification.

The case study presented in this chapter shows the critical role of entrepreneurship, creativity, and technological literacy in establishing a successful business.

Looking ahead, technology adoption will remain a key driver of business transformation. Employers are increasingly seeking candidates with technological proficiency in areas such as AI, big data analytics, and digital literacy (World Economic Forum, 2023). This trend underscores the urgent need to transform educational systems to equip students with the skills required in future technology-driven economies. Technological advances, and particularly artificial intelligence, profoundly impact the role and nature of marketing. To remain competitive, marketing students must cultivate critical thinking, creativity, and entrepreneurial skills. Proficiency in artificial intelligence is a key component of such abilities (Elhajjar et al., 2021).

Reference List

Antczak, D., Gurtatowski, M., Leszczyński, G., Rogala, A., & Lawrynowicz, M. (2025). *NAWA-DIGIT report on: Opportunities and threats of AI for marketing*. https://doi.org/10.17605/OSF.IO/42DRW

Åström, J., Reim, W., & Parida, V. (2022). Value creation and value capture for AI business model innovation: A three-phase process framework. *Review of Managerial Science*, *16*(7), 2111–2133. https://doi.org/10.1007/s11846-022-00521-z

Audretsch, D. B. (1995). *Innovation and industry evolution*. MIT Press. ISBN: 0-262-01146-8.

Audretsch, D. B., Belitski, M., Caiazza, R., Chowdhury, F., & Menteret, M. (2023). Entrepreneurial growth, value creation, and new technologies. *The Journal of Technology Transfer*, *48*(5), 1535–1551. https://doi.org/10.1007/s10961-023-10034-w

Balta, M., Spanaki, K., Papadopoulos, T., & Ravishankar, M. N. (2023). Understanding the use of digital technologies in entrepreneurial startup settings and growth-oriented firms. *International Journal of Information Management*, *69*. https://doi.org/10.1016/j.ijinfomgt.2022.102616

Bruce, H. L., Wilson, H. N., Macdonald, E. K., & Clarke, B. (2019). Resource integration, value creation and value destruction in collective consumption contexts. *Journal of Business Research*, *103*, 173–185. https://doi.org/10.1016/j.jbusres.2019.05.007

Chandra, B., & Rahman, Z. (2024). Artificial intelligence and value co-creation: A review, conceptual framework and directions for future research. *Journal of Service Theory and Practice*, *34*(1), 7–32. https://doi.org/10.1108/JSTP-03-2023-0097

Chen, Y., Chen, Y., & Guo, Y. (2023). Dynamic capabilities for value creation from AI innovation ecosystem: A comparison between IFLYTKE and Amazon. *International Journal of Knowledge Management Studies*, *14*(2), 212. https://doi.org/10.1504/IJKMS.2023.130031

Chesbrough, H., Lettl, C., & Ritter, T. (2018). Value creation and value capture in open innovation. *Journal of Product Innovation Management*, *35*(6), 930–938. https://doi.org/10.1111/jpim.12471

Christensen, C. M. (1997). *The innovator's Dilemma*. Harvard Business School Press. ISBN: 0-87584-585-1.

Elhajjar, S., Karam, S., & Borna, S. (2021). Artificial intelligence in marketing education programs. *Marketing Education Review*, *31*(1), 2–13. https://doi.org/10.1080/10528008.2020.1835492

Elia, G., Margherita, A., & Passiante, G. (2020). Digital entrepreneurship ecosystem: How digital technologies and collective intelligence are reshaping the entrepreneurial process. *Technological Forecasting and Social Change*, *150*, 1–12. https://doi.org/10.1016/j.techfore.2019.119791

Foster, R. N. (1986). *Innovation: The attacker's advantage*. Summit Books. ISBN: 0-671-62250-1.

Foster, R. N., & Kaplan, S. (2001). *Creative destruction: Why companies that are built to last underperform the market – and how to successfully transform them*. Currency/Random House. eISBN: 978-0-307-77931-1.

FT1000. (2025). *Europe's fastest growing companies 2025 ranking*. www.ft.com/content/cb3e317e-e3cc-4e4a-a506-b755b2f94bb1

Giuggioli, G., & Pellegrini, M. M. (2023). Artificial intelligence as an enabler for entrepreneurs: A systematic literature review and an agenda for future research, *International Journal of Entrepreneurial Behavior & Research*, *29*(4), 816–837. https://doi.org/10.1108/IJEBR-05-2021-0426

Grupablix.pl. (2023). *Mediapanel H1*. Blix Group. https://grupablix.pl/wspolpraca/

Gryn, M. (2021, November 3). Poznański start-up zarabia dziesiątki milionów złotych na gazetkach sieci handlowych. *Forbes*. www.forbes.pl/biznes/qponypl-rosna-na-gazetkach-sieci-handlowych/yjdqe5h

Kotler, P., Kartajaya, H., & Setiawan, I. (2024). *Marketing 6.0: The future is immersive*. John Wiley & Sons, Inc.

Lähteenmäki, I., Nätti, S., & Saraniemi, S. (2022). Digitalization-enabled evolution of customer value creation: An executive view in financial services. *Journal of Business Research*, *146*, 504–517. https://doi.org/10.1016/j.jbusres.2022.04.002

Lamine, W., Fayolle, A., Jack, S., & Audretsch, D. (2023). Impact of digital technologies on entrepreneurship: Taking stock and looking forward, *Technovation*, *126*. https://doi.org/10.1016/j.technovation.2023.102823

Mediapanel. (2025). *Data on the number of real users of Blix Group smart shopping applications from 1 to 31 December of 2024*. With permission from Grupa Blix Sp. z o.o.

Mintzberg, H., & Waters, J. A. (1985). Of strategies, deliberate and emergent. *Strategic Management Journal*, 6(3), 257–272. https://doi.org/10.1002/SMJ.4250060306.

Perifanis, N.-A., & Kitsios, F. (2023). Investigating the influence of artificial intelligence on business value in the digital era of strategy: A literature review. *Information*, *14*(2), 85. https://doi.org/10.3390/info14020085

Rafalski, K. (2025, May 8). *AI impact on education: Its effect on teaching and student success*. NetGuru. www.netguru.com/blog/ai-in-education

Rajguru, K. (2024). Artificial intelligence and the perspective of value creation: Present research focus and future directions. In L. Matosas-López (Ed.), *The impact of digitalization on current marketing strategies* (pp. 163–181). Emerald Publishing Limited. https://doi.org/10.1108/978-1-83753-686-320241010

Rogers, E. M. (1983). *Diffusion of innovations*. The Free Press. ISBN: 0-02-926650-5.

Ruokonen, M., & Ritala, P. (2024). How to succeed with an AI-first strategy? *Journal of Business Strategy*, *45*(6), 396–404. https://doi.org/10.1108/JBS-08-2023-0178

Si, S., Hall, J., Suddaby, R., Ahlstrom, D., & Wei, J. (2023). Technology, entrepreneurship, innovation and social change in digital economics. *Technovation*, *119*. https://doi.org/10.1016/j.technovation.2022.102484

Wiraeus, D., & Creelman, J. (2019). *Agile strategy management in the digital age*. Palgrave Macmillan, Springer Nature. ISBN: 978-3-319-76309-5 (eBook). https://doi.org/10.1007/978-3-319-76309-5.

Wirtualnemedia.pl. (2024, October 22), *Grupa Blix przejmuje Proxi.cloud*. www.wirtualnemedia.pl/artykul/grupa-blix-przejmuje-proxi-cloud

World Economic Forum. (2023). *Future of jobs report 2023 (insight report)*. World Economic Forum. https://www3.weforum.org/docs/WEF_Future_of_Jobs_2023.pdf

Zaheer, H., Breyer, Y., & Dumay, J. (2019). Digital entrepreneurship: An interdisciplinary structured literature review and research agenda, *Technological Forecasting and Social Change*, *148*. https://doi.org/10.1016/j.techfore.2019.119735

Zupok, S. (2024). Contemporary tools for creating customer value. *European Research Studies Journal*, *XXVII*(4), 545–559. https://doi.org/10.35808/ersj/3539

9 The Impact of Digital Transformation on the Packaging Industry

Patrycja Wojciechowska, Karolina Wiszumirska, and Marek Hauptmann

Introduction

Industry 4.0 is considered a new industrial stage, reshaping the manufacturing sector by introducing dynamic, interconnected, and complex industrial systems. These systems continuously generate substantial quantities of data, reflecting the growing digitization of production environments. To manage and utilize massive amounts of data effectively, advanced technologies such as artificial intelligence (AI), big data, cloud computing, and the internet of things (IoT) are required. Enhancing the industry through the aforementioned technologies can bring several benefits, such as reducing production costs, facilitating the adaptation to individual customer requirements, and improving quality (Alenizi et al., 2023; Jan et al., 2023; Zeba et al., 2021). AI has significantly transformed the operational dynamics of various sectors. It is successfully applied for predictive maintenance, quality control, supply chain optimization, production planning, process automation, and safety monitoring, enabling timely detection of defects and identifying production configurations that could lead to production problems (Soldatos, 2024). Consequently, it is becoming more prevalent in the packaging sector. The integration of artificial intelligence (AI) in packaging production opens up new perspectives for manufacturers, owing to its capacity for data analysis, machine learning, and swift decision-making based on the gathered information.

The Role of Artificial Intelligence in the Packaging Industry

Artificial intelligence is an advanced computing technology that is inspired by the mechanisms of human thinking and has been transformed from theoretical concepts into practical market implementation. AI is present in practically the entire value chain in the packaging industry, from design and production to quality control and life cycle management. Solutions using AI are perceived by companies as a tool for competitive advantage thanks to increased operational efficiency, the possibility of reducing costs and improving quality parameters, the achievement of which is sometimes too slow or impossible

DOI: 10.4324/9781003659143-12

using previously used tools and methods (Statista, 2024). AI technologies in the packaging industry include machine learning (ML) used to optimize processes; robotic systems (RS) used to perform emerging tasks such as internal transport or palletizing; artificial neural networks (ANNs) used in vision systems; and GenAI (generative artificial intelligence) for the visual design of packaging or advertising (Statista, 2024).

According to McKinsey analysis performed in 2023 across the 63 use cases, generative AI has the potential to generate $2.6 trillion to $4.4 trillion in value across industries. Although a few years ago the packaging sector was slow to embrace new digital technologies, interest in generative AI is currently increasing. The results from the survey conducted with more than 200 paper and packaging executives across substrates and geographies revealed that entrepreneurs recognize the significant potential for generative AI to enhance economic value within their firms and are ready to make investments in it (McKinsey & Company, 2024; Packaging World, 2025).

The global artificial intelligence in packaging market size was USD 2.98 billion in 2024, increased to USD 3.32 billion in 2025, and is projected to grow to approximately USD 8.67 billion by 2034, indicating a strong CAGR of 11.26% between 2024 and 2034 (Precedence Research, 2024).

Leading AI solution providers for the packaging sector include Amazon, Microsoft, GE Digital, ABB, Otto Motors, Universal Robots, Clarifai, Neurala, Basler, Deepsense.ai, Osaro, and SparkCognition. The main users are SIG Combibloc, Tetra Pak, Stora Enso, Metsä Board, Ardagh, Sealed Air, Mondi, Berry Global, Westrock, Verallia, DS Smith, and Georgia-Pacific (Packaging Gateway, n.d.).

The recent advancements in AI technology for food packaging include AI-based vision systems, applied for the assurance of product quality and uniformity while diminishing the necessity for manual inspection. Such systems are able to analyze images or videos of packaged products to detect defects, errors, or anomalies. In the case of smart packaging, AI offers the capacity to improve operational efficiency, refine decision-making, and optimize processes. AI-based systems also have the capability to automate repetitive tasks, optimize workflows, and provide practical insights based on data analysis. This results in cost savings, enhanced productivity, and increased customer satisfaction. Moreover, artificial intelligence algorithms can assess previous sales data and analyze market trends and other factors to precisely forecast demand patterns. It allows optimizing inventory levels, reducing warehouse downtime, and improving supply chain efficiency (Fofana, 2025; Abimbola & Okpara, 2023; Dhal & Kar, 2025).

The Impact of AI on Packaging Design, Personalization, and Compliance

Another example of the beneficial influence of digital transformation on the packaging industry is the possibility to use AI-driven software applications for the design phase, allowing the development of creative and efficient packaging solutions (Hassoun et al., 2023). Some attempts have been made to apply the k-Nearest Neighbor (KNN) algorithm in the development of functional packaging materials to enhance the process of selection of the appropriate amounts of components, for example, antimicrobial agents, which is vital for creating solutions with defined physical characteristics and desired attributes (Silva et al., 2021).

Digital twins based on artificial intelligence have the potential to be a breakthrough solution in many industries, including packaging. A digital twin is a digital clone of a physical object. In case of packaging, the digital replica contains a range of information about its structural and physical, chemical, and mechanical properties. The digital version allows testing of many structural and material solutions before physical prototyping. Thanks to this approach, it is possible to predict design defects and production problems before they materialize. The technology can provide information on the strength of the structure, resistance to internal and external factors, durability and service life, barriers to gases, and even the selection of packaging materials by modeling their recycling scenarios and assessing the impact of the packaging life cycle on the environment (Dabo, 2025).

Related processes also utilize digital twins, including:

- monitoring the performance of production lines in real time, forecasting possible failures and planning preventive maintenance,
- transport management by maximizing transport space and planning shipments,
- automatic creation of legal compliance documents.

ANN methodology has been successfully applied to estimate the box compression strength of corrugated boxes with varied construction (made with perforations and openings, as well as without them). The load capacity of the boxes was analyzed with input parameters such as dimensions of the packaging, material properties of the corrugated board, and the critical buckling forces of the side panels (Gajewski et al., 2024).

AI can support e-commerce packaging management and logistics by selecting optimal packaging. By combining machine learning, text analysis, and computer vision, AI-powered tools can reduce the amount of material used while maintaining transport safety. Millions of delivery data points, including consumer reviews, train the models, thereby enabling continuous improvement. Examples of such solutions include the Package Decision Engine implemented by Amazon and OptiCarton implemented by DHL Supply Chain.

In the context of legal compliance for packaging introduced to the market from 2030, AI will support packers and fillers in fulfilling their responsibility to reduce empty space and minimize the weight, size, and quantity of packaging as required by PPWR (Art. 10, 24). Systems that reduce unnecessary space in shipments by up to 50% directly lead to fewer transport operations and a smaller carbon footprint across production, transport, and recycling processes. Furthermore, packaging optimization translates into lower shipping costs for commercial customers (DHL, 2022; Amazon, 2024; Regulation (EU) 2025/40).

Optimization of packaging dimensions is crucial in light of current legal regulations, which, in accordance with the PPWR (Packaging and Packaging Waste Regulation) (Regulation (EU) 2025/40), impose the obligation to produce packaging with the lowest possible consumption of raw materials, appropriate to provide the needed protection and functionality. This rule is also in line with current packaging design principles, which are consistent with the assumptions of the circular economy model, promoting practices that diminish raw material usage and emissions. Other requirements of the PPWR include the need to use a specified amount of post-consumer recycled materials in plastic packaging. Fulfilling this obligation is a challenge because it is associated with the need to ensure effective sorting and recycling of packaging waste to obtain a recyclate, the quality of which will allow this raw material to be used for the reproduction of packaging intended for contact with food. Currently, the main method of processing plastic packaging waste is mechanical recycling, in which the quality of the recyclate is determined by numerous factors. In this process, obtaining recyclate of a purity suitable for use in packaging intended for contact with food is a significant challenge. For this reason, EFSA has currently approved only two polymers in the EU for contact with food: polyethylene terephthalate and polystyrene.

Besides the mandated purity and safety of the recyclate utilized in package manufacture, another problem pertains to the stability of the recycled raw material concerning its physicochemical properties. This presents numerous challenges in the processing of recyclate and the manufacturing of new packaging incorporating it. In this domain, tools augmented by artificial intelligence can be beneficial. This issue will be discussed in detail later in the last part of the chapter.

AI can be successfully applied in the final phase of the packaging life cycle, particularly for the management of the resulting waste. Investigations and trials are underway to integrate AI into sorting lines to enhance the effectiveness of this procedure. An interesting example is a study that was conducted to explore the potential of support separation systems using Inception-v3, a deep learning model that is based on convolutional neural networks (CNN), as well as ResNet-50, MobileNet-v2, and DenseNet-201. It exhibited substantial potential for the use of AI to separate packaging waste and to provide practical recommendations for enhancing this solution (Pučnik et al., 2024).

The Impact of AI on Consumers

The use of AI tools is becoming increasingly popular in product marketing. The availability of various solutions is used by small and medium-sized companies with limited budgets, as well as corporations in international promotional campaigns. From the point of view of planning and implementing marketing research, AI is also used in audience targeting, analysis and reporting, and content personalization. AI allows for real-time data analysis, identification of new trends, and automation of repetitive tasks, thanks to which teams can work faster and more efficiently. Although AI in marketing offers interesting possibilities for creating products and brands, consumer reactions are sometimes mixed. According to research, trust in brands using AI fell from 57% in 2023 to 46% in 2024. At the same time, more than half of consumers express discomfort related to replacing real celebrities with virtual ambassadors, and almost half do not accept editing product photos using this technology (Statista, 2025). It has been noted that consumer acceptance depends on whether companies openly communicate the use of AI in marketing activities. In the area of targeted use of AI in marketing campaigns, two campaigns are worth noting: Heinz's "A.I Ketchup" campaign from 2023, which used GenAI DALL-E 2. The brand created a campaign featuring ketchup bottle visualizations generated entirely by AI, encouraging collaborative experimentation among consumers; the campaign gained global reach (Ads of the World, n.d.).

VIZIT is an advanced platform using Visual AI. Unlike other AI tools, VIZIT precisely analyzes the visual preferences of specific audiences. The platform can analyze how specific audience segments perceive and respond to given content. "AI Lenses" are VIZIT's proprietary and patented technology that allows brands to "see the world through the eyes of their audience" in real time. They act as advanced perceptual filters that are based on behavioral models of specific audience segments and allow them to predict which visual elements will attract their attention and spark interest. VIZIT uses a new concept called "Intuitive AI," which represents the next evolutionary step in the development of AI, going beyond generative AI. Compared to generative AI, intuitive AI gives machines the ability to see and interpret similarly to humans and uses "synthetic human preferences" to predict audience reactions. VIZIT is used by brands such as Mars, Heineken, and Ghirardelli (Sourceful, n.d.; Barba, 2024; Vizit, 2024).

Path to Digital Transformation in Packaging

It is acknowledged that the mandatory use of recycled content in packaging materials and the value preservation in closed loops is a major challenge that cannot be solved without widespread cooperation and exchange of information in the complete value cycle. Packaging companies are therefore preparing to exploit the opportunities inherent to the consequent and permanent utilization of product-related data and the various available materials, production, and machinery.

Data-driven cooperation and the new information depth far beyond known datasheets are an evolutionary new direction. The basic precondition is an infrastructure for data transfer that preserves the sovereignty of data property rights for each participant. The idea is known from the concept of industrial data dataspaces. In contrast to cloud-based solutions, which store the transferred data separately, the dataspace is a federated system including company-owned data from the respective IT source, operating the data transfer by the use of data interfaces (dataspace connectors) and providing a framework of policies managing rights and the identification of participants (e.g., GAIA X Federated Services). A participant of such a dataspace could be a company, its database, a laboratory, a machine, a single sensor signal (generating physical data), or a model built with methods of AI, but also any other model generating synthetic data. The data needs to be described in a uniform way to enable the automated data transfer without risk of doubling from different wording for the same physical characteristics. The vocabulary is provided by an ontology. It provides a uniform annotation of data and the relationship of data toward each other. Examples in a laboratory test environment are measurement methods, corresponding standards/norms, physical units, test personnel, test machines, and differing test conditions (humidity, temperature, speed). In the production site, data could include: packaging machine type; sensor type; sensor signal; signal unit; corresponding process or process step within the machine; the material; its composition (e.g., layers, layer thickness, material type of each layer), or the packaging component. Its standardization in the normative draft (DIN-Spec 91531, 2025) can be considered as the first step of a way into a digital data-driven economy.

The idea behind the dataspace was initially oriented on the target to enable companies and market actors to get safe and trustworthy access to the capabilities of AI. The evolving growth of AI algorithms has led to a broad toolbox of methods for various application backgrounds.

Use Case Demonstration for an AI Landscape Approach in Packaging Production

To showcase the holistic potential of AI application, an ordinary and simple structured packaging example shall serve as a demonstration case. A typical cylindrical cup is combined with a thin lid membrane and a hard top lid construction (Figure 9.1) made from polypropylene (PP).

The production path of the introduced cup (Figure 9.2) may include compounding of the polymer, film production, material testing, packaging production, and consumer perception of the packaging (Körkemeyer et al., 2025). AI-supported models are introduced for production processes at several places (see Figure 9.2). Their purpose can be structured in the following categories:

1. Process model and optimization, for example:
    - prediction of compound properties and recipe derivation in compounding (Seifert et al., 2024; Seifert et al., 2025a, 2025b)

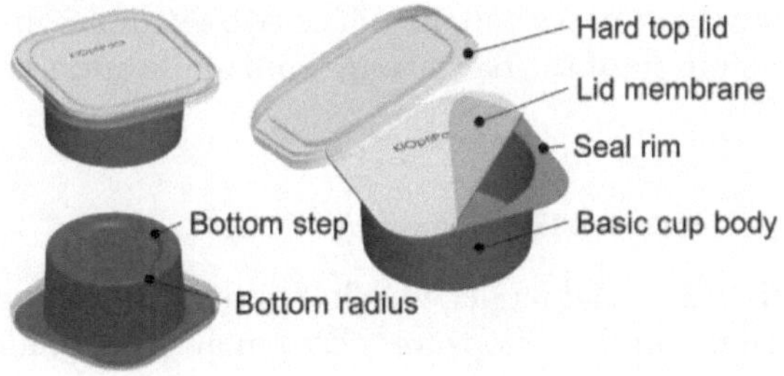

Figure 9.1 Demonstrator packaging case as a cup with sealed membrane and hard top lid.

Source: Author's work.

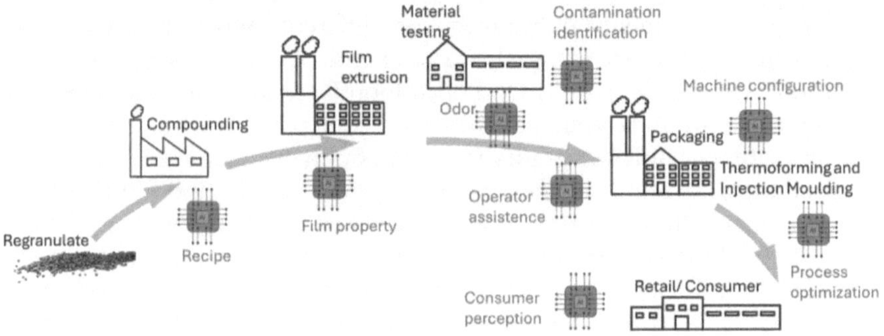

Figure 9.2 Schematic of production chain example with marked places of AI-based model support and example pathways for data exchange and usage.

Source: Author's work.

- injection molding process configuration
- prediction of film properties in film extrusion processes (Stieglitz et al., 2025)

2. Identification and classification of properties, for example:

   - odor classification between recycled and virgin materials
   - inline odor monitoring in extruders

3. Signal processing and extraction of certain attributes, for example, the automated identification of substances or contaminations from a gas chromatographic measurement using peak deconvolution,
4. Assistance systems for human-machine interaction, for example:

   - a defined machine configuration in case of necessary material change
   - operator assistance through the use of models providing advice for operators in case of machine stop.

Out of these categories, we will introduce two examples in more detail to give a better illustration of the background and application scenario of such models.

Example 1: Process Model for Thermoforming of Cups

The first example is a special model, which is developed to support the search for suitable machine configurations for a certain material grade consisting of at least a portion of recycled polymer. Material changes may be necessary due to changes in the produced brand or product or in the case of purchasing advantages. The challenge for the means employed for thermoformed packaging demonstrator (see Figure 9.1) and for the machine that needs to process the materials is that the recycled polymer fraction is likely to cause considerable property variations given the many different origins of the materials. The recycled content can be taken from different sources (post-industrial material, post-consumer material, material from closed-loop or open-loop collection). Especially in the case of open-loop material from post-consumer collection, the secondary material will have different purity and consist of basically different polymer grades (e.g., homopolymer, copolymer, with different additives) from the same type of polymer (e.g., PE and PP) that have their origin in different primary applications (e.g., shampoo bottle, food cup). Further reasons for different qualities are different treatments in the reconditioning, for example, through flake washing in cold water or under elevated temperature and with or without additional chemical treatment, or through filtration of remelt polymer. Even more, it is likely that uncertainty also comes from the degradation state of the polymer (e.g., chain length reductions), which depends on the thermal treatment and the number of thermal processes the material has undergone. In addition to the respectively varying material properties, the geometrical features of the cup may go far beyond the example of Figure 9.1, including, for example, multi-cavity forming, different wall angles, stabilizing beads or stacking steps and noses, and many other features. Together with various process configurations resulting from a certain given machine structure with, for example, single or multiple radiative or conductive heaters,

- different handling and transport distances and times,
- mechanical stretch plug or without,
- pressurized forming air or vacuum application.

At the same time, the forming setup has a strong influence on the permanently changing temperature of the material and the load applied to a certain geometrical region of the cup. This overwhelming number of influences has led to the situation that, in practice, there are often no clear settings to work with any new material, and it takes time to run trials to find the machine settings. Therefore, one step toward a drastic reduction of time is the introduction of an indicative characteristic value. The occurring pressure difference turns out to be characteristic of the forming result (Lange et al., 2025). The pressure difference in the tool correlates well with the evaluated shape of the cup and is represented in a model based on support vector regression in dependency of recycled material content, heater temperature, and heating time for both radiation and conductive heating. The corresponding processing window can be determined with a minimum of physical tests to feed the model and shows necessary adjustments for different fractions of recycled polymer content. The model gives an early processing window to enable thermoforming machines or their operators to react to the changing material properties without the burden of excessive material data. While AI-based models are often dependent on sufficient available data for their learning but still are valid for only one of the aforementioned machine structures, the introduced model relies on a single test value to propose material-specific settings within a few test points. Greater effort would be needed to predict the wall thickness distribution of cups, but it can be expected that such models will be available in the future.

Example 2: Assistance System for Packaging Machine Operators

Another example is the use of operator assistance systems. The origin of this emerging system is the operational behavior of production systems. Typically, packaging machines are sold for a given maximum output. This refers to certain formats, packed products, and other boundary conditions, such as the use of the maximum speed in daily production, which is known to lead to increased probability of failure. Each failure can cause drastic loss in Overall Equipment Efficiency (OEE) due to lost time in which the machine is not working, is running in empty mode, or produces reduced-quality products or full rejects. The reasons are attributed to a systematic time framework in the European standard EN 415–11:2021. The machine operation time is clustered into production time and secondary time, which covers, for instance, all plannable maintenance, cleaning, repairing, changeover, and shift change time. The production time still can be impaired by reasons of technical failure, human mistakes, or organizational issues. The multitude of reasons for a disturbance of machine operation in packaging lines is often more or less well handled by the operators and has proven to be markedly influenced by their basic skills and experiences. A beneficial influence can be a knowledge management system (KMS). However, the packaging sector in this case has issues with the stringent organization of formats and updating and data-holding systems, and even the availability and research ability of stored and documented experiences, cases, or datasets represents a clear techno-psychological challenge. The example of an operator assistance system gives an insight into the challenges appearing during its introduction.

The typical situation in the daily production of many companies is characterized by statistically appearing machine stops, the removal of any material jam, its cleaning, the earliest possible restart, and finally the hope for having found a permanent fix for the disturbance, because machine operators expertise does not extend to every processing step or machine function, and with improvement in automation, they may have to operate a machine park rather than a single machine. Technical support teams are faced with multiple urgent cases, which might arise for very simple reasons, but this does not make them less urgent, since every production stop is expensive. Machine and line observations show differences of 20% and more in OEE, ranging from 90% with the best and most skilled operational personnel to an average of 70%. The difference could be even higher, because the reality of business in the world of production is characterized by insufficient exchange of information between shifts, shortages of skilled labor, changes in production sites, and permanent fluctuations in the work force. The introduction of a KMS shall be a systematic and structured support of workers involved in production. The central question is, however, how the knowledge could be documented, stored, and fed back at a corresponding comparable situation to the worker to solve a problem unerringly and permanently.

Typical issues in the documentation of observations are more human-centered. Pressure from management personal may, for instance, prevent the establishment of enthusiastic use of KMS and create, rather, mistrust. Money is often not a suitable incentive because it could also lead to envy and obstruction, or it is perceived as a manipulation attempt. Moreover, the initial documentation means direct add-on effort for no immediate and direct benefit, and the new system generates a barricade against its use due to the fact that it needs time to get used to it.

Therefore, the pure technical functionality that is incorporated in the decision state has proven to be necessarily accompanied by human psychological comprehension. After (Schult et al., 2024) full initiative of every person in the company is not necessary for a successful KMS and for its substantial filling and use because this engagement is difficult to be achieved by any typical management measure. Instead, practical examples deliver the 90–9–1 thesis, which incorporates the conclusion that 1% of active staff is necessary. The active group draws its motivation from the intention to create added value and contribute to something that is worth the effort, such as a disturbance-free running machine, leaving more free time for planned maintenance and systematic work rather than reactive clearance of interruption. On the other hand, self-efficacy plays a major role. The certainty of value-added operating effectiveness and the recognition of effects can be a powerful motivation and prevent concerns that all the knowledge will be forgotten later on. Important for the active group is a passive group, which receives added value from the given content and gives motivation to the active group by recognition. About 9% will meanwhile react and comment on the content and start improving it (Schult et al., 2024). Still, after acceptance of the system, a joint terminology within the documentation is decisive. Each technical term may have synonyms, the native language can differ, and there may be issues with grammar or at least lack of knowledge about established terms (Schult et al., 2024). Similarities can be drawn to the aforementioned ontology, which annotates signals and physical data and its negotiations. This is even more important since it is reported that the origin of a failure could be at a completely different location compared to the place where the symptom occurs (Tsarouhas, 2012).

Model and Proposal Stage

The event-driven nature of machine and production line behavior inspires the use of machine learning (ML) algorithms to search for recurrent patterns in order to detect the fitting case and origin of failures and prevent quick symptom fixes leading to frequent reoccurrence. One basic approach to compare problems with previous situations and cases is the case-based reasoning (CBR), which consists of four phases: retrieve, reuse, revise, and retain (Aamodt et al., 1994). The retrieve phase requires documented cases in a case database and compares the new occurrence with the available cases using ML-algorithms such as decision trees, nearest neighbor algorithms, genetic algorithms, or Bayesian networks.

Current KMSs are able to represent and include data about human knowledge and experiences as a multisensory source of information, a corresponding event history, and the available machine data covering discrete or continuous signals and conditions. The transfer from human to automatic readable data can be supported by natural language processing (NLP), and its combination with a CBR, as introduced in Rahm et al. (2018), appears to be important for the generation of a sufficiently broad dataset, because the human-machine dialog may contain several observations that cannot be detected by a machine.

The style of presentation to the operator is another element of the psychological domain. Additional image or video documentation, the matching probability, and actual data of failure appearance can help to guide the operator in understanding the cases and choosing accordingly.

All the potential hindrances strongly motivate a stepwise generation of direct use and value generation for all stakeholders in the company when starting to introduce a KMS. It must be considered part of a change management. The acceptance of the system needs early incentives, such as:

- higher productivity based on a better understanding of machines and machine lines leading to a structured work environment rather than unexpected negative events,
- reduction of overload for experienced persons, coming from fewer disturbances to their planned core work,
- visible higher efficiency of the production lines through optimization measures or at least knowledge and awareness of potentials for decision-making with reduced risk for management staff and executive personnel (Schult et al., 2024).

Cooperating Models and Added Value

Each of the introduced model examples is useful within its near environment. Even higher value could be generated by their operational availability and interaction within an industrial dataspace (see Figure 9.3). For instance, recycled materials tend to become malodorous after recycling because of the presence of VOCs in polymers. In the mixed postindustrial collection, they are exposed to several products and substances from the former packaging goods or cross-contamination during their joint collection. Besides common human sensory testing after EN 13725 or VDA 270, it is a fact that recycled polymer grades contain a set of molecules that is responsible for malodorous attributes. The classification of odor between recycled and virgin grades is done by human testers but can also be found by use of a principal component analysis (Haug et al., 2025).

The correlation between analytical data and human sensory evaluation could, for instance, be directly used to provide feedback to the compounding process (black pathways in Figure 9.3), in which odor-reducing additives can be applied. Virtual feedback on learned measures from compounding recipes with regard to their reduction effect on odor could reduce test cycles with human test panels effectively. On the other hand, gas samples taken from the degassing section of extruders, as introduced in Reimringer et al. (2024) could deliver inline information about the expected malodor. The basic strategy of using gas chromatographic data could also be applied to other potentially harmful substances and has high potential to support the monitoring and evaluation of contaminants in the future.

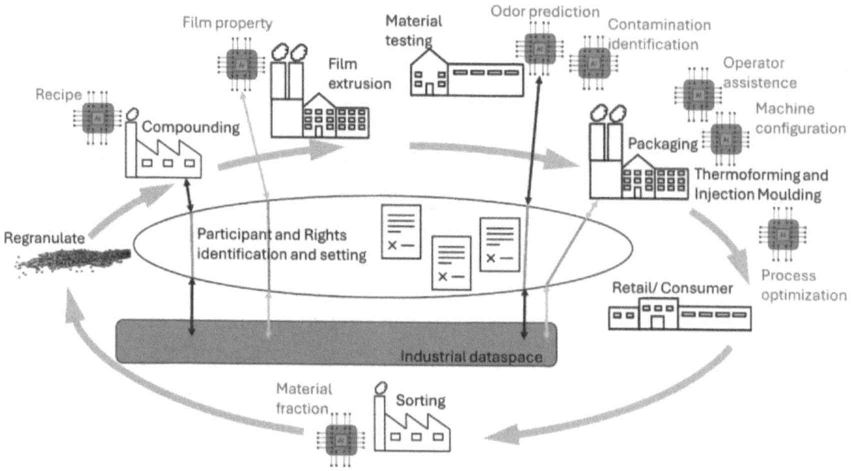

Figure 9.3 Distributed model landscape with a federated industrial dataspace as a communication platform.

Source: Author's work.

Another example scenario is the interaction of predicted or at least digitally provided material data in packaging machines. There are multiple influences of material properties (strength, stiffness, strain, friction, and thermal properties) on the machine, which could be included in digital datasheets or digital product pass to register at the machine or its assistance system for corresponding adjustment. The feedback of models from packaging machines could be a source for the reduction of innovation cycles in material engineering.

The digital environment strongly encourages the introduction of online life cycle assessment to support product development. The availability of data from production processes, different production sites, and facilities containing the specific individual technological equipment will reduce uncertainty of data and assumption-based misinterpretation. This also opens the field for digital data processing using methods of machine learning, which is already a topic within further development of LCA methodology (Romeiko et al., 2024). The development of predictive LCA from such models is a trend in the food value chain (Yu et al., 2024) and has its first approach in the field of packaging (Halstenberg et al., 2024).

There are numerous other potential pathways between distributed models. The models are permanently growing in scientific institutions, and in the near future, we can expect comparable cases of packaging to improve the safety of solutions under a complex profile of requirements and strict regulations.

Conclusion

The integration of AI in packaging production opens up new perspectives for manufacturers, thanks to its ability data, machine learning, and rapid decision-making based on the collected information. However, the implementation of AI in the packaging industry faces several significant barriers. Companies must deal with high initial costs of technological investments and a shortage of specialists with the appropriate skills. The natural resistance of organizations to digital transformation and uneven infrastructure development between regions remains a challenge. Companies express concerns about data protection, potential job reductions, and the loss of human creativity to algorithms. Additionally, integrating advanced AI solutions with existing production systems poses a complex technical challenge. Despite these obstacles, the strategic implementation of AI technology offers unprecedented opportunities to increase operational efficiency and market competitiveness and to achieve sustainability goals in the packaging sector (Statista, 2024).

Reference List

Aamodt, A., & Plaza, E. (1994). Case-based reasoning: Foundational issues, methodological variations and system approaches. *AI Communications*, 7(1), 39–59.

Abimbola, O. F., & Okpara, M. O. (2023). Artificial intelligence in the food packaging industry. In D. Hefft & C. O. Adetunji (Eds.), *Sensing and artificial intelligence solutions for food manufacturing*. CRC Press. https://doi.org/10.1201/9781003207955
Ads of the World. (n.d.). *A.I ketchup*. Retrieved May 18, 2025, from www.adsoftheworld.com/campaigns/a-i-ketchup
Alenizi, F. A., Abbasi, S., Mohammed, A. H., & Rahmani, A. M. (2023). The artificial intelligence technologies in Industry 4.0: A taxonomy, approaches, and future directions. *Computers & Industrial Engineering*, *185*, 109662. https://doi.org/10.1016/j.cie.2023.109662
Amazon. (2024). *How Amazon is using AI to deliver customer orders with less packaging*. Retrieved May 18, 2025, from www.aboutamazon.eu/news/innovation/how-amazon-is-using-ai-to-reduce-packaging
Barba, J. (2024). Vizit raises $25M to enhance visual content with intuitive AI. *P2PI*. Retrieved May 18, 2025, from https://p2pi.com/vizit-raises-25m-enhance-visual-content-intuitive-ai
Dabo, M. (2025). The role of digital twins in packaging development. *Inside Packaging*, 77. Retrieved May 19, 2025, from https://inside-packaging.nridigital.com/inside_packaging_mar25/the_role_of_digital_twins_in_packaging_development
Dhal, S. B., & Kar, D. (2025). Leveraging artificial intelligence and advanced food processing techniques for enhanced food safety, quality, and security: A comprehensive review. *Discover Applied Sciences*, *7*, 75. https://doi.org/10.1007/s42452-025-06472-w
DHL. (2022). *Artificial intelligence saves costs and emissions by optimizing packaging of shipments for DHL Supply Chain customers* [Press release]. https://group.dhl.com/en/media-relations/press-releases/2022/artificial-intelligence-optimizing-packaging-for-dhl-supply-chain-customers.html
DIN-Spec 91531. (2025). *Annotation of recorded measurement and process data for the production of polymer packaging with recycled content.*
Fofana, O. (2025). How AI is reshaping the packaging industry from design to distribution. *Packaging Gateway*. Retrieved May 19, 2025, from www.packaging-gateway.com/features/how-ai-is-reshaping-the-packaging-industry-from-design-to-distribution/?cf-view
Gajewski, T., Grabski, J. K., Cornaggia, A., & Garbowski, T. (2024). On the use of artificial intelligence in predicting the compressive strength of various cardboard packaging. *Packaging Technology and Science*, *37*(2), 97–105. https://doi.org/10.1002/pts.2783
Halstenberg, F., Kerps, A., & Le Rall, F. (2024). *EcoOptiPack – Using openLCA and onlineLCA for an easy-to-use assessment tool for plastic packaging* [Conference presentation]. OpenHubDay Dresden.
Hassoun, A., Boukid, F., Ozogul, F., Aït-Kaddour, A., Soriano, J. M., Lorenzo, J. M., Perestrelo, R., Galanakis, C. M., Bono, G., Bouyahya, A., Bhat, Z., Smaoui, S., Jambrak, A. R., & Câmara, J. S. (2023). Creating new opportunities for sustainable food packaging through dimensions of industry 4.0: New insights into the food waste perspective. *Trends in Food Science & Technology*, *142*, 104238. https://doi.org/10.1016/j.tifs.2023.104238
Haug, H. et al. (2025). Assessing and predicting odor properties of polyolefin plastics and regrinds through correlation of analytical and human sensory data. *Journal of Resources, Conservation and Recycling*. Manuscript under review.
Jan, Z., Ahamed, F., Mayer, W., Patel, N., Grossmann, G., Stumptner, M., & Kuusk, A. (2023). Artificial intelligence for industry 4.0: Systematic review of applications, challenges, and opportunities. *Expert Systems with Applications*, *216*, 119456. https://doi.org/10.1016/j.eswa.2022.119456
Körkemeyer, J. A., Brings, H., Montavon, B., & Schmitt, R. H. (2025). Multi-dimensional perceived quality: Extended level model and case study including

sustainability as a quality dimension in the perception of plastic packaging. *IRP Annals – Manufacturing Technology*, *74*(1), 645–650.

Lange, F., Schaller, F., & Hauptmann, M. (2025). Data-efficient determination of machine-specific processing window in thermoforming using the example of PCR materials. *TAPPI Journal*, *24*(7), 345–357.

McKinsey & Company. (2024). *Generative AI: The packaging and paper industry's next frontier* [Report]. McKinsey & Company report. Packaging & Paper Practice. https://www.mckinsey.com/industries/packaging-and-paper/our-insights/generative-ai-the-packaging-and-paper-industrys-next-frontier

Packaging Gateway. (n.d.). *Artificial intelligence in the packaging industry: Leading AI companies & solutions*. Retrieved May 19, 2025, from www.packaging-gateway.com/buyers-guide/top-ranked-artificial-intelligence-companies-packaging/

Packaging World. (2025). *Annual outlook report: Digitalization* [Report].

Precedence Research. (2024). *Artificial intelligence in packaging market size, share, and trends 2024 to 2034* [Report]. Retrieved May 19, 2025, from www.precedenceresearch.com/artificial-intelligence-in-packaging-market

Pučnik, R., Dokl, M., Fan, Y. V., Vujanović, A., Pintarič, Z. N., Aviso, K. B., Tan, R. R., Pahor, B., Kravnja, Z., & Čuček, L. (2024). A waste separation system based on sensor technology and deep learning: A simple approach applied to a case study of plastic packaging waste. *Journal of Cleaner Production*, *450*, 141762. https://doi.org/10.1016/j.jclepro.2024.141762

Rahm, J., Graube, M., Müller, R., Klaeger, T., Schegner, L., Schult, A., Bonse, R., Carsch, S., Oehm, L., & Urbas, L. (2018). KoMMDia: Dialogue-driven assistance system for fault diagnosis and correction in cyber-physical production systems. In *Proceedings of IEEE 23rd international conference on emerging technologies and factory automation (EFTA)* (pp. 999–1006). IEEE.

Regulation (EU) 2025/40 of the European Parliament and of the Council of 19 December 2024 on packaging and packaging waste, amending Regulation (EU) 2019/1020 and Directive (EU) 2019/904, and repealing Directive 94/62/EC. (2024).

Reimringer, W., Haug, H., Seifert, L., & Sauerwald, T. (2024). Sampling apparatus for the process monitoring of contaminants in polyolefin recycling. In *Proceedings of IEEE international instrumentation and measurement technology conference*. IEEE.

Romeiko, X. X., Zhang, X., Pang, Y., Gao, F., Xu, M., Lin, S., & Babbitt, C. (2024). A review of machine learning applications in life cycle assessment studies. *Science of the Total Environment*, *912*, 168969.

Schult, A., & Windisch, M. (2024). *More production efficiency through knowledge management systems: Best practice guideline for production leaders* (Version 2.0). Peerox GmbH.

Seifert, L., Leuchtenberger-Engel, L., & Hopmann, C. (2024). Development of an analytical model for predicting the tensile modulus of complex polypropylene compounds. *Polymers*, *16*, 3403.

Seifert, L., Leuchtenberger-Engel, L., & Hopmann, C. (2025a). Development of an analytical model for predicting the shear viscosity of polypropylene compounds. *Polymers*, *17*, 126.

Seifert, L., Leuchtenberger-Engel, L., & Hopmann, C. (2025b). Development of PP compound recipes using genetic algorithms and analytical models. *Polymers*, *17*, 1059.

Silva, N. S., Farias, F. S., Freitas, M. M. S., Hernández, E. J. G. P., Dantas, V. V., Oliveira, M. E. C., Joele, M. R. S. P., & Lourenço, L. F. H. (2021). Artificial intelligence application for classification and selection of fish gelatin packaging film produced with incorporation of palm oil and plant essential oils. *Food Packaging and Shelf Life*, *27*, 100611. https://doi.org/10.1016/j.fpsl.2020.100611

Soldatos, J. (Ed.). (2024). *Artificial intelligence in manufacturing: Enabling intelligent, flexible and cost-effective production through AI* (1st ed.). Springer.

Sourceful. (n.d.). *Spring*. Retrieved May 19, 2025, from https://spring.sourceful.com
Statista. (2024). *Artificial intelligence: In-depth market analysis [Market insights report]*. Retrieved May 18, 2025, from www.statista.com/study/50485/in-depth-report-artificial-intelligence/
Statista. (2025). *Artificial intelligence (AI) use in marketing – statistics & facts*. Retrieved May 18, 2025, from www.statista.com/topics/5017/ai-use-in-marketing/#topicOverview
Stieglitz, M., Adomeit, S., Müller, M., Hettwer, K., Schlierf, A., Uhlig, S., David, S., Hopmann, C., & Leuchtenberger-Engel, L. (2025). Model-based prediction of the tensile properties of polypropylene films made from recycled materials. *Polymers, 17*.
Tsarouhas, P. (2012). Reliability, availability and maintainability analysis in food production lines: A review. *International Journal of Food Science & Technology, 47*(11), 2243–2251.
Vizit. (2024). Vizit raises $25M in Series B funding led by Industry Ventures to power the future of e-commerce with its patented visual AI software platform [Press release]. *Business Wire*. Retrieved May 20, 2025, from www.businesswire.com/news/home/20241002832204/en/Vizit-Raises-%2425M-in-Series-B-Funding-Led-by-Industry-Ventures-to-Power-the-Future-of-E-Commerce-with-Its-Patented-Visual-AI-Software-Platform
Yu, C., Xu, G., Cai, M., Li, Y., Wang, L., Zhang, Y., & Lin, H. (2024). Predicting environmental impacts of smallholder wheat production by coupling life cycle assessment and machine learning. *Science of the Total Environment*, *921*, 171097.
Zeba, G., Dabić, M., Čičak, M., Daim, T., & Yalcin, H. (2021). Technology mining: Artificial intelligence in manufacturing. *Technological Forecasting and Social Change*, *171*, 120971.

10 Predictive Analytics and Artificial Intelligence for Greener Product Design

Mariusz Tichoniuk, Joanna Witczak, Wojciech Kozak, Giulio Mario Cappelletti, Pasquale Giungato, and Carlo Russo

Introduction

The development of global economies and the various challenges faced by modern markets result in a constantly growing demand for resources. The world's population consumes about 50% more natural resources than it did 30 years ago (Tchertchian et al., 2024). Despite the development of renewable technologies and the introduction of alternative pro-environmental materials, resource scarcity is still a growing issue (European Commission, 2020). The challenge is not only the constantly increasing consumption of resources but also their waste. The manufacturing sector contributes significantly to worldwide energy consumption, up to 50% of the total (Sahoo & Lo, 2022). Most of the waste is from poor-quality products as well as unused raw materials in the production line. The modern world is increasingly concerned about environmental issues. Despite the growing trends of product reusability and recycling, the production of new goods is still causing accelerated exploitation of raw materials and energy (Psarommatis et al., 2025).

More efficient use of resources and reduction of undesirable environmental impact throughout the product life cycle can be achieved by designing the product in the spirit of ecological awareness. The green design attitude integrates the requirements of product functionality, quality, and environmental neutrality (Kong et al., 2022). Making products "greener" is an iterative process based on stages of design, assessment, and optimization, which requires the collection and analysis of data about the product and its environment at every stage of its life cycle. The assessment for greener design is a multi-criterion decision-making task that takes into account the requirements of consumer needs, the reduction of environmental impact and the availability of resources (Lee et al., 2025).

Finding the best solutions (including the most environmentally friendly ones) can be based on models that combine key factors and constraints. Traditional modeling techniques often involve complex and laborious processes, requiring numerous assumptions to simplify the modeling task (Elsheikh et al., 2025). In recent years, the use of artificial intelligence

DOI: 10.4324/9781003659143-13

(AI), and more specifically, machine learning (ML) techniques has significantly supported this arduous task by offering useful tools for modeling under diverse conditions with reasonable accuracy. According to IBM's survey of global IT leaders on AI adoption (IBM, 2024), over 23% of companies in industries such as automotive, energy, and healthcare already use AI-supported tools, and 44% are exploring their adoption. Another report, prepared for Microsoft and PwC, assumes that AI can immensely benefit environmental sustainability and guide the manufacturing sector to become more eco-friendly and energy-efficient (Joppa & Herweijer, 2019).

Predictive analytics is a branch of advanced analytics that makes predictions about future events, behaviors, and outcomes. The integration of predictive analytics and artificial intelligence into product design has emerged as a transformative approach for developing greener and more sustainable products. These techniques enable designers and manufacturers to optimize resource use, reduce environmental impacts, and promote circular economy principles. The chapter will present key issues of greener product assessment and design, and the possibilities of using AI and predictive analytics tools in this area.

Overview of Key AI Concepts Relevant to Eco-Design

Decisions made at the design stage of a product can influence up to 80% of its environmental impact (Lee et al., 2025). Collecting and analyzing data from the product life cycle is key to anticipating and combining to make predictive decisions. There is a growing awareness of the need for the manufacturing industry to transition toward predictive manufacturing with the increasing popularity and advancement of artificial intelligence tools (Zonta et al., 2020).

The design and development of "smart" technologies is often supported by AI-driven applications based on ML and deep learning (DL) (Mousavizadegan et al., 2023). Similarly, the potential environmental impact of a product and its life cycle can be predicted using ML/DL techniques. The adoption of ML/DL has significantly increased in the last few years in the manufacturing sector due to the generation of a large amount of data (Jamwal et al., 2022). ML focuses on completing the desired analyses utilizing available data through continuous algorithmic optimization (Batool et al., 2025). On the other hand, DL could be defined as a type of advanced ML technique that involves more complex algorithms (so-called neural networks) imitating the network of neurons in the human brain.

ML is made up of three sections (Mousavizadegan et al., 2023): (I) the algorithm, which is the core of the decision-making process; (II) variables that formulate the decision; and (III) the known data and base knowledge that train the algorithm. The created model is first fed with parameter data that has known results. The algorithms are then run until they can develop a predictive model with answers that agree with the answer of the known data. Extracting relevant information is crucial and significant, which DL algorithms can do effectively. Additionally, DL reaches a logical conclusion on tasks involving unstructured data and does not always require labeled data (Batool et al., 2025).

The integration of generative design and innovative manufacturing helps to produce less waste and has fewer adverse effects on the environment than traditional manufacturing processes (Sahoo & Lo, 2022). When used effectively, AI helps to determine product quality issues and to optimize products at inventory levels and the use of resources in the production line (Pratt, 2021).

Product Life Cycle Analysis Supported by AI Tools

In the face of growing global concern about environmental sustainability issues, accurate and comprehensive environmental impact assessments play a key role in achieving sustainability goals. Green design comprehensively integrates the product requirements toward its function, quality, and environmental impact to effectively reduce the emissions from the perspective of the life cycle. Industrial production and consumption generate significant environmental consequences, highlighting the need for robust assessment tools. One of the most widely used methodologies for quantifying sustainability is life cycle analysis (LCA). According to ISO 14040 (ISO 14040:2006), LCA is the systematic analysis of environmental impacts across the whole life cycle of a product, material, process, or other measurable activity. Increasing regulatory pressure and consumer demand for transparent environmental information about products further emphasize the importance of accurate environmental assessments. With advances in technology, AI has emerged as a transformative force across science and industry. AI's ability to handle large data sets, identify patterns, and automate complex tasks opens up new opportunities to improve LCA activities provided during the life cycle stages.

Traditional LCA faces several limitations and challenges (Peña et al., 2021). Data issues are a significant challenge, including difficulties in data acquisition, quality assurance, and availability. Manual data collection is time and resource intensive. Often, there are data gaps, especially for processes before and after the main production process (Bicalho et al., 2017). Examples of data gaps include missing data on food processing or specific materials. Data quality, including accuracy, consistency, and representativeness, is also a challenge. There is often a reliance on secondary data that might be inaccurate or outdated.

ML, natural language processing (NLP), and predictive analytics offer great potential to overcome the limitations of traditional LCA. These primarily include improvements in data processing, predictive accuracy, and efficiency in real-time decision-making. Automating data collection and processing, handling large datasets, improving data accuracy, and increasing speed and scalability can bring great benefits to greener product design (Dostatni et al., 2023). In addition, AI can help fill data gaps, improve modeling techniques, and provide real-time insights. Integrating AI with LCA can represent a shift from traditional expert-based assessments to more automated data-driven approaches (Kong et al., 2022). Traditional LCA relies heavily on manual data collection and interpretation by experts. AI-assisted LCA can use ML and data analytics to automate these processes, thereby leading to greater efficiency and scalability. AI's ability to continuously learn and adapt can lead to more dynamic and accurate LCA models that can respond to changes in data and processes over time. ML algorithms can learn from historical data and adapt to new inputs, enabling the creation of dynamic LCA models that can provide more timely and relevant assessments compared to static traditional ones. NLP can help in automating data extraction from unstructured sources. Predictive analytics projects the environmental effects of future decisions and products. This way, industries may provide and introduce more sustainable practices by making quicker and better-informed decisions.

Application of AI for the Optimization of Materials and Manufacturing Processes

The pro-environmental approach of enterprises is becoming a very important tool for increasing competitive advantage and achieving sustainable development goals (Lin et al., 2024). Many companies have sought practical use of AI to control the environmental impact of their operations. The use of AI is considered by enterprises as an effective way to solve dynamic environmental problems characterized by uncertainty, complexity and interactions with external and internal factors affecting their activities (Dwivedi et al., 2021). AI can help monitor and control the manufacturing processes, extract useful information and insights about the environment. ML and other AI algorithms build predictive models to identify potential environmental risks and support organizations in environmental decisions (Galaz et al., 2021).

Focusing on predictive product analysis, it can be pointed out that ML is the crucial component of the AI algorithms that are currently extensively applied in material science (Li et al., 2020a). The two primary tasks are defined for ML in material development (Wang et al., 2023): predicting the material properties and optimizing its design and manufacturing process. ML represents a revolutionary frame for new materials development, which can realize the synergy of material theory, simulation, synthesis, monitoring, and application (Wang et al., 2023). AI-powered tools also help reduce the trial-and-error cycles of experiments and simulations that are labor-intensive, time-consuming, and resource-intensive, even for single-property improvements (Li et al., 2020b).

ML algorithms, such as decision trees, random forests, and artificial neural networks, are widely used for predictive analytics in sustainable product design. These models can forecast environmental impacts, optimize material properties, and identify opportunities for improving sustainability performance. For example, ML models have been used to predict the environmental performance of construction products with high accuracy, enabling quick decision-making for LCA practitioners (Wang et al., 2023).

AI and predictive analytics play a pivotal role in optimizing product design for sustainability by analyzing vast datasets and identifying optimal solutions. DL-based models can be a suitable choice to provide advanced analytic tools for manufacturing data processing and analysis (Jamwal et al., 2022). Due to the digitalization of manufacturing processes, application of intelligent sensors, and supply chain activities, industry is facing challenges with the generation of high volume and the different variety and velocity of data, which can be very usable in operational management supported by AI-tools. The integration of AI enables sustainable organization management and its long-term development (Zhu & Zuo, 2024).

AI-Supported Product Design for Industry 5.0

When examining the impact of modern technologies on the economy, it was noted that 82% of manufacturing and service companies have increased their efficiency by the implementation of Industry 4.0 technologies associated with AI-based tools and the Internet of Things (IoT) (Jamwal et al., 2022). Further development from Industry 4.0 to Industry 5.0 is associated with the expanded implementation of sustainability in industrial practices, which involves a greater focus on long-term environmental, social, and economic viability (Rame et al., 2024).

Sustainability in Industry 5.0 covers various economic, social, and environmental aspects, including effective resource management and waste reduction. These goals can be achieved by applying a Zero Defect Manufacturing (ZDM) approach (Azamfirei et al., 2023). Successful implementation of ZDM is often connected with the use of AI-based tools, ML, and predictive analytics to anticipate and prevent product' defects, reduce waste, and improve production efficiency. Zero Defect Manufacturing can be applied in single-stage and multi-stage manufacturing systems (Psarommatis, 2021). It is introduced to improve process efficiency and product quality by minimizing, eliminating, or compensating for defects and process errors.

The Industry 5.0 approach focuses on solutions that best meet sustainable development goals. The evaluation of different variants is possible by combining digital technologies and AI tools. The concept of a DT is very useful here, as it is a virtual mirror image of an object or system that exists in the real world (Papacharalampopoulos et al., 2023). The DT enables comparing, analyzing, and predicting the properties of products or processes integrating semi-physical simulations based on the compilation of measurable machine operations and their digital reflections. Digital reality and algorithms using the potential of AI can significantly support the readiness and adaptability of products and processes that are in line with current trends, including greener design (Hadjidemetriou et al., 2023). Compared to traditional modeling, the DT exhibits increased adaptability and flexibility, allowing it to be easily updated and adapted to mirror modifications in their physical counterparts or environment. This ensures a dynamic and responsive model that can evolve continuously. Additionally, the Digital Twin offers predictive maintenance and optimization capabilities that can predict equipment failures, maintenance requirements, and product performance, ultimately leading to increased manufacturing efficiency and reduced cost (Wang et al., 2023).

Examples of the Use of AI in Eco-Design in Different Industries

For certain product groups, the use of AI tools for pro-environmental design is a very good approach that supports sustainable development and green technologies.

Automotive Industry

In the automotive sector, AI and big data analytics are being used to design environmentally friendly products for the circular economy. For instance, smart product platforming (SPP) could be applied to optimize manufacturing processes, reducing material waste and energy consumption while promoting modular design and recyclability in the production of many different parts (Akhtar et al., 2024). ML techniques are useful in the accurate prediction of patterns that can be utilized to better understand and coordinate the processes and to make data-driven decisions about, for example, the use of recycled materials and sustainable manufacturing processes that unlock the circular economy.

ML algorithms can be used to predict the quality of a mechanical product resulting from various manufacturing processes. By employing feature extraction methods, ML algorithms can identify and isolate significant characteristics from raw data, facilitating a deeper understanding of the factors affecting product quality and categorize products based on their attributes (El Melhaoui et al., 2025).

Digital Twin technology facilitates the effective advancement of eco-friendly electric vehicle (EV) technologies, spanning from design to operation (Yalavarthy et al., 2025). It is essential for predictive mobility, autonomous movement control, driver support systems, vehicle condition monitoring, battery supervision, and smart charging of electric powertrain systems. Digital Twin technology enables comprehensive digital life cycle analysis, enhancing battery management efficiency through optimal models for State of Charge (SoC) and State of Health (SoH) assessments.

Construction Industry

AI tools are being applied to optimize the design of green buildings and sustainable construction materials. ML models have been developed to predict the properties of construction materials, achieving high accuracy in optimizing their use for sustainable construction (Hadjidemetriou et al., 2023).

The connection between the construction industry and the environment is essential to the development of effective strategies for energy conservation and sustainable building practices (Wang et al., 2023). Design of buildings, including structural design and visual design, can be improved for energy conservation with the use of AI. The generative DL models, such as generative adversarial network and variational auto-encoder, have demonstrated their excellent ability to generate and optimize 2D and 3D innovative architectural designs, such as energy-efficient building design (Ngo, 2019), planning (Rahbar et al., 2022), interior (Tautkute et al., 2019), and façade design (Jalali et al., 2019). ML and DL can also predict the load capacity and damage degree of existing structures (e.g., crack/corrosion detection) for modification, such as steel structures (Avci et al., 2021) or reinforced concrete structures (Sadeghi et al., 2021).

AI can be applied to create materials that are suitable for the circular economy. Through rearranging innumerable concepts and proposing the particular one that most satisfies requirements for circular design, AI also helps to reduce complexity (Honic et al., 2021). The combination of construction materials intelligent ecosystem (CMIE) and Industry 4.0 can further promote efficiency and safety in the construction industry, which in turn shapes the future direction for construction materials (Wang et al., 2023). CMIE is a new application of AI techniques that integrates material information and its application background from various data sources to enhance the development of next-generation tailored materials.

Electronics Industry

In the electronics industry, AI and ML are being used to design green and flexible electronics. These technologies enable the optimization of material selection, energy efficiency, and design processes, promoting sustainable development in the sector.

AI tools are also applicable in making IT more sustainable (Gloukhovtsev, 2024). AI algorithms can identify inefficiencies in IT equipment manufacturing processes and propose ways to reduce energy consumption (Jamwal et al., 2022). They can also predict when electronic equipment reaches the end of its life (both hardware and software), and schedule servicing before that happens, reducing downtime and the waste of resources on replacement. By analyzing data on the composition of electronics and the availability of raw materials, AI can identify opportunities to recycle components and reduce e-waste (Gloukhovtsev, 2024).

AI tools are also involved in the development of innovative, sustainable, flexible, and self-powered electronic modules that can be applied in smart wearable devices, sensing systems, and other electronic devices. So-called triboelectric nanogenerators (TENG) are designed to use the basic physics phenomena to convert mechanical energy into electrical energy (Wang et al., 2021). The AI tools are applied to overcome the challenges of material selection, output performance prediction, structural design, and durability of the developed electronic items (Swami et al., 2025). The integration of AI tools and advanced materials such as biodegradable polymers, nanomaterials, and high dielectric materials can stimulate further development of next-generation self-powered devices.

Challenges and Prospects for the Development of AI in Eco-Design

While AI and predictive analytics offer significant potential for advancing greener product design, several challenges remain (Dwivedi et al., 2021). Most companies do not have enough knowledge about this new technology, and the current use of AI in organizations remains low. The main limitations concern the need for high-quality training data, the complexity of integrating AI tools into existing design workflows, and the lack of standardized metrics for evaluating product circularity (Psarommatis et al., 2025).

Additionally, the accuracy of predictive models depends on the availability of comprehensive datasets, and the results may vary depending on the specific application and industry. Integrating AI-based LCA tools with existing product life cycle management (PLM) and other enterprise systems can be complex (Raghav et al., 2025). It is also important to mention that the successful development, implementation, and interpretation of AI-assisted LCA results requires expertise in both LCA and AI domains. Currently, there is a lack of standardized methodologies and validation frameworks for AI-assisted LCA, which requires further development in this area (Dostatni et al., 2023). The ethical implications of using AI in environmental assessments, such as data privacy as well as the potential misuse of the technology, should also be noted.

Ensuring data quality and transparency in AI model development is critical to the credibility of AI-assisted LCA. The environmental benefits of using AI in LCA should be weighed against the potential environmental negative impacts associated with energy consumption during AI training and implementation. Running complex AI models requires significant computing power, which translates into energy consumption (De Vries, 2023; Berthelot et al., 2024). It is important to consider the environmental footprint of AI itself when assessing the overall environmental impact of using AI to improve LCA.

To overcome these obstacles, the key areas of AI development should be developed:

- improving the accuracy of predictive models,
- developing standardized metrics,
- encouraging the adoption of AI tools and frameworks across industries,

- addressing the challenges related to availability, computational complexity, and intellectual property of data,
- developing standardized AI-LCA methodologies,
- creating comprehensive LCA databases ready for use with AI.

Despite the noticeable benefits of implementing AI tools, individuals and organizations can exhibit a lack of trust and may have concerns relating to the ethical dimensions of AI systems and their use of shared data (Dwivedi et al., 2021).

AI-based tools, for example, ML and DL algorithms, are an ally of sustainable development, which is significantly supported by the design and production of greener products (Jamwal et al., 2022). They open many opportunities for manufacturing organizations to reduce production losses or errors.

Summary and Conclusion

AI is successfully used to efficiently collect data and analyze product development options, taking into account their environmental impact throughout the entire life cycle. During product design and value chain planning, AI-based predictive analytics can consider many different variants of the product being developed and their impact on the environment. Automatic collection and processing of digitized data from various production and logistics processes contributes to the design of greener products that better contribute to the achievement of sustainable development goals.

Advanced data analytics and ML algorithms enable AI to analyze huge volumes of data, speeding up the product design and development phases and optimizing its performance. The simulation of various options and predictive analytics enables more efficient decision-making and reduces the time to market for sustainable products. Additionally, AI-based tools provide the potential to enhance resource efficiency, minimize waste, and lower overall environmental footprints in the whole product life cycle.

Future research should focus on combining technical advances in AI with the specific methodological requirements of LCA to create a robust and reliable AI-assisted LCA framework. Although AI offers great potential for LCA, its application is still relatively new. Further research is needed to develop standardized methodologies and customized AI algorithms that effectively address the unique complexities and data challenges in LCA. Integrating AI-assisted LCA with other sustainability assessment tools can provide a more comprehensive understanding of product sustainability to facilitate sustainable design.

Reference List

Akhtar, P., Ghouri, A. M., Ashraf, A., Lim, J. J., Khan, N. R., & Ma, S. (2024). Smart product platforming powered by AI and generative AI: Personalization for the circular economy. *International Journal of Production Economics*, *273*, 109283. https://doi.org/10.1016/j.ijpe.2024.109283

Avci, O., Abdeljaber, O., Kiranyaz, S., Hussein, M., Gabbouj, M., & Inman, D. J. (2021). A review of vibration-based damage detection in civil structures: From traditional methods to machine learning and deep learning applications. *Mechanical Systems and Signal Processing, 147*, 107077. https://doi.org/10.1016/J.YMSSP.2020.107077

Azamfirei, V., Psarommatis, F., & Lagrosen, Y. (2023). Application of automation for inline quality inspection, a zero-defect manufacturing approach. *Journal of Manufacturing Systems*, *67*, 1–22. https://doi.org/10.1016/j.jmsy.2022.12.010

Batool, M., Sanumi, O., & Jankovic, J. (2025). Application of artificial intelligence in the materials science, with a special focus on fuel cells and electrolyzers. *Energy and AI*, *18*, 100424. https://doi.org/10.1016/j.egyai.2024.100424

Berthelot, A., Caron, E., Jay, M., & Lefèvre, L. (2024). Estimating the environmental impact of Generative-AI services using an LCA-based methodology. *Procedia CIRP*, *122*, 707–712. https://doi.org/10.1016/j.procir.2024.01.098

Bicalho, T., Sauer, I., Rambaud, A., & Altukhova, Y. (2017). LCA data quality: A management science perspective. *Journal of Cleaner Production*, *156*, 888–898. https://doi.org/10.1016/j.jclepro.2017.03.229

De Vries, A. (2023). The growing energy footprint of artificial intelligence. *Joule*, 7(10), 2191–2194. https://doi.org/10.1016/j.joule.2023.09.004

Dostatni, E., Dudkowiak, A., Rojek, I., & Mikołajewski, D. (2023). Environmental analysis of a product manufactured with the use of an additive technology – AI-based vs. traditional approaches. *Bulletin of the Polish Academy of Sciences Technical Sciences*, *71*(1), e144478–e144478. https://doi.org/10.24425/bpasts.2023.144478

Dwivedi, Y. K., Hughes, L., Ismagilova, E., Aarts, G., Coombs, C., Crick, T., Duan, Y., Dwivedi, R., Edwards, J., Eirug, A., Galanos, V., Ilavarasan, P. V., Janssen, M., Jones, P., Kar, A. K., Kizgin, H., Kronemann, B., Lal, B., Lucini, B., . . . Williams, M. D. (2021). Artificial Intelligence (AI): Multidisciplinary perspectives on emerging challenges, opportunities, and agenda for research, practice and policy. *International Journal of Information Management*, *57*, 101994. https://doi.org/10.1016/j.ijinfomgt.2019.08.002

El Melhaoui, O., El Melhaoui, I., Jeffali, F., Said, S., & Elouaham, S. (2025). Integration of artificial intelligence algorithms for defect detection and shape recognition in mechanical quality control. *Interactions*, *246*, 9. https://doi.org/10.1007/s10751-024-02235-y

Elsheikh, A., Faqeha, H., Hammoodi, K. A., Bawahab, M., Fujii, M., Shanmugan, S., Essa, F. A., Abd-Elaziem, W., Ramesh, B., Sathyamurthy, R., & Egiza, M. (2025). Integrating predictive and hybrid machine learning approaches for optimizing solar still performance: A comprehensive review. *Solar Energy*, *295*, 113536. https://doi.org/10.1016/j.solener.2025.113536

European Commission (2020). *Critical raw materials resilience: Charting a path towards greater security and sustainability*. Communication from the Commission to the European Parliament, the Council, the European Economic and Social Committee and the committee of the regions. COM/2020/474 final. https://ec.europa.eu/docsroom/documents/42849/attachments/2/translations/en/renditions/native

Galaz, V., Centeno, M. A., & Callahan, P. W. (2021). Artificial intelligence, systemic risks, and sustainability. *Technology in Society*, *67*, 101741. https://doi.org/10.1016/j.techsoc.2021.101741

Gloukhovtsev, M. (2024). Transformative role of AI in making IT sustainable. In M. Gloukhovtsev, *Making IT sustainable. Techniques and applications* (pp. 273–282). Academic Press. https://doi.org/10.1016/B978-0-443-13597-2.00015-7

Hadjidemetriou, L., Stylianidis, N., Englezos, D., Papadopoulos, P., Eliades, D., Timotheou, S., Polycarpou, M. M., & Panayiotou, Ch. (2023). A digital twin architecture for real-time and offline high granularity analysis in smart buildings. *Sustainable Cities and Society*, *98*, 104795. https://doi.org/10.1016/j.scs.2023.104795

Honic, M., Kovacic, I., Aschenbrenner, P., & Ragossnig, A. (2021). Material passports forthe end-of-life stage of buildings: Challenges and potentials. *Journal of Cleaner Production, 319*, 128702. https://doi.org/10.1016/J.JCLEPRO.2021.128702

IBM. (2024). *IBM global AI adoption index 2023*. Retrieved April 1, 2025, from https://newsroom.ibm.com/2024-01-10-Data-Suggests-Growth-in-Enterprise-Adoption-of-AI-is-Due-to-Widespread-Deployment-by-Early-Adopters

ISO 14040:2006 / Amd 1:2020, Environmental management – Life cycle assessment – Principles and framework

Jalali, Z., Noorzai, E., & Heidari, S. (2019). Design and optimization of form and façade of an office building using the genetic algorithm. *Journal of Building Performance Simulation* 26, 128–140. https://doi.org/10.1080/23744731.2019.1624095

Jamwal, A., Agrawal, R. Sharma, M. (2022). Deep learning for manufacturing sustainability: Models, applications in Industry 4.0 and implications. *International Journal of Information Management Data Insights*, *2*, 100107. https://doi.org/10.1016/j.jjimei.2022.100107

Joppa, L., & Herweijer, C. (2019). *How AI can enable a sustainable future*. Retrieved April 3, 2025, from www.pwc.co.uk/sustainability-climate-change/assets/pdf/how-ai-can-enable-a-sustainable-future.pdf

Kong, L., Wang, L., Li, F., & Guo, J. (2022). Toward product green design of modeling, assessment, optimization, and tools: A comprehensive review. *The International Journal of Advanced Manufacturing Technology*, *122*, 2217–2234. https://doi.org/10.1007/s00170-022-10021-9

Lee, A. W. L., Seah, K. K. W., Ng, B. F., Zhang, E. T., Lu, W. F., & Low, J. S. C. (2025). Generative ecodesign for mechanical products: A design workflow. *Cleaner Engineering and Technology*, *24*, 100890. https://doi.org/10.1016/j.clet.2025.100890

Li, J., Lim, K., Yang, H., Ren, Z., Raghavan, S., Chen, P. Y., Buonassisi, T., & Wang, X. (2020a) AI applications through the whole life cycle of material discovery. *Matter*, *3*, 393–432. https://doi.org/10.1016/J.MATT.2020.06.011

Li, X., Cai, S., Sun, B., Yang, C., Zhang, J., & Liu, Y. (2020b) Chemically robust covalent organic frameworks: Progress and perspective. *Matter*, *3*, 1507–1540. https://doi.org/10.1016/J.MATT.2020.09.007

Lin, J., Zeng, Y., Wu, S., & Luo, X. (2024). How does artificial intelligence affect the environmental performance of organizations? The role of green innovation and green culture. *Information & Management*, *61*, 103924. https://doi.org/10.1016/j.im.2024.103924

Mousavizadegan, M., Firoozbakhtian, A., Hosseini, & M. Ju, H. (2023). Machine learning in analytical chemistry: From synthesis of nanostructures to their applications in luminescence sensing. *Trends in Analytical Chemistry 167*, 117216. https://doi.org/10.1016/j.trac.2023.117216

Ngo, N. T. (2019). Early predicting cooling loads for energy-efficient design in office buildings by machine learning. *Energy and Buildings*, *182*, 264–273. https://doi.org/10.1016/J.ENBUILD.2018.10.004

Papacharalampopoulos, A., Foteinopoulos, P., & Stavropoulos, P. (2023). Integration ofindustry 5.0 requirements in digital twin-supported manufacturing process selection: A framework. *Procedia CIRP*, *119*, 545–551. https://doi.org/10.1016/j.procir.2023.06.197

Peña, C., Civit, B., Gallego-Schmid, A., Druckman, A., Caldeira-Pires, A., Weidema, B., Mieras, E., Wang, F., Fava, J., Milà i Canals, M., Cordella, M., Arbuckle, P., Valdivia, S., Fallaha, S., & Motta, W. (2021). Using life cycle assessment to achieve a circular economy. *The International Journal of Life Cycle Assessment*, *26*, 215–220. https://doi.org/10.1007/s11367-020-01856-z

Pratt, S. (2021). *How AI can solve manufacturing's waste problem*. World Economic Forum. Retrieved April 1, 2025, from www.weforum.org/stories/2021/04/how-ai-can-cut-waste-in-manufacturing/

Psarommatis, F. (2021). A generic methodology and a digital twin for zero defect manufacturing (ZDM) performance mapping towards design for ZDM. *Journal of Manufacturing Systems*, *59*, 507–521. https://doi.org/10.1016/j.jmsy.2021.03.021

Psarommatis, F., May, G., & Azamfirei, V. (2025). Product reuse and repurpose in circular manufacturing: A critical review of key challenges, shortcomings and future directions. *Journal of Remanufacturing*. https://doi.org/10.1007/s13243-025-00153-y

Raghav, A., Singh, B., Wongmahesak, K., & Chandra, S. (2025). Towards a greener future: Integrating life cycle assessment for sustainability in industry 5.0. In *Sustainable futures with life cycle assessment in industry 5.0* (pp. 1–20). IGI Global Scientific Publishing. https://doi.org/10.4018/979-8-3693-9346-8.ch001

Rahbar, M., Mahdavinejad, M., Markazi, A. H., & Bemanian, M. (2022). Architectural layout design through deep learning and agentbased modeling: A hybrid approach. *Journal of Building Engineering*, *47*, 103822. https://doi.org/10.1016/J.JOBE.2021.103822

Rame, R., Purwanto, P., & Surwanto, S. (2024). Industry 5.0 and sustainability: An overview of emerging trends and challenges for a green future. *Innovation and Green Development 3*, 100173. https://doi.org/10.1016/j.igd.2024.100173

Sadeghi, F., Yu, Y., Zhu, X., & Li, J. (2021). Damage identification of steel-concrete composite beams based on modal strain energy changes through general regression neural network. *Engineering Structures*, *244*, 112824. https://doi.org/10.1016/J.ENGSTRUCT.2021.112824

Sahoo, S., & Lo Ch.-Y. (2022). Smart manufacturing powered by recent technological advancements: A review. *Journal of Manufacturing Systems*, *64*, 236–250. https://doi.org/10.1016/j.jmsy.2022.06.008

Swami, A. K., Verma, D., Soni, R., & Goswami, D. (2025). Artificial intelligence technology in materials selection, device engineering and parameter optimisation for triboelectric nanogenerator. *Materials Today Communications*, *46*, 112553. https://doi.org/10.1016/j.mtcomm.2025.112553

Tautkute, I., Trzcinski, T., Skorupa, A. P., Lukasz, K., & Marasek, K. (2019). DeepStyle: Multimodal search engine for fashion and interior design. *IEEE Access* 7, 84613–84628. https://doi.org/10.1109/ACCESS.2019.2923552

Tchertchian, N., de la Tour, T. R., Millet, D., & Chenouardb, R. (2024). Ecodesign approach for complex systems: Electric vehicle case study. *Procedia CIRP*, *122*, 1006–1011. https://doi.org/10.1016/j.procir.2024.02.035

Wang, H., Han, M., Song, Y., & Zhang, H. (2021). Design, manufacturing and applications of wearable triboelectric nanogenerators. *Nano Energy*, *81*, 105627. https://doi.org/10.1016/j.nanoen.2020.105627

Wang, X. Q., Chen, P., Chow, Ch, L., & Lau, D. (2023). Artificial-intelligence-led revolution of construction materials: From molecules to Industry 4.0. *Matter*, *6*, 1831–1859. https://doi.org/10.1016/j.matt.2023.04.016

Yalavarthy, U. R. S., Kumar, N. B., Babu, A. R. V., Narasipuram, R. P., & Padmanaban, S. (2025). Digital twin technology in electric and self-navigating vehicles: Readiness, convergence, and future directions. *Energy Conversion and Management: X*, *26*, 100949. https://doi.org/10.1016/j.ecmx.2025.100949

Zhu, X., & Zuo, F. (2024). Innovation in operations: Transforming operations management with artificial intelligence and sustainability. In *Reference module in social sciences*. Elsevier. Retrieved April 1, 2025, from https://doi.org/10.1016/B978-0-443-28993-4.00063-9.

Zonta, T., da Costa, C. A., da Rosa Righi, R., de Lima, M. J., Silveira da Trindade, E., & Pyng Li, G. (2020). Predictive maintenance in the Industry 4.0: A systematic literature review. *Computers & Industrial Engineering*, *150*, 106889. https://doi.org/10.1016/j.cie.2020.106889

11 Intelligent Food Automation

How NIR Coupled with AI Can Transform the Food Industry?

Krzysztof Wójcicki and Tomasz Paweł Czaja

Introduction

The modern food industry faces numerous challenges. First and foremost, it must ensure high quality and safety of food products, while at the same time optimizing production costs and meeting strict environmental standards. It must also comply with increasingly stringent food regulations imposed by organizations such as the food authorities and other regulatory bodies (FAO, 2021; Murugan & Vinu, 2024). Additionally, the growing awareness of consumers and changing food trends create even more challenges that the industry must address. On top of that, companies must stay competitive in a rapidly evolving market, continuously innovating to differentiate themselves from their rivals and meet the ever-changing demands of consumers (Guine et al., 2020).

To meet strict regulations, food must undergo thorough analysis at multiple stages of production to ensure safety, quality, and compliance with industry standards. This process begins with the careful screening of raw materials before they enter the production line. Raw ingredients must be tested to verify that they meet the required parameters for quality, safety, and nutritional value. This step is crucial, as any contamination, spoilage, or deviation from the necessary specifications can impact the quality of the final product (Blanchfield, 2005).

Once raw materials pass the initial screening, the next critical step is continuous monitoring during processing. At this stage, ingredients go through various changes such as mixing, heating, cooling, fermenting, or packaging, depending on the type of food being produced. To maintain quality and safety, automated systems and quality control experts closely track key factors like temperature, pH levels, moisture content, and microbial activity. If any issues arise, immediate adjustments can be made to prevent defective or unsafe products from moving further in production (Sørensen et al., 2016).

Sustainability is also a key focus in modern food production. Reducing waste and using resources efficiently not only help the environment but also improve overall operations. By monitoring the production process closely, manufacturers can quickly identify and fix any deviations from expected

DOI: 10.4324/9781003659143-14

standards (Qu et al., 2024). Real-time adjustments ensure that products maintain consistent quality while minimizing unnecessary waste. This approach boosts efficiency, lowers costs, and supports sustainable practices. By combining strict quality control with eco-friendly strategies, food manufacturers can enhance productivity and contribute to a greener for sustainable industry (van den Berg et al., 2013).

Finally, the finished product must undergo rigorous quality evaluation before it reaches consumers. This involves a combination of laboratory testing, sensory assessments, and regulatory inspections to confirm that the product meets all required safety, quality, and labeling standards. Additionally, packaging integrity is checked to verify that food remains protected from contamination and spoilage during transportation and storage. By implementing a comprehensive, multi-stage analysis process, food manufacturers can maintain high standards of quality, safety, and compliance, delivering high quality products to the market.

Despite advancements in food production and quality control, many companies still lack comprehensive analysis methods. Critical production parameters are often only partially monitored, relying on traditional chemical analysis techniques. These methods require extensive sample preparation, specialized equipment, and complex lab procedures, making them time-consuming and expensive. Since these techniques are typically offline analyses, they do not provide real-time results, leading to delays in detecting issues and making necessary adjustments.

Additionally, many of these methods rely on chemical solvents and reagents, generating hazardous waste that is not environmentally friendly (Plotka-Wasylka, 2018). The disposal of these chemicals adds to pollution and increases operational costs, making the process both unsustainable and inefficient. The continued use of such "outdated" techniques raises concerns about the industry's long-term environmental impact and the need for more sustainable solutions. To address these challenges, food manufacturers must adopt greener, more efficient alternatives that minimize waste while maintaining high analytical accuracy and reliability (Meher & Zarouri, 2025).

Another major issue in food analysis is the reliance on univariate techniques, which measure only one parameter at a time. For example, testing for gluten content, which is key parameter for many baking products, might require a long experiment that provides just a single data point. This approach makes it difficult to monitor and control the entire production process effectively. Since food production involves multiple interconnected processes, using separate, slow tests for each factor leads to inefficiencies, delays in decision-making, and challenges in optimizing production. To improve efficiency and accuracy, the industry must shift toward multivariate analysis methods, which allow simultaneous measurement of multiple parameters. One of the solutions is near-infrared (NIR), which has been increasingly implemented in food industry in recent years.

NIR Spectroscopy

Introduction to NIR

NIR is a type of vibrational spectroscopy techniques covered the wavelength range from 750 to 2,500 nm. It makes it possible to perform fast and accurate measurements without any prior sample preparation for the samples in powder and liquid state. When NIR light is directed at a sample, certain wavelengths are absorbed by molecular bonds within the sample – specifically, bonds involving hydrogen atoms, such as O-H (water), N-H (proteins), and C-H (fats and carbohydrates). The absorbed energy causes overtones and combination vibrations of these molecular bonds, and the resulting absorbance or reflectance spectrum serves as a "fingerprint" of the sample's composition (Ozaki et al., 2021). One of the biggest advantages of NIR spectroscopy is that NIR light is transparent to glass, which allows fiber-optic probes to take measurements through glass containers without interference. These probes can be installed in various locations across a facility – such as production lines, tanks, or pipelines – enabling real-time monitoring even in hard-to-reach areas. However, this is only part of the solution. While NIR spectroscopy can rapidly generate detailed spectra, these spectral patterns are often too complex to interpret by simple visual inspection. To extract meaningful information, advanced multivariate data analysis combined with machine learning (ML) and AI techniques is required. Techniques such as Principal Component Analysis (PCA) and Partial Least Squares Regression (PLSR) are commonly used to analyze spectral data. These ML-based methods help build predictive models by correlating specific spectral features with the concentrations of key components, such as moisture, protein, fat, and fiber. As a result, NIR spectroscopy enables fast, non-destructive, and reagent-free analysis, eliminating the need for time-consuming laboratory procedures (Sørensen et al., 2021). When integrated into digitalized production environments, these analytical tools become powerful enablers of food process automation.

NIR and Food Automation

Digital transformation in the food industry is based on the adaptation of Industry 4.0 technologies (Hassoun et al., 2022). A critical aspect of digital transformation in the food industry is quality control. Ensuring that food products meet safety standards and exhibit the desired organoleptic properties is essential for maintaining industry standards. Quality is assessed based on attributes such as nutritional value, physicochemical characteristics, safety measures, sensory properties, and shelf life. Traditionally, food quality assessment relied on destructive and labor-intensive methods with limited analytical capabilities. However, in recent years, automated instrumental techniques have largely supplanted conventional "wet chemistry" methods (Hassoun et al., 2023). According to Misra et al. (2022), spectroscopic sensors and hyperspectral cameras are now widely employed for monitoring food quality and safety. Green NIR technology offer rapid and non-invasive measurements of important food attributes such as moisture, protein, and fat making suitable for in-line quality monitoring. In response to the industry's need for increased efficiency, smaller and faster sensors are being developed for integration throughout production processes (Czaja & Engelsen, 2025). By enabling continuous quality checks without interrupting operation, NIR sensors help streamline decision-making and reduce reliance on manual sampling. Data generated by these sensors can be stored in cloud-based systems to support the regulation of quality standards within Industry 4.0 frameworks (Misra et al., 2022). Emerging technologies such as NIR spectroscopy and hyperspectral imaging (HSI) offer promising, cost-effective, versatile, and user-friendly solutions for quality control in smaller manufacturing operations (Crépon et al., 2023; Lukacs et al., 2025).

The food industry offers significant potential for leveraging big data solutions to optimize operations (Wójcicki, 2021). In agriculture, sensors generate large volumes of data that farmers analyze to make informed decisions (Wolfert et al., 2017). This includes data collected by NIR sensors, which provides insights into crop health, nutrient level and soil condition by non-invasive spectral analysis; drones equipped with NIR sensor further enhance this process by rapid, large-scale field assessment from the air. Integrated across the food supply chain – from farm to fork – NIR enable data supports consistent quality monitoring, helping optimize production, enhance traceability, and ensure food control.

Real-time data captured by NIR sensors can be fed directly into advanced control systems, allowing for automatic adjustments in processing parameters such as mixing, drying, or ingredient dosing. This closed-loop control enhances consistency, minimizes waste, and optimizes efficiency. Furthermore, the incorporation of industrial internet of things (IIoT) devices, cloud-based data platforms, and digital twins enables comprehensive monitoring, predictive maintenance, and remote decision-making. Ultimately, the fusion of smart data analytics with digital technologies is driving the transformation toward fully automated, connected, and intelligent food manufacturing systems (Czaja & Engelsen, 2025).

Artificial Intelligence in Food Industry

Artificial intelligence (AI) plays a crucial role in transforming the food industry by introducing automation at various stages of production, distribution, and consumption, Table 11.1. Through advanced algorithms and technologies, AI helps improve efficiency, enhance product quality, reduce waste, and meet growing consumer expectation (Ding et al., 2023). AI also supports companies in testing and monitoring food safety across the supply chain "from farm to fork" (Wójcicki et al., 2024).

Di Vaio et al. (2020) highlight AI's potential to reduce waste and improve process efficiency for more sustainable food production.

Table 11.1 Examples of AI applications that support food industry

Area	*Application of AI*	*Reference*
Raw Materials	Sorting apples based on their characteristics – enhancing efficiency while minimizing damage during sorting	(Yang et al., 2022)
	Predict risk factors associated with abundance of Vibrio parahaemolyticus in oyster farms in Taiwan	(Ndraha et al., 2021)
	Screening tool for high- and low-risk shipments	(Qian et al., 2023)
	Alert system for food fraud prediction	(Bouzembrak & Marvin, 2016)
	Evaluate fish freshness by analyzing sensory data such as color, odor, and firmness, or chemical markers like pH levels	(Zatsu et al., 2024)
Food processing/ production	Assessing food and agricultural products easier, improving food safety and quality	(Liu et al., 2025)
	Improved food productivity, quality, and nutrition while increasing safety, traceability, and resource efficiency	(Agrawal et al., 2025)
	AI applications in the food business include food chemistry and molecular analysis studies, where AI approaches acquire insights into food composition and attributes	(Tseng et al., 2023)
	Predictive analytical applications, enabling the food and beverage industry to improve operational efficiency and quality using advanced modeling techniques	(Sahni et al., 2021)
	AI has been included in intelligent production control systems, which use ML, IoT, and cloud computing to optimize food production processes	(Abdollahi et al., 2021)
	Optimizing food production systems, improving resource management, and enhancing decision-making capabilities in real-time	(Ogunleye, 2025)
	Predicting pathogen presence in agricultural water.	(Belias et al., 2021)
Packaging	AI-driven solutions can optimize packaging design to reduce environmental impact within the packaging sector	(Chaowei et al., 2023)
	The application of AI allows companies to effectively address the complexities associated with sustainable packaging, thereby enhancing its accessibility and economic viability	(Murugan & Vinu, 2024)

(*Continued*)

Table 11.1 (Continued)

Area	*Application of AI*	*Reference*
Storage, distribution and retail	Customer behavior and demands can be analyzed and identified using ML	(Thapa et al., 2023)
	AI is transforming the *retail value chain* by enhancing efficiency, reducing costs, and improving the customer experience	(Oosthuizen et al., 2020)

Source: Own work, based on Zatsu et al. (2024) and Qian et al. (2023).

In the food industry, there are several key AI technologies that have been adopted, such as: Knowledge Based Expert System (KBES), Fuzzy Logic Technique (FLT), ANN technique and ML, and Deep Learning (DL) (Zatsu et al., 2024).

KBES can be used for recommending optimal storage environments for different food items by considering their specific requirements, such as temperature and humidity (Zatsu et al., 2024). Sottocornola et al. (2023) demonstrated the potential of KBES for diagnosing post-harvest diseases of apple.

FLT has been applied in the food industry to support food modeling, process control, classification, and the resolution of various food-related challenges. It is also employed in the sensory evaluation of products such as bread and cakes, facilitating the assessment of attributes like texture, taste, and visual appeal (Mavani et al., 2022).

In the food sector, ANNs are applied to a wide range of tasks, including sample assessment and classification, performing complex computations such as heat and mass transfer, and analyzing real-time data to support the monitoring and prediction of critical outcomes. ANNs have potential for processing spectral data from NIR sensors, as they can model complex, nonlinear correlations between spectral inputs and process and food quality. Several examples of ANN applications are presented by Thapa et al. (2023).

The integration of AI and ML has the potential to revolutionize data management in the context of food safety and quality by streamlining various processes. Furthermore, ML has demonstrated effectiveness in forecasting sales trends within the food industry and in estimating the amount of food waste generated (Goel et al., 2023; Thapa et al., 2023).

Zhou et al. (2019) demonstrated the utility of DL in areas such as traceability, calorie estimation, quality assessment of fruits, vegetables, and meats, as well as in detecting fraud and contamination. DL plays a significant role in the processing of various fruits, including bananas, dates, walnuts, lemons, avocados, cherries, pears, apples, mangoes, and others. Key applications of DL in fruit processing have been outlined by Nayak et al. (2020). Furthermore, DL has also proven to be an effective tool in fish processing Rauf et al. (2019).

Integration AI with NIR

The swift progress of science and technology has had a profound impact on various aspects of the food industry through the integration of AI. From expert system to fuzzy logic systems, from Adaptive Neuro Fuzzy Interference System (ANFIS) technology to NIRS technology and the application of AI in the food industry, these innovations are bringing advancements in food production processes, quality assurance practices, and safety measures (Ding et al., 2023).

The increasing complexity and volume of spectroscopic data present significant challenges to data analysis. However, recent years have seen the emergence of AI as a transformative solution, enhancing the speed, accuracy, and efficiency of spectroscopic analysis. The majority of AI applications in the field of sensory science are centered around the creation of pattern recognition, classification and regression models through the use of product composition data (Zatsu et al., 2024). Nowadays, the fusion of AI algorithms and NIR technology has enabled effective monitoring of food quality (Ding et al., 2023; Mavani et al., 2022). For example, the NIR hyperspectral images and ML can be used for early detection of mechanical damage in mangoes (Vélez Rivera et al., 2014).

In the meat industry the incorporation of AI-based techniques with NIR spectroscopy has led to significant improvements in the accuracy and reliability of meat quality assessment, as well as authentication in the authentication of high-value products such as Spanish ham. For example, farmers can detect heat stress early, optimize feeding strategies, and maintain superior meat quality, ensuring a more efficient and sustainable livestock industry (Sarker et al., 2024).

The integration of ANN with the VIS-SWNIR (Visible Shortwave Near-Infrared) spectrometer can be used to predict soluble solid substances in pineapple (Nayak et al., 2020). Scientists used four standard datasets to process the pineapple samples. They trained the ANN with one of the four datasets, while the remaining three datasets were used for model validation. They also applied the correlation coefficient, and the performance metrics Root Mean Square Error of Calibration (RMSEC) and Root Mean Square Error of Prediction (RMSEP), claiming that the proposed method is suitable for predicting pineapple properties using VIS-SWNIR spectroscopy. Furthermore, their findings indicated that this spectroscopic technique offers a cost-effective alternative for interpolating pineapple measurements.

El-Sayed et al. (2023) presented the integration of Vis-NIR spectroscopy with AI to predict some soil parameters in South Egypt. Authors obtained a promising result which proved that such integration is faster and more cost-efficient and can be further used in environmental monitoring and precision farming.

Thapa et al. (2023) demonstrated the use of ANNs to forecast the sensory attributes of cheese using NIR data. Their findings indicate that ANNs are capable of reliably predicting sensory responses based on NIR observations.

Table 11.2 The comparison of traditional NIR and NIR with AI

Aspect	*NIR + Human*	*NIR + AI*
Data Interpretation	Relies on expert knowledge	Depends on training data
Accuracy and precision	May very with the operator	High precision only in the domain of trained data
Speed of analysis	Manual data handling	Fast, but with deeper insights and more reliable predictions
Adaptability	Limited to expert experience and training	Can adapt to new patterns and data automatically
Detection of Anomalies	Difficult with traditional chemometric models	Time-series and predictive AI models make it feasible High sensitivity, but can only detect anomalies in trained domain
Scalability	Limited scalability: each new deployment requires significant expert time	Highly scalable; once trained model can be deployed with minimal incremental cost
User-Friendliness	Requires trained analysts	AI-driven interfaces can be simplified for non-experts

Source: Own work

With an accuracy of 95%–100%, the trained ANN and NIRS technique together successfully distinguished between civet and non-civet coffee (Mavani et al., 2022).

Opportunities of Integration NIR with AI

The integration of AI into NIR has resulted in transformative advancements, enhancing data analysis and operational efficiency. A comparison of traditional NIR and NIR with AI is shown in Table 11.2.

As shown in Table 11.2, AI transforms NIR from a "basic" analytical tool into a smart, scalable, and highly efficient system for food quality and safety management.

Challenges of Integration NIR with AI

The integration of AI with NIR technique holds immense potential but also faces several significant challenges. Next are the primary obstacles encountered in this process:

1. Variability – experimental spectra may be affected by noise, baseline drift and instrument to instrument discrepancies. This leads to inconsistencies in spectral resolution and intensity (Guo et al., 2025).

2. Data quality – the raw NIR spectra often requires the mathematical pre-treatment to minimize interference and obtain good quality data (Nduwamungu et al., 2009). If the data used to train these models is biased, AI algorithms, especially those that rely on ML, can inadvertently perpetuate and amplify existing biases (Akinnagbe, 2024).
3. Integration – calibration models developed for one NIR instrument often perform poorly on others due to differences in hardware and measurement conditions. AI models must be robust to variations between different NIR instruments to ensure consistency across multiple locations. Such limitation causes that AI models trained on specific datasets might not generalize well to new samples due to variations in sample composition and instrument conditions. Additionally, model transfer between different hardware is often difficult or even impossible without extensive recalibration or adaptation (Jia et al., 2024; Li et al., 2025).
4. User adoption – the issue of user adoption is a significant barrier to the widespread implementation of AI technologies. Employees may have concerns about the possibility of job displacement due to automation, which can sometimes lead to a reluctance to adopt AI systems in the workplace (Madanchian & Taherdoost, 2025).
5. Transparency – AI models, particularly those based on DL, are often described as "black boxes" because their decision-making processes are not easily interpretable by humans. This characteristic has given rise to concerns regarding the accountability and trustworthiness of AI systems (Akinnagbe, 2024).
6. Investment costs/Investment in AI Infrastructure – developing and deploying AI-enhanced NIR solutions requires financial investment in hardware, software, and expertise. Moreover, continuous maintenance, updates, and training are necessary to ensure the AI systems function properly (Zatsu et al., 2024).

Conclusion

The integration of NIR spectroscopy with AI represents a significant leap forward in the evolution of the food industry. This synergy enables real-time, non-invasive, and highly accurate monitoring of food quality and safety, addressing many of the limitations of traditional analytical methods. AI enhances the interpretability and scalability of NIR data, transforming it into actionable insights that support automation, predictive maintenance, and intelligent decision-making. Despite challenges such as data variability, model generalization, and high initial investment, the benefits of this integration such as improved efficiency, reduced waste, and enhanced sustainability are substantial. As the food industry continues to embrace digital transformation, the adoption of AI-powered NIR systems will be crucial for achieving smarter, greener, and more resilient food production systems.

Reference List

Abdollahi, A., Rejeb, K., Rejeb, A., Mostafa, M. M., & Zailani, S. (2021). Wireless sensor networks in agriculture: Insights from bibliometric analysis. *Sustainability*, *13*(21), 12011. www.mdpi.com/2071-1050/13/21/12011

Agrawal, K., Goktas, P., Holtkemper, M., Beecks, C., & Kumar, N. (2025). AI-driven transformation in food manufacturing: A pathway to sustainable efficiency and quality assurance [Original Research]. *Frontiers in Nutrition*, *12*. https://doi.org/10.3389/fnut.2025.1553942

Akinnagbe, O. (2024). Human-AI collaboration: Enhancing productivity and decision-making. *International Journal of Education, Management, and Technology*, *2*, 387–417. https://doi.org/10.58578/ijemt.v2i3.4209

Belias, A., Brassill, N., Roof, S., Rock, C., Wiedmann, M., & Weller, D. (2021). Cross-validation indicates predictive models may provide an alternative to indicator organism monitoring for evaluating pathogen presence in southwestern US Agricultural water. *Frontiers in Water*, *3*. https://doi.org/10.3389/frwa.2021.693631

Blanchfield, J. R. (2005). Good manufacturing practice (GMP) in the food industry. This chapter copyright © Institute of Food Science & Technology. In *Handbook of hygiene control in the food industry* (pp. 324–347). https://doi.org/10.1533/9781845690533.3.324

Bouzembrak, Y., & Marvin, H. J. P. (2016). Prediction of food fraud type using data from Rapid Alert System for Food and Feed (RASFF) and Bayesian network modelling. *Food Control*, *61*, 180–187. https://doi.org/10.1016/j.foodcont.2015.09.026

Chaowei, W., Lanyu, L., & Zheng, W. (2023, October 10). Development and application of intelligent packaging design under the background of artificial intelligence. *Proceedings of the 2nd International Conference on Intelligent Design and Innovative Technology (ICIDIT 2023)* (pp. 308–318). https://doi.org/10.2991/978-94-6463-266-8_33

Crépon, K., Cabacos, M., Bonduelle, F., Ammari, F., Faure, M., & Maudemain, S. (2023). Using Internet of Things (IoT), Near-Infrared Spectroscopy (NIRS), and hyperspectral imaging (HSI) to enhance monitoring and detection of grain pests in storage and handling operators. *Agriculture*, *13*, 1355. https://doi.org/10.3390/agriculture13071355

Czaja, T. P., & Engelsen, S. B. (2025). Why nothing beats NIRS technology: The green analytical choice for the future sustainable food production. *Spectrochim Acta A Mol Biomol Spectrosc*, *325*, 125028. https://doi.org/10.1016/j.saa.2024.125028

Di Vaio, A., Boccia, F., Landriani, L., & Palladino, R. (2020). Artificial intelligence in the agri-food system: Rethinking sustainable business models in the COVID-19 scenario. *Sustainability*, *12*(12), 4851. www.mdpi.com/2071-1050/12/12/4851

Ding, H., Tian, J., Yu, W., Wilson, D. I., Young, B. R., Cui, X., Xin, X., Wang, Z., & Li, W. (2023). The application of artificial intelligence and big data in the food industry. *Foods*, *12*(24). https://doi.org/10.3390/foods12244511

El-Sayed, M. A., Abd-Elazem, A. H., Moursy, A. R. A., Mohamed, E. S., Kucher, D. E., & Fadl, M. E. (2023). Integration vis-NIR spectroscopy and artificial intelligence to predict some soil parameters in arid region: A case study of Wadi Elkobaneyya, South Egypt. *Agronomy*, *13*(3), 935. www.mdpi.com/2073-4395/13/3/935

FAO. (2021). *The state of food and agriculture 2021*. https://doi.org/10.4060/cb4476en

Goel, A., Goel, A. K., & Kumar, A. (2023). The role of artificial neural network and machine learning in utilizing spatial information. *Spatial Information Research*, *31*(3), 275–285. https://doi.org/10.1007/s41324-022-00494-x

Guine, R. P. F., Florenca, S. G., Barroca, M. J., & Anjos, O. (2020). The link between the consumer and the innovations in food product development. In *Foods* (20200918 ed., Vol. 9). https://doi.org/10.3390/foods9091317

Guo, K., Shen, Y., Gonzalez-Montiel, G., Huang, Y., Zhou, Y., Surve, M., Guo, Z., Das, P., Chawla, N., Wiest, O., & Zhang, X. (2025). *Artificial intelligence in spectroscopy: Advancing chemistry from prediction to generation and beyond.* https://doi.org/10.48550/arXiv.2502.09897

Hassoun, A., Aït-Kaddour, A., Abu-Mahfouz, A. M., Rathod, N. B., Bader, F., Barba, F. J., Biancolillo, A., Cropotova, J., Galanakis, C. M., Jambrak, A. R., Lorenzo, J. M., Måge, I., Ozogul, F., & Regenstein, J. (2022). The fourth industrial revolution in the food industry – Part I: Industry 4.0 technologies. *Critical Reviews in Food Science and Nutrition*, 1–17. https://doi.org/10.1080/10408398.2022.2034735

Hassoun, A., Jagtap, S., Garcia-Garcia, G., Trollman, H., Pateiro, M., Lorenzo, J. M., Trif, M., Rusu, A. V., Aadil, R. M., Šimat, V., Cropotova, J., & Câmara, J. S. (2023). Food quality 4.0: From traditional approaches to digitalized automated analysis. *Journal of Food Engineering*, *337*, 111216. https://doi.org/https://doi.org/10.1016/j.jfoodeng.2022.111216

Jia, W., Georgouli, K., Martinez-Del Rincon, J., & Koidis, A. (2024). Challenges in the use of AI-driven non-destructive spectroscopic tools for rapid food analysis. *Foods*, *13*(6), 846. www.mdpi.com/2304-8158/13/6/846

Li, D., Quansheng, C., Qin, O., & and Liu, Z. (2025). Advances of Vis/NIRS and imaging techniques assisted by AI for tea processing. *Critical Reviews in Food Science and Nutrition*, 1–19. https://doi.org/10.1080/10408398.2025.2474183

Liu, L., Wang, B., Xu, X., & Xu, J. (2025). A tea classification method based on near infrared spectroscopy (NIRS) and transfer learning. *Infrared Physics & Technology*, *145*, 105713. https://doi.org/https://doi.org/10.1016/j.infrared.2025.105713

Lukacs, M., Toth, F., Horvath, R., Solymos, G., Alpar, B., Varga, P., Kertész, I., Gillay, Z., Baranyai, L., Felfoldi, J., Nguyen, Q., Kovacs, Z., & Friedrich, L. (2025). Advanced digital solutions for food traceability: Enhancing origin, quality, and safety through NIRS, RFID, Blockchain, and IoT. *Journal of Sensor and Actuator Networks*, *14*, 21. https://doi.org/10.3390/jsan14010021

Madanchian, M., & Taherdoost, H. (2025). Barriers and enablers of AI adoption in human resource management: A critical analysis of organizational and technological factors. *Information*, *16*(1), 51. www.mdpi.com/2078-2489/16/1/51

Mavani, N., Mohd Ali, J., Othman, S., Hussain, M., Hashim, H., & Abd.Rahman, N. (2022). Application of artificial intelligence in food industry – A guideline. *Food Engineering Reviews*, *14*. https://doi.org/10.1007/s12393-021-09290-z

Meher, A. K., & Zarouri, A. (2025). Green analytical chemistry – Recent innovations. *Analytica*, *6*(1). https://doi.org/10.3390/analytica6010010

Misra, N. N., Dixit, Y., Al-Mallahi, A., Bhullar, M. S., Upadhyay, R., & Martynenko, A. (2022). IoT, big data, and artificial intelligence in agriculture and food industry. *IEEE Internet of Things Journal*, *9*(9), 6305–6324. https://doi.org/10.1109/JIOT.2020.2998584

Murugan, S., & Vinu, V. (2024). AI's role in sustainable packaging: An evolutionary journey from past innovation to future trends. *Proceedings of Tech diplomacy 2.0 India's global strategic alliance in the digital decade*, Bangalore.

Nayak, J., Vakula, K., Dinesh, P., Naik, B., & Pelusi, D. (2020). Intelligent food processing: Journey from artificial neural network to deep learning. *Computer Science Review*, *38*, 100297. https://doi.org/https://doi.org/10.1016/j.cosrev.2020.100297

Ndraha, N., Hsiao, H.-I., Hsieh, Y.-Z., & Pradhan, A. (2021). Predictive models for the effect of environmental factors on the abundance of Vibrio parahaemolyticus in oyster farms in Taiwan using extreme gradient boosting. *Food Control*, *130*, 108353. https://doi.org/10.1016/j.foodcont.2021.108353

Nduwamungu, C., Ziadi, N., Parent, L.-É., Tremblay, G. F., & Thuriès, L. (2009). Opportunities for, and limitations of, near infrared reflectance spectroscopy applications in soil analysis: A review. *Canadian Journal of Soil Science*, *89*(5), 531–541. https://doi.org/10.4141/cjss08076

Ogunleye, O. (2025). Artificial intelligence in smart agriculture: AI applications in optimizing food production, precision farming, and crop management. *Proceedings of third international conference on information systems and emerging technologies (ICISET)*, Johannesburg, South Africa.

Oosthuizen, K., Botha, E., Robertson, J., & Montecchi, M. (2020). Artificial intelligence in retail: The AI-enabled value chain. *Australasian Marketing Journal (AMJ)*, *29*. https://doi.org/10.1016/j.ausmj.2020.07.007

Ozaki, Y., Huck, C., Tsuchikawa, S., & Engelsen, S. B. (2021). *Near-infrared spectroscopy*. https://doi.org/10.1007/978-981-15-8648-4

Plotka-Wasylka, J. (2018). A new tool for the evaluation of the analytical procedure: Green Analytical Procedure Index. *Talanta*, *181*, 204–209. https://doi.org/10.1016/j.talanta.2018.01.013

Qian, C., Murphy, S. I., Orsi, R. H., & Wiedmann, M. (2023). How can AI help improve food safety? *Annual Review of Food Science and Technology*, *14*, 517–538. https://doi.org/https://doi.org/10.1146/annurev-food-060721-013815

Qu, B., Xiao, Z., Upadhyay, A., & Luo, Y. (2024). Perspectives on sustainable food production system: Characteristics and green technologies. *Journal of Agriculture and Food Research*, *15*. https://doi.org/10.1016/j.jafr.2024.100988

Rauf, H. T., Lali, M. I. U., Zahoor, S., Shah, S. Z. H., Rehman, A. U., & Bukhari, S. A. C. (2019). Visual features based automated identification of fish species using deep convolutional neural networks. *Computers and Electronics in Agriculture*, *167*, 105075. https://doi.org/https://doi.org/10.1016/j.compag.2019.105075

Sahni, V., Srivastava, S., & Khan, R. (2021). Modelling techniques to improve the quality of food using artificial intelligence. *Journal of Food Quality*, *2021*(1), 2140010. https://doi.org/https://doi.org/10.1155/2021/2140010

Sarker, T., Al Deen, R., Ghosh, D., Mia, N., Rahman, M., & Hashem, M. A. (2024). AI driven approach and NIRS: A review on meat quality and safety. *Meat Research*, *4*. https://doi.org/10.55002/mr.4.6.105

Sørensen, K. M., Khakimov, B., & Engelsen, S. B. (2016). The use of rapid spectroscopic screening methods to detect adulteration of food raw materials and ingredients. *Current Opinion in Food Science*, *10*, 45–51. https://doi.org/10.1016/j.cofs.2016.08.001

Sørensen, K. M., van den Berg, F., & Engelsen, S. B. (2021). NIR data exploration and regression by chemometrics: A primer. In Y. Ozaki, C. Huck, S. Tsuchikawa, & S. B. Engelsen (Eds.), *Near-infrared spectroscopy: Theory, spectral analysis, instrumentation, and applications* (pp. 127–189). Springer Singapore. https://doi.org/10.1007/978-981-15-8648-4_7

Sottocornola, G., Baric, S., Stella, F., & Zanker, M. (2023). Development of a knowledge-based expert system for diagnosing post-harvest diseases of apple. *Agriculture*, *13*(1), 177. www.mdpi.com/2077-0472/13/1/177

Thapa, A., Nishad, S., Biswas, D., & Roy, S. (2023). A comprehensive review on artificial intelligence assisted technologies in food industry. *Food Bioscience*, *56*, 103231. https://doi.org/https://doi.org/10.1016/j.fbio.2023.103231

Tseng, Y., Chuang, P.-J., & Appell, M. (2023). When machine learning and deep learning come to the big data in food chemistry. *ACS Omega*, *8*. https://doi.org/10.1021/acsomega.2c07722

van den Berg, F., Lyndgaard, C. B., Sørensen, K. M., & Engelsen, S. B. (2013). Process analytical technology in the food industry. *Trends in Food Science & Technology*, *31*(1), 27–35. https://doi.org/10.1016/j.tifs.2012.04.007

Vélez Rivera, N., Gómez-Sanchis, J., Chanona-Pérez, J., Carrasco, J. J., Millán-Giraldo, M., Lorente, D., Cubero, S., & Blasco, J. (2014). Early detection of mechanical damage in mango using NIR hyperspectral images and machine learning. *Biosystems Engineering*, *122*, 91–98. https://doi.org/https://doi.org/10.1016/j.biosystemseng.2014.03.009

Wolfert, S., Ge, L., Verdouw, C., & Bogaardt, M.-J. (2017). Big data in smart farming: A review. *Agricultural Systems*, *153*, 69–80. https://doi.org/https://doi.org/10.1016/j.agsy.2017.01.023

Wójcicki, K. (2021). How big data is changing the food industry: The real examples. In Ś. Hanna (Ed.), *Current trends in quality science: Consumer behavior, logistic, product management* (pp. 367–375). Publishing House of Poznań University of Economics and Business.

Wójcicki, K., Górna, J., & Sikorska, E. (2024). Digitalisation in agri-food sector. In. https://doi.org/10.18559/978-83-8211-209-2/3

Yang, M., Kumar, P., Bhola, J., & Shabaz, M. (2022). Development of image recognition software based on artificial intelligence algorithm for the efficient sorting of apple fruit. *International Journal of System Assurance Engineering and Management*, *13*(1), 322–330. https://doi.org/10.1007/s13198-021-01415-1

Zatsu, V., Shine, A. E., Tharakan, J. M., Peter, D., Ranganathan, T. V., Alotaibi, S. S., Mugabi, R., Muhsinah, A. B., Waseem, M., & Nayik, G. A. (2024). Revolutionizing the food industry: The transformative power of artificial intelligence-a review. *Food Chemistry: X*, *24*, 101867. https://doi.org/https://doi.org/10.1016/j.fochx.2024.101867

Zhou, L., Zhang, C., Liu, F., Qiu, Z., & He, Y. (2019). Application of deep learning in food: A review. *Comprehensive Reviews in Food Science and Food Safety*, *18*(6), 1793–1811. https://doi.org/https://doi.org/10.1111/1541-4337.12492

Part IV
Supply Chains

12 Enhancing Machine Learning Interpretability for Supply Chain Risk Management

An LLM-Powered Approach

Mateusz Wyrembek and George Baryannis

Introduction

Recent advances and successes of artificial intelligence (AI), especially in applications of data-driven methodologies such as machine learning (ML), has led a significant number of supply chain researchers and practitioners to explore AI applications to address long-standing issues such as demand forecasting, inventory management, supplier selection, performance evaluation, and supply chain risk management (SCRM) (Abdulla & Baryannis, 2024). This exploration has delivered advances toward achieving resilience and sustainability but has introduced new challenges related to the explainability and interpretability of AI-supported solutions. Data-driven AI approaches are commonly "black-box," in contrast to earlier knowledge-based and rule-based approaches that are inherently explainable (Baryannis et al., 2016). This lack of explainability and interpretability is especially problematic in the context of SCRM, as it limits applicability and integration of AI outputs and decisions in planning processes, given that these depend on stakeholders understanding the reasoning behind these decisions. One promising approach to address this challenge is to leverage AI itself to understand its outputs; in particular, to use large language models (LLMs) to generate interpretations of ML model outputs.

Researchers have already explored the use of LLMs in the context of model interpretation. Significant amount of work has gone into so-called self-rationalizing models (Marasović et al., 2022) which can generate free-text explanations alongside model outputs. This has led to capabilities such as chain-of-thought prompting and reasoning available in more recent versions of LLM-powered chatbots. Self-rationalization has been shown to improve model interpretation but, in some cases, against the trade-off of reduced robustness to spurious correlations (Ross et al., 2022). It has also been proven beneficial to imbue chain-of-thought capabilities to smaller language models that are learnt from larger ones (Wang et al., 2023). Researchers have also attempted to generalize chain-of-thought structures to overcome limitations of restricting to token-level left-to-right inference, suggesting

DOI: 10.4324/9781003659143-16

the use of tree or graph structures, yielding so-called Tree of Thoughts (Yao et al., 2023) and Graph of Thoughts (Besta et al., 2024) approaches.

The common characteristic of the aforementioned approaches is that they have primarily been developed for the purpose of interpreting LLM outputs, rather than any ML model output. While it can be argued that these approaches can be transferable and/or generalizable to any ML model, this has not yet been established. Employing LLMs to interpret outputs of any ML model, that is, delivering what is increasingly being referred to as "conversational XAI" (Garofalo et al., 2025), has received comparatively less attention, with XAgent (Nguyen et al., 2023) and TalkToModel (Slack et al., 2023) being notable outcomes. Both tools combine a conversational interface with a component that can produce natural language explanations based on outputs from feature importance-based systems such as LIME and SHAP, as well as counterfactual explanations, and feature interaction effects in the case of TalkToModel. While XAgent has not been applied in a specific case study, TalkToModel's capabilities have been demonstrated in relation to disease prediction models. XAIstories (Martens et al., 2025) follows a similar approach but emphasizes more strongly the narrative nature of the generated output. Other approaches and tools that offer similar capabilities include ConvXAI (Malandri et al., 2023), Doctor XAI (Panigutti et al., 2023) and dr_ant (Kuźba & Biecek, 2020).

In this chapter, we explore conversational XAI in the supply chain domain, specifically in the context of SCRM and delay prediction. Similarly to the healthcare domain, supply chains also involve stakeholders with a range of technology knowledge and awareness, including many that are completely non-technical. Understanding ML model outputs is equally paramount, as wrong decisions may have significant operational and financial impact, especially in the case of global supply chains. In contrast to healthcare, the supply chain domain requires a more dynamic approach to explainability, emphasizing real-time adaptability and decision-making transparency. In this context, the contribution of this chapter is an illustration of how conversational XAI can be applied for the particular case of interpreting outputs of delay prediction ML models in order to facilitate understanding and adoption in the case of non-technical supply chain stakeholders.

Illustrative Application of Conversational XAI in SCRM: From a Non-technical Stakeholder Perspective

Delay prediction in SCRM is commonly framed as a classification problem, predicting whether a delay will occur, or as a regression problem, estimating how long the delay might last. As this research area has gained traction, various studies have applied classification (Bassiouni et al., 2024; Mendonça et al., 2024; Zheng et al., 2025) and regression (Camur et al., 2024; Mallidis et al., 2024; Rokoss et al., 2024) models across different domains of the supply chain. While these methodological advances offer significant potential, practitioners frequently express concerns over the "black box" nature of ML models, particularly given the need for accountability in decision-making processes. In response, researchers advocated for the use of interpretable ML approaches, including decision trees (Baryannis et al., 2019), multi-criteria decision-making (Wyrembek & Baryannis, 2024), neurosymbolic AI (Kosasih et al., 2024), and causal machine learning (Wyrembek et al., 2025).

In the remainder of this chapter, we offer an alternative perspective on this challenge by examining two developmental approaches. The first one is predictive modeling, which involves using historical data to predict whether delivery will be on-time or not. The second, less explored, pathway involves the integration of conversational XAI, which aims to enhance supply chain stakeholder understanding of model outputs in an intuitive manner without requiring technical knowledge. This integration not only seeks to support proactive risk mitigation but also enhances transparency and practitioner trust. The problem setting that forms the basis for exploring this complementary approach is described next.

For the case study, we use the publicly available supply chain dataset from Constante et al. (2019), which contains 166,819 orders spanning multiple product categories, including clothing, sports, and electronic parts data from an e-commerce company called DataCo. As every company is interested in minimizing operational risk such as delivery delay to maintain a competitive advantage, the e-commerce supply chain is a strongly relevant example. Its complexity and the high volume of transactions make it an ideal setting for studying such issues, as delays can easily occur and accumulate across multiple stages such as order processing, inventory management and last-mile delivery (Vrhovac et al., 2023). Moreover, due to high customer expectation for timely updates and fast delivery, even minor disruptions can significantly affect customer satisfaction, loyalty, and operational efficiency (Kawa & Zdrenka, 2024).

The dataset contains heterogenous non-IID data (non-identically and independently distributed) which can introduce bias. As with every real-world dataset, it is also affected by data quality issues such as inconsistencies, incomplete fields, duplicates, and outliers. Instead of imputing missing or inconsistent data, we opt for excluding such rows and columns from the dataset entirely. We also discard any duplicate entries that represent the same observations and remove outliers to maintain data quality and reliability. For data transformation, we apply one-hot encoding, a standard method that converts categorical variables into a set of binary features representing the presence or absence of each category (Qiu et al., 2022). Although this approach can lead to high dimensionality, particularly when features have many unique categories as in our case, we choose it for its interpretability and its suitability for further explanation efforts for ML models.

As with any ML process, selecting appropriate features is essential for training a model. This step is crucial, as poor feature selection can negatively affect model performance and introduce bias. Our dataset includes 53 features, from which we focused on those related to delivery performance and product characteristics. We excluded any feature that could lead to data leakage, which refers to the unintended use of information that would not be available at the time of prediction and could give the model an unfair advantage. Ultimately, we selected eight features, which are listed and described in Table 12.1.

A classifier also requires a target variable, which is the outcome the model is trained to predict. In our case, we use a binary variable called Late_delivery_risk where a value of 1 indicates a late delivery and 0 indicates an on-time delivery. This feature shows a slight imbalance, with 43% orders delivered on-time and 57% delayed. However, this moderate imbalance is not expected to significantly impact model performance. Note that the relatively high proportion of delayed deliveries can be attributed to complex network and diverse distribution channels of DataCo.

Next, we split the dataset into training and testing sets using a 70:30 ratio. This split allows the model to learn from the majority of the data while preserving a sufficient portion for unbiased evaluation of its performance. We also applied the MinMaxScaler to normalize the numerical features. This technique scales all feature values to a fixed range, typically between 0 and 1, which ensures that features with larger scales do not dominate the learning process and helps improve the convergence and stability of many ML algorithms (de Amorim et al., 2023).

Following the approach of Baryannis et al. (2019), we selected the decision tree classifier, as it offers a trade-off between performance and interpretability. This classifier is based on a directed acyclic graph and learns by recursively splitting the data into subsets based on feature values that best

Table 12.1 The description of selected features

No.	*Feature name*	*Description*
1	Type	Type of transaction mode (e.g. debit, transfer, payment and cash).
2	Customer City	City where the customer made the purchase.
3	Market	Market to where the order is delivered: Africa, Europe, LATAM, Pacific Asia, USCA.
4	Order City	Destination city of the order.
5	Product Price	Product price.
6	Shipping Mode	Types of shipping (e.g. standard class, first class, second class and same day).
7	Customer Segment	Types of customers: Consumer, Corporate, Home Office.
8	Customer Id	Specific ID of the customer.

Source: Authors' own work.

separate the target classes (Breiman et al., 1984). This model is also easy to understand for non-technical experts, either through its graphical tree structure or as a set of interpretable IF-THEN rules derived from it. Note, however, that other algorithms used for classification or regression could also be suitable depending on the specific trade-offs considered in any given application.

For the training process we limit the maximum depth of tree to 3 to preserve the interpretability of the resulting model. All other parameters were kept at their default settings. We evaluate the trained model using commonly used classification metrics such as accuracy, precision, recall, and F1-score. These metrics are calculated based on a confusion matrix, which compares predicted and actual class labels (Ting, 2011). This means that it compares model predictions to the actual outcomes for delayed and on-time deliveries. Each metric provides particular insights into the model's ability to predict delivery delays (Baryannis et al., 2019; Brintrup et al., 2019):

- **Accuracy** – represents the proportion of all delivery predictions (late or on-time) that were correct. It reflects the overall correctness of the model in making accurate predictions.
- **Precision** – measures the proportion of correctly predicted delays among all deliveries predicted as delay. It reflects how reliable the model is when it predicts a delay.
- **Recall** – indicates the proportion of actual predicted delays that were correctly identified. It reflects the model's ability to detect true delays.
- **F1-score** – is the harmonic mean of precision and recall offering a balance measure that accounts for both false positives and false negatives in delay prediction.

The results of these evaluations are as follows: accuracy was 69%, precision was 85%, recall was 54%, and the F1-score was 66%.

We then visualize the decision tree model to better understand how it makes its predictions. We also export the tree structure in textual form to support interpretation by LLMs. Note that LLMs can analyze decision tree visualizations directly using computer vision techniques, however we opt for extracting decision rules as text as it provides a clearer and more structured representation for conversational XAI models, which should lead to more accurate outputs. The graphical visualization of the decision tree is presented in Figure 12.1, while the textual representation of the tree structure is shown in Figure 12.2.

After training, evaluating, and visualizing the decision tree model, we proceed to apply conversational XAI. In our approach, we select OpenAI's 4o-mini model. This LLM is a compact model that is known for its strong performance in natural language understanding and interactive tasks. The system instructions used to guide the model's behavior are provided in Box 12.1.

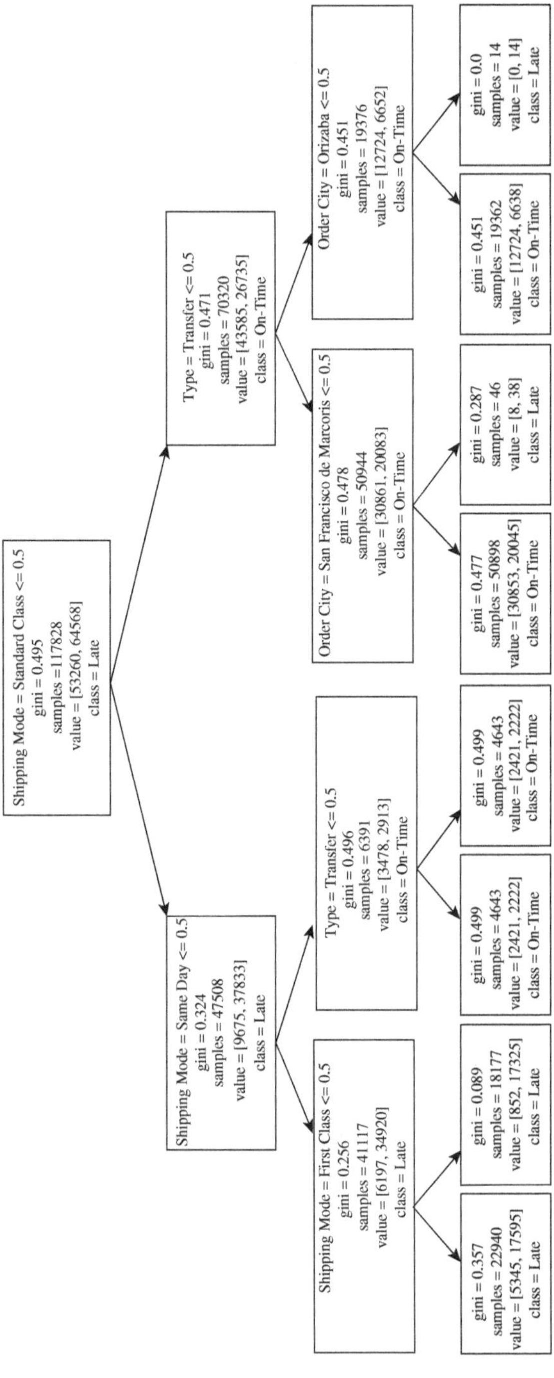

Figure 12.1 Graphical visualization of the decision tree.

Source: Own work.

```
|--- Shipping Mode = Standard Class <= 0.50
|   |--- Shipping Mode = Same Day <= 0.50
|   |   |--- Shipping Mode = First Class <= 0.50
|   |   |   |--- class: Late
|   |   |--- Shipping Mode = First Class >  0.50
|   |   |   |--- class: Late
|   |--- Shipping Mode = Same Day >  0.50
|   |   |--- Type = TRANSFER <= 0.50
|   |   |   |--- class: On-Time
|   |   |--- Type = TRANSFER >  0.50
|   |   |   |--- class: On-Time
|--- Shipping Mode = Standard Class >  0.50
|   |--- Type = TRANSFER <= 0.50
|   |   |--- Order City = San Francisco de Macorís <= 0.50
|   |   |   |--- class: On-Time
|   |   |--- Order City = San Francisco de Macorís >  0.50
|   |   |   |--- class: Late
|   |--- Type = TRANSFER >  0.50
|   |   |--- Order City = Orizaba <= 0.50
|   |   |   |--- class: On-Time
|   |   |--- Order City = Orizaba >  0.50
|   |   |   |--- class: Late
```

Figure 12.2 Textual representation of the tree structure.
Source: Own work.

Box 12.1. System Instructions for GPT 4o-mini Model

You are an AI expert specializing in supply chain management with expertise in machine learning methods. Focus on delivery delays. Your task is to explain the results of a decision tree model (accuracy, precision, recall, F1 score) in simple terms, tailored for non-technical managers. Use accessible language and focus on the practical implications of the metrics. Additionally, interpret the visual representation of a decision tree, highlighting key decision points and their relevance to supply chain operations. Base your response on this exemplary interpretation style: {example}.

Do not use bullet points.

As an example for a model, we followed interpretation approaches inspired by Baryannis et al. (2019) and Wyrembek and Baryannis (2024). Then, we pass to LLM all relevant information including feature descriptions, the textual form of the tree, and model metrics. The temperature of the model was set to 0.5 to ensure that model will follow to the instruction while still allowing some level of creativity. An output generated by the LLM is shown in Box 12.2.

Box 12.2. Output of GPT 4o-mini

The decision tree classifier results show that the model has an accuracy of approximately 70%. This means the model correctly predicted whether a delivery was late or on-time about 70 out of 100 times. While this is a respectable figure, there's still room for improvement, particularly in how well it understands the factors leading to delivery delays. The precision score is quite high at about 85%. This tells us that when the model predicts a delivery will be late, it is correct about 85% of the time. In practical terms, this implies that most of the deliveries flagged as "late" by the model truly are delayed, which is good for planning and resource allocation. However, it also indicates that there could be some instances where the model incorrectly predicts delays, leading to unnecessary operational adjustments. On the other hand, the recall score is lower, at around 54%. Recall measures the model's ability to catch all the real delays. In this case, the model only identifies about half of all the actual late deliveries. This is critical as it suggests there could be significant gaps in anticipating delays, which could result in missed opportunities for proactive measures to address customer dissatisfaction and manage logistics more effectively. The F1 score, which balances precision and recall, stands at approximately 0.66. This score reflects the trade-off between the model's ability to make accurate predictions while also being sensitive enough to catch a larger portion of actual delays. A score of 0.66 indicates that while the model is reasonably effective, improvements could still be made to capture more delays without generating excessive false positives. Looking at the visual representation of the decision tree, we see key decision points that influence the model's predictions. The first major decision is based on the shipping mode. If a package is shipped using "Standard Class," the tree navigates through various conditions to assess whether it will arrive late or on time. For instance, if the shipping mode is "Same Day," the delivery is further classified based on the type of transaction. This highlights how shipping methods significantly affect the timeliness of deliveries. As we delve deeper into the branches of the tree, we recognize that specific factors, such as the order city, play a crucial role. For example, when the order city is "San Francisco de Macorís," the model predicts on-time delivery under certain conditions, while for other cities, the prediction may shift to late. These nuances underscore the practical implications for supply chain managers, emphasizing the necessity to consider various operational elements carefully. In summary, while the decision tree offers valuable insight into how various factors contribute to delivery performance, it underlines the importance of refining the model to minimize missed delays and improve overall service levels in the supply chain. By focusing on the areas highlighted by the decision tree, managers can make more informed decisions to enhance delivery reliability.

To validate our approach, we use another LLM, Grok-2 with the system instructions detailed in Box 12.3.

Box 12.3. System Instruction for Grok-2

You are an AI expert specializing in supply chain management with expertise in machine learning methods. Focus on delivery delays. Your primary task is to validate the GPT-generated interpretations against the decision tree visualization and model results. Provide a validation with accessible and clear language for supply chain managers.

In this case, we provided the same input information as before, but additionally we included the output generated by the first LLM. The results of validation by Grok-2 are presented in Box 12.4.

Box 12.4. Output of Grok-2

To validate the GPT-generated interpretations against the decision tree image and CSV results, I will review each aspect of the analysis provided and ensure it aligns with the data and decision tree structure.

****CSV Results Validation:****

1. ***Accuracy (0.69):***

- *The GPT interpretation states that the model correctly predicted delivery status about 70% of the time. This matches the accuracy value from the CSV, which is indeed 0.69 or approximately 70%. This is a valid interpretation.*

2. ***Precision (0.85):***

- *The GPT interpretation notes that when the model predicts a delivery will be late, it is correct about 85% of the time. This aligns with the precision score of 0.85 or approximately 85%. The interpretation correctly highlights the model's strength in identifying true late deliveries, but also acknowledges potential false positives.*

3. ***Recall (0.54):***

- *The GPT interpretation indicates that the model identifies about half of all actual late deliveries, which aligns with the recall score of 0.54 or approximately 54%. This is an accurate interpretation, emphasizing the model's weakness in capturing all late deliveries.*

4. ****F1 Score (0.66):*****

- *The GPT interpretation states that the F1 score is approximately 0.66, which matches the CSV value of 0.66. The interpretation correctly describes this score as a balance between precision and recall, indicating room for improvement in capturing more delays without excessive false positives.*

Decision Tree Validation:

1. ****Key Decision Points:*****

- *The GPT interpretation mentions that the first major decision is based on the shipping mode, which is correct as seen in the decision tree structure. The tree starts with "Shipping Mode = Standard Class" and branches out accordingly.*

2. ****Shipping Mode Impact:*****

- *The interpretation correctly notes that different shipping modes like "Standard Class," "Same Day," and "First Class" lead to different predictions. For example, "Same Day" shipping leads to further classification based on the type of transaction (TRANSFER), which aligns with the decision tree.*

3. ****Order City Influence:*****

- *The GPT interpretation mentions that the order city plays a crucial role, which is validated by the decision tree. For instance, when the order city is "San Francisco de Macorís," the model predicts on-time delivery under certain conditions, while for other cities like "Orizaba," it predicts late delivery. This matches the decision tree's branches.*

Practical Implications for Supply Chain Managers:

- *The GPT interpretation emphasizes the importance of refining the model to minimize missed delays, which is supported by the lower recall score. Supply chain managers should focus on improving the model's ability to predict all late deliveries more accurately.*
- *The decision tree highlights specific factors like shipping mode and order city, which supply chain managers can use to tailor their strategies. For example, prioritizing faster shipping modes for certain cities could improve delivery reliability.*

- *The interpretation also suggests that managers can make more informed decisions by understanding how different factors contribute to delivery performance, which is a practical takeaway from the decision tree analysis.*

Conclusion:

The GPT-generated interpretations accurately reflect the CSV results and decision tree structure. The analysis provides clear insights into the model's performance and practical implications for supply chain management. Supply chain managers can use this information to enhance delivery reliability by focusing on the areas identified in the decision tree and working to improve the model's recall and overall accuracy.

Discussion and Conclusion

This chapter demonstrated how conversational XAI can serve as a bridge between ML model outputs and non-technical decision-makers in the context of SCRM. By focusing on delivery delay prediction, we illustrated how a relatively interpretable model like a decision tree can be further enhanced through integration with a LLM to deliver natural language explanations tailored to managerial needs. The use of OpenAI's 4o-mini model enabled the transformation of raw evaluation metrics and decision tree logic into human-readable interpretations, while a second LLM (Grok-2) was used to validate the generated explanations. The validation showed strong alignment between the LLM's output and the model's actual structure and performance, providing evidence for the reliability of our approach.

A key insight from our findings is that even when using an inherently interpretable ML model such as a decision tree, LLMs can substantially improve comprehension and communication of model behavior. This is especially valuable in complex, high-stakes domains like supply chain management, where operational decisions must often be made by individuals without technical training. For instance, precision and recall are well-understood in ML literature, but their implications in a supply chain context, such as over-preparing for predicted delays or missing critical ones, are rarely conveyed effectively. Our approach allows these implications to be articulated clearly, including insights derived from decision paths (e.g., the influence of shipping mode and order city) that might otherwise be overlooked in static visualizations. By structuring the prompt and input data carefully, we ensured the LLM-generated interpretations were both accurate and actionable.

This work opens several promising directions for future research. First, while our approach was demonstrated using decision trees, it could be extended to any model by combining LLMs with explanation techniques such as SHAP, LIME, or counterfactual reasoning. Second, integrating real-time or interactive conversational interfaces could further enhance usability, especially in operational dashboards or digital twins. Finally, future work could investigate the use of Mixture-of-Agents framework, which is an ensemble methodology designed to enhance the performance of LLMs through structured collaboration among multiple LLMs. In addition, to further facilitate integration and adoption, it is worth exploring delivery mechanisms for the provided interpretations and explanations, such as in the form of an agent-based or service-based application (Baryannis et al., 2017; Baryannis & Plexousakis, 2014).

Overall, our results suggest that conversational XAI has significant potential to enhance transparency, trust, and operational decision-making in supply chain contexts.

Reference List

Abdulla, A., & Baryannis, G. (2024). A hybrid multi-criteria decision-making and machine learning approach for explainable supplier selection. *Supply Chain Analytics*, *7*, 100074. https://doi.org/10.1016/j.sca.2024.100074

Baryannis, G., Dani, S., & Antoniou, G. (2019). Predicting supply chain risks using machine learning: The trade-off between performance and interpretability. *Future Generation Computer Systems*, *101*, 993–1004. https://doi.org/10.1016/j.future.2019.07.059

Baryannis, G., Kritikos, K., & Plexousakis, D. (2017). A specification-based QoS-aware design framework for service-based applications. *Service Oriented Computing and Applications, 11*(3), 301–314. https://doi.org/10.1007/s11761-017-0210-4

Baryannis, G., & Plexousakis, D. (2014). Fluent calculus-based semantic web service composition and verification using WSSL. In A. R. Lomuscio, S. Nepal, F. Patrizi, B. Benatallah, & I. Brandić (Eds.), *Service-oriented computing – ICSOC 2013 workshops* (Lecture notes in computer science, Vol. 8377, pp. 262–273). Springer. https://doi.org/10.1007/978-3-319-06859-6_23

Baryannis, G., Woznowski, P., & Antoniou, G. (2016). Rule-based real-time ADL recognition in a smart home environment. In J. Alferes, L. Bertossi, G. Governatori, P. Fodor, & D. Roman (Eds.), *Rule technologies. Research, tools, and applications. RuleML 2016* (Lecture notes in computer science, Vol. 9718, pp. 275–289). Springer. https://doi.org/10.1007/978-3-319-42019-6_21

Bassiouni, M. M., Chakrabortty, R. K., Sallam, K. M., & Hussain, O. K. (2024). Deep learning approaches to identify order status in a complex supply chain. *Expert Systems with Applications*, *250*, 123947. https//doi.org/10.1016/j.eswa.2024.123947

Besta, M., Blach, N., Kubicek, A., Gerstenberger, R., Podstawski, M., Gianinazzi, L., Gajda, J., Lehmann, T., Niewiadomski, H., Nyczyk, P., & Hoefler, T. (2024). Graph of thoughts: Solving elaborate problems with large language models. *Proceedings of the AAAI Conference on Artificial Intelligence*, *38*(16), 17682–17690. https://doi.org/10.1609/aaai.v38i16.29720

Breiman, L., Friedman, J., Olshen, R. A., & Stone, C. J. (1984). *Classification and regression trees* (1st ed.). Chapman and Hall/CRC. https://doi.org/10.1201/9781315139470

Brintrup, A., Pak, J., Ratiney, D., Pearce, T., Wichmann, P., Woodall, P., & McFarlane, D. (2019). Supply chain data analytics for predicting supplier disruptions: A case study in complex asset manufacturing. *International Journal of Production Research*. https://doi.org/10.1080/00207543.2019.1685705

Camur, M. C., Ravi, S. K., & Saleh, S. (2024). Enhancing supply chain resilience: A machine learning approach for predicting product availability dates under disruption. *Expert Systems with Applications*, *247*, 123226. https://doi.org/10.1016/j.eswa.2024.123226

Constante, F., Silva, F., & Pereira, A. (2019). *DataCo smart supply chain for big data analysis* (Version 5). Mendeley data. https://doi.org/10.17632/8gx2fvg2k6.5

de Amorim, L. B. V., Cavalcanti, G. D. C., & Cruz, R. M. O. (2023). The choice of scaling technique matters for classification performance. *Applied Soft Computing*, *133*, 109924. https://doi.org/10.1016/j.asoc.2022.109924

Garofalo, M., Fantini, A., Pellugrini, R., Pilato, G., Villari, M., & Giannotti, F. (2025). Conversational XAI: Formalizing its basic design principles. In *Machine learning and principles and practice of knowledge discovery in databases. ECML PKDD 2023* (pp. 295–309). Springer. https://doi.org/10.1007/978-3-031-74627-7_22

Kawa, A., & Zdrenka, W. (2024). Logistics value in e-commerce and its impact on customer satisfaction, loyalty, and online retailers' performance. *The International Journal of Logistics Management*, *35*(2), 577–600. https://doi.org/10.1108/IJLM-02-2023-0078

Kosasih, E. E., Papadakis, E., Baryannis, G., & Brintrup, A. (2024). A review of explainable artificial intelligence in supply chain management using neurosymbolic approaches. *International Journal of Production Research*, *62*(4), 1510–1540. https://doi.org/10.1080/00207543.2023.2281663

Kuźba, M., & Biecek, P. (2020). What would you ask the machine learning model? Identification of user needs for model explanations based on human-model conversations. In I. Koprinska et al. (Eds.), *ECML PKDD 2020 workshops*. ECML PKDD 2020 (pp. 447–459). Springer. https://doi.org/10.1007/978-3-030-65965-3_30

Malandri, L., Mercorio, F., Mezzanzanica, M., & Nobani, N. (2023). ConvXAI: A system for multimodal interaction with any black-box explainer. *Cognitive Computation*, *15*(2), 613–644. https://doi.org/10.1007/s12559-022-10067-7

Mallidis, I., Stamelou, A., Ayfantopoulou, G., & Kanakis, E. (2024). Enhancing supply chain efficiency with predictive analytics: A machine learning approach to dynamic lead time prediction in a chemical industry. *WSEAS Transactions on Business and Economics*, *21*, 2253–2261. https://doi.org/10.37394/23207.2024.21.185

Marasović, A., Beltagy, I., Downey, D., & Peters, M. E. (2022). Few-shot self-rationalization with natural language prompts. In M. Carpuat, M.-C. de Marneffe, & I. V. Meza Ruiz (Eds.), *Findings of the Association for Computational Linguistics: NAACL 2022* (pp. 410–424). Association for Computational Linguistics. https://doi.org/10.18653/v1/2022.findings-naacl.31

Martens, D., Hinns, J., Dams, C., Vergouwen, M., & Evgeniou, T. (2025). Tell me a story! Narrative-driven XAI with large language models. *Decision Support Systems*, *191*, 114402. https://doi.org/10.1016/j.dss.2025.114402

Mendonça, G., Oliveira, S., Lima Jr, O., & Resende, P. (2024). Intelligent algorithms applied to the prediction of air freight transportation delays. I*nternational Journal of Physical Distribution & Logistics Management*, *54*(1), 61–91. https://doi.org/10.1108/IJPDLM-10-2022-0328

Nguyen, V. B., Schlötterer, J., & Seifert, C. (2023). From black boxes to conversations: Incorporating XAI in a conversational agent. In L. Longo (Ed.), *Explainable artificial intelligence. xAI 2023* (pp. 71–96). Springer. https://doi.org/10.1007/978-3-031-44070-0_4

Panigutti, C., Beretta, A., Fadda, D., Giannotti, F., Pedreschi, D., Perotti, A., & Rinzivillo, S. (2023). Co-design of human-centered, explainable AI for clinical decision support. *ACM Transactions on Interactive Intelligent Systems*, *13*(4), 1–35. https://doi.org/10.1145/3587271

Qiu, S., Liu, Q., Zhou, S., & Huang, W. (2022). Adversarial attack and defense technologies in natural language processing: A survey. *Neurocomputing*, *492*, 278–307. https://doi.org/10.1016/j.neucom.2022.04.020

Rokoss, A., Syberg, M., Tomidei, L., Hülsing, C., Deuse, J., & Schmidt, M. (2024). Case study on delivery time determination using a machine learning approach in small batch production companies. *Journal of Intelligent Manufacturing*, *35*, 3937–3958. https://doi.org/10.1007/s10845-023-02290-2

Ross, A., Peters, M. E., & Marasović, A. (2022). Does self-rationalization improve robustness to spurious correlations? *Proceedings of the 2022 Conference on Empirical Methods in Natural Language Processing*, 7403–7416.

Slack, D., Krishna, S., Lakkaraju, H., & Singh, S. (2023). Explaining machine learning models with interactive natural language conversations using TalkToModel. *Nature Machine Intelligence*, *5*(8), 873–883. https://doi.org/10.1038/s42256-023-00692-8

Ting, K. M. (2011). Confusion matrix. In C. Sammut & G. I. Webb (Eds.), *Encyclopedia of machine learning* (pp. 207–209). Springer. https://doi.org/10.1007/978-0-387-30164-8_157

Vrhovac, V., Vasić, S., Milisavljević, S., Dudić, B., Štarchoň, P., & Žižakov, M. (2023). Measuring E-commerce user experience in the last-mile delivery. *Mathematics*, *11*(6), 1482. https://doi.org/10.3390/math11061482

Wang, P., Wang, Z., Li, Z., Gao, Y., Yin, B., & Ren, X. (2023). SCOTT: Self-consistent chain-of-thought distillation. *Proceedings of the 61st Annual Meeting of the Association for Computational Linguistics (Volume 1: Long Papers)*, *1*, 5546–5558. https://doi.org/10.18653/v1/2023.acl-long.304

Wyrembek, M., & Baryannis, G. (2024). Using MCDM methods to optimise machine learning decisions for supply chain delay prediction: A stakeholder-centric approach. *LogForum*, *20*(2), 175–189. https://doi.org/10.17270/J.LOG.

Wyrembek, M., Baryannis, G., & Brintrup, A. (2025). Causal machine learning for supply chain risk prediction and intervention planning. *International Journal of Production Research*, 1–20. https://doi.org/10.1080/00207543.2025.2458121

Yao, S., Yu, D., Zhao, J., Shafran, I., Griffiths, T., Cao, Y., & Narasimhan, K. (2023, December). Tree of thoughts: Deliberate problem solving with large language models. In *Advances in neural information processing systems*, *36*. NeurIPS 2023.

Zheng, G., Ivanov, D., & Brintrup, A. (2025). An adaptive federated learning system for information sharing in supply chains. *International Journal of Production Research*, 1–23. https://doi.org/10.1080/00207543.2024.2432469

13 Effect of AI and Generative AI on Supply Chain Operations and Workforce

Batuhan Kocaoglu and Maciej Szymczak

Introduction

Artificial Intelligence (AI) is poised to transform the global economy and is often likened to a new industrial revolution. Although the full impact remains uncertain, AI is expected to boost productivity, replace some jobs, and enhance others. In advanced economies, approximately 60% of jobs are exposed to AI because of the high share of cognitive tasks. Half may face negative effects, while the other half may benefit from productivity gains. Exposure is lower in emerging (40%) and low-income (26%) economies than in developed economies. If AI-driven productivity gains materialize, they could lead to broad income growth (Cazzaniga et al., 2024).

Workers with higher education are generally better positioned to shift into roles that complement AI, whereas older and less educated workers face greater risks. However, AI also affects high-skilled jobs. Advanced algorithms now handle complex data, recognize patterns, and make decisions, challenging the notion that only routine or low-skilled work is vulnerable. This signals a broader labor market shift than that seen in earlier technological waves.

The integration of AI and generative AI (GAI) is reshaping supply chain operations, from logistics and sourcing to production and distribution. AI-driven systems enhance decision-making and efficiency through real-time data analysis, whereas GAI introduces even greater autonomy and adaptability. Consequently, supply chains are becoming increasingly streamlined, data-driven, automated, and responsive to market changes.

However, these advancements present challenges to the workforce. Although automation boosts efficiency, it raises concerns about job displacement. GAI can even replace the creative roles traditionally held by humans. While new jobs will emerge, transitions often remain within similar job types, limiting labor mobility. Older workers face particular difficulties due to outdated skills and lower reemployment rates. (Cazzaniga et al., 2024).

According to the World Economic Forum's *Future of Jobs 2025* report (World Economic Forum (WEF), 2025), technological advancements,

DOI: 10.4324/9781003659143-17

including AI, robotics, and IoT, are among the macro trends shaping the future of work. These technologies are simultaneously creating new jobs and phasing out repetitive roles, particularly in the supply chain and logistics. Between 2025 and 2030, technology will be the strongest driver of labor transformations. Two major trends stand out (World Economic Forum (WEF), 2025):

1. **Artificial Intelligence (AI)**: 86% of employers expect AI, especially Generative AI, such as ChatGPT, to transform operations by 2030. Investments in GenAI have increased eight-fold since 2022.
2. **Robotics and Energy Transformation:** 58% of employers highlight robotics (e.g., warehouse bots, autonomous vehicles) as a key influence. The global robot density has doubled since 2016, reaching 162 robots per 10,000 workers by 2023.

Overall, 78 million new jobs are expected to grow by 7 %. High-demand roles will include AI specialists and supply chain experts, among others. By 2030, the Supply Chain & Transportation sectors will heavily rely on AI, cybersecurity, and sustainability, requiring a workforce skilled in technology, analytics, and adaptive problem-solving. To remain resilient, companies must invest in digital upskilling, eco-friendly logistics, and workforce adaptability.

(World Economic Forum (WEF), 2025).

AI and GAI

Short on AI

AI involves machines that learn from data, interpret them, and generate outputs and actions aimed at achieving specific goals (Kaplan & Haenlein, 2019). By learning from data, AI can mimic human behaviors. In doing so, businesses seek solutions that automate their workforce and enhance productivity (IOE, 2024). According to an Ipsos survey conducted in 26 countries, the percentage of people who believe AI is beneficial increased from 52% in 2022 to 55% in 2024. Two-thirds of people worldwide believe that AI will significantly impact their daily lives within the next three to five years. Globally, 60% of people think AI will change the way they work, but only 36% believe it will completely take over their jobs (Stanford HAI, 2025). AI boosts efficiency and drives innovation, but it also carries risks, such as bias, misinformation, and a potential decline in critical thinking. Important AI domains include:

1. AI Ethics & Governance
2. General AI (AI agents, personalization, XAI, and deployment tools like Azure and OpenAI Gym)

3. Autonomous Driving (ADAS, LiDAR, routing, and visual tools such as OpenCV).
4. Generative AI (LLMs and tools like ChatGPT, DALL·E)
5. Machine Learning (techniques and tools like PyTorch, TensorFlow).
6. NLP (speech/text understanding models like BERT and platforms like Hugging Face)
7. Neural Networks (CNNs, RNNs, LSTM, and frameworks like Keras and TensorFlow)
8. Robotics (intelligent robotics, motion planning, and systems like Jetson and SLAM.)
9. Visual Recognition (Image analysis, detection, segmentation using ImageNet, MNIST, RealSense.)

Although AI has existed for decades, it has truly surged with the release of ChatGPT in late 2022. Since then, it has rapidly transformed industries, streamlined daily tasks, and powered various modern applications. Many tools are now free or subscription-based, which has accelerated their adoption.

New Generation AI and Generative AI

Traditional AI has long been used to automate routine tasks and optimize operations across industries. However, the emergence of GAI has marked a transformative shift. Unlike conventional AI, which relies on structured programming to respond to tasks, GAI is designed to generate new content, such as text, images, audio, and video, based on vast datasets. This new capability is underpinned by large language models (LLMs), such as ChatGPT and Gemini, which use deep learning to simulate human-like interactions and problem-solving. The GAI signifies the dawn of the "Generative Era" (2022–present), in which AI systems not only answer questions but also simulate, recommend, and even strategize ("What should we do next?") (Oliver Wyman, 2024).

Core Capabilities and Functions of Generative AI: GAI capabilities extend far beyond content generation. Key functions include:

- **Text generation, summarization, and translation**
- **Code writing and debugging** (e.g., GitHub Copilot has improved developer productivity by up to 56%)
- **Research assistance and content creation**
- **Administrative support**, such as drafting reports and emails (World Economic Forum (WEF), 2023).

These features position GAI as a powerful enabler across sectors, including education, healthcare, art, and finance. Within the domain of supply chain management, GAI supports transformative use cases as detailed next.

Generative AI and New Generation AI Applications

AI and GenAI Applications in Supply Chain Management

The convergence of advanced AI technologies with supply chain operations is revolutionizing the field by enhancing its visibility, adaptability, precision, and resilience. AI and GAI enable supply chains to respond dynamically to the increasing global complexity, environmental uncertainty, and customer expectations. AI and GenAI address global supply chain challenges – complexity, volatility, and customer demands – through the following:

Logistics and Transportation:

- **Route Optimization:** GenAI integrates data from traffic, weather, and satellite imagery to generate optimal delivery paths, even in unmapped areas.
- **Smart Cities:** AI-enabled systems can dynamically control traffic lights and routes, thereby reducing congestion and accidents.

Content Automation and Visualization:

- **Text automation:** Automated generation of inventory reports, FAQs, and customer communications.
- **Visual design:** Design of warehouse layouts and packaging solutions.
- **Analytics and Coding:** Generating forecasting models and dashboards.
- **Dashboards:** Generative models assist in the development of predictive dashboards and simulation tools.

Customer-Centric Solutions:

- **Chatbots and E-commerce Automation:** Personalized recommendations and instant support across multiple channels.
- **Sentiment Analysis:** Real-time insights from customer reviews and social media.

Forecasting and Back Office Support:

- **Disruptive Forecasting and Risk Prediction:** AI models analyze patterns to anticipate supply chain disruptions.
- **Warehouse Operations:** AI supports picking, placement, and packing.
- **Administrative Functions:** Summarizing contracts, generating financial reports, and screening resumes.

While these applications optimize existing processes, advanced use cases are reshaping strategic decision-making.

Advanced Use Cases of AI in SCM

AI's impact extends beyond efficiency gains to more strategic and analytical domains.

Contract and legal document analysis: AI-driven tools rapidly scan legal documents to extract key clauses, identify risks, and ensure compliance, thereby streamlining contract life cycle management and due diligence (EY, 2025).

Personalized logistics and scheduling: Personalized logistics platforms adjust delivery schedules based on customer behavior and real-time environmental factors, thereby enhancing service quality and reducing costs (Dekhne et al., 2019).

Predictive maintenance and asset health: Machine learning systems proactively detect equipment deterioration, allowing timely interventions that minimize downtime and extend asset lifespan (Theissler et al., 2021).

Agentic AI systems: Agentic AI refers to systems capable of autonomous decision-making and task execution using reinforcement learning and adaptive algorithm. Key examples include (Acharya et al., 2025):

- **Amazon's Warehouse Robots:** Navigate dynamic environments autonomously.
- **Logistics Platforms:** Automatically detect shipment delays and reroute deliveries (Grewal et al., 2024; Workday US, 2025).

Computer vision and smart systems in logistics: Computer vision (CV), powered by deep learning architectures such as CNNs and Transformers, has emerged as a critical tool in logistics. CV enhances warehouse accuracy (95% sorting efficiency) and safety (real-time hazard detection). CV supports many functions, such as designing warehouse layouts, shipment inspection and dimensioning, real-time personal protective equipment (PPE) detection and hazard alerts, 3D tracking, license plate reading, autonomous robots, and vision-guided inventory and order fulfillment. These innovations pave the way for next-generation delivery technology.

Emerging AI-based Delivery Technologies

The rapid advancement of AI-driven delivery technologies is revolutionizing logistics, with key innovations significantly impacting various applications.

Drones and Aerial Intelligence: Despite regulatory constraints (FAA, EASA), drones are transforming last-mile delivery and infrastructure inspections with AI-powered navigation and 5G connectivity. Some case applications are (Ghazlane et al., 2025; Prakash et al., 2023; Dougherty, 2024):

- Beyond Visual Line of Sight (BVLOS) delivery
- Inventory scanning in large facilities
- Asset inspection and urban drone corridors

Collaborative Robots (Cobots): Cobots are designed to work safely with humans in shared spaces, enhancing throughput and safety through AI-powered sensing. Some use cases are:

- **Material Handling:** Reduced strain, faster movement (Wu et al., 2025)
- **Quality Control:** AI-vision for defect detection (Daios et al., 2025)
- **Order Picking:** Navigation in fulfillment centers (Budhwar et al., 2023)
- **Packaging:** Handling delicate goods (Nozari et al., 2022)
- **Maintenance:** Automated checks and repairs (Wamba et al., 2024)

Autonomous Guided Vehicles (AGVs) and Outdoor Platforms: AGVs use sensors and dynamic maps to operate indoors, transporting materials and managing warehouse flows (Simon & Gogolák, 2025). Outdoor autonomous vehicles are also reshaping port, yard, and airport logistics by driving sustainability and real-time responsiveness.

Coupled with GenAI, these technologies enable strategic supply chain redesign.

Strategic Augmentation with Generative AI

Unlike narrow AI, which is task-specific, GAI augments complex cognitive work in SCM, particularly in strategic and analytical domains.
Examples of Strategic GAI Use:

- **Network Design:** Warehouse network design and location optimization
- **Supplier Selection:** Make-or-buy decisions and simulation-based supplier selection
- **Service Level Planning:** Service level design and scenario-based planning

Mass Personalization in Logistics

Mass *personalization* goes beyond customer choice; it uses AI to *anticipate and fulfill individual preferences*. While *customization* allows for options (e.g., shoe color or delivery time), *AI-driven personalization* predicts needs (e.g., suggesting carbon-neutral delivery or pre-filled orders). In China, *80% of e-commerce purchases* are now influenced by AI recommendations (up from 20% previously). A total of 73% *of customers* expect brands to understand their unique needs, and 50% want brands to *anticipate their preferences* (Salesforce, 2022). Table 13.1 highlights B2C/B2B applications.

Future Outlook: Toward Adaptive and Strategic Supply Chains

By 2025, over 50% of logistics decisions may be automated by AI. Gen Z and Millennial consumers increasingly expect AI-curated shopping experiences

Table 13.1 Key applications in logistics

Area	*AI-Powered Solutions*
B2C Personalization *(Customer-Facing)*	• Flexible last-mile delivery (lockers, same-day, neighbor drop-off) • Sustainable options (cargo bikes, green packaging) • Smart suggestions (e.g., default recycled packaging for eco-conscious buyers)
B2B Personalization *(Retail & Fulfillment)*	• Predictive inventory placement (e.g., personalized vitamin kits) • Real-time routing and stock adjustments via APIs • Sustainable logistics (EV fleets, biodegradable packaging)
Generative AI Use	• Forecasting customer needs (e.g., DHL's tailored delivery options) • Auto-reordering & dynamic pricing based on AI insights
Collaboration	• Support retailers in mass-personalized fulfillment • Maintain cost-efficiency with smart routing and returns

Source: Own work based on DHL Logistics Trend Radar 7.0, 2024.

and sustainable delivery methods. Retailers unable to adapt may lose competitiveness to tech-savvy rivals (DHL Logistics Trend Radar 7.0, 2024).

The key enablers of the future supply chain are:

- Seamless AI-human collaboration
- Workforce development and digital upskilling
- Governance frameworks for ethical AI deployment

According to World Economic Forum, WEF (2025), human-exclusive tasks will decrease from 47% to 33% by 2030. Hybrid AI-human roles are expected to dominate the future. Therefore, upskilling in AI literacy and analytical thinking will be essential for future supply chain professionals.

Workforce Transformation: Challenges and Strategies

The Economic Impact of AI and GAI on Supply Chains and Job Disruption

The widespread adoption of generative AI has the potential to revolutionize industries. Since the launch of ChatGPT, the world has been grappling with how generative AI will reshape economies, industries, and individual lives in the future. According to estimates, generative AI could contribute up to $20 trillion to the global GDP by 2030 and save an estimated 300 billion work hours annually. However, this massive economic boost is accompanied by potential disruptions. The World Economic Forum estimates that AI technologies could displace up to 85 million jobs globally by 2025. Traditionally, automation narratives have focused on blue-collar workers, but the rise of GAI has shifted this concern to white-collar jobs. Approximately three in five white-collar workers now fear that their roles could become redundant or automated as AI's capabilities continue to evolve, impacting knowledge-based professions.

Generative AI is not only automating entry-level tasks but also disrupting traditional career paths. As AI handles routine work, such as customer service bots and automated reporting, junior employees are fast-tracked into semi-managerial roles, leaving mid-level managers in uncertain positions.

- **Task Automation:** Routine functions, such as customer support and reporting are increasingly AI-driven.
- **Career Path Disruption:** Junior roles are being elevated to strategic functions, bypassing traditional mid-level management (Oliver Wyman, 2024).

The Impact of Automation and Augmentation by GAI in Supply Chains

Automation and AI augmentation are reshaping the roles in supply chains. According to (World Economic Forum (WEF), 2023), job exposure varies according to the task type.

1. **General and operations managers** face *low automation risk* but *high augmentation potential* because their tasks require judgment and leadership beyond LLM capabilities.
2. **Drivers** (light truck, bus, heavy vehicle) may experience *moderate augmentation* (e.g., route optimization), but only *partial automation* owing to the physical nature of their work.
3. **Manual roles** (stock clerks, packers, material movers, industrial truck operators) face *high automation risk* and *low augmentation potential* because their tasks are largely repetitive and do not benefit significantly from LLMs.

Overall, jobs involving physical labor are more susceptible to automation, whereas managerial positions are more likely to be augmented by AI technologies (World Economic Forum (WEF), 2023).

The Impact of AI and GAI on the Workforce in Supply Chains

The rise of AI and GAI is reshaping work across supply chains. Routine, rule-based tasks are increasingly automated, whereas complex decisions are enhanced through AI. This shift reduces the demand for certain roles while creating opportunities that require skills in intelligent systems. Job exposure varies across supply chain functions.

1. **Highest Total Exposure (Procurement Clerks):** Procurement clerks face the most automation and augmentation because of repetitive, rule-based tasks.
2. **Medium Exposure (Logistics Specialists, Production Planners, and Shipping, Receiving, and Stock Recording Clerks):** These roles have moderate exposure, with a mix of automatable and lower-exposure tasks.
3. **Managerial Roles (Procurement, Industrial Production, and Transport, Storage, and Distribution Managers):** These roles have low automation exposure but high augmentation potential; AI will enhance, not replace, their work.
4. **Lowest Automation Exposure (Drivers, Sales Representatives, Procurement Specialists, and Procurement Officers):** These positions are least affected by automation but can benefit from AI in tasks such as route optimization, inventory management, and customer interactions.
5. **Non-language (LLM) Tasks:** Jobs not reliant on language, often physical or logistical, are less impacted by LLMs but may still be transformed through robotics or process redesign (World Economic Forum (WEF), 2023).

Supply chain jobs are rapidly evolving with AI. Routine tasks are being automated, whereas managerial roles are increasingly augmented. (Hazan et al., 2024). By 2030, the demand for technical and socio-emotional skills will rise as some cognitive skills decline. Generative AI is accelerating this shift – 40% of executives expect reskilling and 98% of workers recognize the need for it (Oliver Wyman, 2024). With skill relevance lasting under five years (Harward Business Review, 2023), the talent gap is urgent, yet only 39% of companies feel prepared. Affected sectors include supply chain, transport, healthcare, manufacturing, and retail (World Economic Forum (WEF), 2024b)

Digitalization, driven by AI, big data, and autonomous technology such as electric trucks and drones, is transforming logistics and transportation. Simultaneously, climate adaptation and rising costs fuel the demand for green and efficient innovations (World Economic Forum (WEF), 2024b). New roles are emerging, such as last-mile delivery drivers and EV infrastructure specialists, requiring AI-based analytics, cybersecurity, and tech literacy (O*NET Resource Center, 2025). Encouragingly, 57% of workers have reskilled, which is above the industry average. Encouragingly, 57% of workers have reskilled – above the industry average.

However, talent shortages in technology and green skills threaten innovation. Sector-specific needs vary: consumer goods prioritize automation and materials, whereas transportation focuses on digital infrastructure. Both

Table 13.2 AI-enabled innovative solutions for flexible logistics work

Application	*Solutions/Examples*
AI-Driven Scheduling	AI platforms enable self-scheduling and shift swapping (e.g., DHL reduces staffing shortages).
Hybrid Roles	Admin, training, and monitoring tasks are performed remotely via IoT/AR. Autonomous warehouse vehicle pilots allow for remote control.
Cross-Industry Seasonal Jobs	Logistics + tourism/retail collaboration = year-round contracts and reduced layoffs.
Gig Worker Integration	On-demand labor with rating-based platforms (e.g., Uber-style) is available, though QC and reliability remain issues.
Health & Safety (H&S)	AI wearables can detect unsafe actions. Exoskeletons reduce the strain. Mental health tools: quiet rooms and resilience training.
Skills Gaps	AI-powered microlearning and micro-credentials support faster skill development.

Source: Own work based on DHL Logistics Trend Radar 7.0, 2024.

sectors demand labor and immigration policy reforms. By 2030, targeted strategies for technology adoption, green transitions, and skill development will be vital (World Economic Forum (WEF), 2025).

AI-Enabled Flexible Working Models

Workforce expectations are shifting toward flexibility and purposefulness. Most employees (77%) prefer flexible schedules, and 81% resist returning to full-time offices. In logistics, 59% favor hybrid work, although physical demands limit options. Shift patterns hinder alternatives such as four-day workweeks. Workers increasingly value upskilling (60%) and sustainability; 48% accept lower pay for green employers. Gen Z and Millennials often quit over poor digital tools usage. Technologies such as AR glasses enhance warehouse productivity. By 2027, 60% of logistics firms will adopt AI-driven scheduling to increase flexibility, integrate gig workers, and enable self-scheduling, as seen in DHL platforms (Table 13.2).

Recommendations for *workers* include:

- Embrace flexible roles and upskilling opportunities.
- Prioritize digital and sustainability skills for long-term employability.
- Wearable technology and mobile applications are used to enhance safety and productivity.

Recommendations for *educators*:

- Offer micro-credential programs tailored to logistics roles (e.g., AR tools and AI scheduling).
- Teach hybrid skillsets by combining tech literacy and operational know-how.
- Promote awareness of green logistics and mental health in work design (DHL Logistics Trend Radar 7.0, 2024).

Recommendation for Supply Chains

Preparing for AI-driven transformation depends on digital infrastructure and a skilled workforce. *Digital infrastructure* is vital for AI adoption but requires a capable workforce to maximize its benefits. *Human capital policies* are essential for distributing digital skills and supporting workers affected by AI transition.

Developed economies should focus on regulatory frameworks and innovation, while emerging markets should prioritize investment in ***digital infrastructure*** and ***human capital*** to fully leverage AI (Cazzaniga et al., 2024):

- Targeted *skill development programs* should focus on high-demand sectors, such as *technology*, *telecommunications*, *logistics*, and *finance*, with an emphasis on *AI, IoT automation*, and *data analytics.*
- Efforts to reskill workers from *manual labor* to *technology-aided roles* are on the rise, especially to adapt to automation and digital changes.
- To reduce inequalities in access to training, *government incentives*, *public-private partnerships*, and *flexible learning models* (e.g., micro-certifications and online platforms) should be utilized.
- *Training ROI* should be tracked through *productivity*, *employee engagement*, and *promotion rates*, with AI-supported assessments helping to create *personalized learning paths.*
- Despite progress in reskilling, *inequities in access* and *future competency gaps* remain significant challenges for the workforce. Employers should prioritize strategic sectors and create inclusive solutions that balance human and AI capability.

Recommendations for the Use of GAI in Supply Chains

Recommendations for *logistics professionals:*

- Start with *content automation* and *route optimization* to reduce manual workload
- Use *AI assistants* for supply chain visibility and planning
- Engage GenAI to improve *customer interaction* and internal processes

- Logistics firms should *pilot Gen AI in sandbox environments* (like DHL's GenAI Hub: Sandbox environment for testing automation, content generation, and process improvements) to explore automation, content generation, and predictive analytics use cases. (DHL Logistics Trend Radar 7.0, 2024)

Gen AI is set to revolutionize logistics through automation, optimized planning and enhanced customer interactions.

Recommendations for *educators*:

- Explain the difference between GANs and Transformers
- Use DHL's *GenAI Hub* as a case study for safe experimentation
- Show live demos of ChatGPT, image generators, or code-writing AI in class
- Encourage students to brainstorm GenAI use cases for warehouse, fleet, or customer service scenarios

Conclusion

The integration of AI and GAI is revolutionizing supply chains, shifting from automation to intelligent adaptive systems. While these technologies enhance efficiency, predictive analytics, and decision-making, their full potential requires investment in workforce development, ethical governance, and organizational changes.

AI and GAI are reshaping labor dynamics by automating routine tasks while augmenting strategic roles. Emerging economies must strengthen their digital infrastructure, while advanced economies face job displacement risks. Key technologies, such as autonomous robots and AI-driven drones, optimize operations but necessitate workforce upskilling in AI literacy and analytical thinking.

Success depends on balancing innovation and human collaboration. Businesses must foster AI-augmented roles, prioritize continuous learning, and implement ethical frameworks to mitigate biases and support job transitions. Governments, educators, and industries must collaborate to bridge skill gaps and ensure equitable adaptation.

Ultimately, AI is redefining, not replacing, human roles. Organizations that combine digital transformation with workforce resilience will lead the next wave of supply chain innovation. The future lies in adaptive, data-driven supply chains where AI and human potential synergize for sustainable, inclusive growth.

Reference List

Acharya, D., Kuppan, K., & Divya, B. (2025). Agentic AI: Autonomous intelligence for complex goals: A comprehensive survey. *IEEE Access*, *13*, 18912–18936.

Budhwar, P., Chowdhury, S., Wood, G., Aguinis, H., Bamber, G., Beltran, J., . . . Varma, A. (2023, July). Human resource management in the age of generative artificial intelligence: Perspectives and research directions on ChatGPT. *Human Resource Management Journal*, *33*(3), 606–659. https://doi.org/10.1111/1748-8583.12524

Cazzaniga, M., Jaumotte, F., Li, L., Melina, G., Panton, A., Pizzinelli, C., . . . Tavares, M. (2024, January). *Gen-AI: Artificial intelligence and the future of work*. International Monetary Fund (IMF). www.imf.org/en/Publications/Staff-Discussion-Notes/Issues/2024/01/14/Gen-AI-Artificial-Intelligence-and-the-Future-of-Work-542379

Daios, A., Kladovasilakis, N., Kelemis, A., & Kostavelis, I. (2025, March). AI applications in supply chain management: A survey. *Applied Sciences*, *15*(5), 2775. www.mdpi.com/2076-3417/15/5/2775/htm

Dekhne, A., Hastings, G., Murnane, J., & Neuhaus, F. (2019, April). Logistics automation: Big opportunity, bigger uncertainty | McKinsey. *McKinsey & Company*. www.mckinsey.com/industries/logistics/our-insights/automation-in-logistics-big-opportunity-bigger-uncertainty#/

DHL Logistics Trend Radar 7.0. (2024). *DHL logistics trend radar. Insights. Shaping tomorrow. – DHL – United Kingdom*. Retrieved April 29, 2025, from www.dhl.com/gb-en/home/innovation-in-logistics/logistics-trend-radar.html

Dougherty, Z. (2024, February 1). *Understanding Drone Regulations: The FAA's role and challenges – Coruzant Technologies*. Retrieved May 16, 2025, from https://coruzant.com/opinion/understanding-drone-regulations-the-faas-role-and-challenges/

EY. (2025). *GenAI in contract management*. www.worldcc.com/Resources/Content-Hub/details/

Ghazlane, Y., Hajar, B., Hajar, E., Saida, H., & Mourad, E. (2025). artificial intelligence in drone and anti-drone systems: Cutting-edge advances and applications. *Sustainable Civil Infrastructures*, 167–174. https://link.springer.com/chapter/10.1007/978-3-031-86705-7_16

Grewal, D., Satornino, C., Davenport, T., & Guha, A. (2024, December). How generative AI Is shaping the future of marketing. *Journal of the Academy of Marketing Science*, 1–21. https://link.springer.com/article/10.1007/s11747-024-01064-3

Harward Business Review. (2023, September). *Reskilling in the age of AI*. Retrieved May 18, 2025, from https://hbr.org/2023/09/reskilling-in-the-age-of-ai

Hazan, E., Madgavkar, A., Chui, M., Smit, S., Maor, D., Dandona, G., & Huyghues-Despointes, R. (2024). *A new future of work: The race to deploy AI and raise skills in Europe and beyond*. McKinsey Global Institute. www.mckinsey.de/~/media/mckinsey/locations/europe%20and%20middle%20east/deutschland/news/presse/2024/2024%20-%2005%20-%2023%20mgi%20genai%20future%20of%20work/mgi%20report_a-new-future-of-work-the-race-to-deploy-ai.pdf

IOE. (2024). *The impact of AI on work and employment – AI's impact on work and employment examined in new publication*. International Organisation of Employers (IOE). Retrieved April 29, 2025, from www.ioe-emp.org/news/details/ais-impact-on-work-and-employment-examined-in-new-publication

Kaplan, A., & Haenlein, M. (2019, January). Siri, Siri, in my hand: Who's the fairest in the land? On the interpretations, illustrations, and implications of artificial intelligence. *Business Horizons*, *62*(1), 15–25.

Nozari, H., Szmelter-Jarosz, A., & Ghahremani-Nahr, J. (2022, April). Analysis of the challenges of Artificial Intelligence of Things (AIoT) for the smart supply chain (case study: FMCG Industries). *Sensors*, *22*(8), 2931. www.mdpi.com/1424-8220/22/8/2931/htm

O*NET Resource Center. (2025). *About O*NET at O*NET Resource Center*. Retrieved May 7, 2025, from www.onetcenter.org/overview.html

Oliver Wyman. (2024). *How generative AI Is transforming business and society*. www.oliverwymanforum.com/global-consumer-sentiment/how-will-ai-affect-global-economics.html

Prakash, K., Ravva, S., Rathnamma, M., & Suryanarayana, G. (2023, May). AI applications of drones. *Drone Technology: Future Trends and Practical Applications*, 153–182. https://doi.org/10.1002/9781394168002.ch7

Salesforce. (2022, May). *Customer engagement research 2022 – Salesforce*. Retrieved May 18, 2025, from www.salesforce.com/news/stories/customer-engagement-research/

Simon, J., & Gogolák, L. (2025). Supply chain management using automatic guided vehicle systems in smart factory logistics. *Advanced Sciences and Technologies for Security Applications, Part F136*, 611–624. https://link.springer.com/chapter/10.1007/978-3-031-78544-3_49

Stanford HAI. (2025). *The 2025 AI index report | Stanford HAI*. Stanford HAI. https://hai.stanford.edu/ai-index/2025-ai-index-report

Theissler, A., Pérez-Velázquez, J., Kettelgerdes, M., & Elger, G. (2021, November). Predictive maintenance enabled by machine learning: Use cases and challenges in the automotive industry. *Reliability Engineering & System Safety*, *215*, 107864. www.sciencedirect.com/science/article/pii/S0951832021003835

Wamba, S. F., Guthrie, C., Queiroz, M. M., & Minner, S. (2024, August). ChatGPT and generative artificial intelligence: An exploratory study of key benefits and challenges in operations and supply chain management. *International Journal of Production Research*, *62*(16), 5676–5696. www.tandfonline.com/doi/pdf/10.1080/00207543.2023.2294116

Workday US. (2025). *What Is agentic AI? Definition, types, examples | Workday US*. Retrieved May 19, 2025, from www.workday.com/en-us/topics/ai/agentic-ai.html

World Economic Forum (WEF). (2023, September). *Jobs of tomorrow: Large language models and jobs*. World Economic Forum. Retrieved April 30, 2025, from www.weforum.org/publications/jobs-of-tomorrow-large-language-models-and-jobs/

World Economic Forum (WEF). (2024b, January). *Putting skills first: Opportunities for building efficient and equitable labour markets*. World Economic Forum (WEF). Retrieved April 29, 2025, from www.weforum.org/publications/putting-skills-first-opportunities-for-building-efficient-and-equitable-labour-markets/

World Economic Forum (WEF). (2025, January). *The future of jobs report 2025*. World Economic Forum. Retrieved April 29, 2025, from www.weforum.org/publications/the-future-of-jobs-report-2025/

Wu, H., Li, G., & Ivanov, D. (2025, March). The transformative power of generative AI for supply chain management: Theoretical framework and agenda. *Frontiers of Engineering Management*, *12*(2), 425–433. https://link.springer.com/article/10.1007/s42524-025-4240-x

14 AI and the Development of Mobility

Marcin Jurczak

What can artificial intelligence do today? If we ask this (artificial intelligence, of course), we get the answer that these include areas such as data analysis, pattern recognition, and natural language processing, which can analyze and interpret visual information from the world and make speech recognition and generation (this is how chatGPT describes its possibilities). Artificial intelligence means today also refers to automation and robotics, decision-making and optimization, implementation of creative tasks (e.g., creation of images), personalization and recommendation, learning and self-improvement, simulation, and virtual environments (the author's intention here is to point out how wide the current scope of AI's possibilities is and the potential for their use in transportation and the creation of mobility). With such a wide range of AI capabilities, are there areas that will not be able to support? These point out, for example, AI's problems in common sense analysis and general understanding, interpreting selected events, or lack of understanding of human behavior. Are these areas used for AI in the transportation development? How can we combine a wide range of possibilities for creating and supporting reality with the world of transportation? The potential for the use of AI in transportation is incredible, as it offers the opportunity to support virtually every mode of transportation in many key areas.

The purpose of this chapter is not to create another literature review on the use of AI in transportation, as such reviews can already be found in global literature. The author focuses on indicating the areas of practical use of AI in transportation, a broad view of the issue of AI in transportation and the opportunity to improve, thanks to it, the efficiency of processes, reduce costs, improve the quality of services. The concept of AI is capacious and allows for the classification of many different tools or models. Hence, it is worth citing examples of algorithms and methods used in the transportation industry. Researchers here point to Artificial Neural Networks (ANN), genetic algorithms (GA), Simulated Annealing (SA), Artificial Immune system (AIS), Ant Colony Optimizer (ACO), Bee Colony Optimization (BCO), or fuzzy logic Model (FLM) (Abduljabbar et al., 2019). On the solution and technology audience side, there are four main groups (attitudes): AI neutral, AI optimist, AI pessimist, and AI skeptics (Qian et al., 2025). The wide range

DOI: 10.4324/9781003659143-18

of tools that comprise the concept of AI increases the possibility of its use. It should also be noted that not everyone or everywhere is positive regarding AI. There is a perception that behind the obvious benefits of implementing AI in transportation, there are many dangers, primarily concerning the loss of jobs (including in public transportation, driving, or cargo operations) related to data security, potential AI taking control of vehicles, etc.

For years, technology has been a way to help mankind and solve problems such as banking, insurance, healthcare, and sports. It continues to help humans today, including, among others, in solving problems in the transportation industry, such as traffic congestion, unexpected delay and routing problems – areas that also generate financial losses for organizations (Iyer, 2021). Innovation in transportation can be found in many areas, including physical infrastructure and transport units (especially planes, ships, and trucks) and people and ICT infrastructure (De Liso & Zamparini, 2022). The reliability of a transportation system is primarily its ability to provide services and transport passengers and cargo in response to internal and external disruptions (Janić, 2021).

Changes in Mobility Over the Years

Mobility is defined in many different areas of human activity, such as interpretation of selected physical phenomena or telecommunications. It is also sometimes used in transportation analysis. Mobility is defined as the freedom of a person to move around. Freedom is understood as the ability to travel certain distances for various purposes – professional or social – and is related to the generation of GDP or one's own development and fulfillment of needs of different levels.

Globally, changes in consumer behavior have an impact on mobility. The development of cities and agglomerations lead to greater travel distances (on the way to work or school). The labor market expects employees to be flexible; flexibility is often understood as a willingness to work far from home. In recent years, the trend of working remotely has been strongly noticeable – people's occupational mobility is decreasing, while the need to move for other purposes (related to tourism, etc.) is increasing. The increase in the level of mobility can also be influenced by changes of a systemic nature – urban sprawl, or even – the emergence of so-called "black swans" (when macroeconomic changes lead to changes in the behavior of the individual and the associated change in mobility). Human mobility habits provide valuable information for assessing human behavior, building settlement units, traffic prediction, and public health planning. All human activities are embedded in time, so it is even more important to have tools that make it possible not only to analyze the activities already happening but also to forecast the next ones (Huang et al., 2015). An interdisciplinary perspective is important for assessing human mobility. Researchers as early as 2000 created the term "globility" – allowing to combine the concepts of global change and human mobility (Domínguez-Mujica, 2016).

Today, transportation is undergoing several key changes, which have led, among other things, to the concept of new mobility. This new mobility is increasingly identified with treating transportation as a service, which allows to realize mobility, in the system of "mobility as a service" (MaaS), that is, without the need to acquire one's own means of transportation (Kamargianni et al., 2016). Among the elements of new mobility that support the use of AI are (in addition to MaaS) certain types of vehicles: Connected and Autonomous Vehicles (CAVs), autonomous Personal and Unmanned Aerial Vehicles (PAVs and UAVs) – in example drones (Nikitas et al., 2020; Zhang & Kamargianni, 2023). New mobility includes ride-hailing solutions, on-demand transit, and other tools to support individual mobility, such as dockless shared bikes (Palm et al., 2021). The term "new mobility" refers to the emergence of new, highly automated transportation systems. This is also an evolutionary scenario in the automotive industry (Pisarov & Mester, 2021). New mobility has also been identified in autonomous vehicles (Lenz & Fraedrich, 2016; Pisarov & Mester, 2021).

Does this new mobility merge with AI? It naturally does. New modes of transportation, a different organization of processes, and the ubiquity of digital tools all make new mobility susceptible to the use of AI. The individual solutions of new mobility will be discussed later in this chapter in relation to the transportation of passengers and cargo. Already at this point, however, it is worth noting that AI strongly supports the concept of new mobility.

Mobility vs Pandemia

Human mobility can also change dynamically because of external factors. Pandemia is an excellent example of this. A sharp drop in the level of mobility was recorded during the pandemic in many areas of transportation. The research showed that the decline was pronounced for different destinations and modes of transportation, regardless of the size of the household, age of respondents, or gender. The more feared the coronavirus is, the more travel time is reduced (Borkowski et al., 2021). Interestingly, some researchers point out that the reduction in mobility associated with the pandemic may have a positive impact on how mobility is implemented in general, making mobility more sustainable (by reducing unnecessary movements) or healthier (by promoting walking or cycling). This can also have a long-term impact, though, of course, keeping in mind that this is the result of less use of public transportation (Musselwhite et al., 2021). Similar effects concerning less use of public transportation and a sharp increase in the cycling population have also been pointed out by Bucsky (2020), who analyzed the impact of the pandemic on transportation in Budapest. At the same time, it was pointed out that the long-term determination of the impact of the pandemic on transportation at this stage was not yet possible (Bucsky, 2020).

Simultaneously, it should be noted that social distancing, case isolation, and shielding are keyways to combat the virus. Thus, distancing policies have been rapidly implemented in individual countries and understanding how mobility policies affect virus transmission is key (Nouvellet et al., 2021). A separate group of studies in the literature focused on the relationship between transportation behavior and virus transmission; for example, a 10 percent decrease in infections was found with the use of masks in public transportation (Zargari et al., 2022). The cited pandemic example shows that human mobility can also be affected by random events. In this case, the sharp reduction in mobility was influenced by the pandemic. However, we can also find potential applications for artificial intelligence, if only in data analysis, forecasting, or simulation (of the surrounding reality).

Sustainable Mobility

In recent years, the concept of "sustainable mobility" has also been gaining career. This means mobility is carried out with respect to the environment. Is there a field of AI here as well? Naturally, wherever there is talk about optimizing processes and the distance traveled, prediction influences more efficient management of resources or automatic performance of tasks and activities in a way that leads to saving resources. By the way, there is a natural question about the meaningfulness of selected elements of human mobility. New mobility and sustainable mobility indicate, among other things, the need to reduce air travel "in favor" of rail transportation.

To what extent does AI support sustainable mobility? Eco-friendly and energy-efficient mobility is increasingly using AI to improve safety and comfort, as well as in terms of traffic management (Elbroumi et al., 2025). With the availability of AI, optimization in transportation is much broader, supporting the MaaS concept (Servou et al., 2023). AI-supported information technologies also represent a revolution in route planning, which will dramatically change public transportation thinking (Jadhav et al., 2025). AI also supports the implementation of new technologies. Thus, for example, real-time data management using machine learning can support energy management systems in the future, supporting, among other things, the development of hydrogen technologies in transportation based on hydrogen-powered vehicles such as fuel cell electric vehicles (FCEVs) (Polymeni et al., 2024).

To what extent can AI provide digital support for transportation? Regardless of the branch, this will mean traffic management, increased safety, and better efficiency. However, these are the areas that fit into the skills that AI has today. Therefore, are there areas that are non-automatized, according to the current state of knowledge and level of development of AI? Areas and competencies related to solving unique problems that do not fit typical AI templates are indicated here. At the decision-making stage in a changing environment, many areas of transportation activity are still dominated by humans today.

AI in Passenger Transportation

AI has great potential to support passenger transportation in three basic areas: it can carry on a conversation and be a travel assistant, drive vehicles autonomously, and robotize and automate all types of processes. Thus, there are many potential applications with different spectrums of benefits. The benefits of AI are emerging today, especially in areas of passenger transportation where innovation is high: in air transportation, rail transportation, or in the implementation of smart city concepts.

Air transportation changed significantly during and after the pandemic. Here, AI offers an opportunity to improve competitiveness and customer satisfaction in terms of using predictive technologies and to enhance comfort and real-time information (Chiang, 2025). AI can also be a way to improve passenger experience at airports with the support of sensors and automatically tailored services (Mäkelä, 2024). Increasingly, we are even talking about the "digital passenger" – who, because of the widespread use of digital technologies, will be able to appreciate the opportunities arising from the implementation of AI, such as in air transportation (Mayer, 2019).

The mobility of the future will also be challenged by other expectations from the new generation. There is growing talk that millennials and gen-Z are paying and will pay more attention to the development of sustainable mobility, which will have a major impact on shaping sustainable transportation infrastructure. New technologies, smart realities, and other needs all influence the availability of "green alternatives" in transportation (Vávrová et al., 2025).

AI's support for smart city concepts has received considerable attention in scientific literature. Technology is used to manage the flows of growing metropolises and indirectly improve the standard of living of residents (Bharadiya, 2023). Modern cities are integrating a variety of technologies such as the Internet of Things, blockchain, Artificial Intelligence, Machine Learning or Deep Reinforcement Learning (Szpilko et al., 2023). AI in smart city development also includes cloud infrastructure and pattern recognition (Navarathna & Malagi, 2018). AI affects the selected functional areas of cities today; in the future, it will comprehensively affect the design and management of cities (Alahi et al., 2023). Some researchers have proposed to go even further when evaluating the use of AI in smart cities. Because AI algorithms provide opportunities to process large datasets, detect patterns, and change many areas of traditional thinking, combined with wireless sensors and the aforementioned data analysis, we can even talk about XAI – "explainable artificial intelligence," for the kind of "smart monitoring" smart monitoring' present in the smart city (Luckey et al., 2021). In the long term, AI will become a source of urban transformation, although it will take decades to move cities into this new era. This will include cities as whole organizations as well as their individual components – autonomous vehicles (including flying vehicles) or MaaS, with the use of the Internet of Things, the Internet in general, and wider concepts such as Industry 4.0 (Mahor et al., 2022).

The potential for AI use includes autonomous vehicles (AVs). In passenger transportation, we discuss both alternatives to personal automobiles (i.e., robo-taxis) and public transportation. AI also has a significant effect on rail transportation. The authors of a literature review on the impact of AI on rail transportation indicated that it is a real game changer for the industry (Tang et al., 2022).

Two concepts have appeared in the literature. "Autonomous vehicles" – meaning vehicles that autonomously move through space and around other vehicles, and "automated vehicles" – vehicles that do not have a person driving them, moving on their own along a dedicated track. The second group has been present in public spaces for many years; they appeared many years before the AI discussion of autonomous vehicles began. According to the International Union of Public Transportation (UITP) classification, automated vehicles are divided into four levels, depending on the level of automation. At the two highest levels, the vehicle was driven by automation. At the GoA3 level, there is no driver in the cabin, but there are separate on-board personnel (known as driverless train operations (DTO). At the GoA4 level (Unattended Train Operation – UTO), the train is fully automatic, without any staff member on board (Lemonnier et al., 2023). In practice, therefore, automatic (but not autonomous) systems have been known, at least in rail transportation for years, and a great many vehicles can be found around the world also operating at the GoA4 level. AI offers the possibility of data analysis (on a previously unknown scale), extending automation to include systems that move in normal traffic, respond to signals from the environment, and exhibit reactions with stakeholders.

The technology of automated train operation (also known as Automatic Train Operation (ATO)) is typically based on traditional automation systems, with the first systems based on artificial intelligence being introduced. At the same time, it is seen as a great opportunity related to AI, concerning data processing, machine learning with reinforcement in decision-making processes, improving security, energy efficiency, or control, by integrating AI into ATO systems (Barruffo et al., 2024). The ability of AI to support ATO systems is the next revolution in railroads. This topic is eagerly addressed by researchers; the use of AI in ATO will provide opportunities to reduce costs and improve safety and efficiency (Plissonneau et al., 2021). This is related to the possibility of the extensive use of new technologies, such as cameras, lidars, radars, and ultrasonic sensors (Tagiew et al., 2023).

AI in Freight Transportation

Tools that enable us to optimize routes (or supply networks more broadly) have been present in logistics for years. With the advent of AI, the question of the possibility of optimizing various transportation processes from an operational perspective has arisen. from tactical to strategic. However, optimization of routes and deliveries is not the only area of AI use in freight transportation.

The rapid development of road transport is currently charted by electrification and automation, among other factors. Driverless technologies combined with the development of the concept of sustainable transport have led to clear process changes, but also in terms of propulsion, batteries, infrastructure or control systems (Natarajan et al., 2023). Changes in road transportation are determined by technology and algorithms, but also by social aspects; an important area for analysis remains the human factor and social questions of future mobility concepts (Dartmann et al., 2021).

The logistics industry is seeing the potential of AI to optimize delivery networks in real time. The optimization distribution also includes last-mile deliveries, including the use of intelligent robots. With AI-drive robots, it is possible to observe a clear improvement in the efficiency of deliveries made within the last mile. Challenges here include issues of delivery cooperation or user authorization: the robot must find the right customer and make the delivery automatically (Wang et al., 2022). AI-based technologies also make it possible to re-shape processes already underway, both in terms of distribution and, for example, product delivery tasks, including internal transportation (Reis et al., 2020). A separate group of potential benefits is associated with the implementation of AI in warehousing. However, this is not the subject of discussion in this chapter.

We are also increasingly talking about "smart logistics," that is, one that makes extensive use of modern technology (including AI) by improving efficiency and ensuring the intelligent development of the entire logistics industry. This development can be derived from path and route optimization, intelligent planning, data mining and predictive logistics algorithms. A separate group of solutions also includes intelligent algorithms for warehouses that support both storage and internal transportation (Li et al., 2024). Route and movement planning can also be a source of benefit for maritime transportation (Chen et al., 2024). In recent years, there has been marked by a generally great fascination with artificial intelligence. One can find researchers who are skeptical, seeing no clear and unequivocally confirmed by research on the benefits of AI (Okrepilov et al., 2022); however, these are few voices. It should also be kept in mind that one of the most important elements in the evolution of entire economic systems is the development of supply chains (Zamparini, 2022).

How will this be secure? There is a widespread opinion that AI in transportation will increase safety. However, looking at the current crucial role of humans, according to Salmon (2024) the introduction of AI will not raise the level of safety in transportation, although it will play an important role in prevention around safety in future transportation systems (Salmon, 2024).

Summary

AI drives changes in all business models. Instead of analyzing the drivers' working time, we analyzed the energy consumption and planned the

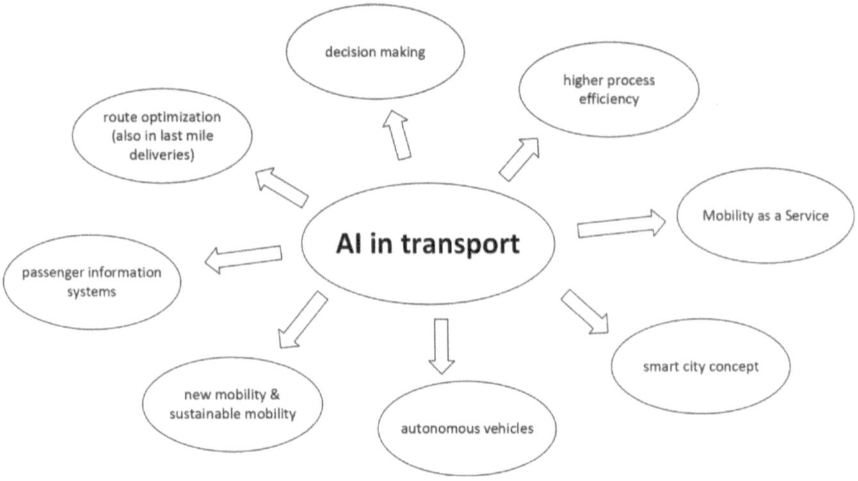

Figure 14.1 AI use in transportation.

Source: Own elaboration.

appropriate charging of the vehicles. The pace of change in transportation (especially road transport) is determined by decarbonization, among other factors. AI has several applications in transportation. They are schematically simplified, as presented in Figure 14.1.

Today, AI brings incredible possibilities. The focus is on supporting transportation and improving efficiency. In the future, we can expect fundamental changes related to the widespread use of autonomous vehicles or new energy sources. Artificial intelligence, by gaining the ability to learn, will be able to create new business models on its own – vehicles, delivery methods, or process organization. Fortunately, if people still need to move from one place to another, their mobility seems to be secure.

Reference List

Abduljabbar, R., Dia, H., Liyanage, S., & Bagloee, S. A. (2019). Applications of artificial intelligence in transport: An overview. *Sustainability*, *11*(1), 189.

Alahi, M. E. E., Sukkuea, A., Tina, F. W., Nag, A., Kurdthongmee, W., Suwannarat, K., & Mukhopadhyay, S. C. (2023). Integration of IoT-enabled technologies and artificial intelligence (AI) for smart city scenario: Recent advancements and future trends. *Sensors*, *23*(11), 5206.

Barruffo, L., Caiazzo, B., Petrillo, A., & Santini, S. (2024). A GoA4 control architecture for the autonomous driving of high-speed trains over ETCS: Design and experimental validation. *IEEE Transactions on Intelligent Transportation Systems*, *25*(6), 5096–5111.

Bharadiya, J. P. (2023). Artificial intelligence in transportation systems a critical review. *American Journal of Computing and Engineering*, *6*(1), 35–45.

Borkowski, P., Jażdżewska-Gutta, M., & Szmelter-Jarosz, A. (2021). Lockdowned: Everyday mobility changes in response to COVID-19. *Journal of Transport Geography*, *90*, 102906.

Bucsky, P. (2020). Modal share changes due to COVID-19: The case of Budapest. *Transportation Research Interdisciplinary Perspectives*, *8*, 100141.

Chen, X., Ma, D., & Liu, R. W. (2024). Application of artificial intelligence in maritime transportation. *Journal of Marine Science and Engineering*, *12*(3), 439.

Chiang, C. H. (2025). AI in airport operations: Enhancing competitiveness and satisfaction. *Enterprise Information Systems*, 2454003.

Dartmann, G., Schmeink, A., Lücken, V., Song, H., Ziefle, M., & Prestiflippo, G. (Eds.). (2021). *Smart transportation: AI enabled mobility and autonomous driving* (1st ed.). CRC Press. https://doi.org/10.1201/9780367808150

De Liso, N., & Zamparini, L. (2022). Innovation, transport security and supply chains: A review. *Transport Reviews*, *42*(6), 725–738.

Domínguez-Mujica, J. (2016). *Global change and human mobility*. Springer Nature.

Elbroumi, S., Idrissi, M. A., Chaaouan, M., & Eddahmouny, H. (2025). Exploring trends, perspectives, and challenges of artificial intelligence in sustainable mobility: A systematic review. *Utilizing Technology to Manage Territories*, 207–238.

Huang, W., Li, S., Liu, X., & Ban, Y. (2015). Predicting human mobility with activity changes. *International Journal of Geographical Information Science*, *29*(9), 1569–1587.

Iyer, L. S. (2021). AI enabled applications towards intelligent transportation. *Transportation Engineering*, *5*, 100083.

Jadhav, B., Kulkarni, A., Khang, A., Kulkarni, P., & Kulkarni, S. (2025). Beyond the horizon: Exploring the future of artificial intelligence (AI) powered sustainable mobility in public transportation system. In *Driving green transportation system through artificial intelligence and automation: Approaches, technologies and applications* (pp. 397–409). Springer Nature Switzerland.

Janić, M. (2021). An approach to analysing and modelling the reliability of transport services. *Transportation Planning and Technology*, *44*(6), 647–678.

Kamargianni, M., Li, W., Matyas, M., & Schäfer, A. (2016). A critical review of new mobility services for urban transport. *Transportation Research Procedia*, *14*, 3294–3303.

Lemonnier, A., Adelé, S., & Dionisio, C. (2023). Acceptability of autonomous trains with different grades of automation by potential users: A qualitative approach. *Travel Behaviour and Society*, *33*, 100641.

Lenz, B., & Fraedrich, E. (2016). New mobility concepts and autonomous driving: The potential for change. *Autonomous Driving: Technical, Legal and Social Aspects*, 173–191.

Li, A., Zhuang, S., Yang, T., Lu, W., & Xu, J. (2024). Optimization of logistics cargo tracking and transportation efficiency based on data science deep learning models. *Applied and Computational Engineering*, *69*, 71–77.

Luckey, D., Fritz, H., Legatiuk, D., Dragos, K., & Smarsly, K. (2021). Artificial intelligence techniques for smart city applications. In *Proceedings of the 18th international conference on computing in civil and building engineering: ICCCBE 2020* (pp. 3–15). Springer International Publishing.

Mahor, V., Bijrothiya, S., Mishra, R., Rawat, R., & Soni, A. (2022). The smart city based on AI and infrastructure: A new mobility concepts and realities. *Autonomous Vehicles Volume 1: Using Machine Intelligence*, 277–295.

Mäkelä, M. (2024). Artificial intelligence to benefit the passenger experience at the airport.

Mayer, C. (2019). Digital passengers: A great divide or emerging opportunity? *Journal of Airport Management*, *13*(4), 335–344.

Musselwhite, C., Avineri, E., & Susilo, Y. (2021). Restrictions on mobility due to the coronavirus Covid19: Threats and opportunities for transport and health. *Journal of Transport & Health*, *20*, 101042.
Natarajan, J., Kantipudi, M. B., Yang, C.-H., & Shiao, Y. (Eds.). (2023). *The future of road transportation: Electrification and automation* (1st ed.). CRC Press. https://doi.org/10.1201/9781003354901
Navarathna, P. J., & Malagi, V. P. (2018, December). Artificial intelligence in smart city analysis. In *2018 International conference on smart systems and inventive technology (ICSSIT)* (pp. 44–47). IEEE.
Nikitas, A., Michalakopoulou, K., Njoya, E. T., & Karampatzakis, D. (2020). Artificial intelligence, transport and the smart city: Definitions and dimensions of a new mobility era. *Sustainability*, *12*(7), 2789.
Nouvellet, P., Bhatia, S., Cori, A., Ainslie, K. E. C., Baguelin, M., Bhatt, S., Boonyasiri, A., Brazeau, N. F., Cattarino, L., Cooper, L. V., Coupland, H., Cucunuba, Z. M., Cuomo-Dannenburg, G., Dighe, A., Djaafara, B. A., Dorigatti, I., Eales, O. D., van Elsland, S. L., Nascimento, F. F., . . . Donnelly, C. A. (2021). Reduction in mobility and COVID-19 transmission. *Nature Communications*, *12*, 1090. https://doi.org/10.1038/s41467-021-21358-2
Okrepilov, V. V., Kovalenko, B. B., Getmanova, G. V., & Turovskaj, M. S. (2022). Modern trends in artificial intelligence in the transport system. *Transportation Research Procedia*, *61*, 229–233.
Palm, M., Farber, S., Shalaby, A., & Young, M. (2021). Equity analysis and new mobility technologies: Toward meaningful interventions. *Journal of Planning Literature*, *36*(1), 31–45.
Pisarov, J., & Mester, G. (2021). Implementing new mobility concepts with autonomous self-driving robotic cars. *IPSI Transactions on Advanced Research (TAR)*, *17*(2), 41–49.
Plissonneau, A., Trentesaux, D., Ben-Messaoud, W., & Bekrar, A. (2021, May). AI-based speed control models for the autonomous train: A literature review. In *2021 third international conference on transportation and smart technologies (TST)* (pp. 9–15). IEEE.
Polymeni, S., Pitsiavas, V., Spanos, G., Matthewson, Q., Lalas, A., Votis, K., & Tzovaras, D. (2024). Toward sustainable mobility: AI-enabled automated refueling for fuel cell electric vehicles. *Energies*, *17*(17), 4324.
Qian, Y., Polimetla, T., Sanchez, T. W., & Yan, X. (2025). How do transportation professionals perceive the impacts of AI applications in transportation? A latent class cluster analysis. *Transportation*, 1–26.
Reis, J., Amorim, M., Cohen, Y., & Rodrigues, M. (2020). Artificial intelligence in service delivery systems: A systematic literature review. In *Trends and innovations in information systems and technologies* (pp. 222–233). Springer.
Salmon, P. M. (2024). These aren't the droids you're looking for: Artificial intelligence and safety in future transport systems. *Transportation Planning and Technology*, 1–5.
Servou, E., Behrendt, F., & Horst, M. (2023). Data, AI and governance in MaaS – Leading to sustainable mobility? *Transportation Research Interdisciplinary Perspectives*, *19*, 100806.
Szpilko, D., Naharro, F. J., Lăzăroiu, G., Nica, E., & de la Torre Gallegos, A. (2023). Artificial intelligence in the smart city – A literature review. *Engineering Management in Production and Services*, *15*(4), pp. 53–75. Sciendo.
Tagiew, R., Leinhos, D., von der Haar, H., Klotz, C., Sprute, D., Ziehn, J., Schmelter, A., Witte, S., & Klasek, P. (2023). Sensor system for development of perception systems for ATO. *Discover Artificial Intelligence*, *3*(1), 22.
Tang, R., De Donato, L., Bešinović, N., Flammini, F., Goverde, R. M. P., Lin, Z., Liu, R., Tang, T., Vittorini, V., & Wang, Z. (2022). A literature review of Artificial

Intelligence applications in railway systems. *Transportation Research Part C: Emerging Technologies*, *140*, 103679.
Vávrová, L., Nacházelová, E., & Bůhová Foltýnová, H. (2025). Shaping mobility futures: Understanding Millennials and Gen Z transport choices for sustainable policy design. *Sustainable Communities*, *2*(1), 2483250.
Wang, W., Gope, P., & Cheng, Y. (2022). An AI-driven secure and intelligent robotic delivery system. *IEEE Transactions on Engineering Management*, *71*, 12658–12673.
Zamparini, L. (2022). A review of models for transport security and of their relevance for supply chains. *Transport Reviews*, *42*(6), 784–800. https://doi.org/10.1080/01441647.2022.2056255
Zargari, F., Aminpour, N., Ahmadian, M. A., Samimi, A., & Saidi, S. (2022). Impact of mobility on COVID-19 spread – A time series analysis. *Transportation Research Interdisciplinary Perspectives*, *13*, 100567.
Zhang, Y., & Kamargianni, M. (2023). A review on the factors influencing the adoption of new mobility technologies and services: Autonomous vehicle, drone, micromobility and mobility as a service. *Transport Reviews*, *43*(3), 407–429.

15 The Adoption of Autonomous Technologies in the Polish TFL Sector and the Implications of Digital Transformation

Sylwia Konecka, Anna Lewandowska-Ciszek, and András Keszthelyi

The Importance of Artificial Intelligence for Logistics and Logistics Education

Artificial intelligence (AI) is a significant factor in supporting economic efficiency across various sectors. According to analyses by Accenture (2020), by 2035, AI could increase the annual GDP growth rate by an average of 1.7 percentage points across 16 sectors. The highest projected growth is expected in the information and communication sector (4.8%), the financial sector (4.3%), and the manufacturing sector (4.4%). In the transport and warehousing sector, the expected growth is 1.3 pp, from 2.7% to 4.0%, primarily driven by automation processes, transport route optimization, and tools supporting supply chain management. Simultaneously, the education sector, a key driver in developing competencies necessary for implementing and using AI, is projected to grow by 0.9 percentage points. This growth is mainly attributed to personalized learning and the implementation of augmented and virtual reality (AR/VR) technologies, as confirmed by Hoffmann and Mehta (2024). A comparative overview presented in the McKinsey report (Mayer et al., 2025) indicates a significantly higher value added by AI technologies compared to conventional solutions, particularly in the tourism (+128%), logistics (+89%), automotive (+87%), and financial services (+85%) sectors.

Additionally, the World Economic Forum report (Mayer et al., 2025) highlights that 48% of employers in the delivery and logistics sector, and 56% in the education sector, find AI and big data analysis skills as critical for 2025–2030. Specific areas of AI application include inventory management (40%) and quality control (34%). Market forecasts estimate that by 2026, the global warehouse automation market will exceed USD 30 billion, while the cargo drone sector is expected to reach USD 17.88 billion by 2030. High levels of AI adoption are also seen in the retail and consumer goods sectors, where up to 90% of companies report implementation plans. Simultaneously, challenges related to cybersecurity and skills shortages are emphasized (Mayer et al., 2025). AI-based technologies are being increasingly implemented, particularly in such areas as order fulfillment and financial

DOI: 10.4324/9781003659143-19

management. By 2025, the logistics robotics market in the MENA region is projected to reach USD 2.56 billion. Technological advancements are also influencing shipment tracking methods, which are especially valued by younger consumer groups (Saleh, 2022).

AI is increasingly used in the Transport, Forwarding, Logistics (TFL) sector, as well as industries highly dependent on efficient supply chains, such as automotive, tourism, healthcare, and consumer goods sectors. Increasingly important is the inclusion of AI in TFL-related education. Therefore, it is justified to conduct an in-depth analysis of implemented technological solutions, with particular attention to their practical applications, achieved results, and potential threats.

Key AI Technologies in Logistics

The review of scientific literature was conducted using the Web of Science (WoS) database, employing a combination of keyword searches and the functionality of the Research Assistant tool. In the initial stage, 10,995 documents containing the phrases "logistics" and "AI" were identified, which were then narrowed down to 483 records by applying the "AI tools" filter. From this group, 409 publications dated from 2021–2025. Further selection, based on selected WoS thematic categories (including Computer Science AI, Management, Transportation), resulted in a final research sample of 147 documents, that is, 91 journal articles, 37 conference papers, ten review articles, eight early access items, and one book chapter. The dominant countries of publication origin included the United States (19), the United Kingdom (18), India (17), China (13), and Spain (11).

The literature indicates the growing role of AI as a tool enhancing operational efficiency, flexibility, and resilience of supply chains. The most implemented AI technologies in the TFL sector include machine learning (ML), predictive analytics, mobile robotics (AMR, AGV), natural language processing (NLP), image recognition, and process automation using RPA technology. These tools are used, among others, for route optimization, demand forecasting, inventory management, and real-time decision support (Riad et al., 2024; Nozari et al., 2025).

Evolutionary algorithms such as Genetic Algorithm (GA), Particle Swarm Optimization (PSO), or Grey Wolf Optimizer (GWO) are applied to solving complex logistics problems, including the distribution of temperature-sensitive products. In the context of warehouse automation, artificial intelligence supports the development of mobile robotics, enhancing precision, scalability, and safety of warehouse operations (Hangl et al., 2022).

Contemporary applications of generative AI (e.g., ChatGPT and Bard) include the creation of training materials, automation of stakeholder communication, and support for decision-making processes (Raman et al., 2024). The role of IoT devices should also be emphasized, although not themselves AI technologies, they perform an essential function in feeding intelligent systems with data used, for instance, in predictive maintenance and real-time shipment tracking (Idrissi et al., 2022; Nozari et al., 2025).

AI constitutes an integral component of Industry 4.0 and Logistics 4.0 ecosystems, cooperating with technologies such as blockchain, big data, cyber-physical systems, and cloud computing. The integration of these solutions supports the enhancement of supply chain resilience and enables the implementation of sustainable development strategies (Amejwal et al., 2022; Modgil et al., 2022). Nevertheless, the implementation of AI technologies encounters significant technical and organizational barriers, including insufficient digital infrastructure, resistance to change, and concerns about the impact of automation on the labor market (Hangl et al., 2022).

The use of the Research Assistant tool supported the selection of documents and the formulation of a response to the research question regarding the key AI technologies utilized in the TFL sector. An excellent literature review in the field of production logistics was presented by Zafarzadeh et al. (2021), who identified 47 technologies classified into 10 groups based on 142 scientific articles:

- Auto-identification: RFID, barcode, QR code, Fingerprint of Things, tag-free traceability.
- Vision systems and image recognition: vision systems, point cloud.
- Mobile and industrial robots: industrial robots, drones, AGV, mobile robots.
- Internet of Things: IoT, IoS, RTLS, Node-RED.
- Smart devices: AR/VR, Pick-by-X, smartwatches, tablets, smart gloves.
- Artificial intelligence and big data: ML, AI, Apache Flume, Hadoop, Kafka, MQTT.
- Wireless communication and networking: 2G–5G, Wi-Fi, Bluetooth, GPS, ZigBee.
- Cloud and edge computing: cloud computing, fog/edge computing.
- Cyber-physical systems and simulations: digital twin, embedded systems, simulation, SoA.
- Blockchain.

In the study by Winkelhaus and Grosse (2020), seven main categories of technologies typical of the Logistics 4.0 concept were identified, such as IoT, CPS, big data, cloud computing, mobile technologies, social media, and blockchain. The authors demonstrated that major keywords in the analyzed publications included RFID, augmented reality, production logistics, smart logistics, warehouse management, and 3D printing.

In both the classical and Research Assistant-supported approaches, documents were classified according to their association with AI technologies, "smart technologies," and the concepts of Industry 4.0/5.0. The analysis clearly indicates that AI technologies – such as ML, big data analytics, and autonomous systems – form the foundation of modern logistics solutions. Many of the remaining technologies (e.g., vision systems, digital twins, IoT) use AI in an indirect manner, confirming their complementary character in creating intelligent, integrated logistics systems.

During the original research, six individual in-depth interviews (IDIs – Individual In-Depth Interviews) were conducted. The research sample included exhibitors of the International MODERNLOG Fair – from among 75 companies participating in the event, six enterprises delivering or using solutions dedicated to the logistics sector were selected. The respondents were industry experts representing various levels and areas of activity. The research group consisted of an employee of a scientific institution who is also employed in a company specializing in the distribution of collaborative robots (cobots), with over ten years of professional experience, a robotics specialist with more than ten years of experience, two warehouse managers with experience ranging from five to ten years and from three to five years, respectively, a key account manager with three to five years of professional experience, and a company vice president, also with three to five years of experience. The respondents represented three medium-sized enterprises (employing from 50 to 249 employees) and three corporations (employing over 500 employees). Four of these companies have operated in the market for over ten years, while two have been active for between one and five years. Geographically, three enterprises operated in the European market, and the remaining three conducted business on a global scale. The interviews were conducted between June 3 and June 5, 2024.

During the research, 31 of the most frequently used technological tools in the TFL industry were identified. The responses obtained indicated that 83% of companies used warehouse management systems (WMS), transport management systems (TMS), and ERP systems, and also employ Jungenrich high-lift forklifts; 67% of enterprises implemented autonomous internal transport vehicles (AMR – Autonomous Mobile Robots). 50% of the respondents utilized technologies related to robotics and automation, including robotic systems for goods handling, RFID chips and AI, 33% of companies applied solutions such as pick-to-light systems, robotic palletizers, automated warehouse stackers, internet of things (IoT), automated transport systems (AGV), virtual reality (VR), and intelligent transport systems (ITS), 17% of enterprises used advanced technologies, such as big data, cobots, automatic conveyors and racks, blockchain, Supply Chain 4.0 (IoT & analytics), and digital twins. Additionally, cloud services (cloud computing & storage) and MRO (Maintenance, Repair, and Operations) were also employed, although their exact share was not precisely determined. However, respondents did not indicate the use of solutions such as smart glasses, exoskeletons, 3D printing, AR (augmented reality), AIDC (Automatic Identification and Data Capture), or anthropomorphic robots, despite the questions also covering these technologies.

Potential Barriers and Risks for TFL Sector Enterprises in Implementing AI Technologies

Analysis of the subject literature allowed for the identification of key risks associated with the implementation of AI technologies in the TFL sector. One of the main risks is the security of logistics systems, which, due to their complexity and numerous access points, are vulnerable to malware attacks and data breaches by cybercriminals. Modern distribution centers may have hundreds of such points, significantly increasing the risk of incidents resulting in financial losses, operational disruptions, loss of customer trust, and in extreme cases, threats to human life and health (Efthymiou & Ponis, 2021; Chung, 2021). Despite the existence of security standards such as ISO/IEC 27000 and IEC 62443, there is a need for further work on standard unification and expansion to meet the challenges of Logistics 4.0 and ensure comprehensive protection (Chung, 2021).

The process of implementing AI technologies and Industry 4.0 solutions in the TFL sector is often hindered or delayed by insufficient regulatory frameworks and a lack of consistent technical standards. Gaps in legal regulations concerning commercial issues, security, and system interoperability constitute a significant barrier to the widespread adoption of these technologies (Efthymiou & Ponis, 2021; Chung, 2021). The current industrial environment is characterized by a fragmented approach to standards, which limits both the scalability and reliability of implemented solutions (Chung, 2021).

The high complexity of AI-based systems and related technologies generates difficulties related to their integration, interoperability, and management. Specific challenges occur when connecting new solutions, such as blockchain or the IoT, with the existing IT infrastructure of enterprises, which can lead to operational disruptions and reduced supply chain efficiency (Zafarzadeh et al., 2021). Additionally, investments in technologies with a low level of technological maturity carry the risk of ineffective implementation and operation.

The development of infrastructure necessary for the implementation of AI technologies and Industry 4.0 solutions in logistics requires ensuring flexibility, scalability, advanced networking, and communication capabilities. Building a fully functional logistics ecosystem, including autonomous systems and interoperability among network nodes, is a significant technological and organizational challenge (Trkman et al., 2010). High investment costs related to creating such systems represent an additional barrier, especially when previous investments have not yielded the expected returns.

Many enterprises experience a shortage of employees with the competencies and knowledge required to implement and manage AI technologies. Insufficient workforce preparation and the lack of specialized skills constitute significant obstacles to the effective use of intelligent logistics systems (Chung, 2021). The increasing automation of systems, such as robotics or autonomous vehicles, also raises concerns about the potential negative impact on employment in the TFL sector, particularly in warehousing and transportation areas.

Table 15.1 Potential risks arising from the use of AI technologies in transportation and warehousing

How Important Do You Consider the Risks Associated with the Use of Autonomous Solutions in Transportation and Warehousing?	*Average*
Data security	4.67
Security threat arising from machine error	4.67
Inadequately adapted infrastructure	4.50
Risk of hacker attacks	4.00
Security threat arising from human error	4.00
High failure rate of vehicles	3.83
Insufficient level of technological preparedness	3.67
Lack of accountability in case of accident/collision	3.67
Inadequate legal regulations regarding commercial issues	3.50
Erroneous AI decisions	3.20
Privacy threats	3.00
Inadequate legal regulations regarding vehicle technical inspection requirements	3.00
Job loss among warehouse workers	2.83
Excessively high implementation costs	2.83
Inadequate legal regulations regarding operations on public roads	2.83
Reduction of vehicle owners' prestige	2.50
Inadequate legal regulations regarding infrastructure and connected vehicles	2.50
Inadequate legal regulations regarding licensing and registration	2.50
Excessively high purchase costs	2.33
Inadequate legal regulations regarding operator requirements	2.33
Job loss among drivers	2.17

Source: Authors' own work.

Based on original research and individual interviews, respondents identified the most critical risks, including data security, machine or human errors, inadequate infrastructure, and threats related to hacking attacks. The evaluations were provided on a five-point scale where 1 meant "completely unimportant," 2 – "slightly important," 3 – "neither important nor unimportant," 4 – "fairly important," and 5 – "very important." All risks identified in the original study are presented in Table 15.1.

The analysis of responses obtained during the primary research concerning financing models and implementation barriers of autonomous logistics solutions allows for the identification of a diverse approach among enterprises toward investing in new technologies, as well as specific challenges arising during their deployment. The most frequently indicated financing model was the operating lease option, selected by 41.7% of respondents. This preference may reflect companies' tendency to spread investment costs over time, thereby reducing the one-time burden on the operating budget. The second most frequently chosen solution was the service model known as RaaS (Robots as a Service), accounting for

25.0% of responses, which confirms the growing interest in flexible access to advanced technologies without the necessity of full purchase. In contrast, full upfront payment and other subscription models were selected by 16.7% of the surveyed enterprises. Models based on performance metrics, such as "pay per pick," "pay per mile," or "pay per peak day" (0%, 0%, and 8.3%, respectively), attracted negligible interest, possibly due to implementation difficulties and their inadequacy relative to the nature of the conducted operations.

The most frequently identified barriers in the implementation process of automation solutions included employee resistance to organizational change and the shortage of qualified personnel (each accounting for 26.7% of responses). These factors highlight the significance of social and competency-related aspects in the technological transformation process. Other notable barriers included limited financial resources (20.0%) and the lack of suitable technological and implementation partners (13.3%). Issues related to the availability of training were less significant; only 6.7% of respondents reported a lack of training, while 13.3% indicated an insufficient number of training opportunities. Importantly, the quality of training and other factors were not identified as major constraints.

The organizational units studied also reported a range of technical and organizational barriers, which included difficulties integrating multiple, often independent, IT systems, prolonged preparation and execution times of investments (averaging four to five years), spatial limitations, such as the inability to expand warehouse space adjacent to the production facility, and low flexibility of automation systems under conditions of high product assortment variability.

The respondents further emphasized that automation implementation did not result in workforce reduction but rather modified its structure – repetitive tasks were taken over by technical systems, while employees were relocated to tasks requiring higher qualifications. The need to invest in the development of employee competencies was also stressed, not only in terms of operating automated systems but also with respect to language and managerial skills. At the same time, the inadequacy of the existing educational programs in view of the dynamically changing sector needs was highlighted, both regarding vocational training and academic curricula.

The frequently mentioned risks also included issues related to occupational safety, data access management (including Big Data systems), the requirement to ensure high availability of solutions (SLA – Service Level Agreement), and the necessity to adapt organizational culture to the working conditions in automated environments. In this context, the challenges arising from cultural differences among employees of international operational teams were noted, one example being difficulties in managing teams employed in warehouses in Central and Eastern Europe, where a significant group of workers came from the Philippines.

Potential Benefits of Artificial Intelligence in the TFL Sector

According to the findings of Edirisuriya et al. (2018) and Zhong et al. (2017), the technologies encompassed within the Industry 4.0 ecosystem, including the IoT, cloud computing, big data analytics, AI, automation, and augmented and virtual reality (AR/VR), exert a significant impact on enhancing operational efficiency in logistics and transportation. The integration of these solutions enables the automation of logistics processes, optimization of resource utilization, shortening the delivery cycles, inventory reduction, and decreased reliance on manual labor. Additionally, these technologies contribute to improving punctuality in production and distribution, facilitate the identification and elimination of bottlenecks within the supply chain, and support precise demand and sales forecasting.

Similar perspectives are expressed by Winkelhaus and Grosse (2020) and Nagy et al. (2018), who emphasize the importance of digital technologies in real-time monitoring of operational processes, dynamic optimization of activities, and efficient warehouse space management. Consequently, this leads to increased productivity and reliability of logistics systems.

The implementation of AI-based systems and big data analytics also contributes to the reduction of operational costs. By enhancing transparency in supply chain processes, automating tasks, and enabling more precise inventory management, losses and warehousing expenses can be significantly curtailed (Winkelhaus & Grosse, 2020; Nagy et al., 2018). Furthermore, a high level of information integration allows managers to make more informed decisions, resulting in more effective resource allocation and reduced operational risk.

Modern technologies also support the flexibility and adaptability of logistics systems in volatile market conditions. The ability to rapidly respond to demand fluctuations and dynamically adjust processes to individual customer needs fosters the development of services tailored to consumer expectations, which in turn enhances the competitiveness of TFL sector enterprises (Zhong et al., 2017; Zafarzadeh et al., 2021).

The application of advanced solutions, such as blockchain technology, real-time CRM systems, and intelligent analytical platforms, strengthens the collaboration among supply chain participants (Nagy et al., 2018). Process integration and ensuring transparency of information flow promote better coordination, minimize disruptions, and improve customer service quality. In the vision presented by Winkelhaus and Grosse (2020), the future of logistics is an integrated environment where resources, machines, and products communicate autonomously, and operational decisions are made in real time. Products equipped with digital identities and their continuous tracking make it possible to create intelligent warehouses and self-organizing transport systems, thereby increasing the efficiency and reliability of operational activities.

The findings from the present study corroborate these observations. The respondents evaluated the benefits of implementing autonomous solutions

Table 15.2 Potential benefits of implementing AI technologies in transportation and warehousing

How Significant Are the Benefits of Implementing Autonomous Solutions in Warehousing and Transportation?	*Average*
Reduction in the time required to perform logistics activities	5.0
Increased efficiency of logistics processes	4.8
Improved information flow within logistics operations	4.2
Optimization of goods placement within warehouses	4.2
Reduction in the number of warehouse workers	4.0
Enhanced customer service	3.8
Ability to prioritize logistics tasks	3.8
Reduction of errors	3.8
Lower transportation costs for cargo	3.8
Independence from the physical presence of forklift operators	3.8
Decreased number of road accidents	3.8
Elimination of empty runs in internal transport processes	3.6
Elimination of empty runs in external transport processes	3.6
Improved workplace safety	3.4
Higher return on investment in autonomous warehouse solutions	3.4
Reduction in the number of drivers	3.2
Lower warehousing costs	3.2
Higher return on investment in autonomous vehicles	3.2
Reduction of road congestion	3.2
Decreased consumption of raw materials	3.0
Independence from the physical presence of drivers	3.0
Reduction of emissions (autonomous vehicles)	3.0
Increased fleet efficiency (autonomous vehicles)	3.0
Reduced electricity consumption in warehouses	2.4

Source: Authors' own work.

in warehousing and transportation as significant, particularly with respect to reducing logistics operation times and increasing process efficiency. The highest-rated benefits were those related to operational improvements and internal process optimization. The ratings were provided on a five-point scale, where 1 indicated "completely insignificant" and 5 "very significant." The results are presented in Table 15.2.

The in-depth interviews examined external factors influencing the decisions of the TFL sector companies regarding the implementation of autonomous and environmentally friendly solutions. The study explored whether these decisions were driven by technological and operational benefits, the availability of financial support (e.g., subsidies), the absence of regulatory frameworks, or the necessity to choose between automation and environmental objectives due to regulatory pressure or the risk of sanctions. The respondents answered using a three-point scale: "yes," "no," or "I don't know."

The collected data indicate that autonomous technologies are, in most cases, based on electric propulsion, suggesting a complementary relationship with electric vehicles rather than a competitive one. The respondents perceived autonomous technologies as more cost-effective and less burdened by regulatory constraints than purely ecological solutions. Most participants rejected the view that the implementation of such technologies in Polish TSL firms would be driven by legislative changes or depend on external funding. Instead, investment decisions appear to be primarily based on internal assessments of operational benefits.

Furthermore, more than half of the respondents disagreed with the notion that Industry 4.0 technologies automatically lead to higher profit margins through improved resource utilization and enhanced product value. Similarly, they did not support the claim that integrating autonomous functions was easier in electric vehicles than in conventional combustion-engine vehicles. In other areas, such as prioritizing autonomy over environmental initiatives, the legal status of autonomous technologies in Poland, or vehicle ownership models, no clear consensus was found.

Qualitative data analysis also revealed key factors motivating companies to automate the logistics processes, including both warehousing and transportation operations. The most frequently cited reasons for adopting automation were

- Limited access to qualified labor, especially in regions with high employment levels and for repetitive tasks or those performed in challenging environmental conditions (e.g., cold storage facilities).
- Inappropriate level of automation, either too low, restricting efficiency, or too high relative to the scale of operations, a phenomenon mainly observed in small and medium-sized organizations.
- Long return on investment (ROI) periods, often exceeding 3 to 5 years. which contributes to cautious investment behavior.
- Issues with the quality and availability of operational data, complicating the assessment of implementation effectiveness and the integration of new solutions with the existing IT infrastructure.
- High share of labor costs in the cost structure of TFL companies, reaching up to 50% of operating expenses, making automation an attractive tool for cost reduction.
- High variability in the product assortment structure, including the presence of hazardous goods (e.g., ADR) that limits the possibility of full automation in certain processes.

In practice, automation is primarily applied in areas with large operational scales and where order fulfillment time is a key competitive advantage. A notable example is the automotive sector, where companies such as Inter Cars deliver spare parts within 45–60 minutes, and the implementation of automation solutions in the goods issuance process significantly shortens the so-called last mile.

This issue is also reflected in the literature. Lim et al. (2018) revisited last-mile logistics (LML) models in the context of digital supply chains in e-commerce, highlighting the need to integrate the automation systems with AI technologies. Similar observations were reported by those survey respondents who indicated an operational efficiency increase of approximately 8–12% using AI for remote technical problem-solving.

In summary, AI plays a pivotal role in logistics and logistics education by significantly enhancing operational efficiency, optimizing transportation routes, supporting supply chain management, and automating warehouse processes. However, we should keep in mind that both the benefits and the risks of using AI are strongly linked to the quality of the data it relies on and the level of advancement of the models being used. The projected economic growth in the transportation and warehousing sector attributable to AI is estimated at 1.3 percentage points, with added value in logistics potentially increasing by up to 89%. In education, AI enables personalized learning and the use of AR/VR technologies, fostering the development of key competencies necessary for implementing advanced logistics solutions. There is a growing demand for skills related to AI and data analytics, alongside an emphasized need to adapt educational programs to evolving technological challenges.

Technologies such as machine learning, mobile robotics, predictive analytics, and digital twins are applied in demand forecasting, inventory management, and real-time decision support, contributing to the creation of more resilient and adaptive supply chains. However, these implementations face multiple limitations, including technological, regulatory, and social challenges, with particular concern given to data security and the integration of existing IT infrastructure. Moreover, the threats identified in the original study are interrelated and may reinforce or weaken each other, which should also be considered as an area for further analysis.

The identified benefits of AI adoption primarily include process automation, cost reduction, shortened lead times, and improved coordination across the supply chain. Respondents also highlight the increased return on investment and enhanced workplace safety conditions, while academic literature stresses the importance of increased flexibility in logistics systems and process integration, ultimately leading to greater competitiveness of enterprises.

Reference List

Amejwal, M., El Jaouhari, A., Arif, J., Fellaki, S., & Jawab, F. (2022). Production flow management based on Industry 4.0 technologies. In *2022, 14th international colloquium of logistics and supply chain management (LOGISTIQUA2022)*. https://doi.org/10.1109/LOGISTIQUA55056.2022.9938064

Chung, S.-H. (2021). Applications of smart technologies in logistics and transport: A review. *Transportation Research Part E: Logistics and Transportation Review, 153*, 102455. https://doi.org/10.1016/j.tre.2021.102455

Edirisuriya, A., Weerabahu, S., & Wickramarachchi, R. (2018). Applicability of lean and green concepts in Logistics 4.0: A systematic review of literature. In *Proceedings of the 2018 international conference on production and operations management society (POMS)*, Peradeniya, Sri Lanka.

Efthymiou, O. K., & Ponis, S. T. (2021). Industry 4.0 technologies and their impact in contemporary logistics: A systematic literature review. *Sustainability*, *13*(21), 11643. https://doi.org/10.3390/su132111643

Hangl, J., Behrens, V. J., & Krause, S. (2022). Barriers, drivers, and social considerations for AI adoption in supply chain management: A tertiary study. *Logistics-Basel*, *6*(3). https://doi.org/10.3390/logistics6030063

Hoffmann, J., & Mehta, D. (2024, April). *Artificial intelligence: In-depth market analysis (Market Insights report)*. Statista. www.statista.com/

Idrissi, Z. K., Lachgar, M., & Hrimech, H. (2022). Blockchain, IoT and AI revolution within transport and logistics. In *2022 14th international colloquium of logistics and supply chain management* (LOGISTIQUA2022). https:/doi.org./10.1109/LOGISTIQUA55056.2022.9938035

Lim, S. F. W. T., Jin, X., & Srai, J. S. (2018). Consumer-driven e-commerce: A literature review, design framework, and research agenda on last-mile logistics models. *International Journal of Physical Distribution & Logistics Management*, *48*(3), 308–332.

Mayer, H., Yee, L., Chui, M., & Roberts, R. (2025, January 28). *Superagency in the workplace: Empowering people to unlock AI's full potential* [Report]. McKinsey & Company. www.mckinsey.com/

Modgil, S., Gupta, S., Stekelorum, R., & Laguir, I. (2022). AI technologies and their impact on supply chain resilience during COVID-19. *International Journal of Physical Distribution & Logistics Management*, *52*(2). https://doi.org/10.1108/IJPDLM-12-2020-0434

Nagy, J., Oláh, J., Erdei, E., Máté, D., & Popp, J. (2018). The role and impact of Industry 4.0 and the Internet of Things on the business strategy of the value chain – the case of Hungary. *Sustainability*, *10*(10), 3491. https://doi.org/10.3390/su10103491

Nozari, H., Rahmaty, M., Foukolaei, P. Z., & Bayanati, M. (2025). Optimizing cold chain logistics with artificial intelligence of things (AIoT): A model for reducing operational and transportation costs. *Future Transportation*, *5*(1). https://doi.org/10.3390/futuretransp5010001

Raman, R., Sreenivasan, A., Suresh, M., Gunasekaran, A., & Nedungadi, P. (2024). AI-driven education: A comparative study on ChatGPT and Bard in supply chain management contexts. *Cogent Business & Management*, *11*(1). https://doi.org/10.1080/23311975.2024.2412742

Riad, M., Naimi, M., & Okar, C. (2024). Enhancing supply chain resilience through artificial intelligence: Developing a comprehensive conceptual framework for AI implementation and supply chain optimization. *Logistics-Basel*, *8*(4). https://doi.org/10.3390/logistics8040111

Saleh, S. (2022, April 26). *Warehouse automation market size MENA 2014–2025*. Statista. www.statista.com/

Trkman, P., McCormack, K., de Oliveira, M. P. V., & Ladeira, M. B. (2010). The impact of business analytics on supply chain performance. *Decision Support Systems*, *49*(3), 318–327. https://doi.org/10.1016/j.dss.2010.03.007

Winkelhaus, S., & Grosse, E. H. (2020). Logistics 4.0: A systematic review towards a new logistics system. *International Journal of Production Research*, *58*(1), 18–43. https://doi.org/10.1080/00207543.2019.1612964

Zafarzadeh, M., Wiktorsson, M., & Baalsrud Hauge, J. (2021). A systematic review on technologies for data-driven production logistics: Their role from a holistic and value creation perspective. *Logistics*, *5*(2), 24. https://doi.org/10.3390/logistics5020024

Zhong, R. Y., Xu, C., Chen, C., & Huang, G. Q. (2017). Big data analytics for physical Internet-based intelligent manufacturing shop floors. *International Journal of Production Research*, *55*(9), 2610–2621. https://doi.org/10.1080/00207543.2015.1086037

Part V

Finance

16 Application of AI and RPA in Accounting and Corporate Finance

Economic and Social Consequences

Marzena Remlein, Ana Rep Romić, Dariusz Nowak, and Marlena Napierała

Introduction

Artificial intelligence (AI) and robotic process automation (RPA) are widely utilized across various domains of corporate operations, with significant adoption in finance and accounting, as indicated by research findings (Kroll et al., 2016; Borowiec, 2022; Remlein, Bejger, et al., 2022; Žager et al., 2020). The processes most frequently subjected to automation include invoice processing, transaction recording and analysis, receivables and payables management, financial reporting, internal audit and compliance, data analysis and visualization, expenditure control and budgeting, financial forecasting (Gotthardt et al., 2019; Kaya et al., 2019; Huang & Vasarhelyi, 2019; Moffitt et al., 2018; Rozario & Vasarhelyi, 2018), and tax settlement (Mezzio et al., 2019; Łada & Mierzejewska, 2021; Remlein et al., 2022).

The implementation of AI and RPA in corporate accounting and finance can produce various economic outcomes, which may differ based on industry, geographic location, and specific market conditions. The primary effects include reduced operating costs, increased efficiency, and improved accuracy. The main social implications involve shifts in employment, education, and skills requirements, as well as ethical and accountability considerations.

The aim of the chapter is to present the significance of applying AI and RPA in the field of accounting and corporate finance, with a particular focus on their impact on the operational and organizational efficiency of enterprises. The chapter discusses the potential benefits of implementing modern automation technologies in accounting practices and identifies key challenges associated with the deployment of automation solutions within organizational structures. Particular attention is given to the issues related to the impact of automation on changes in employee competencies and the organizational structure of financial units.

Case Context and Research Perspective

The study employed a qualitative approach based on a semi-structured interview method conducted with the chief financial officer (CFO) responsible for

DOI: 10.4324/9781003659143-21

implementing automation processes in the area of finance and accounting. This methodological choice enabled the collection of in-depth empirical data and the capture of the respondent's subjective experiences. The interview was open-ended, allowing for flexible exploration of key issues. To enhance data validation, method triangulation was applied, combining interview results with an analysis of the company's internal documentation and a review of data related to implemented technological solutions. This combination of research techniques provided a comprehensive view of automation processes in accounting and allowed for the identification of factors determining the success of implementations.

The study on the potential applications of AI and RPA in corporate accounting and finance, as well as their economic and social consequences, was conducted in the second quarter of 2025 at FCW company. The company was chosen due to its high level of advancement in business process automation, particularly in the areas of finance, accounting, controlling, and data management. FCW company, part of the global FCW group, specializes in industrial automation solutions and connection technology, providing advanced systems for the energy, automotive, and manufacturing industries, which translates into extensive and modern administrative and financial support processes. Additionally, the company is located in Poland and specializes in the production of electrical and electronic connectors, as well as serving as a shared services center.

The respondent in the study was CFO responsible for managing automation processes in finance and accounting, with many years of practical experience in designing, implementing, and optimizing AI and RPA – based tools within corporate structures. Due to their daily work with these technologies, the respondent was able to provide information not only about current applications but also about the strategic challenges associated with their further development. In her opinion, the automation of business processes at FCW company primarily results from limitations in employee availability and the need to increase cost efficiency. The main challenge is to improve the efficiency of business processes, both administrative and production-related. The respondent emphasized that rising employment costs are partially offset by the implementation of modern automation technologies. Automation enables significant improvements in efficiency regarding lead time and the cost of performing individual processes, particularly in financial and production data reporting, where obtaining results as quickly as possible is crucial.

Furthermore, the interviewee highlighted that automating administrative processes improves reporting quality by using standardized algorithms and eliminating errors resulting from a lack of specialization in global reporting. The implementation of automation also supports improving the quality of master data in ERP/SAP systems, which significantly affects the consistency and accuracy of reports. According to the interlocutor, one of the challenges in automating administrative processes is also providing employees with modern work tools necessary to perform their duties optimally and efficiently. The use of automation helps avoid monotonous and repetitive tasks, which increases employee satisfaction and retention, especially in the context of growing expectations for working in an innovative environment.

In the study, the authors focused on four main areas: (1) identifying the applications of AI and RPA in corporate finance and accounting, (2) analyzing the economic effects of the implemented solutions, (3) assessing the social and organizational consequences of automation, and (4) discussing the organization's strategic approach to the development of these technologies. The selection of these areas was driven by their critical importance for a comprehensive understanding of the impact of modern tools on the functioning of financial departments, both at the operational and strategic levels. It was essential not only to determine which processes were automated but also to analyze the economic outcomes and social changes brought about by these transformations, as well as how they shape the future competency structure within the organization.

The interview was conducted in a direct, qualitative, and semi-structured format, allowing for a free-flowing conversation around predefined topics while maintaining the flexibility to explore new, emerging themes. The direct form of the interview facilitated relationship building and enabled obtaining more honest and comprehensive responses, which are difficult to achieve in surveys or fully structured interviews. The qualitative nature of the study not only captured factual information but also provided a deeper understanding of the respondent's perspective, motivations, experiences, and opinions regarding the use of AI and RPA, which would be challenging to achieve through quantitative methods. The semi-structured format, based on a set of key topics, ensured conversation consistency while allowing questions to be adapted to the interview flow and delving into particularly important subjects.

To ensure high-quality research results, methodological triangulation was applied, involving the supplementation of interview data with an analysis of the company's internal process documentation and a review of available data on implemented automation solutions. This approach enhanced the credibility of the obtained information by enabling its verification and enrichment with organizational and technological context.

Such an approach made it possible not only to discuss the identified areas in detail but also to build a broader picture of the role that AI and RPA technologies play in shaping modern corporate finance and their impact on the organizational and social structure of enterprises.

At the outset, the respondent presented and discussed the various stages of automation implementation in the studied company, highlighting key activities and challenges encountered during the deployment process. The individual stages are illustrated in Table 16.1.

Table 16.1 Stages of implementing automated solutions in the operational activities of FCW company

Pre-implementation analysis

- Business process analysis
- Identyfication of areas requiring optimization
- Definition of automation objectives (cost-, time- , quality-related)
- Consultations with stakeholders and IT teams

Cost-benefit analysis

- Costs of purchasing software licences (eg. RPA tools, AI platforms)
- IT infrastructure costs (servers, databases)
- Expenses for system integration (ERP, CRM) and configuration
- Costs of employee training and technical support

Design

- Selection of tools and technologies (AI, RPA, ERP)
- Designing the system architecture
- Creating prototypes and process models
- Considering compliance issues (eg. GDPR)

Implementation

- Installation and configuration of automation tools
- Development and testing of RPA bots and AI algorithms
- Integration with existing systems (EPR, CRM)
- Training of teams

Monitoring

- Monitoring the operation of bots and algorithms
- Detecting errors and their prompt resolution
- Regular system updates
- Performances analysis and results reporting

Optimization

- Analysis of usage data (KPIs, savings)
- Identification of new automation opportunities
- Updating and development of systems according to organizational needs
- Creating future plans (scaling and expansion)

Source: Own elaboration.

Identifying the Applications of AI and RPA in Corporate Finance and Accounting

As noted, the first area of analysis focused on identifying the scope of application of AI and RPA solutions in the financial and accounting activities of the studied company. The respondent indicated that the company implements RPA solutions in a pragmatic, rational, and practical manner, driven by current needs, capabilities, and conditions. The selection of areas for automation is based on a detailed analysis of the efficiency of existing processes. The respondent emphasized that automation primarily covers the areas of finance, controlling, procurement, and production. This indicates a well-thought-out strategy and a practical approach that integrates support for processes critical to the functioning of the entire company.

When analyzing the scope of automation, the respondent noted that certain subprocesses within larger organizational processes have been fully automated. The most significant examples include the update of master data for inventory indexes, the transaction verification procedure for AML reporting purposes, automatic posting of invoices in EDI format, and the preparation of financial reporting, including investment reporting. This practice reflects a typical trend in modern organizations, where repetitive, standardizable, and high-precision processes are prioritized for automation while maintaining compliance with regulatory requirements.

The respondent also addressed the objectives of the implementation, indicating that the primary goal of deploying AI and RPA solutions in finance and accounting was multidimensional optimization, covering both cost and time aspects. In the conversation, the interviewee emphasized the need for more efficient technological solutions in response to the organization's limited internal resources and the availability of ready-made RPA tools on the market at a reasonable implementation cost. In our opinion, this indicates a conscious and responsible approach to investing in new technologies, focused not on mere innovation but on achieving real operational and strategic benefits.

It is also worth noting the area of compliance processes and internal audit, which at FCW company has been systematically automated. As part of the AML procedure, a technical solution was implemented to enable daily transaction monitoring and monthly archiving of results. This solution, complementing the existing internal procedure, allows for the real-time detection of potential irregularities and serves as evidence of the company's consistent approach to minimizing operational risks using modern technological tools.

Furthermore, during the conversation, it was highlighted that automation was primarily achieved through the implementation of dedicated BOT robots configured to perform specific process tasks. In our view, this choice confirms the growing role of low-code or no-code solutions in the practical application of RPA, enabling quick implementation and easy modification in line with the organization's dynamically changing needs.

In summary of the analysis of the first area, it should be emphasized that the implementations carried out at FCW company are characterized by a high degree of pragmatism, a focus on efficiency, and conscious management of technological risk. This case clearly illustrates how companies can integrate new technologies not through their mass deployment but through selective automation of processes with the greatest operational and economic significance.

Analyzing the Economic Effects of the Implemented Solutions

After a detailed analysis of the areas of AI and RPA application in finance and accounting, a natural next research step was to assess the economic effects of these implementations. The focus was on the outcomes of automation, particularly to what extent the implemented processes translated into real, measurable financial and operational benefits for the company.

The respondent clearly indicated that the implementation of AI and RPA solutions resulted in significant cost savings. They emphasized that reducing operational workload, eliminating some repetitive tasks, and minimizing the need for multiple processing of the same data led not only to lower labor costs but also to more efficient use of internal resources. From a managerial perspective, such outcomes should be considered particularly important in the context of rising operational costs and the pressure to increase the efficiency of business support units.

Regarding work efficiency, the respondent emphasized the reduction in the time required to complete key processes, such as invoice processing and report generation, while simultaneously improving the quality of their execution. It can be noted that such an outcome is characteristic of organizations that consistently implement automation in carefully selected, well-prepared processes where the risk of automation-related errors is minimized through prior data and procedure standardization.

When analyzing the cost and investment challenges associated with technology implementation, it is noteworthy that the main issue was not the technological costs themselves but the need to obtain organizational acceptance for creating new structures dedicated to automation management and convincing specialists to collaborate with the newly established department. This confirms a well-known thesis in the literature that one of the greatest challenges in implementing new technologies is not the technical process itself but organizational adaptation and cultural change (Hubbart, 2023; Wiese et al., 2024; Kuchel et al., 2023; Lenberg et al., 2016).

An important aspect discussed during the interview was the quality of financial processes after automation was implemented. The respondent indicated that thanks to the precise definition of algorithms controlling the robots, there was a significant tightening of processes, reducing the risk of errors. However, she emphasized that automation did not completely eliminate the need for human involvement but rather changed the human role – from an operational executor to a verifier and controller of robot actions. This can be highlighted as a typical example of the evolution of an employee's role in a highly automated environment, moving from manual tasks to operational responsibilities and eventually to supervisory and analytical functions. Furthermore, in terms of measuring the effects of implementations, the company adopts a pragmatic approach based on calculating time savings, which are then converted into a financial equivalent in the applicable currency. This method, while operationally simple, allows for a clear presentation of the actual benefits of technology implementation, supporting the process of justifying further investments in automation.

In summary, analyzing the second area, it should be noted that in the case of FCW company, the automation of financial and accounting processes brought not only significant cost savings but also contributed to organizational transformation. The structure of work, competency requirements, and the approach to process quality management have all changed.

Assessing the Social and Organizational Consequences of Automation

The analysis of the social and organizational consequences of automating financial and accounting processes constituted the third key area of the study. The choice of this area for analysis was based on the assumption that any technological change, particularly those related to automation and robotics in the workplace, generates not only economic effects but also significant transformations in employment structure, competency requirements, and organizational dynamics.

According to the respondent, the implementation of AI and RPA solutions in the discussed entity has led to a limitation in the growth of employment in financial and accounting departments. She emphasized that the company's management places great emphasis on developing new automation solutions that optimize key business processes. This process does not result in direct job reductions but serves as an essential mechanism for managing the dynamics of employment growth, which, in the long run, contributes to transforming the employment structure and changing the approach to human resource management.

Additionally, with the implementation of automation, there has been a significant change in employee competency requirements. Specialists have been systematically directed to focus on evaluating current processes and seeking new opportunities for optimization. It should be noted that the shift from performing operational tasks to an analytical and design role indicates a profound transformation in the competency profile of employees in financial departments.

In terms of competency support, the company undertakes initiatives aimed at building a solid foundation for the development of the department responsible for RPA. One element of this strategy is the internal promotion of implemented solutions through publications and presentations designed to disseminate knowledge about the functioning of automation. Such educational activities help foster a positive image of new technologies within the organization, although they do not entirely eliminate the natural resistance associated with their implementation.

In the context of the team's reaction to organizational changes, a characteristic phenomenon was the emergence of standard defense mechanisms, such as denial and resistance to new solutions. These reactions were particularly strong in the relationships between the newly established department responsible for RPA and the existing IT Department, which saw the new structure as potential competition and a threat to its traditional areas of influence.

The automation of financial processes also led to ethical and organizational dilemmas. The main issue was the lack of a full understanding of the purpose of implementing RPA solutions among operational employees. In many cases, new initiatives were perceived as a threat to job stability. From the management's perspective, there was a clearer understanding of the need to develop RPA solutions, especially in the context of the decision to limit further employment growth.

Another significant organizational challenge remained the proper definition of needs by internal clients using the services of the RPA department. In the model adopted by the organization, the internal client specifies the requirements, while the RPA team develops the solution without interfering with the organizational aspects of the process. While the speed of solution delivery is undoubtedly an advantage, it requires clients to precisely define the expected outcomes and fully understand the business process.

In summary, analyzing the third area reveals that automation at CFW company has led to significant organizational and competency changes. Although this process was associated with certain social tensions and ethical challenges, it aligns with a broader trend of organizational transformation, where digital technologies change not only how work is performed but also the operating model of the organization as a whole.

Discussing the Organization's Strategic Approach to the Development of These Technologies

The fourth and final area of analysis, focusing on the strategic approach to automation development and future plans, served as a summary of the study and allowed for identifying directions for further process improvements within the organization. This area of analysis was particularly important from the perspective of assessing the sustainability and maturity of ongoing initiatives and planning the development of structures leveraging artificial intelligence and robotic process automation.

According to the respondent's statements, the company's further plans for automation development at FCW company include integrating an increasing number of departments and organizational processes into the optimization project using RPA solutions. This strategy involves gradually expanding the use of automation beyond the initially selected areas of finance and accounting, indicating a process of systematic technological expansion within the organizational structure of the company.

The interlocutor also indicated that the company is actively considering and implementing the use of RPA in additional areas of its operational activities. The intensification of efforts in this regard is based on the development of appropriate organizational structures and strong strategic support provided by the company's top management. Such anchoring of automation initiatives at the management level is one of the key success factors for the effective implementation of new technologies.

In terms of monitoring the effectiveness of implemented solutions, a pragmatic approach has been adopted, focused on measuring time savings achieved in individual processes. Such indicators, while operationally simple, provide clear data that enables the assessment of the profitability of implemented projects and supports decision-making regarding further investments.

In relation to cooperation with external partners, the interlocutor emphasized that the company typically develops automation solutions internally, which demonstrates a high level of in-house expertise. At the same time, the company remains active in the business and academic environment, enabling it to draw inspiration and benchmark against best market practices.

Key Takeaways

It is also worth noting that the analysis identified key success factors for the effective implementation of automation in finance. These include: strong anchoring of initiatives at the management level and securing funding, identifying actual optimization needs while avoiding solution duplication, fostering openness and readiness for change among process owners, maintaining a fast pace of automation project implementation, deploying partial solutions where full optimization is not necessary, redefining the role of the process owner as a verifier or coordinator of actions performed by robots, and adopting an open communication strategy regarding employment policy in the context of automation.

Particular attention was also paid to the need for defining and monitoring indicators of process owners' workload reduction as a result of RPA implementation, which allows for transparent management of automation outcomes and prevents uncontrolled decisions regarding workforce reduction.

In summary, the automation development strategy at FCW company is based on sound business foundations, strong managerial support, and a consistent pursuit of efficiency in process management, providing a solid foundation for the organization's further digital transformation.

The qualitative study conducted at FCW company enabled an in-depth analysis of the applications of AI and RPA in the areas of finance and accounting, as well as an assessment of their economic and socio-organizational consequences. The case study revealed that automation within the organization is not an incidental activity but part of a broader, systematically implemented process transformation strategy. A synthetic summary of the study, indicating benefits, barriers, and challenges, is presented in Table 16.2.

The implementation of RPA-based solutions brought tangible benefits in the form of reduced process execution time, lower operational costs, and increased accuracy and consistency in administrative and financial tasks. Automation was applied to those elements that demonstrated the highest optimization potential, particularly repetitive, formalizable processes such as EDI invoice posting, AML reporting, and master data updating. Simultaneously, efforts were made to support the development of structures responsible for building and implementing automation solutions, indicating the long-term nature of these initiatives.

The results of the study indicate a significant impact of AI and RPA on improving the efficiency of business processes in finance and accounting, which aligns with numerous studies demonstrating the positive impact of automation on organizational efficiency. The literature unequivocally highlights the benefits of implementing automation technologies in accounting and finance, particularly in reducing operating costs and shortening process execution times (Gotthardt et al., 2019; Kaya et al., 2019; Mamić Sačer & Oluić, 2013). Similar to FCW company, where the implementation of RPA resulted in significant cost savings and reduced report generation times, the studies by Moffitt et al.

Table 16.2 RPA in accounting: Key benefits, challenges, and recommended strategies in the studied enterprise

Description	*Implementation Details*
Benefits of RPA Implementation	
Increased operational efficiency	Automation of routine processes, error reduction
Reduction of operational costs in the long term	Shortened time for accounting and reporting
Improved data accuracy and consistency	Automatic processing of invoices and transactions
Challenges of RPA Implementation	
High initial implementation costs	Purchase of licenses, infrastructure upgrades
Integration issues with existing systems	Modernization of ERP systems
Cybersecurity threats	Risk of data leakage, need for protection
Changes in employee competencies	Need for training and adaptation
RPA Implementation Strategies	
Gradual automation deployment	Pilot projects before full implementation
Investment in data security	Encryption, system monitoring
Employee training	Courses and workshops on new technology usage

Source: Own elaboration.

(2018) also indicate the operational efficiency provided by robotic automation in finance. The reduction of operational workload and the elimination of errors arising from manual data handling confirm the validity of implementing these technologies, as reflected in the analyses of Gotthardt et al. (2019) and the results obtained in the studied entity. It is also worth noting that one of the key aspects of implementing RPA, emphasized in the conducted study, is the improvement of data quality in ERP/SAP systems, which significantly affects the consistency and accuracy of financial reports. Similar conclusions were presented by Lahtinen et al. (2023), who indicated that automation in accounting allows for the elimination of human errors and ensures high data consistency through the use of standardized algorithms.

The analysis also showed that digital transformation has significant organizational consequences. Not only have organizational structures and functions changed, but the roles of employees have also evolved – from performing operational tasks to taking on supervisory and analytical functions. The increased importance of skills in process evaluation and design responded to the organization's new needs, while training and internal communication activities aimed to mitigate tensions arising from the introduction of new technologies. According to the literature (Jędrzejka, 2019), such a process is a natural outcome of digital transformation, where automation frees human resources from routine tasks, enabling them to engage in more complex and analytical activities.

Certain barriers, including resistance to change and an incomplete understanding of the purpose of automation implementation, were consistent with typical organizational reactions accompanying technological transformations. Ethical and organizational dilemmas were also identified, relating to the redefinition of roles and responsibilities, as well as the need for transparent management of automation efficiency indicators, including the so-called release of operational capacity of process owners. Costa et al. (2022), as well as Nema and Sonwaney (2020), emphasize that one of the main challenges in automation is employee resistance, stemming from fears of job loss and uncertainty regarding new systems. In the studied company, this challenge was partially mitigated through intensive training and employee involvement in the automation process, which is also supported in the literature as best implementation practices (Crisan et al., 2023; Nowak & Remlein, 2025).

Conclusion

The findings of the study confirm that effective automation in organizations requires not only appropriate technological tools but also a comprehensive strategic approach, including: securing decision-making at the management level, clearly defining project needs and scopes, ensuring adequate competency resources, adopting a dynamic implementation model, and consciously managing changes in workforce structure.

In a strategic context, FCW company adopted a pragmatic approach to measuring the effects of implementations, based on calculating time savings and their financial equivalence. Lahtinen et al. (2023) indicate that such an approach is particularly effective in justifying investments in automation technologies, as it presents concrete data on return on investment.

It is also worth noting that during the interview, the respondent highlighted challenges related to integrating new technologies with existing IT systems. This is reflected in the literature. For example, Marciniak and Stanisławski (2021) point out that RPA implementation is primarily limited by internal barriers arising mainly from difficulties associated with integrating new technologies into existing IT infrastructure, especially in organizations using heterogeneous IT systems. Similar issues are described by Nema and Sonwaney (2020), who emphasize that integration difficulties primarily result from outdated ERP systems being incompatible with modern RPA tools. Many organizations also experience IT infrastructure gaps that hinder effective management and scaling of automated processes.

In summary, the findings of the study at FCW company are consistent with the current literature. The benefits of implementing AI and RPA, such as improved cost efficiency, reduced process execution times, and enhanced data quality, are widely confirmed in scientific literature. At the same time, challenges related to organizational adaptation and system integration represent typical barriers mentioned by many authors. Thanks to a rational approach to implementation and openness to change, FCW company can be considered an example of conscious and effective use of modern technologies in finance and accounting, and the study results should be seen as a contribution to the discussion on the processes of implementing automation in business operations.

Reference List

Borowiec, L. (2022). The cost-benefit of robotizing selected accounting processes. *Theoretical Journal of Accounting*, *46*(2), 11–26. https://doi.org/10.5604/01.3001.0015.8807

Costa, S. A. S., Mamede, H. S., & Silva, M. M. (2022). Robotic Process Automation (RPA) adoption: A systematic literature review. *Engineering Management in Production and Services*, *14*(2), 1–12. https://doi.org/10.2478/emj-2022-0012

Crisan, E. L., Chis, D. M., Bodea, E. E., & Buchmann, R. (2023). Mechanisms for robotic process automation implementation in organizations: A systematic literature review. *Journal of Advances in Management Research*, *20*(5), 920–946. https://doi.org/10.1108/JAMR-04-2023-0100

Gotthardt, M., Koivulaakso, D., Paksoy, O., Saramo, C., Martikainen, M., & Lehner, O. (2019). Current state and challenges in the implementation of robotic process automation and artificial intelligence in accounting and auditing. *ACRN Oxford Journal of Finance & Risk Perspectives*, *8*, 90–102.

Huang, F., & Vasarhelyi, M. A. (2019). Applying robotic process automation (RPA) in auditing: A framework. *International Journal of Accounting Information Systems*, *35*.

Hubbart, J. (2023). Organizational change: The challenge of change aversion. *Administrative Sciences*, *13*(7), 1–9. https://doi.org/10.3390/admsci13070162

Jędrzejka, D. (2019). Robotic process automation and its impact on accounting. *Zeszyty Teoretyczne Rachunkowości*, *105*(161), 137–166. https://doi.org/10.5604/01.3001.0013.6061

Kaya, C. T., Turkyilmaz, M., & Birol, B. (2019). Impact of RPA technologies on accounting systems. *Journal of Accounting & Finance*, *85*, 235–250.

Kroll, C., Bujak, A., Volker, D., Wolfgang, E., & Esser, M. (2016, May 5). *Robotic process automation: Robots conquer business processes in back offices*. Capgemini Consulting. www.scribd.com/document/574157450/robotic-process-automation-study

Kuchel, T., Neumann, M., Diebold, P., & Schön, E.-M. (2023). Which challenges do exist with agile culture in practice? In *Proceedings of the 38th ACM/SIGAPP symposium on applied computing (SAC '23)* (pp. 1018–1025). Association for Computing Machinery https://doi.org/10.1145/3555776.3578726

Lahtinen, L., Mahlamäki, T., & Myllärniemi, J. (2023). Benefits and challenges of robotic process automation. In *Proceedings of the 15th international joint conference on knowledge discovery, knowledge engineering and knowledge management (IC3K 2023)* (Vol. 3, pp. 249–255). https://doi.org/10.5220/0012208700003598

Łada, M., & Mierzejewska, M. (2021). Robotyzacja procesów podatkowych w przedsiębiorstwie. *Zeszyty Naukowe Uniwersytetu Ekonomicznego w Krakowie*, *3*(993), 109–120.

Lenberg, P., Wallgren, L. G., & Feldt, R. (2016). Software engineers' attitudes towards organizational change: An industrial case study. arXiv:1601.05837, https://doi.org/10.48550/arXiv.1601.05837

Mamić Sačer, I., & Oluić, A. (2013). Information technology and accounting information systems' quality in Croatian middle and large companies. *Journal of Information and Organizational Sciences*, *37*(2), 117–126. https://hrcak.srce.hr/file/164977

Marciniak, P., & Stanisławski, R. (2021). Internal determinants in the field of RPA technology implementation on the example of selected companies in the context of industry 4.0 assumptions. *Information*, *12*(222), 1–19. https://doi.org/10.3390/info12060222

Mezzio, S., Stein, R., & Stein, S. (2019). Robotic process automation for tax. *Journal of Accountancy*. Issue December 1, 2019, https://www.journalofaccountancy.com/issues/2019/dec/robotic-process-automation-for-tax/

Moffitt, K. C., Rozario, A. M., & Vasarhelyi, M. A. (2018). Robotic process automation for auditing. *Journal of Emerging Technologies in Accounting*, *15*(1), 1–10.

Nowak, D., & Remlein, M. (2025). Office work automation: Implementation, costs and benefits. A case study. *Scientific Papers of Silesian University of Technology. Organization & Management/Zeszyty Naukowe Politechniki Slaskiej. Seria Organizacji i Zarzadzanie*, (216).

Nema, K., & Sonwaney, V. (2020). Analysis on barriers to implementation of RPA: An interpretive structural modelling (ISM) *Approach, Psychology and Education*, *57*(9), 1958–1964.

Remlein, M., Bejger, P., Olejnik, I., Jastrzębowski, A., & Obrzeżgiewicz, D. (2022). The application of Robotic Process Automation in the financial accounting in entities that operate in Poland. *Theoretical Journal of Accounting*, *46*(1), 47–65. http://doi.org/10.5604/01.3001.0015.7988

Remlein, M., Jastrzębowski, A., & Obrzeżgiewicz, D. (2022). The impact of legislation on the development of accounting digitisation in Poland. *Zeszyty Teoretyczne Rachunkowości*, *46*(4), 115–127.

Rozario, A. M., Vasarhelyi, M. A. (2018). How robotic process automation is transforming accounting and auditing. *The CPA Journal*, *88*(6), 1–6.

Wiese, S. A., Lehmann, J., & Beckmann, M. (2024). Organizational culture and the usage of Industry 4.0 technologies: Evidence from Swiss businesses. *arXiv* arXiv.10.48550/arXiv.2412.12752

Žager, K., Dečman, N., & Rep, A. (2020). The impact of artificial intelligence on the accounting process. In *Proceedings of the RED 2020–9th international scientific symposium "Region, entrepreneurship, development"* (pp. 1430–1444). Josip Juraj Strossmayer University of Osijek, Croatia, ISSN: 1848-9559.

17 Advancing EU VAT Systems with AI and E-Invoicing

Remigiusz Napiecek, Milena Stróżyna, and Elżbieta Lewańska

Introduction

Digitalization is transforming the EU's financial sector, with the VAT in the Digital Age (ViDA) initiative ushering in e-invoicing, real-time reporting, simplified VAT collection, and single VAT registration for businesses across the EU. Although some EU member states have already begun adopting e-invoicing solutions, full compliance with ViDA will become mandatory for all EU countries by 2028. This initiative presents a series of challenges, ranging from the development of regulations, systems, and tools, through its implementation by governments and private enterprises, to verification of data collected in the e-invoicing systems and its utilization by governments.

Researchers and financial professionals already rely on artificial intelligence (AI) techniques (supervised, unsupervised, and reinforcement learning methods) to address various problems in domains such as credit evaluation, fraud detection, algorithmic trading, and wealth management (Yeo et al., 2025). Furthermore, large language models (LLMs) have become increasingly popular in the financial domain. Both general-purpose models (such as GPT) and specialized ones, specifically trained for financial text processing (e.g., BloombergGPT and open-source FinGPT), are gaining traction in financial applications (H. Yang et al., 2023).

This chapter seeks to address the research question: How can AI tools support the verification and analysis of data collected in the e-invoicing system, while preparing future professionals for AI-driven transformations in the financial sector? The primary research objective is to evaluate the applicability of AI-driven solutions for ViDA by analyzing viable use cases and proposing strategies for mitigating the limitations of AI in the financial accounting sector.

The chapter begins with a brief overview of the legislative framework for e-invoicing systems and the structure of electronic invoices. It then turns to AI-based analytical scenarios tailored to the data derived from e-invoicing systems, emphasizing the importance of data quality and method-specific constraints. Practical examples of AI applications are subsequently discussed. Finally, the chapter examines the critical need to redesign educational

DOI: 10.4324/9781003659143-22

frameworks for finance students, ensuring they acquire future-proof competencies that are essential for AI literacy.

Legislative Framework

Value-added tax (VAT) constitutes a core revenue source for EU Member States, contributing 7.2% of EU's GDP and 15.7% of total government revenue in 2023 (Poniatowski et al., 2024). However, VAT collection faces significant challenges, resulting in the VAT gap – the difference between expected and actual VAT revenues. This shortfall is primarily attributed to inefficiencies in collection systems, as well as fraud and tax evasion. Figure 17.1 summarizes VAT revenues in 2022, presenting the VAT gap as a percentage of projected revenue.

The ViDA initiative is a legislative package introduced by the European Commission (EC) to modernize the EU's VAT system in response to accelerating digitalization and the emergence of new business models. Initially proposed in 2022 and formally adopted in March 2025, ViDA aims to reduce the VAT gap, combat fraud, and improve efficiency for businesses operating within the EU (European Commission, 2025a). The reforms rest on three key pillars:

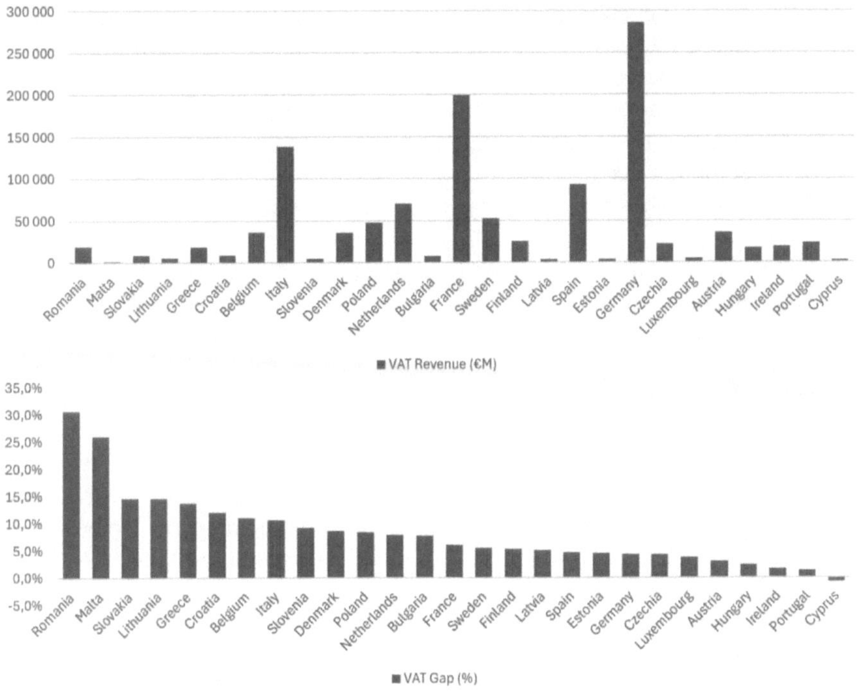

Figure 17.1 VAT revenue and VAT GAP in EU countries in 2022.

Source: Own elaboration based on Poniatowski et al., 2024.

- Introducing standardized Digital Reporting Requirements (DRR) and mandatory e-invoicing for intra-EU transactions.
- Addressing challenges in the platform economy by clarifying existing rules and imposing greater responsibilities on digital platforms in VAT collection.
- Reducing registration burdens for businesses through the expansion of the One-Stop Shop (OSS) and broader application of the reverse charge mechanism.

These ViDA measures will be phased in between 2027 and 2035, necessitating substantial modifications of invoicing, reporting, and compliance processes across the EU (European Commission, 2025a).

To ensure interoperability and compliance across the EU, the EC has developed the European eInvoicing standard EN 16931 (CEN, 2018). Its core objective is to enable sellers to send invoices to multiple customers using a single standardized format, eliminating the need for customization. At the heart of EN 16931 is a semantic data model that defines the essential business terms and rules for electronic invoicing, ensuring consistent interpretation and automated processing across different systems.

Directive 2014/55/EU (European Parliament, 2014) designates two mandatory syntaxes for B2G e-invoicing: Universal Business Language (UBL) and UN/CEFACT Cross Industry Invoice (CII). The CII standard provides a comprehensive data set covering multiple sectors and types of commodities, though most transactions use only a subset of the full model. This approach allows flexibility while maintaining a common structure, making it easier to identify specific invoice formats.

ViDA distinguishes three main types of e-invoices:

- Legal invoices, which comply with tax regulations and contain mandatory fields and authentication features. These serve as original, valid invoices for tax and auditing purposes, typically comprising 8 to 16 essential data fields. They must be stored in a compliant digital format and may be exchanged directly between suppliers and buyers, via service providers, or through tax authority platforms.
- Core invoices, which conform to VAT, sales tax, and trade invoicing standards, such as EN 16931, and are used EU-wide for B2G and B2B e-invoicing. Often generated by information systems, they include between 150 and 500 fields and support automated processing and electronic tax reporting.
- Commercial invoices, based on standards like ISO/IEC 19845 and UBL, are designed for broader electronic exchange of business documents, including invoices, purchase orders, and shipping notices. These invoices may include up to 4,000 data fields. UBL subsets, such as OpenPeppol,[1] are tailored to specific industries (e.g., healthcare and logistics), supporting end-to-end process automation.

E-Invoice Data Structure

Part 1 of the EN 16931 standard defines the core business terms through a semantic data model, specifying the required invoice elements, their meaning, and the common business rules governing structured and valid e-invoices. The model accommodates rules for optional and conditional content, developed with particular attention to public administration requirements and VAT legislation. Within its semantic scope, the model covers key areas such as process control, invoice identification, seller, buyer and payee details, tax representation, delivery details, invoice terms, payment instructions, VAT breakdowns, totals, and supporting documents.

This semantic data model is mapped to machine-readable syntaxes (technical structure) that determine how the content is presented. Two main message standards (syntaxes) are recognized as compliant with EN 16931 (European Commission, 2025b):

- Universal Business Language (UBL): an XML format designed for the exchange of a wide range of electronic business documents, including invoices. The UBL invoice contains all information required by EN 16931 and is widely used across the EU.
- Cross Industry Invoice (CII): an XML format developed by UN/CEFACT, also compliant with EN 16931.

Part 3 of the European standard outlines the specific mappings in the core invoice into each message format. The following example shows how the business term BT-27 (Seller Name) is bound to both UBL and CII syntaxes.

Example of Syntax Binding

According to Part 1 of the EN 16931 standard, semantic information is specified for each data element in an electronic invoice. For instance, the seller's name is defined in the standard invoice as follows:

- **Business term:** "The Production Company"
- **Term ID:** BT-27
- **Definition:** The full formal name by which the seller is registered in the national registry of legal entities or as a taxable person, or under which it otherwise operates commercially.
- **Cardinality:** 1..1 (indicating that the field must appear at least once (1..) and no more than once (..1)

In an electronic message, the seller's name must be provided as shown in Figure 17.2. When the seller's name is read from a message using syntax, it should be understood in accordance with the definition specified in the standard.

Syntax mapping to UBL

```
<Invoice>
  <cac:AccountingSupplierParty>
    <cac:Party>
      <cac:PartyLegalEntity>
        <cbc:RegistrationName>The Production Company</cbc:RegistrationName>
```

Syntax mapping to UN/CEFACT

```
<rsm:CrossIndustryInvoice>
  <rsm:SupplyChainTradeTransaction>
    <ram:ApplicableHeaderTradeAgreement>
      <ram:SellerTradeParty>
        <ram:Name>The Production Company</ram:Name>
```

Figure 17.2 Example of binding semantic information to UBL and UN/CEFAST standards according to EN 16931 standard.

Source: Own elaboration.

In practice, national regulations specify further implementation requirements for e-invoicing. For example, in Poland, structured e-invoices are issued and received via the National e-Invoicing System (KSeF),[2] as mandated by domestic legislation (*Ustawa z Dnia 11 Marca* 2004 *r. o* Podatku Od Towarów i Usług, 2024). Each e-invoice receives a unique identification number assigned by the system and must conform to a legally prescribed electronic template (Ustawa o Informatyzacji Działalności Podmiotów Realizujących Zadania Publiczne, 2024). Structured invoices are submitted in XML format, with fields categorized as:

1. Mandatory – fields that must always be completed, as required by law and defined in the template's logical structure (e.g., the Tax Identification Number).
2. Optional – fields that must be included only under specific legal conditions; and are not required for the semantic validity of the file.
3. Voluntary – fields not required either by law or for the file's semantic validity (e.g., the PKWiU field), but potentially necessary under other regulations.

Each structured invoice is a detailed database entry in the KSeF system, recording details of a transaction, including the parties involved, transaction amount, and date. Among these data, particularly valuable, but not yet explored on a wider scale, are fields describing the subject of the transaction, that is, the data stored as the Product entity. This entity holds all attributes of the traded product, provided in a standardized form with both mandatory and optional fields. From an AI application perspective, details of particular interest include date of delivery for each line item, good or service name, Global Trade Item Number (GTIN), a worldwide classification of goods and services, the numeric equivalent of an EAN code), Polish Classification of Goods and Services (PKWiU), and the Combined Nomenclature (CN) symbol. This structured product-level information offers an excellent source for advanced AI analysis, promising to provide previously unexplored insights.

AI-Based Analytics in E-Invoicing Systems

E-invoicing systems, such as ViDA and KSeF, enable tax authorities to access high volumes of data on transactions occurring on the market. These data are captured automatically, in a structured format, in (near) real time, providing significant opportunities for further analysis, both at the national and, in the future, international level once ViDA is fully implemented across EU countries. While the rapid advances in AI technologies unlock new possibilities for analyzing data collected in e-invoicing systems, this potential hinges on the ability of finance professionals to adapt to and leverage those tools. Discussed next are possible analytical AI application scenarios focusing on anomaly detection and fraud analysis, entity relationship mapping, and automatic understanding of invoice content.

Anomaly Detection

A study by Forrester (2023) reveals that over 70% of businesses in countries such as Denmark, Spain, Germany, the Netherlands, and Italy experienced an increase in invoice-related fraud losses during 2022. The application of AI and advanced machine learning (ML) algorithms offers promising avenues for combatting invoice fraud by efficiently and accurately identifying irregularities, suspicious patterns, and potential instances of fraud. Key AI methods applicable to anomaly detection in e-invoicing include (Comarch, 2024):

- Clustering – Identifying groups of invoices with similar characteristics and flagging statistical outliers within each group.
- Neural networks – Particularly autoencoders, which are trained to learn the patterns of legitimate invoices and identify records that significantly diverge from those patterns.
- Decision trees and random forests – Algorithms that progressively isolate anomalies by recognizing rare combinations of invoice attributes.

Practical applications areas of AI for anomaly detection in e-invoicing include:

- Historical invoice data analysis to establish baseline transaction patterns. These encompass vendor profiles, pricing, frequencies, line-item breakdowns, etc. Deviations from these patterns, such as atypical pricing or frequencies, can be flagged as potential fraud (Constantinou & Kabiri, 2021; Tang et al., 2020).

- AI-based validation of invoice data against taxpayer registries and product databases to detect inconsistencies, for example, invalid VAT IDs and mismatched product codes. According to the OECD, this is crucial for combating false invoicing in cross-border transactions (OECD, 2017, 2022).
- Automating checks against evolving tax regulations, for example, VAT rates and invoice formatting rules.

LLMs and NLP[3] techniques can be applied to analyze unstructured invoice text and detect semantic inconsistencies, such as mismatched product descriptions and billed amounts.

Entity Relationship Mapping

AI enables tax authorities to uncover complex and previously hidden business relationships by analyzing e-invoicing data. These capabilities are of critical importance in combating VAT fraud schemes, such as carousel fraud. In this context, several AI techniques may be effectively applied.

One of them, graph-based network analysis of transactional data (Alexopoulos et al., 2020), can be employed to map interactions among entities, exposing suspicious patterns that often elude traditional auditing methods. For example, multi-hop transaction chains can be traced using path-finding algorithms to identify indirect connections that reveal fund funneling between ostensibly unrelated entities and high-risk actors. Additionally, centrality algorithms can be used to identify critical intermediaries (fraudulent hubs) that process disproportionate transaction volumes, often aggregating small deposits before routing large sums to offshore accounts.

Another technique, algorithm clustering, can support pattern recognition within transaction graphs by grouping entities that exhibit similar transactional behaviors. An example of algorithm clustering is the detection of circular trading loops, where goods are repeatedly resold without ever reaching an end consumer (Alexopoulos et al., 2020). LLMs can further enhance this analysis by supporting entity identification, reconciling disparate business names to expose shell companies.

Finally, entity relationships and transaction flows can be visualized to provide authorities with a systematic overview of business ecosystems, enabling early intervention before fraudulent invoices propagate through the system (Alexopoulos et al., 2020).

Understanding the Invoice Content

Another category of solutions uses NLP techniques to analyze invoice content by converting item descriptions into a structured form (e.g., vectors) and then grouping similar purchases. This facilitates the detection of product categories with shared functions and the monitoring of their relative importance in the overall purchases of a company (Tang et al., 2020).

Recent advances in LLMs have also been recognized in finance. Both general domain models (e.g., OpenAI GTP-series, Google AI BERT, and Meta LLaMA) and models trained to process financial texts (e.g., BloombergGPT, FinGPT) have been successfully implemented to perform a wide range of tasks, including text classification (e.g., grouping similar invoice items), relationship extraction, event detection, and document understanding (Lee et al., 2025). These models can also support automated completion of voluntary fields within e-invoices and provide more context for analysis. For example, based on item line descriptions, GTIN or PKWIU codes can be identified.

Data Quality

High-quality invoice data are a cornerstone of effective tax administration, providing the necessary foundation for both regulatory compliance and the further application of analytics tools (OECD, 2022). Although the adoption of e-invoicing standards, as outlined in earlier sections, aims to ensure a standardized structure for invoices, ongoing quality control is required. This quality assurance should address both master data (related to trading partners and products) and transactional data (details contained within individual invoices).

Ensuring high-quality e-invoice data is crucial for a variety of reasons, such as:

- Regulatory compliance: The fact that incorrect or incomplete invoice fields may result in tax reporting errors and regulatory misfilings, potentially exposing businesses to fines and penalties from tax authorities (OECD, 2022).
- Traceability: Complete, timestamped, and verifiable invoice records support end-to-end traceability, enabling authorities to determine who submitted an invoice, when edits were made, etc. (Ciricello & Gray, 2024).
- Processing delays: Even minor errors or incorrect information can lead to invoice rejections or delays, thereby disrupting cash flow, damaging business relationships, and diminishing operational efficiency (European Innovation Council and SMEs Executive Agency & EY, 2024).
- Limited AI effectiveness: As per the standard rule of data processing, "garbage-in, garbage-out," highlighting that ML and AI algorithms are highly sensitive to training data quality. Feeding low-quality data into AI systems inevitably leads to unreliable outputs (Zha et al., 2023).

To assure sufficient data quality, AI-based validation tools might perform basic format checks and assess the completeness and correctness of e-invoice content. Such quality checks typically fall into two categories: syntactic verification (which ensures structural correctness of the e-invoice and adherence to predefined formats) as well as semantic verification (which assesses the logical coherence and business validity of invoice content).

A range of AI solutions can support this quality assurance process, including:

- NLP and LLMs, which can understand text data, extract and validate relevant information from invoices that deviate from standard templates, and evaluate whether the items, quantities, and prices make logical sense (Eerola, 2024).
- Pattern recognition and anomaly detections algorithms (Tang et al., 2020).

These AI-based tools can calculate data quality metrics and flag incorrect entries or manipulated data (e.g., mismatched tax rates, duplicated invoices, and implausible values).

Explainable and Interpretable AI

While often used interchangeably, the concepts of explainability and interpretability are distinguished within the AI domain. Explainability refers to the capability to identify which data contributed to a model's decision, while interpretability pertains to the capability to understand how decisions were made (Zhao et al., 2024). Both of these terms are referred to as Explainable AI (XAI).

Explainability and interpretability are especially important in the finance domain, where regulatory obligations and trust constitute fundamental pillars of business transactions (Bussmann et al., 2021; Yeo et al., 2025). XAI in finance (FinXAI) has attracted considerable attention in both academia and industry (Achituve et al., 2019; Bussmann et al., 2021; Yeo et al., 2025). Unlike general XAI, FinXAI combines accurate explanations with financial expertise to ensure credibility. Stakeholders across the realm of finance require varying levels of detail and scope of explanation (Berg & Kuiper, 2020; Yeo et al., 2025). Customers need simple and concise justifications for decisions that affect them, while auditors and regulators demand comprehensive details on model behavior and development, training data, and regulatory compliance.

Significant variation exists in XAI between supervised, unsupervised, and reinforcement learning methods. Some such methods are easier to understand and interpret (known as white-box methods), while others (referred to as black-box methods) present more difficulties (Yeo et al., 2025). FinXAI advocates the use of transparent, easier to understand methods such as decision trees and linear models when possible, as these build trust and reduce misinterpretation. For black-box models, post-hoc explanation methods are employed (Rudin & Radin, 2019).

Interpretability may be improved at various stages of model development: at the input stage by analyzing variables or removing irrelevant features, at the modeling stage by simplifying the model, and at the output stage by highlighting key features or generating counterfactuals to show how changes in inputs affect the outcome. Methods such as LIME and SHAP are commonly used for these purposes (Davis et al., 2022; Dikmen & Burns, 2022; L. Yang et al., 2020).

LLMs require different approaches as their internal complexity exceeds the computational capabilities of standard methods. Such approaches include self-explanation mechanisms (e.g., chain-of-thought), feature-attribution-based explanations (e.g., perturbation-based methods and surrogate modeling), attention-based explanations (e.g., visualizations, debate over attention), and example-based explanations (e.g., adversarial examples and counterfactual explanations) (Zhao et al., 2024).

Another critical concern is harmful bias, which can influence model outcomes. Common bias types include outcome fairness (when results are equally distributed among categories), procedural bias (arising from the decision-making process), and interpretation bias (arising in models whose explanations rely on stereotypical assumptions). A number of tools have been developed to identify model biases. These include IBM AI Fairness 360,[4] Microsoft Fairlearn,[5] R library: Themis,[6] and the general Bias Detection and Fairness Evaluation (BDFE) Framework (Vats et al., 2025).

AI bias in financial services can give rise to significant issues across various sectors (Vats et al., 2025), for example, algorithmic lending platforms may disproportionately deny loans to certain demographic groups, even when applicants are equally eligible, or charge higher interest rates to minority borrowers (Bajracharya et al., 2023).

AI Applications

Case Studies from EU Member States

As discussed in the preceding section, the adoption of e-invoicing systems presents substantial opportunities for tax authorities to leverage AI for anomaly detection and entity relationship mapping. Several EU Member States have already demonstrated significant success in such applications.

Italy stands as one of the EU's early adopters of e-invoicing. Having started with B2G transactions in 2014, the system was gradually extended to encompass B2B transactions across all companies by 2022. Italy's system, Sistema di Interscambio (SDI), processes approximately 2 billion B2B invoices annually and has contributed to a significant reduction of the VAT gap by 10.7 percentage points in 2021 (European Commission, 2024). The data collected through SDI is analyzed using AI-based data systems (referenced to the VeRa algorithm) to identify high-risk taxpayers. This approach contributed to the detection of over one million high-risk cases in 2021 (Radhi et al., 2024).

Poland's System Teleinformatyczny Izby Rozliczeniowej (STIR) is another advanced case of AI use for VAT fraud detection in the EU. STIR conducts daily data collection and analysis from banks and credit unions, focusing on taxpayers and transactions. The system supports taxpayer risk scoring and anomaly detection by conducting network analysis (examining links between taxpayers), identification of unusual trading patterns, and alert generation based on taxpayer activity. Between the system's deployment in 2017 and 2022, Poland's VAT gap declined from 15% to 8.4% (Poniatowski et al., 2024). Moreover, in 2022, Poland implemented the KSeF system that is compliant with the EN-16931 standard and will become mandatory for B2B transactions by 2026 (European Commission, 2024). KSeF provides real-time invoice data to tax authorities, creating a supplementary data stream for AI-based analytics (Brodzka & Biernacki, 2024). Nevertheless, the Polish authorities emphasize the need for expert review of AI-generated decisions, with rigorous validation protocols for system alerts, to prevent unintended actions (e.g., wrongful account freezes).

Another example of AI application in tax administration is provided by Alexopoulos et al. (2020), who examined Bulgaria's nationwide VAT e-invoicing data with a view to detecting fraud. Based on data from over 300,000 taxpayers and their monthly transactions, the researchers employed XGBoost for individual risk scoring alongside spectral clustering to identify suspicious trader communities within transaction networks. Their approach achieved a 92% detection rate of known high-risk traders and revealed previously undetected fraud cases. The study also demonstrated how AI-driven methods can uncover sector-specific risk patterns and support real-time, scalable fraud monitoring, offering a powerful tool for tax authorities to enhance audit targeting and reduce VAT revenue losses.

Shift in Accountants' Competencies

AICPA&CIMA[7] conducts research on the changing skill requirements for finance professionals at the time of ongoing digitalization of industry. As an international organization, AICPA&CIMA collaborates with entrepreneurs worldwide to identify the skills sought by businesses. An AICPA&CIMA report on the impact of digitization on financial professional competencies (Farrar, 2019) outlines a notable paradigm shift: as automatization accelerates the execution of numerous accounting tasks, it becomes imperative for finance professionals to not only acquire basic technical skills but also become highly proficient in emerging technologies and develop a mindset attuned to navigating complexity, engaging in lifelong learning, and adopting agile working practices. AICPA&CIMA monitor the impact of AI and LLMs on the finance domain and accordingly revise training recommendations for finance professionals, emphasizing the competencies that are vital for the responsible and efficient use of AI and LLMs (Rutt, 2023).

AI's impact on the accountant's role is both significant and far-reaching, with implications that extend to the evolution of the profession itself and the related educational processes. AI can revolutionize the work of accountants, automating routine tasks, reducing costs through increased efficiency and productivity, improving accuracy by minimizing human error, and enabling the processing of large amounts of data to predict trends and outcomes. To adapt, accountants need new skills, such as (Rutt, 2023):

1. Technical proficiency in data analytics, machine learning, and automation.
2. Understanding the business environment, including a broader understanding of organizational goals, external factors, and strategic thinking.
3. Critical thinking abilities for evaluating and interpreting AI outputs. Accountants will need a deeper understanding of AI, allowing them to ask the right questions and assess the results.
4. Understanding of the ethical aspects, biases, and risks involved in using AI in financial decision-making.
5. Communication skills necessary to explain complex financial information as well as technical concepts to a variety of stakeholders.

Conclusion

This chapter explores the application of AI to the analysis of e-invoicing data, with particular focus on anomaly and fraud detection, the discovery of inter-entity relationships, and the automated interpretation of invoice content, including better identification of buyers, sellers, and the products sold. The capabilities of these AI tools are particularly valuable in uncovering complex fraud, money laundering, and coordinated tax evasion schemes by revealing business relationships. By leveraging these tools, authorities may gain a holistic overview of business ecosystems and identify individual anomalies and broader fraud networks.

The chapter also addresses the crucial role of data quality, emphasizing that the effectiveness of AI-driven analysis depends on the accuracy and completeness of the underlying data. Furthermore, it discusses the limitations of these methods, particularly the challenges associated with explainable and interpretable AI.

In order to realize the full potential of these technologies, finance professionals need to acquire new AI skills not previously included in their education. As many accounting tasks are easy to automate, demand for traditional accounting roles may decline. Moreover, successful AI adoption requires a combination of domain knowledge and technical skills. The latter entails understanding the operational logics of AI systems (e.g., anomaly detection algorithms) and their limitations (e.g., bias risk and interpretability challenges). Future graduates in finance-related fields will be expected to master the technical competencies necessary to effectively and ethically utilize the opportunities offered by AI technologies.

Acknowledgment

This research was supported by funds granted by the Minister of Science of the Republic of Poland under the "Regional Initiative for Excellence"

Programme for the implementation of the project "The Poznań University of Economics and Business for Economy 5.0: Regional Initiative – Global Effects (RIGE)."

Notes

1 https://peppol.org/about/
2 KSeF refers to the National e-Invoicing System (Krajowy System e-Faktur)
3 Natural Language Processing
4 https://aif360.res.ibm.com/
5 https://fairlearn.org/
6 https://themis.tidymodels.org/
7 The American Institute of CPAs® (AICPA) The Chartered Institute of Management Accountants® (CIMA).

Reference List

Achituve, I., Kraus, S., & Goldberger, J. (2019). Interpretable online banking fraud detection based on hierarchical attention mechanism. *2019 IEEE 29th International Workshop on Machine Learning for Signal Processing (MLSP)*, 1–6. https://doi.org/10.1109/MLSP.2019.8918896

Alexopoulos, A., Dellaportas, P., Gyoshev, S., Kotsogiannis, C., & Pavkov, T. (2020). *Detecting network anomalies in the value added taxes (VAT) system*. A TARC Policy Analysis Report.

Bajracharya, A., Khakurel, U., Harvey, B., & Rawat, D. B. (2023). Recent advances in algorithmic biases and fairness in financial services: A survey. In K. Arai (Ed.), *Proceedings of the future technologies conference (FTC) 2022, Volume 1* (Vol. 559, pp. 809–822). Springer International Publishing. https://doi.org/10.1007/978-3-031-18461-1_53

Berg, M. van den, & Kuiper, O. (2020). *XAI in the financial sector. A conceptual framework for explainable AI (XAI)*. Hogeschool Utrecht, Lectoraat Artificial Intelligence. www.internationalhu.com/-/media/hu/documenten/onderzoek/projecten/whitepaper-xai.pdf

Brodzka, A., & Biernacki, K. (2024). Fighting the VAT gap – the polish experience. *Knowledge and Digitalisation, 88*.

Bussmann, N., Giudici, P., Marinelli, D., & Papenbrock, J. (2021). Explainable machine learning in credit risk management. *Computational Economics, 57*(1), 203–216. https://doi.org/10.1007/s10614-020-10042-0

CEN. (2018). *The European standard on eInvoicing (EN 16931)*. https://ec.europa.eu/digital-building-blocks/sites/display/DIGITAL/European+Standard+and+Specifications

Ciricello, C., & Gray, E. (2024). *Report on the evolution of eInvoicing in the digital age*. European Commission. https://data.europa.eu/doi/10.2873/104234

Comarch. (2024). *AI-powered Fraud Prevention in E-invoicing*. https://www.comarch.com/trade-and-services/data-management/news/ai-powered-fraud-prevention-in-e-invoicing/

Constantinou, V., & Kabiri, M. (2021). Detecting anomalous invoice line items in the legal case lifecycle. *arXiv* arXiv:2012.14511

Davis, R., Lo, A. W., Mishra, S., Nourian, A., Singh, M., Wu, N., & Zhang, R. (2022). Explainable machine learning models of consumer credit risk. *SSRN Electronic Journal*. https://doi.org/10.2139/ssrn.4006840

Dikmen, M., & Burns, C. (2022). The effects of domain knowledge on trust in explainable AI and task performance: A case of peer-to-peer lending. *International*

Journal of Human-Computer Studies, *162*, 102792. https://doi.org/10.1016/j.ijhcs.2022.102792

Eerola, T. (2024). *Enhancing automatic invoice coding performance with unstructured data* [Tampere University]. https://trepo.tuni.fi/bitstream/handle/10024/155981/EerolaTeemu.pdf?sequence=2

European Commission. (2024). *Report from the Commission to the European Parliament and the Council on the effects of Directive 2014/55/EU on the Internal Market and on the uptake of electronic invoicing in public procurement*. https://eur-lex.europa.eu/legal-content/EN/TXT/HTML/?uri=CELEX:52024DC0072

European Commission. (2025a). *Adoption of the VAT in the digital age package*. https://taxation-customs.ec.europa.eu/news/adoption-vat-digital-age-package-2025-03-11_en

European Commission. (2025b). *Compliance with eInvoicing standard*. https://ec.europa.eu/digital-building-blocks/sites/display/DIGITAL/Compliance+with+eInvoicing+standard

European Innovation Council and SMEs Executive Agency & EY. (2024). *How electronic invoicing helps reduce late payments in commercial transactions: 3rd thematic report*. https://doi.org/10.2826/60250

European Parliament. (2014). *Directive 2014/55/EU of the European Parliament and of the Council of 16 April 2014 on electronic invoicing in public procurement Text with EEA relevance*. http://data.europa.eu/eli/dir/2014/55/oj

Farrar, M. (2019). *Re-inventing finance for a digital world. The future of finance*. CGMA, AICPA, and CIMA.

Forrester. (2023). *Defeating fraud*. https://experianacademy.com/forrester-fraud-research-report-2023/

Lee, J., Stevens, N., & Han, S. C. (2025). Large language models in finance (FinLLMs). *Neural Computing and Applications*. https://doi.org/10.1007/s00521-024-10495-6

OECD. (2017). *Technology tools to tackle tax evasion and tax fraud*. OECD. https://doi.org/10.1787/g2g77afa-en

OECD. (2022). *Tax Administration 3.0 and Electronic Invoicing: Initial Findings* (OECD Forum on Tax Administration) [OECD Forum on Tax Administration]. https://doi.org/10.1787/2ffc88ed-en

Poniatowski, G., Bonch-Osmolovsky, M., Braniff, L., Harrison, G., Luchetta, G., Neuhoff, J., Śmietanka, A., & Zick, H. (2024). *VAT gap in the EU: 2024 report*. European Commission. https://data.europa.eu/doi/10.2778/2476549

Radhi, W. A., Hamdan, A., & Binsaddig, R. (2024). Assessing the role of artificial intelligence (AI) on tax fraud detection. In A. Hamdan & A. Harraf (Eds.), *Business development via AI and digitalization: Volume 1* (pp. 359–364). Springer Nature Switzerland. https://doi.org/10.1007/978-3-031-62102-4_30

Rudin, C., & Radin, J. (2019). Why are we using black box models in AI when we don't need to? A lesson from an explainable AI competition. *Harvard Data Science Review*, *1*(2). https://doi.org/10.1162/99608f92.5a8a3a3d

Rutt, T. (2023). *Reimagining professional accounting: The impact of artificial intelligence on knowledge and educational processes*. AICPA & CIMA.

Tang, P., Qiu, W., Huang, Z., Chen, S., Yan, M., Lian, H., & Li, Z. (2020). Anomaly detection in electronic invoice systems based on machine learning. *Information Sciences*, *535*, 172–186. https://doi.org/10.1016/j.ins.2020.03.089

Ustawa o informatyzacji działalności podmiotów realizujących zadania publiczne. (2024). [Act of 17 February 2005 on the Computerization of the Activities of Entities Performing Public Tasks]. Dz.U.2024.0.1557 t.j. (Pol).

Ustawa z dnia 11 marca 2004 r. O podatku od towarów i usług. (2024). [Act of 11 March 2004 on Goods and Services Tax]. Dz.U.2024.0.361 t.j. (Pol.).

Vats, R., Agrawal, S., & Chippada, S. S. (2025). Bias detection and fairness in large language models for financial services. *International Journal of Scientific Research in Computer Science, Engineering and Information Technology*, *11*(2), 1329–1345. https://doi.org/10.32628/CSEIT25112461

Yang, H., Liu, X.-Y., & Wang, C. D. (2023). FinGPT: Open-source financial large language models (Version 1). *arXiv*. https://doi.org/10.48550/ARXIV.2306.06031

Yang, L., Kenny, E., Ng, T. L. J., Yang, Y., Smyth, B., & Dong, R. (2020). generating plausible counterfactual explanations for deep transformers in financial text classification. *Proceedings of the 28th International Conference on Computational Linguistics*, 6150–6160. https://doi.org/10.18653/v1/2020.coling-main.541

Yeo, W. J., Van Der Heever, W., Mao, R., Cambria, E., Satapathy, R., & Mengaldo, G. (2025). A comprehensive review on financial explainable AI. *Artificial Intelligence Review*, *58*(6), 189. https://doi.org/10.1007/s10462-024-11077-7

Zha, D., Bhat, Z. P., Lai, K.-H., Yang, F., & Hu, X. (2023). Data-centric AI: Perspectives and challenges. In *Proceedings of the 2023 SIAM international conference on data mining (SDM)* (pp. 945–948). https://doi.org/10.1137/1.9781611977653.ch106

Zhao, H., Chen, H., Yang, F., Liu, N., Deng, H., Cai, H., Wang, S., Yin, D., & Du, M. (2024). Explainability for large language models: A survey. *ACM Transactions on Intelligent Systems and Technology*, *15*(2), 1–38. https://doi.org/10.1145/3639372

18 Digital Transformation in Banking

How Artificial Intelligence Can Transform Legacy Core Banking Systems

Joanna Aleksandrowicz, Agata Kliber, and Hans Michael Egelhoff

Core Banking

The term "core banking" refers to the fundamental banking services and the resources necessary to deliver these services. Acronym "Core" refers to the Centralized Online Real-time Exchange (Haralayya, 2021). A core banking system is a suite of banking services implemented through software. It primarily relies on a centralized database, which allows all branches and sub-branches of the bank to access the same information from a single location (Naimi-Sadigh et al., 2022). It is a back-end system that processes everyday banking transactions and updates their records. Core banking systems typically include functions for processing deposits, loans, and mortgages, along with an interface for main ledger systems (Aleksandrowicz et al., 2022; Alcazar et al., 2024; Undurraga, 2023).

Services of core banking can be divided into primary and ancillary (Alcazar et al., 2024). The *primary services* are the essential functions that the core systems have to provide. They include:

- Account management – managing different types of accounts, including checking accounts, savings accounts, loans, and credit cards.
- Customer management – creating and managing customer profiles, tracking customer activities, handling customer relationships;
- Processing of deposits and withdrawals – processing deposits to customer accounts and withdrawals from them;
- Loans processing – managing the issuance, processing, and administration of various types of loans;
- Finance and accounting – managing the general ledger, accounts payable, asset and liability management, and developing credit loss models.

On the other hand, *ancillary services* are the additional functions that the core system may offer, such as:

- Payments – authorizing and verifying funds for outgoing payments (such as automated clearinghouse transactions, wire transfers, instant payments,

DOI: 10.4324/9781003659143-23

and card transactions), capturing checks remotely, providing gateway services to payment networks and operators, managing and processing ATMs, offering merchant services, and delivering enterprise and business account payment services;
- Bank product interfaces – providing applications for online and mobile banking, as well as teller systems;
- Customer support – providing technical support for the call center and online chat;
- Fraud and risk management – monitoring transactions for suspicious activities and issuing alerts to address potential bank fraud risks and vulnerabilities.
- Compliance and audit – managing compliance and risk-related functions such as anti-money laundering, counter-terrorism financing checks, and know-your-customer verification;
- Reporting and analytics – creating financial reports like balance sheets and income statements, analyzing data to understand customer behavior and market trends;
- Supporting third-party applications – providing third-party access to customer data and integrate third-party applications to online/mobile banking apps.

Evolution of Core Banking Systems

Banking systems developed in the 1970s provided the basic functionality required for executing and processing typical banking transactions. Over the years, the philosophy behind these systems has evolved.

In the realm of core banking, there are references to six generations of systems (Advapay, 2024). *The first generation*, from the 1970s to the 1980s, involved monolithic central systems (now referred to as legacy systems) that were developed internally to meet institutional needs. Prior to the 1980s, core banking systems primarily functioned on large mainframe computers, which were specifically designed to manage vital operations such as account management, transaction processing, and ledger updates. This approach resulted in delays in updating account balances, requiring customers to wait until the subsequent day for their transactions to be accurately reflected in their accounts. Despite these challenges, mainframe systems established a foundational framework for the development of more sophisticated banking technologies. They provided a dependable, albeit slow, basis for managing and processing financial data (Advapay, 2024).

The *second generation* of banking systems spanned from 1980 to 1990, when banks began implementing the client-server architecture. This shift from centralized mainframe models to distributed computing improved system performance and scalability. Banks were able to handle larger transaction volumes more efficiently. The introduction of graphical user interfaces (GUIs) replaced command-line interfaces, enabling comfortable access to account information and faster transaction processing. Thus, the client-server model laid the groundwork for more responsive and user-friendly banking systems (Advapay, 2024).

The third generation of banking systems (1990–2000) is the era of internet banking when customers started to reach their accounts, perform transactions, and manage their finances online. In the *fourth generation*, spanning from 2000 to 2010, banking systems shifted toward modular and component-based architectures. That enabled banks to customize their systems by adding or removing modules like account management and loan processing. Service-oriented architecture (SOA) further transformed core banking by enabling interoperability and seamless integration with third-party services such as payment gateways and fraud detection. That fosters innovation and collaboration, allowing banks to partner with FinTech's to enhance customer experiences easily (Advapay, 2024).

The fifth generation of the systems emerged in 2010 when banks started the transformation of their core systems to cloud-based ones (see also Aleksandrowicz et al., 2022). Meanwhile, the banking industry has been experiencing a digital transformation driven by digital-first strategies and regulatory initiatives like the European Payment Services Directive 2 (PSD2), which promotes open banking. Nowadays, we are witnessing a transformation to the *sixth generation*, driven by Artificial Intelligence (further: AI) and machine learning (further: ML) solutions (Advapay, 2024).

Challenges for Modern Banking and Their Consequences for Core Banking

The recent rise of digital banking signifies a remarkable acceleration in technological advancements fueled by factors such as the COVID-19 pandemic and evolving demographics. At the forefront of these transformative shifts are FinTech providers, who leverage innovations like cloud computing, APIs (application programming interfaces), and ML to offer seamless, around-the-clock financial services (Wang et al., 2021; Kasturi, 2023).

Banks must effectively respond to the rapid transformations occurring within the industry. However, they encounter significant challenges, including outdated legacy systems, siloed operations, an extensive array of potential enhancements, and the need to comply with regulations. In contrast, typical FinTech companies often operate with fewer constraints, enabling them to adapt more swiftly to the changing landscape (Wang et al., 2021; Kasturi, 2023). As a result of these challenges, some experts have suggested that FinTech solutions could potentially replace banks in certain areas (see e.g., Bunea et al., 2016; Będowska-Sójka et al., 2023; Shpachuk & Trinh, 2024). However, it has become evident that cooperation is often more beneficial for both sides, leading modern banks to partner with FinTech companies to enhance customer experiences. This partnership presents another challenge for traditional banks – integrating their older systems with modern services.

As previously discussed, the core banking system has undergone significant changes over the years. This evolution is essential since core banking systems must operate continuously without substantial interruptions. Maintaining uninterrupted service is critical for building customer trust and ensuring compliance with regulatory standards. Core banking systems should provide a reliable IT infrastructure, which includes state-of-the-art hardware (for on-premises systems), efficient software solutions, and a robust network architecture. They must be capable of handling high transaction volumes and offer seamless service while preventing downtime. Another requirement for the core banking system is regulatory compliance because institutions are obligated to adhere to a range of local and international regulations, which are frequently updated. Core banking systems should also be flexible and scalable, able to integrate with third-party providers, and operate seamlessly during peak hours. Additionally, they need to offer reliable accounting, process automation, and real-time transactions. They should support the automation of routine processes and provide immediate services such as processing fund transfers, payments, and balance inquiries. Security is also paramount. Core banking systems must protect against cyber threats through comprehensive security measures, including encryption, multi-factor authentication, and intrusion detection systems. Furthermore, data protection and privacy initiatives must comply with stringent regulatory standards.

However, despite intensive technology growth, a significant number of basic banking systems are still based on older designs (Alcazar et al., 2024). Traditional systems with a monolithic architecture combine all their complex functions into a single application with a puzzle-like structure. Over time, this structure can lead to a codebase that becomes overwhelmingly complex and difficult to understand. As a result, making improvements and adding features to such a system using modern technologies becomes quite challenging (Aydemir & Başçiftçi, 2022). Therefore, older systems struggle to integrate with modern technologies and applications. The costs of maintaining outdated systems is also high. Many of them were developed using COBOL, a programming language created in the 1950s, which is still in use today (Lau, 2025). There is a lack of specialists in typical core banking technologies, and a low level of interest in such technologies among candidates on the job market (see e.g., Aleksandrowicz et al., 2022). Additionally, these legacy systems often lack adequate documentation, making it even more difficult to find specialists who can maintain them or address potential issues. Therefore, such banks are now under increasing pressure to transition to modern core banking software in order to improve their services and stay competitive.

However, it is important to acknowledge that implementing this new generation of core banking software is quite challenging (Haralayya, 2021). First of all, core banking software implementation projects typically have extended timelines, making them susceptible to project delays. As a result, these projects often face the risk of escalating costs. Secondly, such an operation results in lengthy pay-off periods and involves substantial investments. Third, implementation of core banking software can lead to significant organizational restructuring. Consequently, stakeholders with a vested interest in the project's outcome can introduce considerable risks to the implementation process. Furthermore, implementing a new core banking system requires seamless integration with other components of the banking architecture, such as customer relationship management (CRM) systems and middleware solutions. This is challenging because these channels are often costly to replace entirely, given a bank's substantial investment in them. Lastly, successfully implementing core banking software necessitates effective business process re-engineering and ample resources (Haralayya, 2021). Technological challenges include tasks such as accurately defining a comprehensive set of functional and technical requirements based on established best practices for the core banking system. Additionally, selecting the right core banking system vendor is crucial to securing the best deal, considering a bank's dynamics, and ensuring that the core banking system implementation does not disrupt existing services (Johri, 2014).

Applications of AI in Modernizing Core Banking Systems

According to a McKinsey report (McKinsey & Company, 2020), to deliver value and stay competitive, banks must adopt an AI-first strategy that transforms their entire operating model. To build fundamentals for the entire organization, banks need to build capabilities in four areas: an engagement layer, a decision layer, a core technology layer, and a platform operating model.

First-layer adjustments require redesigning the *customer engagement layer* through seamless, omnichannel experiences that are personalized and embedded in customers' daily digital journeys. AI enables banks to shift from standardized offerings to intelligent, context-aware services that anticipate and solve customer needs.

To support this, banks must build an AI-powered *decision-making layer* that delivers real-time insights and personalized actions across customer touchpoints. That requires robust data infrastructure and modern APIs (*core technology layer*) to ensure data liquidity, interoperability, and agility. Cloud-based platforms and intelligent infrastructure further enable scalability, cost efficiency, and continuous innovation.

A strategy must also ensure security, compliance, and a plan for sourcing or internally building capabilities. Banks should adopt a *platform operating model* with cross-functional teams aligned around products, technology, and agreed shared outcomes. Becoming AI-first must be a strategic goal that focuses on transforming capabilities holistically across customer engagement, AI decision-making, core technology, and operating models (Refer to "AI Bank of the Future model," Exhibit 6 of the McKinsey & Company, 2020).

Building an AI-first bank requires the six fulfillment stages:

1. **Preparation of an AI-first strategy**
   Before a transformation, banks should create a clear AI-first vision and strategy, focusing on three key areas: faster time to market, alignment of demand with capacity, and effective coordination of transformation. The strategy aims to improve governance, efficiency, and value generation.
2. **Ensuring high-quality customer experiences**
   The goal of this stage is to design seamless, efficient, and personalized *omnichannel customer journeys*. This requires integrating various systems and using APIs for real-time data exchange. Banks should focus on reusable enterprise-level products and microservices that automate backend processes.
3. **Scalability of data and analytics platform**
   Delivering personalized services requires a strong data infrastructure supported by AI and ML models. Banks need to incorporate feedback loops into their systems for continuous optimization.
4. **Scalable hybrid infrastructure**
   Banks need to implement hyper-scalable infrastructure, combining on-premises and cloud resources, to handle high volumes of transactions and ensure low-latency performance. Cloud-based solutions offer elastic capacity and self-healing features while maintaining high availability for critical operations.
5. **Configurable core product processors**
   To stay competitive, banks must ensure core product processors can scale and adapt to customer needs. This enables the creation of innovative, real-time products that meet customer expectations.
6. **Cybersecurity strategy**
   Strong security measures have to be applied to protect technology infrastructure, especially during movement to hybrid cloud environments. AI can enhance security by detecting threats and vulnerabilities (McKinsey & Company, 2020).

The modernization of core banking systems is one of the critical challenges of the banking industry. Banks are currently exploring Generative AI (further: GenAI) to help transform and modernize their core banking systems efficiently. GenAI can support this modernization effort in multiple ways, as listed next:

1. **Documenting legacy code**
   By analyzing mainframe applications, GenAI tools can produce detailed technical and functional documentation that outlines program logic, data flows, key features, and system dependencies. This documentation of corporate knowledge streamlines the onboarding process for development teams. AI models can be used to remove redundant or unused code (dead code detection) or suggest more efficient coding patterns to rewrite it in a

cleaner format. Since legacy systems often lack accompanying documentation, they require in-depth system analysis to understand the business logic and overall functionality (Nandedkar et al., 2024).

2. **Automated code translations**
   Along with automatically translating code from COBOL and other legacy coding languages to Java, AI can also help with code conversion and updating legacy systems more efficiently (Lau, 2025; Amazon Web Services, 2025). For example, leveraging GenAI, Capgemini's A2B translator can redefine code translation by extracting semantic meaning in blocks, ensuring a more automated and accurate transition than traditional methods (Capgemini, 2024).
3. **Facilitating data exchanges and defining migration project waves**
   Another use case of AI automation is data mapping between old and new systems during data migration. Modernized core technology with an API and streaming architecture enables continuous and secure data exchanges between the centralized data infrastructure and decision-making layer. It ensures faster development and minimizes human errors (Nandedkar et al., 2024). Moreover, GenAI can help prioritize modernization wave sequences based on multiple factors, like code and data dependencies, code volume, or business priorities (Amazon Web Services, 2025).
4. **Generating automated test code**
   GenAI can be used to test automation in migration and modernization processes. AI can also be used in the quality assurance area to improve the quality, accuracy, and security of testing activities by bug detection during refactoring. AI models can examine large datasets to identify risks and forecast outcomes (Doshi, 2024).
5. **Identifying groupings for decomposition**
   GenAI can assist banks in decomposing complex mainframe applications into smaller, domain-specific modules. By analyzing system architecture, project scope, and requirements, it identifies key components and prepares work breakdowns and phased modernization programs.

Amazon Web Services (further: AWS) is a leader and key enabler in infrastructure transformation, helping banks move to a composable architecture, cloud-native core banking solutions, and a data-driven and AI-first approach. AWS provides a range of tools, including Amazon Q Developer (automating code translation, documentation, and modernization planning) and Amazon Bedrock (building and scaling GenAI applications using foundational models). These platforms facilitate the intelligent orchestration of AI agents, scalable computing environments, and real-time analytics, which are crucial for managing large-scale modernization projects.

An AWS report (see Amazon Web Services, 2025) documents GenAI implementation benefits gained by organizations that already implemented GenAI solutions to support core banking modernization. AWS presents the following steps of a modernization journey along with proven benefits:

1. **Initial assessment of legacy platforms**
   Gen AI supports the reverse engineering of legacy code, documents and extracts business logic that achieves a 50% reduction in time spent on business rule extraction.
2. **Execution**
   AI based tools assist in planning migration waves, defining new architecture, codebase, and data migration to achieve 60% faster translation time of legacy components into modern equivalents.
3. **Post-migration validation**
   AI tools help to test, validate, and document new functionality, resulting in 30% improvement in application performance by identifying bottlenecks in translated code and implementing optimizations. They also contribute to a 40% reduction in coding defect rate.
4. **Monitoring and optimization**
   GenAI plays a role in maintaining and managing the modernized platform by automating routine tasks and supporting continuous improvement, resulting in 40% reduction in maintenance costs and 25% increase in productivity.

As emphasized in the report, legacy modernization is not a final destination; it is an ongoing project to build a composable architecture for banking services. GenAI, particularly when integrated with cloud infrastructure and services, is helping financial institutions reach this next stage with greater efficiency, security, and confidence.

Another area of adoption of AI and ML solutions to support core banking is the modernization of core technology and data infrastructure. The challenge with existing legacy banking systems is making decisions based on massive and different sources of data, which generates huge costs. About 20 to 30% of decisions go wrong due to incomplete and inappropriate data (Ris et al., 2020).

Banks that are facing dual challenges from innovation pressure and the need for operational efficiency should transform and increase their critical technology capability in order to continuously respond to changing market demands, regulatory environments, and customer needs.

One important aspect to highlight is the Accenture digital core approach in banking, which consists of three interconnected technology layers: the Data and AI Backbone, Digital Platforms, and Digital Foundation. The Data and AI Backbone are responsible for intelligent decision-making and automation, while Digital Platforms support agility and scalable service delivery. The Digital Foundation covers cloud-first infrastructure, security, composable integration, and a continuum control plane that ensures secure, flexible, and scalable operations (Accenture, 2024).

In terms of AI support for core technology and data modernization, the following areas should be highlighted:

1. **Automated Cloud Provisioning** – AI can automate the provisioning of cloud infrastructure essential for modernizing core banking systems by enabling

a shift from legacy infrastructure to scalable, resilient, cloud-native solutions. It accelerates the process of development, reduces IT overhead and creates the foundations for AI/ML initiatives such as deployment of data environments and integration of AIOps (AIOps uses AI to automate and improve IT operations through data analysis and pattern recognition.) for resilience and efficiency (Caban et al., 2025).

2. **API and Streaming Architecture** – AI can facilitate the development and implementation of API and streaming architectures, enabling continuous and secure data exchange between the modernized core and other layers. API is crucial in connecting layers by providing controlled access to services, data, and products within and outside the bank. Internally, an API helps to reduce silos, increase the reusability of technology assets, and promote flexibility in the technology architecture. Externally, it makes it possible to accelerate integrations with a partner solution ecosystem to deliver better customer experiences. To establish an efficient API and streaming architecture, several key factors must be addressed. These include the development of scalable and standardized APIs and integration methodologies, thorough performance testing, and the implementation of an API-first strategy. Additionally, adhering to standards such as the Open API Banking Industry Architecture Network (BIAN) is crucial for enhancing readiness for modernization. (Accenture, 2025).
3. **Improved Data Management** – AI plays an important role in managing the growing volumes of data, ensuring its accuracy, relevance, better analysis, and adherence to privacy regulations. However, improved data management is essential for modernizing banking systems and is a key factor enabling the implementation and scaling of AI. High-quality and unified data forms the basis for effective AI, as data is the fuel that powers AI.

Meanwhile, banks face significant challenges with outdated data management, including data silos that impede integration and timely access to information. Poor data quality, limited scalability, lack of MLOps infrastructure (MLOps is the practice of managing and automating the life cycle of ML models in production), and fragmented tools reduce the effectiveness of AI systems and decision-making processes. Additionally, much of the data is locked in documents and spread across disconnected systems, preventing a unified, real-time view of operations.

To overcome outdated data challenges, banks must adopt modern data management strategies that centralize and unify data across internal and external sources, enabling real-time access, streaming, and analytics through advanced platforms like data lakes. Implementing decentralized data mesh architecture empowers business units to own and manage their data as a product, supported by strong governance, security, and self-serve infrastructure for trusted and compliant collaboration. Ensuring high data quality and serving both structured and unstructured data from different sources enhances AI and ML capabilities (KPMG, 2025; Ris et al., 2020; Capgemini, 2024).

This unification of data enables banks to create an accurate 360° view of the customer. This holistic view enhances offering personalization, streamlines decision-making, and allows for proactive engagement across all touchpoints. Leveraging real-time analytics and ML, institutions can deliver tailored experiences that adapt to each customer's behavior, preferences, and needs (Backbase, 2025).

Despite the significant potential benefits, the implementation of AI in core banking modernization faces many challenges and barriers that need to be identified and addressed:

1. Outdated legacy systems and integration complexity are often incompatible with new processes and can lead to poor AI performance.
2. Fragmented and low-quality data – without consistent, reliable, and accessible data, building accurate and effective AI models is difficult.
3. Ensuring data security and privacy protection.
4. There are ethical concerns and potential biases in AI algorithms.
5. The need for appropriate AI skills – talent gap slows the pace of transformation and acquiring or upskilling employees with the necessary AI skills.
6. Regulatory compliance and governance – navigating complex regulatory frameworks is a significant challenge, especially across different jurisdictions.
7. Ethical concerns and trust – the "black box" nature of some AI systems is undermining trust among customers and regulators. Banks must ensure that their AI systems are transparent and explainable.
8. Changing organizational culture and employee acceptance of new technologies – the introduction of AI solutions can cause anxiety and uncertainty among employees regarding potential job automation and job loss.
9. Lack of a clear AI strategy and difficulty in scaling – many banks struggle to move from experimenting with select AI use cases to scaling them across the organization. Most banks are historically organized in silos around products, which makes the shift to value streams and customer-centricity difficult.
10. Risk aversion and balancing innovation with risk – as banks are risk-averse institutions, concerns associated with data governance and regulatory scrutiny can create barriers to progress.
11. Cost and ROI measurement – banks are experiencing management pressure to demonstrate immediate ROI of AI investments. There are concerns about the uncertain returns on investment and appropriate metrics to measurement adoption.
12. Sustainability concerns – balancing AI adoption with sustainability objectives is a challenge, as the energy usage of AI can conflict with banks' environmental goals (Lau, 2025; KPMG, 2025; World Economic Forum, 2025).

AWS has significantly contributed to the modernization of core banking systems by providing solutions that enhance operational efficiency and customer experience. AI and ML services include Amazon SageMaker, which supports model development, Amazon Fraud Detector, which enables real-time fraud prevention, Amazon Personalize, which delivers customer recommendations, and Amazon Comprehend, which supports document processing. For legacy system modernization, AWS offers tools such as: AWS Lambda for serverless computing, Amazon Aurora for modernizing databases, AWS Outposts for hybrid deployment, and API Gateway to support a microservices architecture.

The number of success stories involving the use of AI/ML tools to modernize banks' legacy infrastructure has been growing recently. For example, one of the implementation examples is NatWest Group, which utilized Amazon SageMaker to develop personalized customer journeys, leveraging ML to understand and serve their clients better (AWS, 2023). Standard Chartered Bank re-architected its core banking system using Amazon Aurora, achieving a tenfold increase in transaction throughput and enhancing disaster recovery capabilities across 26 global markets (AWS, 2024). Database modernization is another area where AWS supports the financial sector. For example, due to its scalability and reliability, Amazon Aurora became the preferred database engine for several core banking software vendors, including 10x Banking and Thought Machine (AWS, 2024). AI-driven legacy code modernization enables financial institutions to convert outdated languages into modern ones; JPMorgan Chase uses GenAI tools like its in-house GenAI assistant LLM Suite to extract and modernize COBOL-based core systems as part of a broader $17 billion tech transformation (Banking Dive, 2025).

To summarize, this chapter discusses the challenges the banking sector faces in modernizing its core systems. These challenges include maintaining outdated legacy systems and the potential transition to modern core banking software. It highlights how AI technology can help address these problems. Specifically, AI tools can generate detailed technical and functional documentation that outlines program logic, data flows, key features, and system dependencies. Additionally, AI can automatically translate code from COBOL and other legacy programming languages to Java.

Furthermore, it can facilitate data mapping between old and new systems during data migration. GenAI, combined with test automation, can significantly enhance migration and modernization efforts. Finally, AI can aid banks in breaking down complex mainframe applications into smaller, domain-specific modules.

We note that some banks have already implemented AI and reinforced the value of these solutions, for example, NatWest Group leveraged Amazon SageMaker for personalized customer journeys, Standard Chartered Bank re-architected its core systems using Amazon Aurora, and JPMorgan Chase is modernizing legacy COBOL systems using its internal LLM Suite. These examples demonstrate a clear trend that banks are strategically adopting AI/ML tools to modernize legacy core systems and infrastructure to increase system resilience and deliver better digital banking focused on customer experiences.

Reference List

Accenture. (2024). *Reinventing with the digital core in banking*. www.accenture.com/us-en/insights/banking/reinventing-digital-core-banking

Accenture. (2025). *Core banking modernization: Unlocking long-term value through generative AI*. Accenture Banking Blog: Core banking modernization: Unlocking legacy code with generative AI | Accenture Banking Blog

Advapay (2024, February 24). *Core banking unveiled: Evolution, key components, types, challenges, and opportunities*. Retrieved May 1, 2025, from https://advapay.eu/core-banking-what-is-evolution-key-components-types-challenges-opportunities/

Alcazar, J., Baird, S., Cronenweth, E., Hayashi, F., & Isaacson, K. (2024, February 28). *Core banking systems and options for modernization*. Federal Reserve Bank of Kansas City, Payments System Research Briefing. Retrieved May 1, 2025, from www.kansascityfed.org/documents/10016/PaymentsSystemResearchBriefing24AlcazarBairdCronenwethHayashiIsaacson0228.pdf

Aleksandrowicz, J., Kliber, A., & Marszałek, M. (2022). *The future of the core systems. Is it the time for the cloud?* Technical Report, Przyszłość systemów centralnych. Retrieved May 1, 2025, from https://www.gft.com/pl/pl/business/banking/corebanking

Amazon Web Services. (2025). *Banking on the cloud*. https://pages.awscloud.com/banking-on-the-cloud-ebook-2025-learn.html

Anusha, S. N., Kamurthy, J., Mustafa, M., Mohit, S., Shabeer, S., & Jeevan. (n. d.). Revolutionizing banking: The path to an AI-driven future with a special reference to Union Bank. *International Journal for Multidisciplinary Research (IJFMR)*. E-ISSN: 2582-2160.

AWS. (2023). *Accelerate time to business value using Amazon SageMaker at Scale with NatWest Group*. Accelerate Time to Business Value Using Amazon SageMaker at Scale with NatWest Group | Case Study | AWS

AWS. (2024). *Amazon Aurora for core banking systems*. Retrieved May 4, 2025, https://aws.amazon.com/blogs/industries/amazon-aurora-for-core-banking-systems/

Aydemir, F., & Başçiftçi, F. (2022). Building a performance efficient core banking system based on the microservices architecture. *Journal of Grid Computing*, *20*(37), 2–37. https://doi.org/10.1007/s10723-022-09624-z

Backbase. (2025). *Customer data & AI services: Harness enterprise-wide intelligent automation*. www.backbase.com/

Banking Dive. (2025). *How JPMorgan Chase's infrastructure chief keeps the AI engine humming*. Retrieved May 4, 2025, from How JPMorgan Chase's infrastructure chief keeps the AI engine humming | Banking Dive

Będowska-Sójka, B., Kliber, A., & Laidroo, L. (2023). Has the pandemic changed the relationships between fintechs and banks? *Operations Research and Decisions*, *33*(4), 15–33. https://doi.org/10.37190/ord230402

Bunea, S., Kogan, B., & Stolin, D. (2016). Banks versus FinTech: At last, it's official. *Journal of Financial Transformation, Capco Institute*, 44, 122–131.

Caban, W., Nesheim, S., & Harmon, R. L. (2025). *AI strategies for scalable, secure and compliant banking* [Webinar report]. Red Hat.

Capgemini. (2024). *World retail banking report 2024. Capgemini Research Institute for financial services*. https://worldretailbankingreport.com/

Doshi, K. (2024). Harnessing the power of AI in banking. *International Journal of Science and Research (IJSR)*, *13*(5), 362–366. https://doi.org/10.21275/SR24506091158

Haralayya, B. (2021). Core banking technology and its top 6 implementation challenges. *Journal of Advanced Research in Operational and Marketing Management*, *4*(1), 25–27.

Johri, S. (2014). Core banking-redefining banking operations – A critical. *JSSGIW Journal of Management*, *1*(2), 107–117.

Kasturi, S. (2023). Evolving consumer expectations and the future of digital banking. *Journal of Digital Banking*, *8*(1), 37–48.

KPMG. (2025). *Intelligent banking: A blueprint for creating value through AI-driven transformation*. KPMG International: Intelligent Banking.

Lau, T. (2025). *Banking on (artificial) intelligence: Navigating the realities of AI in financial services*. Springer Nature Switzerland AG. https://doi.org/10.1007/978-3-031-81647-5

McKinsey & Company. (2020). *Building the AI bank of the future*. www.mckinsey.com/capabilities/mckinsey-digital/our-insights/building-the-ai-bank-of-the-future

Naimi-Sadigh, A., Asgari, T., & Rabiei, M. (2022). Digital transformation in the value chain disruption of banking services. *Journal of the Knowledge Economy*, *13*, 1212–1242. https://doi.org/10.1007/s13132-021-00759-0

Nandedkar, R., & Maniyar, A. (2024, November). AI use in application modernization for banking applications. *International Journal of Scientific Research in Engineering and Management (IJSREM)*, *8*(11). https://doi.org/10.55041/IJSREM38472

Ris, K., Stankovic, Ž., & Avramovic, Z. (2020). Implications of implementation of artificial intelligence in the banking business with correlation to the human factor. *Journal of Computer and Communications*, *8*, 130–144. https://doi.org/10.4236/jcc.2020.89010

Shpachuk, V., & Trinh, V. Q. (2024). FinTech companies: Trends and opportunities in the banking sector. In *Modern banking and digitalization. Contributions to finance and accounting*. Springer. https://doi.org/10.1007/978-3-031-71422-1_6

Undurraga, M. (2023). *Bank of AI: Transforming financial services with artificial intelligence: Unlocking value and revolutionizing banking operations through artificial intelligence* (Kindle ed.). Amazon Digital Services.

Wang, Y., Xiuping, S., & Zhang, Q. (2021). Can fintech improve the efficiency of commercial banks? – An analysis based on big data. *Research in International Business and Finance*, *55*, 101338. https://doi.org/10.1016/j.ribaf.2020.101338

World Economic Forum. (2025). *Artificial intelligence in financial services*. In collaboration with Accenture. WEF_Artificial_Intelligence_in_Financial_Services_2025.pdf

Part VI

Foundational Issues (Law, Ethics, Education)

19 Calling the Tune!

How AI Act Recitals Set the Tone for AI Governance

Krzysztof Durczak and Rasmus Nykvist

Directing Technological Progress

Technology is often viewed as an inevitable force advancing civilization. Yet history shows that progress is neither inherently good nor bad – it is shaped by choices and directed by those in power. Acemoglu and Johnson (2023) illustrate this across centuries: while technological advancements have driven economic growth, they have also reinforced inequalities, from the displacement of medieval peasants to the exploitation of industrial workers. Today, artificial intelligence (AI) follows a similar trajectory (Haenlein & Kaplan, 2019), often favoring corporate actors over shared social benefits and potential threats. Technological progress does not automatically serve the common good; it reflects the interests of those who control its direction (Dant, 2006).

Conversely, it means that technological advancement can be steered. Because innovation does not unfold in isolation, it can be deliberately directed by social priorities. AI, for instance, can be developed to complement human labor rather than replace it (Acemoglu & Johnson, 2023). Although this may be challenging at the organizational level (Raisch & Krakowski, 2021), achieving this may require regulatory action and incentives that shape its trajectory. In this context, the AI Act (Regulation (EU) 2024/1689, 2024) deserves attention as one of the most comprehensive up-to-date attempts to achieve this goal (Butt, 2024).

Although its enactment is recent, the AI Act reflects a long-standing discourse (Jobin et al., 2019) shaped by both ambitious expectations and ongoing concerns. Discussions on AI governance started in 2018 (European Commission, 2019), gradually signaling the need for transparency, accountability, and oversight – needs that only recently translated into regulatory action for trustworthy AI. Therefore, the AI Act should not be viewed merely as a legal framework but as the culmination of a broader discussion about the transformative potential of these technologies and the risks they pose. As such, this single document represents both principles and ideological commitments, conveying the envisioned direction in which AI systems should be woven into the fabric of European societies (Ho & Caals, 2024).

DOI: 10.4324/9781003659143-25

This chapter, then, aims to examine the AI Act through the lens of institutional theory (Selznick, 2008; Scott, 2013), identifying and articulating the values embedded within the text to offer insights into the principles guiding AI development. Legal language is often difficult to navigate without formal training, making it inaccessible to the general public (Martínez et al., 2023). However, understanding the underlying values can serve as a more intuitive proxy – not through legal interpretation, but through a comprehension of the rhetoric that justifies and explains the character of rights, restrictions, and obligations.

To achieve this goal, this chapter zooms in on a distinct aspect of the AI Act's composition: the recitals. EU Regulatory texts are typically composed of *operative provisions*, which form the legally binding core, and *recitals*, serving to inform, explain, and justify relevant parts and the regulation as a whole (den Heijer et al., 2019). While operative provisions dictate enforceable obligations, recitals provide the backdrop for legal interpretation, offering insights into the principles and motivations that underpin the text. Although recitals do not carry the same legal force, they set the tone and signal the regulation's normative direction. This is also what *Calling the Tune* is eluding to: if operative provisions compose regulatory actions, the *recitals* offer guidance on how those actions should be understood.

By analyzing these recitals, we aim to surface the values embedded in the AI Act and construct an axiologically informed map that articulates the direction taken by the EU in the domain of AI governance. Although it is difficult to consider regulatory rhetoric as a mirror of collective values, the fact remains that operative provisions rely on principles expressed via recitals – meaning they inevitably shape the regulatory landscape and, by extension, everyday life (Celsi, 2023). In this context, grasping the underlying values may offer a more accessible way to engage with the AI regulation.

Values in Context

Institutional theory proposes three fundamental domains to explain how people and organizations position themselves within a broader context (Scott, 2013). These domains are shaped by coercive, normative, and cultural pressures that guide social behavior (DiMaggio & Powell, 1983). The regulative pillar refers to governance through coercion, compelling conformity to formal rules and laws (Scott, 2013, pp. 59–64). The normative pillar consists of norms that define acceptable behavior, promote cooperation through shared expectations, and sanction deviations (ibid. 64–66). The cultural-cognitive pillar encompasses shared beliefs and mental models that influence how people interpret experiences and act within their (ibid. 66–70). Taken together, these aspects represent interdependent yet distinct forces shaping behaviors and their underpinnings in social contexts (Friedland & Alford, 1991).

Values – understood as a kind of belief that lends positive or negative valence to social judgments – play a crucial role in this frame, as they conceptually cut across all three domains. In the regulative terms, values influence compliance with laws and regulations, encouraging conformity to societal standards (Peton & Pezé, 2014). Within the normative pillar, values are embedded in collective norms that guide organized practices, foster a sense of obligation, and establish what is considered appropriate. In the cultural-cognitive domain, values shape identities and shared cognition within institutions, providing the context for judging actions and decisions in light of institutional demands.

This framework's implicit interest in values draws significant inspiration from Max Weber's foundational analysis of authority and rationalization (Weber & Tribe, 2019). While Weber never spoke about institutions explicitly as later scholars would (Selznick, 2008), his work on bureaucracy laid the groundwork for understanding how formal structures gain legitimacy through normative and cultural frameworks. Weber's typology of authority – traditional, charismatic, and legal-rational – emphasized how the values underpinning rationalization processes influence both rule-bound compliance and broader patterns of organized behavior. In this sense, the integration of values into institutional theory is not incidental; it is central to how organizations establish legitimacy, navigate social expectations, and respond to institutional pressures (Krygier, 2012, pp. 29–42).

Underlying this view is Weber's distinction between instrumental and value rationality. While the former refers to action aimed at achieving goals through calculated means, value rationality involves action guided by commitment to intrinsic ideals, pursued regardless of the outcomes (Rutgers & Schreurs, 2006). Instrumental rationality supports rule-bound procedures and optimization, which are central to formal structures; value rationality introduces normative commitments that define legitimate goals. This distinction highlights that institutions not only emerge for efficiency but also reflect socially embedded values.

Thematizing Values

Weber's ideas offer a valuable point of departure for examining how values are embedded in AI governance at the regulatory level. Accordingly, value and instrumental rationality were adopted as sensitizing concepts for thematic analysis (Clarke & and Braun, 2017) of the 180 recitals in the AI Act. Values were operationalized as ideals that lend positive or negative valence to justify regulatory ideas, with the distinction between:

- Autotelic values – concepts expressed as ends in themselves.
- Instrumental values – concepts expressed as means to an end.

For clarity, these concepts are discussed in tandem with the findings to contextualize the empirical results. They served, nevertheless, as the initial departure points for the analysis.

Against their initial instincts, the authors decided to employ an AI-assisted approach – somewhat mischievously – to explore how an AI tool (chatGPT-4o) might help uncover insights into the spirit of AI regulation. This idea arose from an initial reading of recitals, which presented a dense mix of vagueness and technical language that proved overwhelming to unravel and thematize. Given the transformer models' high sensitivity to linguistic nuance, using an AI-assisted approach appeared to be a functional method for discovering and tracing thematic patterns. This required careful research design, including the development of tailored personas and constraints suitable for close reading – ultimately forming an augmented environment for qualitative analysis. The process unfolded in four phases:

1. **Open Coding.** The first 45 recitals were analyzed inductively, one at a time. The interface included the verbatim text of the recital, a summary of its regulatory intent, a list of proposed themes based on linguistic clues, and a critical evaluation of the proposed themes. This process yielded an unwieldy collection of 47 themes as proxies for values, many of which were either too broad or overly specific. These were examined for semantic overlap in order to begin clustering thematically similar items.
2. **Integrated Approach.** The authors narrowed the collection to 17 themes based on interpretative judgment. These then served as a deductive frame for analyzing the next 45 recitals. The interface was constrained to detect linguistic clues against refined definitions while remaining open to new, uncaptured themes. The result was a collection of 22 themes, which were further refined.
3. **Deductive Coding.** The refined set of themes was used to code the remaining 90 recitals in a fully deductive manner. Each theme was examined individually, with the interface displaying only excerpts from recitals triggered by the working definitions. This allowed the authors to crystallize a final thematic structure and retroactively apply it to earlier materials. Though the themes catalogue was expected to be fixed at this stage, one additional value emerged and was incorporated.
4. **Final Readings.** As a robustness check, the authors reread all the recitals without AI assistance.

Although the research design was structured, the actual practice required constant cross-checking, error tracing, managing bloated context windows, resolving memory artifacts, and correcting misapplied constraints – often necessitating repeated iterations. Despite the tedium, this iterative approach fostered focus and prompted re-evaluation of previously crystallized themes. In this sense, the analysis remained as delightfully messy as any qualitative study must be to reach a proper interpretation. This suggests that – even with AI-assistance – the process of disentangling meanings embedded in the regulatory act remains a deeply human endeavor.

Regulatory Tones

As discussed in the previous section, the working definitions of autotelic and instrumental values underline their functional distinctiveness for analytical purposes. However, during the analysis, further distinctions turned out to be relevant for interpretation. Therefore, in the two following subsections, the authors begin by expanding the original conceptualization to contextually account for an empirically informed split within both categories. Autotelic values are discussed in terms of *foundational* and *substantive* types, while instrumental values are divided into *instrumental per se* and *epistemic* values.

Autotelic Values

This category captures the cultural fabric of human societies, wherein certain symbolic ideas are valued "just because." There are multiple ways that attempt to explain why, for instance, freedom may be valuable (Carter, 2022), and how it ought to be conceptualized to translate into positive outcomes. Nonetheless, the essential point is that such values are considered desirable social conditions by virtue of their recurring cultural manifestations. These values resist disregarding them as well as reduction to anything beyond themselves, and this self-referential quality guided this part of the analysis.

In applying this lens, it soon became apparent that clustering values based solely on this quality conflated two different questions that the AI Act seeks to answer: *What justifies this regulatory action*? And: *What goals does this intervention aim to pursue?* Accordingly, the authors decided to address those themes separately by dividing uncovered themes into two interrelated, but distinct types: *foundational* and *substantive* values.

Foundational values define the legitimacy of the AI Act. They are drawn from constitutional frameworks such as the Treaty on European Union or the Charter of Fundamental Rights, comprising the EU framework for civic rights. These values are not policy goals but normative preconditions for AI governance. They signify the existence and relevance of the boundary conditions – principles that cannot be crossed or altered under any circumstances.

Substantive values, by contrast, represent the core policy objectives that the AI Act is designed to achieve. They translate foundational commitments into more tangible priorities, while still preserving the self-referential quality of being pursued as ends in themselves.

Foundational values *(dignity, freedom, democracy, equality, and rule of law)* serve as anchors for the EU's constitutional, ethical, and civic frameworks, translating them into institutionally grounded governance principles. They are intended to equip the AI Act with regulatory legitimacy by embedding it within the broader context in which it is meant to operate. These values encompass both individual rights and collective-level commitments, safeguarded by the procedural legitimacy guaranteed by the rule of law. They

Table 19.1 Autotelic values in AI Act by foundational and substantive types (N – recitals count)

Value	*Normative Function*	*Rhetorical Function in Recitals*	*N*
Foundational values – articulate non-negotiable basis for AI governance			
Dignity	Points at the intrinsic worth and autonomy of a person, which is not to be treated as a mere object of computation or inference. It safeguards the person as a moral subject.	Protecting people from reduction to data proxies, scores, or categories, especially if AI overrides judgment, erodes consent, or substitutes identity with statistical estimates.	53
Freedom	Defends against the erosion of autonomy through subtle control. Affirms the right to think, speak, associate, and act without coercion, surveillance, or manipulation.	Affirming negative freedoms from profiling, behavioral nudging, or opaque surveillance and positive freedoms to participate, express, and dissent without algorithmic suppression.	34
Democracy	Ensures retaining civic control over technologies, shaping the public life in terms of electoral integrity, participation, and oversight over AI governance.	Demanding not to distort deliberation, silence dissent, or centralize power in unaccountable infrastructures. Without it, managing AI risks may be feasible but politically hollow.	28
Equality	Demands that discrimination or systematic bias do not intensify or replicate. It prevents unequal treatment based on race, gender, age, disability, or economic status.	Enforcing how data and algorithms might produce disparate outcomes intentionally or through neglect, justifying proactive measures to detect and mitigate unfair treatment.	21
Rule of law	Ensures embeddedness within a clear, predictable, and enforceable regulatory framework at national and Union-wide levels to safeguard legal authority.	Stressing that rights, obligations, and remedies must be defined by law in terms of legal thresholds for classification, guarantees for redress, and the obligation to maintain public registers and explainability schemes.	42
Substantive values – expand foundational values into policy goals of AI governance			
Solidarity	Strengthens the infrastructures that support collective welfare. It requires that vulnerable people and communities are not left behind by structural redistribution of opportunity.	Nudging AI systems designed to sustain access to public infrastructures that support social cohesion – education, healthcare, housing, and welfare – and involve civil society in decisions that affect them.	19

(*Continued*)

Table 19.1 (Continued)

Value	*Normative Function*	*Rhetorical Function in Recitals*	*N*
Safety	Guarding against physical, psychological, and systemic damage, particularly in sensitive domains such as healthcare, mobility, access control, and critical infrastructure.	Justifying the restriction, prohibition, or withdrawal of AI systems, posing unacceptable risks. It underlies duties to mitigate adversarial threats and uphold baseline protection.	48
Privacy	Safeguards informational autonomy in terms of collecting, processing, inferring, storing, and acting upon personal data. It limits the reach over personal identity, exposure, and behavior so that people retain control over what is known about them.	Imposing privacy-by-design constraints on what AI may infer, remember, or act upon. It is not reducible to ethics or formal rights discourse – it is a deliberate choice to preserve boundaries against expanding surveillance, inference, and automated categorization.	61
Health	Protects human wellness in clinical, diagnostic, therapeutic contexts. It entails early detection, treatment accuracy, psychological well-being, equitable care access, and population-level resilience.	Justifying restriction of harmful systems across individual and institutional settings and exceptional regulatory treatment where the medical advancement warrants deviation from standard procedures.	32
Flourishing	Stresses the role to promote individual development across the life course in terms of personal growth or distorting thereof. It pleads to empower people to thrive, contribute, and shape their futures.	Promoting autonomy and participation in domains that shape long-term capabilities and access to opportunity – including education, employment, healthcare, housing, or credit – which underlie life prospects.	27
Prosperity	Focuses on progress in terms of economic development for individuals and society. It encompasses inclusive material growth, productivity gains, and broad access to the benefits of innovation.	Advocating for structural changes like labor market transitions, access to economic resources, and public sector modernization to harmonize and support shared economic benefit across all levels.	31

(*Continued*)

Table 19.1 (Continued)

Value	*Normative Function*	*Rhetorical Function in Recitals*	*N*
Work	Ensures dignity and procedural justice in workplaces. It protects the rights, roles, or recognition of workers but also implies the aim to foster employment.	Stressing the role of protection against de-skilling, workplace surveillance, and the automation of managerial authority. It applies wherever AI reshapes the organization, supervision, or value of human labor.	52
Ecosystem	Iterates the role of care for ecological sustainability. It is usually a confounding reference alongside health, safety, and fundamental rights.	Working as a governance trigger which justifies environmental concern to ensure alignment with industrial and ecological strategies to mitigate climate change.	12

Source: Based on own interpretative work.

are origin points, articulated as conditions that must be met for any regulatory outcome to be deemed legitimate.

Together, these values compose a mutually reinforcing tone of singular qualities. *Dignity* functions as the moral baseline, affirming that individuals must not be reduced to proxies. *Freedom* extends this protection into the sphere of autonomy, safeguarding individuals from unjustified interference, profiling, or coercive inference. Yet freedom only becomes meaningful when accompanied by *equality*, which ensures that algorithmic systems do not reproduce or reinforce structural disadvantages. The logic of *democracy* builds upon these to affirm that AI governance requires collective participation, public oversight, and institutional transparency. All of them, however, ultimately depend on the *rule of law* to be transformed into enforceable norms. The tone emerging from this interaction reflects a vision of AI governance that is not only lawful but also human-centric, not only transparent but also socially embedded, not only fair but also protective of the common good.

While this orchestrated ideal sets the stage for other values to play their part, it does not remain entirely harmonious when the recitals begin to invoke substantive values – those aimed at transforming foundational conditions into tangible outcomes. These include concerns for *solidarity, safety, privacy, health, flourishing, prosperity, work*, and *ecosystem* – values that the AI Act aspires to foster through its governance.

The disharmony arises from a tension between preserving present concerns and nurturing future possibilities. For instance, *solidarity*, usually invoked implicitly, is more about protecting structural conditions under which people live together than promoting any future-orientated transformation. This orientation is even more pronounced in reference to *safety* and *privacy*, which enable people to feel secure in the digital realm and shield them from potential harms.

The tone shifts subtly when *health* is invoked – both as a call for responsible treatment and as an opportunity to improve collective well-being through medical innovation. These themes continue through the notions of *flourishing*, which emphasizes life opportunities, and *prosperity*, which suggests economic conditions that support the distribution of benefits across European societies. While *work* is occasionally framed in terms of fostering employment, it is more commonly rendered in a protective tone – safeguarding workers from AI-driven exploitation rather than advancing new labor paradigms.

Perhaps the most ambivalent treatment concerns the *ecosystem*. While the energy-intensive nature of the AI industry would warrant protective concern, the recitals addressing this value are notably vague and, in general, suspiciously silent.

The common tone set by the foundational values begins to fall out of tune when concrete outcomes are considered. This tonal dissonance reflects a broader discursive clash: on one side, the technocratic enthusiasm for AI-driven transformation; on the other, a deep concern for preserving culturally entrenched values. Rhetorically, the latter appears more pronounced – unsurprising, given the risk-based approach adopted for this regulation. Yet, the language around recognizing and mitigating risks is louder than the language around embracing them.

Instrumental Values

In contrast to autotelic values, Weber also points at the other type of rationality grounded in a different kind of ideals. While these also function as cherished concepts that justify action, the instrumental values operate more as mediators in a broader chain of legitimization – means to an end rather than the end in themselves. *Competition*, for example, is often positively associated with structuring market economies (Hayek, 2016). From this perspective, however, competition is only valued insofar as it leads to prosperity – unlike *war*, which also involves competition but typically does not yield comparably positive outcomes. In this sense, instrumental values may carry normative weight, but the positive or negative evaluation they receive depends on their alignment with more ultimate, autotelic ideals.

Following this logic, the analysis of the AI Act also considered instrumental values. However, a further interpretative distinction emerged. The authors observed that while some values are articulated to justify how societal-level goals are to be achieved, others relate to the qualities of AI systems themselves – specifically, how they should function to serve those goals effectively. Based on this collection, instrumental values were further divided into two types: *instrumental per se* and *epistemic* values.

Table 19.2 Values ordered by instrumental per se and epistemic (N – recitals count)

Value	*Normative Function*	*Rhetorical Function in Recitals*	*N*
Values instrumental per se – expressed as means to achieve autotelic values			
Risk	Articulates concern for rational recognition and structured engagement with uncertainty, variability, and potential harm.	Grounding the governance framework to differentiate, contextualize, and control AI system obligations across their life cycle. It is a key object to be managed.	118
Legibility	Stresses the role of structuring regulatory complexity to make governance intelligible, navigable, and enforceable across contexts, actors and international jurisdictions.	Ensuring that obligations are rendered clear, non-arbitrary, and operationally traceable – even in hybrid, evolving, or cross-sectoral use cases across multiple actors.	90
Innovation	Enables conditions for safe experimentation, technical exploration, and iterative improvement across the product life cycle.	Creating a regulated space for adaptive progress and experimentation. It affords structured flexibility, reduced compliance for SMEs, start-ups, and open-source ecosystems.	46
Competition	Affirms the value of open, diverse, and non-concentrated markets. It supports fair access for smaller actors to limit monopolization.	Structuring conditions for a plural and accessible AI ecosystem by integrating the single market and empowering small actors lacking the economy of scale.	34
Maintenance	Stresses the relevance and necessity to preserve operational and technical capacity for performance and refinement over time.	Ensuring that AI systems remain functional, intelligible, and compliant not just at the point of deployment, but as they evolve, degrade, or move across domains and actors.	77
Epistemic values – expressed as means for AI systems to serve well all previous values			
Reliability	Grounds the concern for epistemic integrity and operational soundness, such that any outputs can be faithfully treated as valid and consistent.	Assuring that inferences, classifications, or recommendations stem from quality-data and can be treated as robust particularly in high-stakes or risk-sensitive environments.	62

(*Continued*)

Table 19.2 (Continued)

Value	*Normative Function*	*Rhetorical Function in Recitals*	*N*
Transparency	Mandates the structured disclosure of information to ensure intelligibility, traceability, and procedural accessibility reasonably open to inspect.	Forcing AI systems to be governed and inspected to ensure explainability and traceability. It entails standardized documentation formats and auditing.	65
Control	Requires capacity for human actors to oversee or interrupt the automated operations to preclude them from evading comprehension or constraint.	Structuring where, how, and by whom the intervention is possible by human-in-the-loop design affording validation and authorization to guarantee human authority.	53
Accountability	Demands the structured attribution of responsibility so that decisions can be traced to specific actors able to explain or remedy arising issues.	Anchoring responsibility for AI systems in specific, enforceable roles. It ensures that actors can be identified, monitored, and called to account across the AI life cycle.	85
Trust	Designates the desirable state of collective perception of trustworthiness amid complexity, black boxing, or limited technical understanding.	Enabling AI systems to be accepted and used even under uncertainty. It serves legitimacy arising from visible constraint, responsible governance, and truthful accountability.	52

Values *instrumental per se* reflect a similar tension between immediate concerns and AI-mediated potential, much like substantive values. The key theme in this category is *risk*, which is framed as an object to be rationally assessed and governed through regulation. It underpins the classification of AI systems into risk categories, with the high-risk designation serving as the benchmark for the strictest regulatory obligations, while general-purpose AI and low-risk systems – are relieved of certain duties. This regulatory strategy is accompanied by *legibility* (or *legal certainty*), which is framed as the provision of clear guidance through restrictions and obligations to ensure harmonious implementation. It is reiterated throughout the Act as a justification for EU-level intervention to prevent more fragmented or more rigid regulatory responses at the national level.

Counterintuitively, this logic is also tied to the promotion of *innovation*, which is to be supported by exemptions for research and development activities and the establishment of "regulatory sandboxes" as structured testing environments. *Competition* is discussed in a similar vein, with an emphasis on reducing compliance burdens for smaller actors that may lack the resources to meet full regulatory demands. In the background – but consistently present – is the value of *maintenance*, which underlies cost-inducing demands of purposeful system design, post-market monitoring, and ongoing refinement, signaling that AI systems are here to stay and evolve regardless of associated concerns.

This instrumental tone is clearly supported by epistemic values, which frame AI development as transformative for how knowledge is produced and how collective cognition might be reshaped. These values are closely related semantically and axiologically, as they play the same normative tune while pointing toward different operational ends. *Reliability* is strongly connected to *transparency*, with the assumption that system robustness depends on external evaluability. This, in turn, underpins the value of *control* and *human oversight*, conceived as a continuum from systemic to end-user levels. These afford the realization of *accountability*, since the demand for control necessitates naming those responsible for specific actions or outcomes.

Together, these values form the idea of trustworthy AI – a recurring ideal throughout the AI Act. *Trust* itself is frequently mentioned as the mediating factor that enables AI systems to be meaningfully inscribed in the pursuit all previously discussed values further along the legitimization chain.

Summary

The analysis of the AI Act demonstrates that values cut across regulatory, normative, and cultural dimensions of institutional theory – all of which informed different parts of the interpretation. The resulting discussion explicates an unequivocal symphony. While *foundational* and *epistemic* values play on the same note coherently, the *substantive* values and *instrumental per se* echo the broader drift between ongoing concerns for cherished social ideals and the transformative potential of AI-mediated progress. Given the discursive resonance of the Draghi report on European Competitiveness (European Commission, 2024), one can see its resounding impact in the outset as expressed in the second AI Act recital:

> This Regulation should be applied in accordance with the values of the Union enshrined as in the Charter, facilitating the protection of natural persons, undertakings, democracy, the rule of law and environmental protection, while boosting innovation and employment and making the Union a leader in the uptake of trustworthy AI.
>
> (Regulation (EU) 2024/1689, 2024, p. 1)

However, despite the AI Act's stated ambition to foster the EU's competitive advantage, the overtone stressing the need to mitigate the negative outcomes remains more pronounced throughout the text. This suggests that the European approach for AI development follows a logic of "two steps back, one step forward" – in subtle contrast to the opening narrative. Whether this approach represents a cautious strength or a limiting conservatism is left open. In classic Weberian fashion, the authors withhold their normative judgment, as they meant only to provide a map of the value landscape that the AI Act delineates.

Acknowledgments

This chapter has been supported by the Polish National Agency for Academic Exchange under the NAWA Partnerstwo Strategiczne program, project BNI/PST/2023/1/00082.

Reference List

Acemoglu, D., & Johnson, S. (2023). *Power and progress: Our thousand-year struggle over technology and prosperity*. PublicAffairs.

Butt, M. J. S. (2024). Analytical study of the world's first EU Artificial Intelligence (AI) act, 2024. *International Journal of Research Publication and Reviews*, *5*(3). https://doi.org/10.55248/gengpi.5.0324.0914

Carter, I. (2022, Spring). Positive and negative liberty. W E. N. Zalta (Red.), *The stanford encyclopedia of philosophy*. Metaphysics Research Lab, Stanford University. https://plato.stanford.edu/archives/spr2022/entries/liberty-positive-negative/

Celsi, L. R. (2023). The Dilemma of rapid AI advancements: Striking a balance between innovation and regulation by pursuing risk-aware value creation. *Information*, *14*(12). https://doi.org/10.3390/info14120645

Clarke, V., & Braun, V. (2017). Thematic analysis. *The Journal of Positive Psychology*, *12*(3), 297–298. https://doi.org/10.1080/17439760.2016.1262613

Dant, T. (2006). Material civilization: Things and society. *The British Journal of Sociology* *57*(2), 289–308. https://doi.org/10.1111/j.1468-4446.2006.00110.x

Den Heijer, M., Abeelen, T. V. O. V. D., & Maslyka, A. (2019). On the use and misuse of recitals in European Union Law. *SSRN Electronic Journal*. https://doi.org/10.2139/ssrn.3445372

DiMaggio, P. J., & Powell, W. W. (1983). The iron cage revisited: Institutional isomorphism and collective rationality in organizational fields. *American Sociological Review*, *48*(2), 147–160. https://doi.org/10.2307/2095101

European Commission. (2019). *Ethics guidelines for trustworthy AI*. https://digital-strategy.ec.europa.eu/en/library/ethics-guidelines-trustworthy-ai

European Commission. (2024). *The future of European competitiveness: Report by Mario Draghi*. https://commission.europa.eu/topics/eu-competitiveness/draghi-report_en#paragraph_47059

Friedland, R., & Alford, R. (1991). Bringing society back in: Symbols, practices, and institutional contradictions. In W. W. Powell & P. J. DiMaggio (Eds.), *The new institutionalism in organizational analysis* (pp. 232–267). University of Chicago Press, Chicago.

Haenlein, M., & Kaplan, A. (2019). A brief history of artificial intelligence: On the past, present, and future of artificial intelligence. *California Management Review* *61*(4), 5–14. https://doi.org/10.1177/0008125619864925

Hayek, F. A. (2016). The meaning of competition. *Econ Journal Watch*, *13*(2), 359–372.

Ho, C. W.-L., & Caals, K. (2024). How the EU AI act seeks to establish an epistemic environment of trust. *Asian Bioethics Review*, *16*(3). https://doi.org/10.1007/s41649-024-00304-6

Jobin, A., Ienca, M., & Vayena, E. (2019). The global landscape of AI ethics guidelines. *Nature Machine Intelligence*, *1*(9). https://doi.org/10.1038/s42256-019-0088-2
Krygier, M. (2012). *Philip selznick: Ideals in the world*. Stanford Law Books.
Martínez, E. J. A., Mollica, F., & Gibson, E. (2023). Even lawyers do not like legalese. *Proceedings of the National Academy of Sciences*, *120*(23). https://doi.org/10.1073/pnas.2302672120
Peton, H., & Pezé, S. (2014). The unsuspected dynamics of the regulative pillar: The case of faute inexcusable in France. *Management*, *17*(3). https://doi.org/10.3917/mana.173.0001
Raisch, S., & Krakowski, S. (2021). Artificial intelligence and management: The automation: Augmentation paradox. *Academy of Management Review*, *46*(1), 192–210. https://doi.org/10.5465/amr.2018.0072
Regulation (EU) *2024/1689, European Parliment* (2024). https://eur-lex.europa.eu/eli/reg/2024/1689/oj/eng
Rutgers, M. R., & Schreurs, P. (2006). The morality of value- and purpose-rationality: The Kantian roots of weber's foundational distinction. *Administration & Society*, *38*(4), 403–421. https://doi.org/10.1177/0095399706290632
Scott, W. R. (2013). *Institutions and organizations: Ideas, interests, and identities*. SAGE Publications.
Selznick, P. (2008). *A humanist science: Values and ideals in social inquiry*. Stanford University Press.
Weber, M., & Tribe, K. (2019). *Economy and society: A new translation*. Harvard University Press. https://doi.org/10.4159/9780674240827

20 (E)DIHs Strengthening the Adaptability of SMEs in the AI-Driven Digital Transformation

Dorota Czyżewska-Misztal, Piotr Idczak, and Sébastien Bourdin

20.1 Introduction

Digital transformation powered by AI has gained particular interest among academics and policymakers in recent years. Increased digitalization is a key tool for addressing some of the major challenges that European businesses face. Digital innovations are powerful leverage that can be channeled in support of actions against climate change or the challenges of the Fourth Industrial Revolution under the umbrella of the twin transition (Meijer, 2024; Muench et al., 2022). AI, as a key part of the Fourth Industrial Revolution, is considered to be a game changer (especially with the exponential growth of more and more powerful GenAI technologies) with the potential to revolutionize almost everything, meet societal challenges, and create new possibilities but also threats at the same time (Chalmers et al., 2020; Holmström, 2022; Escoz Barragán et al., 2025; Storey et al., 2025).

European SMEs are often perceived as reluctant or hesitant to embrace the digital transition of the European economy, despite its potential to enhance productivity, competitiveness, and resilience. This hesitancy should not be considered, however, irrational. Instead, it is rooted in a complex interplay of internal constraints, external uncertainties, and systemic policy failures. Implementing solutions based on advanced technologies requires substantial upfront investments in hardware and software, training, and maintenance. Since SMEs operate with limited cash flow and insufficient access to financial resources, they favor short-term investment timelines, thereby avoiding excessive capital commitments for activities unrelated to their core operating expenses (Botsari et al., 2024; EIB, 2024). Furthermore, they often struggle with a lack of in-house digital expertise, a scarcity of a digital transformation mindset, and a clear strategic vision for driving change. This results in inertia caused by a fear of implementation failure (OECD, 2021). Digital change is seen as a threat to existing business models, workforce roles, and long-standing routines. In fact, employees may resist due to fears of job loss, role changes, and the need for reskilling or upskilling, and managers, in turn, express concerns about losing control or disrupting customer relationships and processes, which often hinder digital progress (Autio et al., 2018;

DOI: 10.4324/9781003659143-26

Nambisan, 2017). Most ready-made digital tools are designed with large companies and their standardized workflows in mind. In contrast, SMEs require adaptable, cost-effective, and modular digital solutions tailored to their size and industry needs (Abel-Koch et al., 2019; Seppänen et al., 2025). Consequently, there is a reluctance to invest in software perceived as overly complex or difficult to integrate, leading many to favor familiar analogue or legacy systems instead (EIB, 2020; Eurochambres, 2021; Seppänen et al., 2025). This situation causes SMEs to express apprehension toward the digital transition of the European economy.

Addressing these fears requires an ecosystemic approach that reduces complexity and uncertainty, lowers operational costs, builds skills, and provides trustworthy support systems at the European territorial level. Such an interconnected and location-specific collaboration, which establishes multiple avenues for stimulating economic progress, can be ignited by an innovation ecosystem. Co-locating knowledge institutions such as universities and research and development centers with firms can accelerate the diffusion of new technologies and practices across various sectors (Cooke et al., 1997; Adner, 2006; Jackson, 2011). Innovation ecosystems often incorporate incubators, accelerators, and capital networks that help startups concentrate on high-value niches, which enhances regional competitiveness (Autio & Thomas, 2014). The multilevel governance and stakeholder coordination within these ecosystems enable better alignment of resources with local priorities. This results in increased efficiency and effectiveness of public investments and supports long-term structural transformation that aligns with regional strengths. Ongoing collaboration among these stakeholders fosters institutional trust and promotes mutual learning. At the same time, it builds the adaptive capacity to respond to economic shocks and strengthens the resilience and sustainability of growth pathways.

In the sense outlined earlier, Digital Innovation Hubs (DIHs) followed by the European Digital Innovation Hubs (EDIHs) network were designed to accelerate the digital transformation of businesses and public sector organizations in the EU through a one-stop-shop model. In this chapter, we are using DIHs and EDIHs or (E)DIHs to refer to these two groups of DIHs interchangeably. DIHs comprise a broad and diverse category of institutions that serve as regional one-stop shops for companies, particularly SMEs, seeking to adopt digital technologies. These hubs typically arise from national or regional initiatives and are often anchored in research organizations, universities, or industry clusters. EDIHs, in contrast, represent a formally designated subset of DIHs that have been selected through a competitive process under the Digital Europe Programme. This initiative, launched in 2021, aims to create a pan-European network of excellence, with EDIHs supporting both regional ecosystems and transnational digital priorities. While both DIHs and EDIHs strive to enhance the digital maturity of European industry, EDIHs fulfill a more strategic, structured, and internationally connected role.

EDIHs have been introduced as key components of the European Digital Strategy that help businesses, mainly SMEs, meet digital challenges and increase their competitiveness. EDIHs are seen as digital transformation agents that should operate within and through innovation ecosystems, enhancing the local capacity to adopt and benefit from advanced digital technologies. They are crucial in translating regional innovation policies into concrete digital support services while aligning with smart specialization priorities. EDIHs should strengthen the digital capacities of SMEs and public institutions and foster cross-border innovation through integration into European networks. EDIHs also offer training and skills development and guide entities in accessing various financing sources to ensure they can effectively utilize new digital technologies and foster digital transformation.

However, integrating new digital technologies, which utilize AI, into existing systems often presents many difficulties for SMEs. Therefore, EDIHs are expected to play a pivotal role in fostering the development of AI agents in SMEs by providing tailor-made resources, expertise, and network opportunities.

The original contribution of this chapter is to examine the role of (E)DIHs as territorial intermediaries supporting the digital transition of businesses and public sector organizations across Europe. However, the main objective is to demonstrate how (E)DIHs contribute to shaping a sustainable innovation ecosystem that supports the continuous digital transition of European business models.

The rest of the chapter is structured as follows: Section 20.2 presents our theoretical background, Section 20.3 describes the (E)DIH network from the perspective of the European Digital Strategy, Section 20.4 presents the embeddedness of (E)DIHs in a territorial context, followed by results from the interviews. Section 20.5 concludes this chapter.

20.2 Territorial Intermediation as the Foundation for Digital Transition

The theoretical framework used in the study refers to territorial intermediation. According to Nadou and Pecqueur (2020), territorial intermediation can be defined as "modes and processes regulating behaviors and relationships between actors in the territorial system." The concept of territorial intermediation can be referred to as a plethora of concepts under the umbrella of territorial innovation models (TIM) coined by Moulaert and Sekia (2003). Of all the territorial innovation models, the regional innovation system (RIS) concept has attracted the most interest from researchers and policymakers. Cooke et al. (1997) define regional innovation systems as sets of interdependent actors (companies, universities, and public institutions, etc.) that collaborate within a region in order to promote innovation and economic development. Knowledge sharing, R&D activities, and entrepreneurship are considered to be the activities at the heart of the stimulation of regional innovation (Asheim et al., 2019). In the era of the digital economy, these RIS are likely to undergo significant changes (Antipina et al., 2021), as the role of digital technology in innovation processes has become decisive (Mura & Donath, 2023).

Innovation economists tend to characterize the third-party actors that are essential to the development of innovation processes between companies (Howells, 2006; Dalziel & Parjanen, 2012). These key actors, called "intermediaries," are part of the panorama and ecosystems of innovation actors. They can play multiple roles within the regional innovation system, among others: i) help companies to network, ii) lead to building joint projects, iii) facilitate the exchange of best practices, iv) raise awareness, v) lead the ecosystem, which is made up of members, partners, and other structures, vi) facilitate access to finance, vii) promote the network to external stakeholders, and viii) participate in developing innovation/development strategies for the region (Bourdin et al., 2020; Kanda et al., 2025; Laur & Kanda, 2025). However, the significance and role of intermediaries in digital innovation have been very little studied to date (Caloffi et al., 2023; Lepore, 2024; Howells, 2024). Our study aims to fill the research gap by investigating the role of EDIHs in the digital transformation of SMEs and public sector organizations.

20.3 European Digital Strategy with the Focus on (E)DIHs

Recognizing the importance of digital transformation, the European Union has been taking steps for years to, among other things: (1) develop strategies in this field, (2) actively involve member states and stakeholders at international, national, regional, and local levels in its actions, (3) define indicators and monitor progress toward the results set, (4) invest in actions at the pan-European level to help increase the digitization of players, and (5) network the players involved in this process.

The origins of the DIH program are linked to the European Commission's announcement of the first call in April 2016 as part of the Digital Single Market package. The Commission's intention was to increase the interest of businesses in digitization, boost the level of investment in this strategic area, and create the framework conditions for the Fourth Industrial Revolution in the EU. One of the most important pillars of this program was the creation of DIHs, which would operate on a one-stop-shop basis offering tailored services aimed at increasing the competitiveness and innovation of small and medium-sized enterprises in particular (Czyżewska-Misztal, 2024). A tailor-made approach following the digitization needs of SMEs was a distinguishing feature of this program compared to other rather numerous initiatives aimed at increasing innovation, technology transfer, or building digital skills of employees. Here, the focus was on offering a range of services dedicated to the specific needs of businesses in response to the barriers to SME innovation and digitization identified in the literature (see Section 20.1). While networking and digital skills-building services are also offered to companies as part of other initiatives, the distinctive feature of the DIH program was the possibility of using the "test before invest" service, which allowed for testing within the company without the need to make an investment, thus providing the opportunity to assess whether a given technological solution could actually contribute to the digital transformation of the company.

Based on the experience of the DIH network, in 2021, the European Commission announced a call for EDIHs. EDIHs represent a key operational instrument within the European Union's digital policy architecture. Their establishment stems from the strategic objective of facilitating the digital transformation of both private and public actors across European regions, with a particular focus on small and medium-sized enterprises (SMEs), which often lack the internal capacity to adopt and deploy advanced technologies (OECD, 2021). Conceived as decentralized infrastructures embedded in regional ecosystems, EDIHs aim to foster innovation diffusion while responding to territorial specificities and economic structures.

As of May 2025, there are 168 EDIHs funded under the Digital Europe Program. Moreover, 86 EDIHs, coined as Seals of Excellence, are positively evaluated in a European competitive call but are funded exclusively by national or regional resources. The EDIH Network catalogue comprises 206 EDIHs funded by other initiatives – former DIHs (https://european-digital-innovation-hubs.ec.europa.eu/pl/edih-catalogue?f%5B0%5D=edih_soe%3Asoe). Their geographical distribution reflects not only the economic weight and digital maturity of different Member States but also the European cohesion objective, which seeks to ensure territorial balance in access to innovation infrastructure (De Nigris et al., 2023). While Western and Northern Europe host a large proportion of hubs, a deliberate effort has been made to strengthen digital support in Central, Eastern, and Southern regions. This ambition aligns with the Digital Europe Program and its concern for reducing digital divides across EU territories (EIB, 2020; Meijer, 2024).

The institutional configurations of EDIHs are diverse. Some are embedded within universities and research centers; others operate through regional development agencies, technological parks, or clusters. In many cases, EDIHs operate as consortia, bringing together complementary institutions that can align technological expertise with business needs while anchoring their actions within regional smart specialization strategies (S3) (Rissola & Sörvik, 2018).

Each EDIH provides a structured portfolio of services designed to enhance digital maturity. These include digital readiness assessments, access to testing facilities, technical guidance in areas such as artificial intelligence and cybersecurity, skills development, and navigation of financing opportunities (Czyżewska-Misztal, 2024; Carpentier et al., 2025). These services are not offered in isolation but are part of a broader mission of territorial intermediation (Nadou & Pecqueur, 2020). Through their proximity to local actors, EDIHs are positioned to interpret regional needs, facilitate stakeholder coordination, and promote innovation uptake.

Beyond their local anchoring, EDIHs also contribute to a pan-European innovation infrastructure. The network operates through shared governance and is supported by the European Commission to ensure consistency, mutual learning, and cross-border synergies (De Nigris et al., 2023). This dual positioning – local and transnational – enhances the potential of EDIHs to serve as policy integrators capable of translating EU digital strategies into locally relevant actions (Chalmers et al., 2020; Holmström, 2022).

Ultimately, the EDIH network must be understood not merely as a technical infrastructure for digital diffusion but as a governance device enabling multi-level coordination across the digital policy landscape. Its success depends on the hubs' ability to navigate the complexities of territorial dynamics, support SMEs in overcoming structural barriers to digitalization, and contribute to building a more cohesive and innovative European economy (Storey et al., 2025; Escoz Barragán et al., 2025).

20.4 Embeddedness of (E)DIHs in a Territorial Context: First Evidence

The primary data for this research were gathered through semi-structured interviews that were conducted between April and August 2023, lasting between 25 and 100 minutes. The distribution of interview participants is as follows: 2 interviews with representatives from the European Commission working in the DIH and EDIH areas, 3 interviews with DIH network coordinators, 1 interview with a representative of a fundraising organization for DIHs, and 38 interviews with DIH and EDIH representatives.

This section reports the key findings stemming from the study, composed of the following: (1) an exploration of the specific roles (E)DIHs are expected to play in reshaping the business strategies and models of SMEs, guiding them toward the future business landscape; (2) an investigation of the causal capacities of (E)DIHs, measured through their embeddedness in a particular territorial context and their ability to build trust; and (3) an identification of the key support activities offered by (E)DIHs to SMEs, as well as the main industries that have been supported so far.

20.4.1 Functional Roles of (E)DIHs in SME Digitalization

The results of the correspondence analysis, which illustrate the involvement of (E)DIHs in the digital transformation of SMEs, are depicted in Figure 20.1a. The visualization indicates that (E)DIHs, particularly those with legal forms such as associations, development agencies, or technology parks, are primarily associated with the orchestration and facilitation of two out of five support activities. The scores for these two categories are approximately equally spaced, except for the three remaining support activities – incubation, innovation, and others – indicating that a majority of (E)DIHs engage in purposeful actions aimed at integrating SMEs into specified innovation networks for collaborative transformation, thereby facilitating easier achievement of digitalization goals. It is also observed that (E)DIHs with public institution status are less common and uniquely focus on innovation. Additionally, the relationship between the scores and the impact context suggests a positive association between sectoral and geographical influences and the features mentioned earlier, indicating strong mutual relationships. However, very few (E)DIHs operate within the sectoral and geographical contexts; those that do often function as research centers, likely providing a broader spectrum of action. Conversely, development agencies and the geographical context are closely linked, suggesting that these agencies primarily operate regionally, while associations show a stronger link to the sectoral context, indicating a wider influence. Interestingly, and not surprisingly, most variable scores are arranged and approximately equally spaced around the "Yes" category, indicating that nearly all (E)DIHs participate in some form of cooperation or collaboration network. However, (E)DIHs classified as public institutions or private companies are less likely to engage in networking. Additionally, the category points corresponding to different country groups are dispersed and spread out across most other categories, indicating no significant differences between (E)DIHs from various countries in terms of their commitment to SMEs' digital transformation.

20.4.2 *Territorial Embeddedness and Trust-Building Dynamics*

Regarding the embeddedness of (E)DIHs in a particular territorial context (Figure 20.1b), evidence suggests a positive association between the dominant roles of (E)DIHs (specified as orchestrators, facilitators, and consultants) and their territorial position as being sufficiently close to the companies to influence desirable transformative changes. These (E)DIHs are also regarded as trusted third parties with adequate capabilities to build trust and understanding of objectives and expectations related to the strategy for developing digital and green innovations. The geographical context reveals a strong relationship between the scores of (E)DIHs located in CEE and WE countries and their embeddedness in the territorial context and the trust function. A relatively weak relationship to these categories is plotted concerning NE, SE, and N-EU countries. Remarkably, (E)DIHs situated in NE countries are less likely to be viewed as trusted third parties and less embedded in the territorial ecosystems. In contrast, those in SE and N-EU countries are seen as more territorially rooted and capable of building trust. However, their role is considered intermediate in facilitating the digital and ecological transition. This discrepancy may stem from the need for (E)DIHs to clarify their role in assisting companies, as businesses often doubt that research institutions can enhance their competitiveness through digital technologies.

20.4.3 Digital Demand and Perceived Need for Support

The results of plotting the categories corresponding to the importance of the digital dimension and the need for support in digital transformation can be compared in Figure 20.1c. The layout of the scores can be interpreted as showing that the profiles of these two variables are ordered, and their relationship can be explained as a positive association between the importance of the digital dimension and the need for support in digital transformation. This relationship, considered from a geographical perspective, is especially strong in terms of (E)DIHs operating in CEE and SE countries. However, the scores for (E)DIHs in NE countries show a characteristic opposite corner pattern of the relationship, suggesting that these two variables are less relevant.

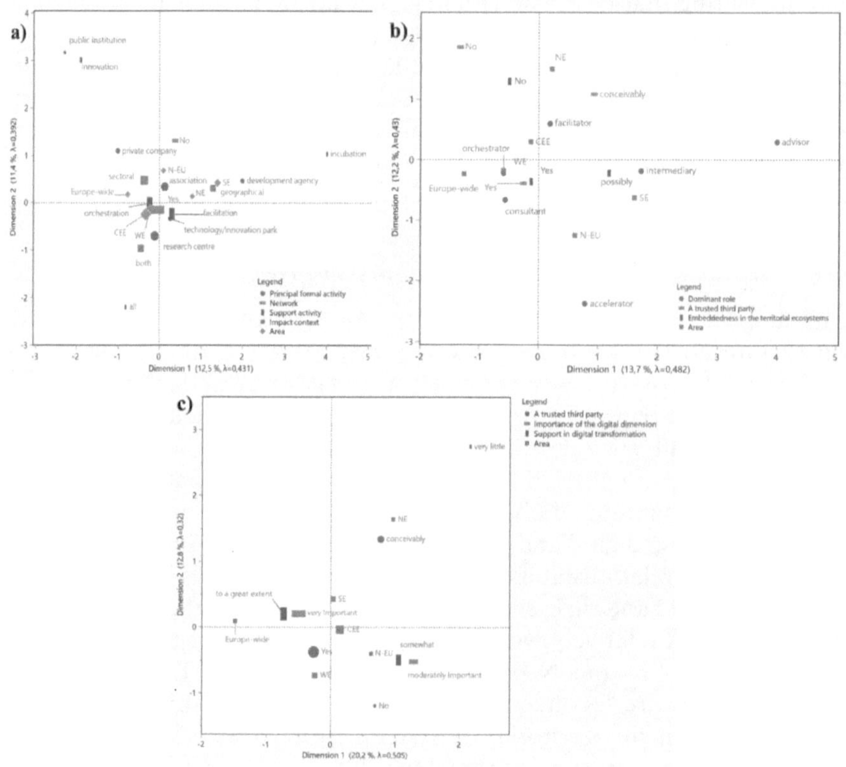

Figure 20.1 Correspondence analysis solutions: (a) regarding the characteristic and specific role of (E)DIHs; (b) concerning the embeddedness of (E)DIHs in a territorial context and their trust-building capacities; (c) highlighting the importance of the digital dimension.

Source: Authors' own elaboration.

20.4.4 Types of Services Provided and Industries Supported

In order to identify the main support activities provided by (E)DIHs to SMEs and the primary industries that have received support thus far, a textual analysis was carried out using the word cloud technique. The visual representations of word frequency related to both features analyzed are presented in Figure 20.2. As shown in Figure 20.2a, the two most prominent words highlighted are "networking" and "events." Only a slightly smaller size is displayed in the case of "workshops" and "raising awareness." This finding conforms to the main goal of (E)DIHs, which is to connect companies with research and other institutions, thus fostering collaboration that should lead to innovation.

As shown in Figure 20.2b, the word "manufacturing" occurs with the highest frequency of all the industries being supported so far. The target industries are given as "agriculture," "robotics," and "health care," which are also significant, reflecting the key industries that are most active in undertaking digital transformation activities.

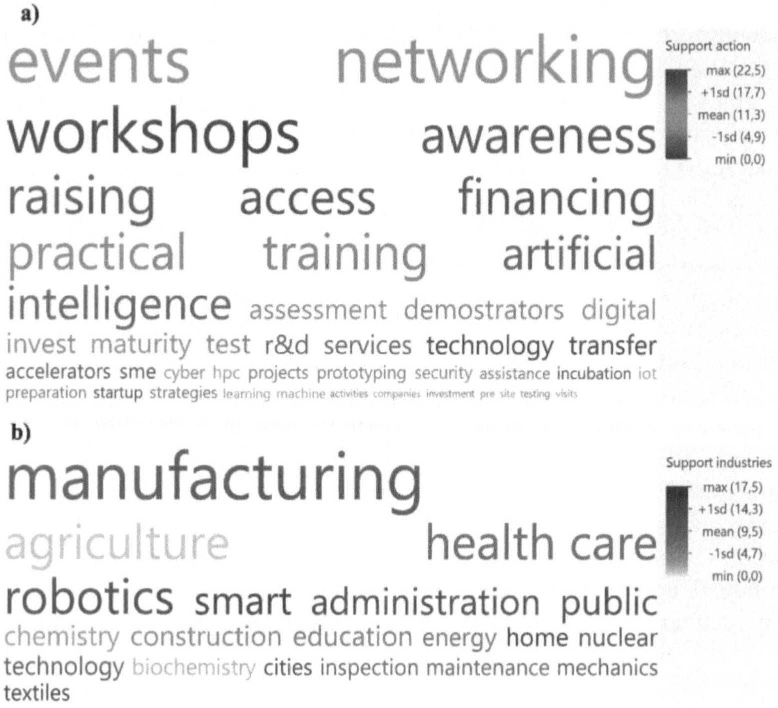

Figure 20.2 Word clouds: (a) depicting the key support activities provided by (E)DIHs; (b) illustrating the main industries supported by (E)DIHs.

Source: Authors' own elaboration.

20.4.5 Limits and Evolution of (E)DIH Activities

Based on the interviews conducted, it can be indicated that (E)DIHs perceive themselves as a vital link connecting the actors of the regional innovation ecosystem. They can play the role of orchestrators, being able to offer services both to technologically advanced entities and to companies at an early stage of digital transformation. However, overall, they provided pilot services, raising awareness of digital transformation rather than offering test-before-invest services or advanced AI-based solutions. Digital maturity assessment, a roadmap for digital transformation, networking, and webinars were the main types of services provided to companies. Services related to AI were treated rather as additional ones by companies. If offered, they were related to raising awareness about this technology. Interviewed (E)DIHs expect to come up with more tangible results from their activity in this second wave of the EDIH program (2025).

5. Conclusion

The analysis conducted in this chapter highlights the strategic and operational importance of (E)DIHs in supporting the digital transformation of SMEs within the broader framework of innovation ecosystems. Confronted with persistent structural barriers – financial, technological, organizational, and cognitive – European SMEs often struggle to fully engage with the digital transition, particularly when it involves advanced technologies such as artificial intelligence. (E)DIHs, as intermediary institutions, have emerged as pivotal actors in addressing these challenges by offering locally embedded, demand-driven, and modular forms of support that resonate with the specific constraints of small and medium-sized firms.

The chapter demonstrates that (E)DIHs operate at the intersection of European strategic priorities and regional development trajectories. Their institutional diversity and territorial anchoring enable them to act as bridges between technological opportunity and business capability. Through their one-stop-shop model, they provide a portfolio of services that not only facilitate access to digital tools but also encourage strategic reorientation and organizational learning among SMEs. This function is especially relevant in a context marked by rapid technological change and the imperative of the twin transition – digital and ecological – driven by European policy frameworks.

Empirical evidence suggests that the effectiveness of (E)DIHs depends heavily on their degree of embeddedness within regional ecosystems and their ability to foster trust, coordination, and mutual learning among stakeholders. The findings presented in the chapter confirm that (E)DIHs contribute to shaping territorially differentiated responses to digital transformation by adjusting their support to the local economic fabric, sectoral specializations, and institutional arrangements. Notably, the most embedded hubs – those recognized as orchestrators or facilitators – appear better positioned to generate transformative impacts, particularly when they integrate digital strategies with workforce upskilling and inter-organizational cooperation.

Nevertheless, the chapter also identifies several limitations. Despite their potential, (E)DIHs still face governance challenges, including coordination asymmetries, variable levels of engagement across regions, and sometimes limited recognition by SMEs unfamiliar with public innovation infrastructures. Furthermore, the full integration of AI-based solutions into SME business models remains largely aspirational, with current support often limited to awareness-raising rather than applied adoption. These findings underscore the necessity for sustained investment in capacity building, long-term policy commitment, and improved alignment between the EDIH initiative and complementary regional and European instruments.

In conclusion, (E)DIHs should not be viewed as isolated instruments, but rather as central nodes within multi-scalar innovation systems that seek to reconcile technological ambition with territorial cohesion. Their contribution extends beyond the simple provision of services: they help construct a more inclusive and adaptive model of economic modernization, where SMEs can become not only recipients of digital innovation but active agents in its development and appropriation. Future research and policy evaluation should focus on measuring the long-term impact of (E)DIHs, understanding the dynamics of territorial coordination, and identifying the conditions under which these hubs can evolve into permanent infrastructures for resilience in the digital age.

Reference List

Abel-Koch, J., Al Obaidi, L. El Kasmi, S. Acevedo, M. F., Morin, L., & Topczewska, A. (2019). Going digital. The challenges facing European SMEs. *European SME Survey 2019*. www.british-business-bank.co.uk/sites/g/files/sovrnj166/files/2022-11/going-digital-the-challenges-facing-european-smes-european-sme-survey-2019_2.pdf

Adner, R. (2006). Match your innovation strategy to your innovation ecosystem. *Harvard Business Review*, *84*(4), 98–148.

Antipina, O., Kireeva, E., Ilyashevich, N., & Odoeva, O. (2021, November). Digitalization of regional economies in the context of innovative development of the country. In *International scientific and practical conference digital and information technologies in economics and management* (pp. 224–235). Springer International Publishing.

Asheim, B. T., Isaksen, A., & Trippl, M. (2019). *Advanced introduction to regional innovation systems*. Edward Elgar Publishing.

Autio, E., Nambisan, S., Thomas, L. D. W., & Wright, M. (2018). Digital affordances, spatial affordances, and the genesis of entrepreneurial ecosystems. *Strategic Entrepreneurship Journal*, *12*(1), 72–95. https://doi.org/10.1002/sej.1266

Autio, E., & Thomas, L. (2014). Innovation ecosystems: Implications for innovation management? In M. Dodgson, D. M. Gann, & N. Phillips (Eds.), *The Oxford handbook of innovation management* (pp. 204–228). Oxford University Press.

Botsari, A., Gvetadze, S., & Lang, F. (2024). *The European small business finance outlook. European investment fund*. Working Paper 2024/101. www.eif.org/news_centre/publications/eif-working-paper-2024-101.pdf

Bourdin, S., Nadou, F., & Obermöller, A. (2020). Comment les politiques publiques favorisent-elles les dynamiques collaboratives d'innovation? Analyse du management de l'intermédiation territoriale. *Revue d'Économie Régionale & Urbaine*, (2), 311–335.

Caloffi, A., Colovic, A., Rizzoli, V., & Rossi, F. (2023). Innovation intermediaries' types and functions: A computational analysis of the literature. *Technological Forecasting and Social Change*, *189*, 122351. https://doi.org/10.1016/j.technovation.2024.103022

Carpentier, E., D'Adda, D., Nepelski, D., & Stake, J. (2025). *European digital innovation Hubs Network's activities and customers*. Publications Office of the European Union. https://data.europa.eu/doi/10.2760/7784020, JRC140547.

Chalmers, D., MacKenzie, N. G., & Carter, S. (2020). Artificial intelligence and entrepreneurship: Implications for venture creation in the fourth industrial revolution. *Entrepreneurship Theory and Practice*, *45*(5), 1028–1053. https://doi.org/10.1177/1042258720934581

Cooke, P., Uranga, M. G., & Etxebarria, G. (1997). Regional innovation systems: Institutional and organisational dimensions. *Research Policy*, *26*(4–5), 475–491. https://doi.org/10.1016/S0048-7333(97)00025-5

Czyżewska-Misztal, D. (2024). The European Union's approach to artificial intelligence from a territorial perspective: The case of DIHs and EDIHs programmes. *Prace Naukowe Uniwersytetu Ekonomicznego we Wrocławiu*, *68*(2), 1–11. https://doi.org/10.15611/pn.2024.2.01

Dalziel, M., & Parjanen, S. (2012). Measuring the impact of innovation intermediaries: A case study of Tekes. In H. Melkas & V. Harmaakorpi (Eds.), *Practice-based innovation: Insights, applications and policy implications*. Springer. https://doi.org/10.1007/978-3-642-21723-4_7

De Nigris, S., Kalpaka, A., & Nepelski, D. (2023). *Characteristics and regional coverage of the European digital innovation hubs network*. Publications Office of the European Union. https://doi.org/10.2760/590526, JRC134620.

EDIH Catalogue. (2025). Retrieved May 21, 2025, from https://european-digital-innovation-hubs.ec.europa.eu/pl/edih-catalogue?f%5B0%5D=edih_soe%3Asoe.

EIB. (2020). *European Union overview. EIB investment survey*. www.eib.org/en/publications/flip/eibis-2020-european-union/#p=1

EIB. (2024). *Do financing conditions pose a threat to the performance and transformation of SMEs?* Economics – Working Papers 2024/08. www.eib.org/attachments/lucalli/20240358_economics_working_paper_2024_08_en.pdf

Escoz Barragan, K., Hassan, S. S., Meisner, K., & Bzhalava, L. (2025). Dynamics of digital change – measuring the digital transformation and its impacts on the innovation activities of SMEs. *European Journal of Innovation Management*, *28*(4), 1625–1648. https://doi.org/10.1108/EJIM-05-2023-0432

Eurochambres. (2021). *Eurochambres economic survey*. www.eurochambres.eu/wp-content/uploads/2020/11/EES2021-Report-Final.pdf

Holmström, J. (2022). From AI to digital transformation: The AI readiness framework. *Business Horizons*, *65*(3), 329–339. https://doi.org/10.1016/j.bushor.2021.03.006

Howells, J. (2006). Intermediation and the role of intermediaries in innovation, *Research Policy*, *35*(5), 715–728. https://doi.org/10.1016/j.respol.2006.03.005

Howells, J. (2024). Innovation intermediaries in a digital paradigm: A theoretical perspective, *Technovation*, *129*, 102889. https://doi.org/10.1016/j.technovation.2023.102889

Jackson, D. J. (2011). *What is an innovation ecosystem?* National Science Foundation. https://erc-assoc.org/sites/default/files/topics/policy_studies/DJackson_Innovation%20Ecosystem_03-15-11.pdf

Kanda, W., Klofsten, M., Bienkowska, D., Audretsch, D. B., & Geissdoerfer, M. (2025). Orchestration in mature entrepreneurial ecosystems towards a circular economy: A dynamic capabilities approach. *Business Strategy and the Environment*. https://doi.org/10.1002/bse.4229

Laur, I., & Kanda, W. (2025). Navigating conflicts between niche and regime intermediaries in the energy transition. *Energy Research & Social Science*, *124*, 104070. https://doi.org/10.1016/j.erss.2025.104070

Lepore, D. (2024). Intermediaries in innovation systems: Match or mismatch? *Journal of the Knowledge Economy*, *15*(3), 12678–12708. https://doi.org/10.1007/s13132-023-01566-5

Meijer, A. (2024). Perspectives on the twin transition: Instrumental and institutional linkages between the digital and sustainability transitions. *Information Polity*, *29*(1), 35–51. https://doi.org/10.3233/IP-230015

Moulaert, F., & Sekia, F. (2003). Territorial innovation models: A critical survey. *Regional Studies*, *37*(3), 289–302. https://doi.org/10.1080/0034340032000065442

Muench, S., Stoermer, E., Jensen, K., Asikainen, T., Salvi, M., & Scapolo, F. (2022). *Towards a green and digital future*. Luxembourg: Publications Office of the European Union.

Mura, P. O., & Donath, L. E. (2023). Digitalisation and economic growth in the European Union. *Electronics*, *12*, 1718. https://doi.org/10.3390/electronics12071718

Nadou, F., & Pecqueur, B. (2020). For a socioeconomics of territorial intermediation a conceptual approach. *Géographie, économie, société*, *22*(3), 245–263. https://shs.cairn.info/journal-geographie-economie-societe-2020-3-page-245?lang=en.

Nambisan, S. (2017). Digital entrepreneurship: Toward a digital technology perspective of entrepreneurship. *Entrepreneurship Theory and Practice*, *41*(6), 1029–1055. https://doi.org/10.1111/etap.12254

OECD. (2021). *The digital transformation of SMEs. OECD studies on SMEs and entrepreneurship*. OECD Publishing. https://doi.org/10.1787/bdb9256a-en

Rissola, G., & Sörvik, J. (2018). *Digital innovation hubs in smart specialisation strategies*. Publications Office of the European Union.

Seppänen, S., Ukko, J., & Saunila, M. (2025). Understanding determinants of digital transformation and digitizing management functions in incumbent SMEs. *Digital Business*, 100106. https://doi.org/10.1016/j.digbus.2025.100106

Storey, V. C., Yue, W. T., Zhao, J. L., & Lukyanenko, R. (2025). Generative artificial intelligence: Evolving technology, growing societal impact, and opportunities for information systems research. *Information Systems Frontiers*. https://doi.org/10.1007/s10796-025-10581-7

21 Evaluation and Verification of the Quality of AI-Generated Information Using ChatGPT as an Example

Mirosława Kaczmarek

ChatGPT: Benefits and Risks for Users

ChatGPT has become a popular tool for students to find information, generate ideas, and create content. The rapid adoption of ChatGPT by users is mainly due to two factors – ease of use and usability, which are consistent with the Technology Acceptance Model (TAM) in the field of information systems. ChatGPT's usability is positively influenced by its natural language processing capabilities and interactive interface, and its perceived usefulness is enhanced by the generation of appropriate responses (Mambile & Ishengoma, 2024). Through real-time interactions and feedback, ChatGPT adapts its language models to meet the changing needs of its audience (Ray, 2023). ChatGPT's growing popularity is also due to the presence of network effects – the more people use it and upload data to it, the more its performance improves. Moreover, ChatGPT's ability to continuously learn and adapt to user needs is consistent with the principles of adaptive structuration theory, which emphasizes the existence of strong links between technology and social systems (Mambile & Ishengoma, 2024).

The OpenAI lab is constantly updating ChatGPT, culminating in the version released in March 2023, which is based on the GPT-4 artificial intelligence language model. Compared to earlier versions, the model has better conversational capabilities, that is, more creativity and consistency in generating content, handles context well, and can understand even quite complex queries, resulting in more nuanced responses. It also responds to both textual and pictorial queries and is available in multiple languages, including Polish, in addition to English. Empirical studies have revealed both the strengths and weaknesses of ChatGPT from a user's perspective and their experiences in using the tool. Among the main strengths highlighted are: the ability to mimic human conversation patterns and generate authentic-sounding and nuanced responses (Choudhury & Shamszare, 2023), the provision of personalized responses in real time (Farrokhnia et al., 2023; Xu et al., 2024), and quick responses and the generation of a wide range of information (Pasca & Arcese, 2025). ChatGPT also stands out due to its minimalist and user-friendly interface (Xu et al., 2024; Xiaoyu et al., 2025), with its social

DOI: 10.4324/9781003659143-27

presence and legitimacy contributing to the positive attitude toward using the tool (Tiwari et al., 2024).

The weaknesses of ChatGPT include limited critical thinking skills (Sun & Hoelscher, 2023), ethical issues such as encouraging plagiarism and cheating (Gašević et al., 2023), and privacy risks associated with chat room data collection (Pasca & Arcese, 2025). However, the most frequently raised problem is the creation of false information (Tlili et al., 2023) and inaccurate and inconsistent information (Sun & Hoelscher, 2023; Xiaoyu et al., 2025). It should be added the OpenAI lab has warned about the phenomenon of hallucination, that is, ChatGPT providing information that sounds plausible but is in fact completely made up. This can include definitions, dates or facts, quotes, and research. False content and claims may be interspersed with true information and presented in a convincing manner, making them difficult to detect without close scrutiny (OpenAI, 2025). In addition, ChatGPT is not free of biases and stereotypes, and may be biased in providing information, so users should critically evaluate any content that may perpetuate such bias (OpenAI, n.d.). In this context, limited access to expertise and lack of fact-checking tools should also be noted (Xiaoyu et al., 2025).

As ChatGPT evolves, the catalog of advantages and disadvantages will change, and eliminating the weaknesses of earlier versions does not mean that new disadvantages will not appear, especially since successive versions offer users more and more options. It would seem that when using ChatGPT as an information retrieval tool, the fundamental problem remains the risk of receiving false information that misleads the recipient, resulting in misinformation. Therefore, a key research problem is to determine the competence of users in verifying the quality of information generated by ChatGPT. This research thus seeks answers to the questions: How do users assess the quality of the information they receive through ChatGPT, and how do they verify this information? This chapter attempts to answer these questions based on the results of an empirical survey conducted by CAWI (Computer-Assisted Web Interviewing) and a real-world experiment among ChatGPT users from Generation Z, which is among the most active in using AI-based tools.

Evaluation of the Quality of Information Generated by ChatGPT

Information quality is a complex, multidimensional construct, which is well-illustrated by the numerous proposals for information quality models. Among the best-known models is Wang's model (1998) for improving the quality of information systems, which identifies 15 dimensions of information quality. Another proposal is the conceptual model of information quality by Khan et al. (2002), known as the PSP/IQ model (Product and Service Performance for Information Quality). In this model, information quality is considered from the perspective of the receiver and the producer, and is assessed on the basis of 16 dimensions. Information users are the focus of the model proposed by Bovee et al. (2003), in which only seven information quality criteria are extracted based on the sequence of information processes. Among the most comprehensive is the list of 23 quality dimensions proposed by Delone and McLean (1992). It should be added that information quality models, unlike data quality models, do not focus only on formal quality dimensions, but also take into account subjective criteria such as usability and understandability. Based on an analysis of 20 articles from 2002 to 2013, Shamala et al. (2017) identified the 13 most commonly used dimensions of quality in the online environment. These dimensions, regardless of the existence of differences in their number between models, can generally be grouped into the four categories proposed by Wang (1998). The "big five" most frequently analyzed dimensions of information quality are timeliness, accessibility, believability, completeness, and understandability. These were also the subject of a CAWI survey (n = 442) conducted in November–December 2024 among members of Generation Z in Poland who use ChatGPT.

The results of this survey indicate that the respondents are relatively critical of the quality of information from this source. On a scale from 1 (very bad) to 5 (very good), the mean rating did not exceed 4 points for any of the five dimensions of information quality analyzed. The highest relative rating was given to the understandability of the information generated by ChatGPT (mean value of 3.60). Timeliness (3.57) and believability (3.55) received slightly lower mean ratings, while accuracy (3.45) and completeness (3.41) received the lowest mean ratings. The understandability of the information generated by ChatGPT was rated very highly by 27% of Generation Z users. In terms of timeliness, the information obtained through ChatGPT is rated very highly by 16% of people, and 13% of users have no objections to its believability. The accuracy of the information obtained from this source is rated very highly by 12% of people, and its completeness by 10% of people.

With the spread of the Internet and the development of technology, the gender gap in digital consumer behavior is clearly blurring, especially among the younger generations who have grown up with it. This regularity is confirmed by numerous empirical studies, including those conducted in the United Kingdom (Helsper, 2010), Germany (Gnambs, 2021), the United States (McGloin et al., 2016), and Poland (Ochnik & Dembińska, 2018). Of course, there are still some gender differences, especially in the type of information searched for and the level of activity, for example, women are more likely to visit health and wellness sites, while men spend significantly more time playing games and are more likely to use generative AI tools (Ofcom, 2024). In addition, men are more likely to provide informational assistance, while women are more likely to make friends and to be emotionally biased (Sun et al., 2020).

The CAWI survey indicates that gender is a characteristic that statistically significantly differentiates the evaluation of the quality of information generated by ChatGPT. The results of the Mann-Whitney U test confirm that there are statistically significant differences between male and female users of this AI tool (at a significance level of $P < 0.05$) in the evaluation of three of the five dimensions of information quality analyzed. The first is accuracy, with a mean of 3.34 for women and 3.56 for men. There are similar differences in the ratings for completeness and detail of information. Here, the mean scores are 3.32 and 3.48 for women and 3.52 and 3.74 for men. In terms of these criteria, the information generated by ChatGPT is rated as good by 28–30% of women and 39–41% of men. The relatively low assessment of the quality of information provided by ChatGPT is reflected in the attitudes toward this language model. The CAWI survey shows that only 17% of Generation Z representatives fully agree with the statement "I am usually satisfied with the results I get using ChatGPT" and opinions in this case are significantly differentiated by gender. Only 14% of women and 22% of men are completely satisfied with the information they receive. In addition, only 5% of young people admit that they "rarely check the information provided by ChatGPT." The relatively critical assessment of the quality of the information received through chat explains why only 7% consider it "the first tool I turn to when looking for information," with statistically significant differences by gender – it is more often the first-choice tool for men (12%) than for women (4%). Not surprisingly, only 13% of Generation Z users say: "I can no longer imagine functioning without being able to use ChatGPT," and one in four strongly agree with the statement that "using ChatGPT is intellectually lazy."

Kendall's tau correlation analysis shows that there are statistically significant correlations between attitudes toward ChatGPT and ratings for information quality (Table 21.1). For both men and women, the strongest positive correlation is between ratings for information quality in each of the five dimensions, as well as satisfaction with search results when using ChatGPT. Thus, the lower they rate the quality of information, the more often they disagree with the statement "I am generally satisfied with the results obtained using ChatGPT." For women, this attitude is most strongly correlated with believability (tau = 0.47), and for men with accuracy (tau = 0.45). Interesting gender differences are found in correlation analysis between information quality ratings and attitudes toward verifying chat-generated information. For women, there is only one statistically significant correlation – for the believability criterion (tau = 0.21). The situation is different for men, who are more likely to agree with the statement "I rarely verify information I receive through ChatGPT" the higher they rate the believability (tau = 0.34), timeliness (tau = 0.33), accuracy (tau = 0.27), and completeness (tau = 0.28) of the information.

In the case of female ChatGPT users, a relatively weak positive correlation is observed between their rating of each dimension of information quality and their attitude toward the statement "ChatGPT is the first tool I turn to when looking for information." Thus, the lower they rated the quality of information from this source, the more often they disagreed with the statement. Low correlation coefficients are also found for male ChatGPT users for the dimensions of believability (tau = 0.16), accuracy (tau = 0.26),

Table 21.1 Kendall's tau correlation analysis between attitudes toward ChatGPT and assessment of the quality of information from this source

Variable	*I Rarely Check the Information I Receive Through ChatGPT.*	*I Am Usually Satisfied with the Results I Get from ChatGPT.*	*ChatGPT is the First Tool I Turn to When Looking for Information.*	*I Cannot Imagine Working Without Using ChatGPT.*	*Using ChatGPT Makes Me Intellectually Lazy*
Women					
Believability	0.21*	0.47*	0.31*	0.25*	-0.31*
Timeliness	0.10	0.23*	0.17*	0.16*	-0.12
Accuracy	0.07	0.28*	0.20*	0.19*	-0.15*
Understand-ability	0.11	0.32*	0.13*	0.14*	-0.05
Completeness	0.11	0.37*	0.24*	0.25*	-0.23*
Men					
Believability	0.34*	0.39*	0.16*	0.12	0.01
Timeliness	0.33*	0.35*	0.11	0.10	-0.02
Accuracy	0.27*	0.45*	0.26*	0.15*	-0.16*
Understand-ability	0.13	0.25*	0.21*	0.15*	-0.12
Completeness	0.28*	0.38*	0.11	0.11	-0.03

* These results are significant at $P < 0.05$.

Source: Own calculations.

and understandability (tau = 0.21). For this group of users, there is also a weak positive correlation between attitudes toward the statement "I can no longer imagine functioning without being able to use ChatGPT" and ratings for the understandability and accuracy of information (for both dimensions tau = 0.15). For women, statistically significant but weak correlations were found for all dimensions of information quality. Thus, the lower they rated the quality of information, the more often they indicated that ChatGPT was not an essential tool for them. Negative values for Kendall's tau correlation coefficients were obtained in only one case, that is, in analysis of the relationship between the evaluation of the quality of information generated by ChatGPT and the attitude to the statement "Using ChatGPT makes me intellectually lazy." For female chat users, a negative correlation was found for the information dimensions of believability (tau = -0.31), completeness (tau = -0.23), and accuracy (tau = -0.15). Thus, the study shows that gender is an important factor differentiating the evaluation of the quality of information provided by ChatGPT and the attitudes toward this AI tool. When evaluating information, women are more insightful and critical, indicating the need to diversify the content provided by AI and take this characteristic into account when personalizing information.

Both the relatively low evaluation of the quality of information generated by ChatGPT and the critical attitude toward chat as a source of information were reasons to ask respondents whether they actually perceived differences between information from different sources. An experiment-based study conducted for this purpose showed no statistically significant differences in the evaluation of information quality between the experimental group (n = 13), which was informed that the text was generated using ChatGPT, and the control group (n = 12), in which ChatGPT was not indicated as the source of the text (the text was about the advantages and disadvantages of using mobile payments and the percentage of users of such a service in different generations). In both groups, statistics on the percentage of consumers using banking applications and mobile payments, as well as the source of the data, were identified among the information selected for further validation, with respondents following different motivations. Respondents in the experimental group mainly emphasized the possibility that ChatGPT could falsify or even invent data, while the control group pointed out that there were differences in the numbers depending on the report they came from, and stressed the need for the latest, most up-to-date data. Thus, it can be concluded that people from Generation Z are characterized by a high awareness of the occurrence of errors in ChatGPT's "work" with numbers, and that using this tool to search for numbers automatically triggers a reaction of limited trust in the search results.

The Process of Verifying the Information Generated by ChatGPT

The critical assessment of the quality of information generated by ChatGPT raises the question of how to verify the content provided by the tool. The process of verifying the content generated by ChatGPT, which emerges from the description made by the participants of the experimental survey, includes the following steps (Figure 21.1):

1) initial verification – intuitive assessment of information generated by ChatGPT,
2) in-depth verification – evaluation of information using other sources,
3) acceptance of information.

The course of this process depends on such factors as the complexity of the issue under investigation, the type of information sought and its purpose. The initial evaluation of information is intuitive, based on existing knowledge, and the recipient evaluates it primarily for internal consistency. If no objections are raised, the information is accepted. When a ChatGPT user is satisfied with the quantity and quality of the information provided, the search process is completed. Their level of satisfaction is influenced by both their knowledge and the complexity of the question. If the user's expectations are not met, they will formulate further questions, which most often are aimed at detailed information in relation to selected issues of the researched topic. In the case of poor knowledge of the topic, the "hints" suggested by

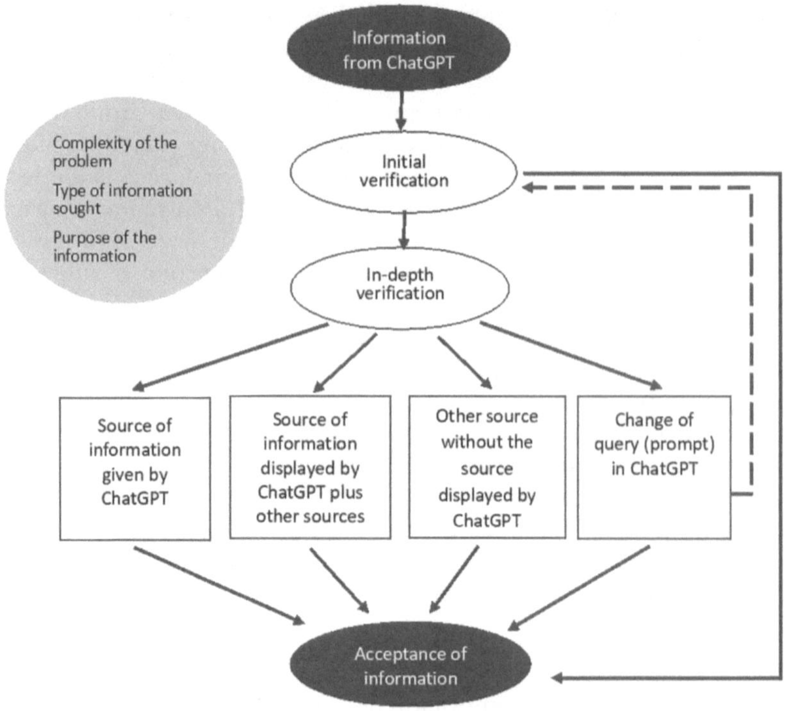

Figure 21.1 The procedure for verifying information generated by ChatGPT.
Source: Own elaboration.

ChatGPT on the direction of the search for additional information become more important when directing further queries (prompts). In such a situation, ChatGPT begins to act as a moderator of the dialog with the user. To ensure the quality of information, ChatGPT also provides users with additional tools such as "Reason" and "Explore Deeply." If the user is satisfied with the results of the chat "work" in terms of the quantity and quality of information provided, the search is terminated. According to such a sequence of actions, skipping the verification of the information in other sources, we are de facto dealing with its apparent verification.

Therefore, in most cases, the next step is to verify the information provided by the chat room in independent sources. The course of this step depends on two factors: the type of information sought and its purpose. Almost always, factual information, which deals with specific facts and figures, is additionally verified, while this is less often the case with information in descriptive form, such as a presentation of the characteristics of a phenomenon. In the latter case, details are not further verified or are verified at random. Additional verification is most often performed when the information obtained through ChatGPT is used for work and study purposes, that is, when the user bears specific responsibility for the content presented and is aware of the negative consequences for themselves or the environment resulting from the presentation of false information. The verification stage is most often skipped for information obtained for private purposes.

There are several "ways" to verify information provided by ChatGPT. Users conduct such verification using:

(1) the source of information given by ChatGPT,
(2) the source of information displayed by ChatGPT plus other sources,
(3) another source than the source displayed by ChatGPT,
(4) a change of query (prompt) in ChatGPT.

When using ChatGPT for educational or professional purposes, users are most often encouraged to use two-step verification. First, they check the consistency of the information generated by ChatGPT with the content of the source referenced in the chat, and in situations where this is not provided, an additional request is made for a link to the source from which the information came. In the next step, users compare the consistency of the information from this source with information available in other sources. For this purpose, they most often use Wikipedia, Google Search and Google Scholar, as well as sites they consider reliable, such as sites with the domain "org.pl," "gov.pl," and industry portals. It is worth noting that it is relatively unpopular – at least at the moment – to verify information using online search engines based on generative AI. The most widely used is Perplexity AI, which is appreciated by users because it provides answers based on sources that actually exist. What is more, if it cannot answer a given query, it does not gloss over the answer, but instead asks users to refine the content of the query. Therefore, when verifying the information generated by ChatGPT, it is rare to rely solely on the sources it cites.

Another solution used to verify the information generated by ChatGPT is to check it in other sources, excluding those cited by the chat room. The reason for using this option are previous negative experiences resulting from hallucinations and ChatGPT citing non-existent sources. Another solution is to verify information by starting a new conversation in ChatGPT with a modified prompt, or by directing a request to a specific passage of text from the source cited by the chat. The refinement of the conversation skills in the current version of ChatGPT and previous positive experiences of repeatedly checking different prompt variants by asking the same thing a few times in different ways are reasons for choosing this solution. The improvement of ChatGPT's communication capabilities leads to its personification, which is reflected in the style of conversation. Its characteristic feature is an appeal to empathy or honesty, which takes the form of messages like "Aren't you dimming?", "Are you sure you're not wrong?" It should be noted, however, that such unconventional solutions are rarely practiced. This situation should be distinguished from typical phrases used in conversations with chat rooms, such as the greeting at the beginning ("good morning," "hello") or using the words please and thank you.

The presented information retrieval algorithm confirms that users appreciate ChatGPT as an information retrieval tool, but that they are also aware of its limitations and therefore follow the "I trust, but verify" principle. The level of verification of the generated content depends on the type of information, its purpose and the user's knowledge of the subject. Therefore, it sometimes ends with an intuitive assessment of the credibility of the information, while at other times it turns into a multi-step process. Of great importance is previous experience of using ChatGPT, especially the negative experience of receiving false information. Several "ways" are used to verify the content provided by the chat, which indicates the lack of a uniform standard in this area. What is surprising is the low level of use of tools based on other AI language models and reliance on well-known and widely used sources such as Wikipedia and Google Search.

ChatGPT: The Next Challenges

With the development of generative AI, its access to larger and larger datasets, and equipping it with more and more "human" competencies (creativity, use of language adapted to the level of the recipient), the quality of the information received and the length of the chat conversation will depend on the lexical competence of the people conducting it. A key challenge would seem to be improving users' competence in the ability to formulate queries correctly, that is, to write prompts. The quality of the response received will depend on such factors as the vocabulary and syntax used (simpler syntax and understandable language generally lead to more accurate results), the precision of the query (the more detailed the prompt, the more tailored the response), defining the requirements for the structure of the chat response, and providing context, that is, additional information that will help the chat bot understand the user's intentions. The training of prompt writing skills is certainly one of the main challenges for users of generative AI, and is a prerequisite for effective chat conversations. However, it is crucial to have knowledge of the topic ChatGPT is asked about, without which it is impossible to conduct a proper initial verification of the information, let alone effectively assess its quality. This is certainly not helped by the observed decline in general knowledge among students, the best illustration of which is the continuing and seemingly unthreatened popularity of Wikipedia.

ChatGPT, while easy to use, does not meet the expectations of many young users. In addition to concerns about the quality of information generated, its use is discouraged by the limitations of the content provided and the high cost of subscriptions, especially for long-term use. Given young people's limited financial resources and the availability of alternative, free content generation tools, this could quickly lead to a decline in popularity. In addition, there is a lack of tools to verify the information generated by ChatGPT. Meanwhile, an attempt has been made to meet the need to increase protection against confabulation, with the availability of features such as "Reason" and "Examine Deeply," but their free use is also limited. Therefore, other content search tools that use large language models to answer queries, such as Perplexity, Gemini and Claude AI, will become more popular. Expanding the features available in the free version of ChatGPT that improve the quality of the information provided by ChatGPT, without restricting its availability, seems to be an obvious direction for the development of this information retrieval tool.

Users must understand both the capabilities and limitations of ChatGPT as an information generation tool. Critical evaluation of the quality of the information indicates an awareness of the need to be cautious and critical in the use of this tool, and to apply the principle of limited trust in the content generated. With the growing popularity of AI in education, the issue of ethical use of this tool is becoming paramount. Unresolved problems that remain are the lack of effective methods for distinguishing authored text from ChatGPT-generated text, and the limited effectiveness of educating users about the potential negative consequences of providing plagiarized text generated by AI.

Reference List

Bovee, M., Srivastava, R. P., & Mak, B. (2003). A conceptual framework and belief-function approach to assessing overall information quality. *International Journal of Intelligent Systems*, *18*(1). http://dx.doi.org/10.1002/int.10074

Choudhury, A., & Shamszare, H. (2023). Investigating the impact of user trust on the adoption and use of ChatGPT: Survey analysis. *Journal of Medical Internet Research*, *25*(e47184), 1–11. www.jmir.org/2023/1/e47184/PDF

Delone, W. H., & McLean, E. R. (1992). Information systems success: The quest for the

dependent variable. *Information Systems Research*, *3*(1), 60–95. https://doi.org/10.1287/isre.3.1.60

Farrokhnia, M., Banihashem, S. K., Noroozi, O., & Wals, A. (2023). A SWOT analysis of ChatGPT: Implications for educational practice and research. *Innovations in Education and Teaching International*, *61*(3), 460–474. https://doi.org/10.1080/14703297.2023.2195846

Gašević, D., Siemens, G., & Sadiq, S. (2023). Empowering learners for the age of artificial

intelligence. *Computers and Education: Artificial Intelligence*, *4*(100130), 1–4. https://doi.org/10.1016/j.caeai.2023.100130

Gnambs, T. (2021). The development of gender differences in information and communication technology (ICT) literacy in middle adolescence. *Computers in Human Behavior*, *114*(106533), 1–10. https://doi.org/10.1016/j.chb.2020.106533

Helsper, E. J. (2010). Gendered internet use across generations and life stages. *Communication Research*, *37*(3), 352–374. https://doi.org/10.1177/0093650209356439

Khan, B. K., Strong, D. M., & Wang, R. Y. (2002). Information quality benchmarks: Product and service performance. *Communications of the ACM*, *45*(4), 84–192. https://web.mit.edu/tdqm/www/tdqmpub/KahnStrongWangCACMApr02.pdf

Mambile, C., & Ishengoma, F. (2024). Exploring the non-linear trajectories of technology adoption in the digital age. *Technological Sustainability*, *3*(4), 428–448. https://doi.org/10.1108/TECHS-11-2023-0050

McGloin, R., Richards, K., & Embacher, K. (2016). Examining the potential gender gap in online health information-seeking behaviors among digital natives. *Communication Research Reports*, *33*(4), 370–375. https://doi.org/10.1080/08824096.2016.1224169

Ochnik, D., & Dembińska, A. (2018). Gender differences and areas of Internet behavior in seven years' perspective. *Polish Psychological Bulletin*, *49*(3), 383–390. https://doi.org/10.24425/119506

Ofcom. (2024). *Online nation 2024 report*. www.ofcom.org.uk/siteassets/resources/documents/research-and-data/online-research/online-nation/2024/online-nation-2024-report.pdf?v=386238

OpenAI. (2025). *Does ChatGPT tell the truth?* https://help.openai.com/en/articles/8313428-does-chatgpt-tell-the-truth

OpenAI. (n.d.). *Is ChatGPT biased?* https://help.openai.com/en/articles/8313359-is-chatgpt-biased

Pasca, M. G., & Arcese, G. (2025). ChatGPT between opportunities and challenges: An empirical study in Italy. *The TQM Journal*, *37*(3), 637–652. https://doi.org/10.1108/TQM-08-2023-0268

Ray, P. P. (2023). ChatGPT: A comprehensive review on background, applications, key challenges, bias, ethics, limitations and future scope. *Internet of Things and Cyber-Physical Systems*, *3*, 121–154. https://doi.org/10.1016/j.iotcps.2023.04.003

Shamala, P., Ahmad, R., Zolait, A., & Sedek, M. (2017). Integrating information quality dimensions into information security risk management (ISRM). *Journal of Information Security and Applications*, *36*, 1–10. https://doi.org/10.1016/j.jisa.2017.07.004

Sun, B., Mao, H., & Yin, C. (2020). Male and female users' differences in online technology community based on text mining. *Frontiers in Psychology*, *11*(806), 1–11. https://doi.org/10.3389/fpsyg.2020.00806

Sun, G. H., & Hoelscher, S. H. (2023 May–June). The ChatGPT storm and what faculty can do. *Nurse Educator*, *48*(3), 119–124. https://doi.org/10.1097/NNE.0000000000001390

Tiwari, C. K., Bhat, M. A., Khan, S. T., Subramaniam, R., & Khan, M. A. I. (2024). What drives students toward ChatGPT? An investigation of the factors influencing adoption and usage of ChatGPT. *Interactive Technology and Smart Education*, *21*(3), 333–355. https://doi.org/10.1108/

Tlili, A., Shehata, B., Adarkwah, M. A., Bozkurt, A., Hickey, D. T., Huang, R., & Agyemang, B. (2023). What if the devil is my guardian angel: ChatGPT as a case study of using chatbots in education. *Smart Learning Environments*, *10*(1), 1–15. https://doi.org/10.1186/s40561-023-00237-x

Wang, R. Y. (1998). A product perspective on total data quality management. *Communications of the ACM*, *41*, 58–65. https://doi.org/10.1145/269012.269022

Xiaoyu, W., Zainuddin, Z., Leng, C. H., Wenting, D., & Li, X. (2025). Evaluating the efficacy of ChatGPT in environmental education: Findings from heuristic and usability assessments, *On the Horizon*, ahead-of-print No. ahead-of-print. https://doi.org/10.1108/OTH-11-2024-0079

Xu, X., Wang, X., Zhang, Y., & Zheng, R. (2024). Applying CHATGPT to tackle the side effects of personal learning environments from learner and learning perspective: An interview of experts in higher education. *Plos One*, *19*(1), 1–19. https://doi.org/10.1371/journal.pone.0295646

22 Cultural Conditions of Scientific Discourse on AI Ethics

Karolina Anna Nowak and Damian Luty

The issue of artificial intelligence (AI) axiology – that is, the values through which we think about, use, design, and develop AI – is fundamental, requiring philosophical and ethical reflection. This chapter emphasizes the significance of axiological determinants in contemporary academic debates on AI ethics and addresses which axiological shifts dominant in these discussions. To achieve this, we conducted a literature review based on selected axiological domains that seem key in shaping the scientific discourse around the ethics and ethicality of AI-related practices. We identified five key final values, treated as autotelic – that is, values in and of themselves: freedom, dignity, justice, safety, and beneficence.

The study focused on academic publications on AI ethics from the past five years available on the Scopus platform. The justification for this timeframe (2020–2025) lies in a series of events that significantly influenced the development of and debate on AI. These include the release of the GPT-3 language model by OpenAI in 2020, marking the beginning of the era of large language models (such as ChatGPT); the rapid deployment of AI in combating the COVID-19 pandemic (e.g., predicting infection waves, vaccine research, patient chatbots, and vision systems); high-profile ethical controversies such as the dismissal of Timnit Gebru, then head of Google's AI ethics team, following the publication of a critical paper on large language models; and the initiation of legislative work by the European Union, ultimately leading to the formulation of the AI Act.

We employed a systematic literature review method based on the SALSA model (Grant & Booth, 2009). In the first stage of the review (Search), we used five keyword phrases reflecting the axiological areas, focusing on their presence in the scholarly discourse of three disciplines: social science, medicine, and business, management and accounting. The search phrases were: "ai AND ethics AND freedom/dignity/justice/safety/beneficence," limited to the years 2020–2025 and to articles. The initial search across all axiological domains retrieved a total of 527 articles. After assessing their relevance and quality, 51 articles were selected for further analysis. In the next phase (Appraisal), we assessed the quality and relevance of the selected publications.

DOI: 10.4324/9781003659143-28

This was followed by the Synthesis phase, where we integrated themes, topics, and methodological approaches to construct a comprehensive perspective. Finally, in the Analysis stage, an in-depth examination of patterns and emerging trends in academic debates on AI ethics allowed us to identify the main types of discursive trends within this field.

The first part of our review focused on the medical literature. By connecting the recurring themes running throughout the reviewed literature, we constructed a synthesized perspective revealing three dominant axiological constellations: freedom and dignity, justice and beneficence, and freedom and safety.

In the freedom and dignity domain, we identified two healthcare-related applications for which these values were explicitly cited as axiological justifications: neuro-robotics and care robots, and diagnostics. Each application is associated with unique ethical issues and considerations. In medical robotics, the ethical discourse surrounding the promotion of dignity and the expansion of freedom (along with the responsibilities that follow) was primarily situated in the context of long-term care and terminal extubation, particularly regarding the formulation of guidelines for implementing such AI models. Scholars emphasized the need to complement the ethical focus on enhancing patient autonomy and freedom with the value of dignity, especially when setting guidelines for everyday tasks typically performed in solitude – situations where recipients of care may prefer robotic assistance over human help (Felber et al., 2022). The ethical impact of AI assistants on human life has also been considered a potential threat to individual freedom and autonomy (Bauer & Dubljević, 2020). In the context of terminal extubation, dignity and freedom (understood as freedom from pain) were cited as the axiological basis for introducing palliative general anesthesia, aimed at safeguarding patients from potential suffering at the end of life (Lazaridis, 2025). Freedom and dignity also feature prominently in bioethical debates on bioenhancement (Kneer & Christen, 2024). Hertz (2023) argues that the right to freedom of thought can be coherently interpreted as offering comprehensive protection for cognitive processes and brain data, thereby providing a normative basis for regulating neurotechnologies. The role of AI in expanding knowledge and enabling more accurate diagnoses – as well as the associated need for educational reform within the medical profession – was framed in the literature as a necessary response to modern demographic and health-related challenges (Coeckelbergh, 2025).

Discussions on AI within the field of medical sciences have primarily focused on the functioning of Beauchamp and Childress' biomedical ethical principles (respect for autonomy, non-maleficence, beneficence, and justice) in the context of AI use in medical practice. These discussions have also addressed humanitarian crises – particularly the use of medical AI during and after the pandemic – the design and implementation of healthcare programs, and environmental pollution associated with AI-integrated healthcare systems. Westerstrand (2024) explicitly calls for the development of

AI ethics, including within medical sciences, centered on the idea of justice, understood in Rawlsian terms as fairness. Biomedical ethics must evolve to sensitize developers, healthcare professionals, and legislators to the challenges and limitations of opaque algorithms in medical AI. This is especially critical in the context of clinical ethics education (Zhui et al., 2024). The physician-patient relationship, social realities, resource redistribution, equitable access, and data-related aspects of AI-driven systems may conflict with the bioethical principles (Vilaza & MacCashin, 2021).

We also identified concerns the use of AI during crises and post-pandemic challenges. Particular attention has been given to the use of data during the pandemic (Kreutzer et al., 2025), as well as to the issue of equitable distribution of technological innovations during the pandemic and public trust in AI models during that time (Cave et al., 2021). The axiological dimension of justice also emerges in discussions on the post-pandemic "costs," such as the current mental health crises (Tortora, 2024) and the growing sense of loneliness and social isolation (Jecker et al., 2024). The principles of justice and beneficence also arise in debates on the implementation of diagnostic and prognostic AI tools when algorithmic systems lack adequate representation of all patient groups (Kerasidou, 2021). Patients' and families' openness to the adoption of AI models in healthcare is also discussed in the context of social justice, particularly in pediatrics (Coghlan et al., 2024). Katirai (2024) draws attention to the issue of distributive justice in relation to the environmental burdens borne by society due to the energy demands generated by the implementation of AI in medicine. These environmental costs are not necessarily borne directly by those who benefit from the technology, which raises serious questions in the context of social justice.

The value of safety was invoked as an axiological justification almost exclusively in the context of one major thematic area: debates surrounding patient data. Biobanks are recognized as valuable resources for scientific research; however, accessing and utilizing the data stored within them raises numerous legal, ethical, and social challenges, primarily due to the difficulty in ensuring and managing the cybersecurity of sensitive health-related data (Staunton et al., 2024). Crucial issues that demand careful consideration when regulating the use of medical data for AI purposes include the conceptual boundaries between privacy and personal data, the impact of technological development on the model of informed consent, and the tensions between freedom and safety in cross-border data flows (Wang et al., 2022). It has been argued that AI systems in healthcare must align with core ethical principles and standards enshrined in research ethics and law, even when this alignment poses significant implementation challenges. Data-sharing frameworks, in particular, are expected to emphasize strict integration with high data security standards, robust oversight mechanisms, and the preservation of patient control over their personal information (Murdoch et al., 2022). Kellmeyer (2021) highlights the ethical, legal, and social challenges associated with ensuring the responsible and secure use of "big brain data." Therefore, safety must be ensured through hardware- and software-level safeguards, alongside efforts to improve data literacy across society. These measures are essential for increasing the security of neurotechnological devices and for safeguarding the privacy of personal brain data.

In the second part of our review, we examined the axiological foundations of debates conducted within the social sciences. The synthesis produced two main axiological constellations: freedom, justice, and safety, and freedom and dignity.

In the domain encompassing freedom, justice, and safety, research by social scientists investigating educational contexts – though not exclusively focused on pedagogical theory – frequently highlights these three values. Such studies recognize that freedoms are increasingly challenged by concerns surrounding data privacy and the potentially hazardous extraction of personal data, particularly as educational technologies progressively incorporate AI. Consequently, it is argued that establishing risk assessment metrics that explicitly incorporate considerations of freedom is necessary (Marshall et al., 2022). From another perspective, freedom is examined through the interaction between students and AI within educational settings.

Justice, more broadly, is discussed within educational contexts as a rationale for promoting specific pedagogical practices. It is addressed not solely in direct relation to artificial intelligence (AI) but also within the broader framework of a world increasingly shaped by AI technologies (Burris & Leander, 2024). In their study, the authors argue that regulations governing AI in educational settings must conceptualize the interaction between students and AI as a partnership to meaningfully and effectively ensure fair usage. Additionally, the concept of justice is invoked to critically examine the fundamental purposes of education and pedagogy in an era increasingly influenced by AI, particularly concerning AI's transformative effects on our understanding of intelligence (Baker et al., 2023).

Data privacy, previously discussed in relation to freedom, is closely linked to issues of justice in education through the concept of "data justice." This concept posits that the availability of personal data can have varying socio-political impacts depending on the social group to which an individual belongs (Dencik & Sanchez-Monedero, 2022). When applied to educational contexts, this framework has been proposed as a foundation for designing AI-based teaching practices (Picasso et al., 2024). Similar to the discourse on freedom, the integration of AI in education is often associated with the personalization of learning experiences, with the goal of enhancing inclusivity (Kamalov et al., 2023). However, it is explicitly acknowledged that, given AI's potential to replicate and reinforce harmful biases, its application in education must be critically assessed and guided by an appropriate ethical framework.

Another area in which social scientists analyze the use of AI in education is higher education. One study developed a framework for integrating AI into adult education, with a particular emphasis on lifelong learning (Adarkwah,

2024). Notably, the framework, known as GenAI-ALE (Generative AI Adult Learning Ecology), emphasizes the importance of digital safety for adult learners. In a separate line of research, the application of AI in adult education is explored within the context of medical education.

In the axiological domain of freedom and dignity, research in the social sciences concerning human rights frequently references these two fundamental values. In our study, a central theme concerning freedom is the legal implications of AI implementation, particularly the need to ensure that AI technologies do not infringe upon fundamental freedoms. One study highlights the challenges UNESCO member states face in implementing the *Recommendation on the Ethics of Artificial Intelligence*, largely due to sociopolitical disparities and the non-binding nature of the Recommendation (Natorski, 2024). Reflecting related concerns, other scholars advocate for the establishment of regulatory bodies designed to assess the risks and societal impacts of AI deployment (Ashraf & Islam, 2023). Discussions around freedom often center on freedom of expression, particularly given AI's potential to reinforce existing discrimination and generate new forms of bias. A more critical perspective is offered by Teo (2022), who contends that conventional legal instruments may be inadequate for protecting human rights in the context of AI.

The value of dignity has been explored in the context of immigration and refugee issues (Ahmad, 2020). The author critiques the algorithmization of humanitarian assistance, whereby automated decisions regarding individual cases are made based on AI-driven analysis of data collected from refugees, asylum seekers, and migrants. These processes are highly susceptible to manipulation and may result in the inadequate or unjust treatment of individuals. Ahmad contends that algorithmic humanitarianism operates independently of the *Human Rights Act* and calls for a reconsideration of data collection practices involving migrants and refugees.

The final literature review aimed to identify ethical challenges related to AI models as recognized in debates within the field of business, management, and accounting.

In the axiological configuration encompassing freedom, justice, and dignity, the field of business, management, and accounting reveals two major thematic areas where these values are actively engaged. First, there is a focus on the preservation of human rights in the use of AI tools within the workplace and in interactions with customers. Second, there is a concern with the transformation of the workplace resulting from the implementation of AI technologies. Notably, in the scope of our study, these transformations are not primarily concerned with the replacement of human workers by AI, but rather with broader structural and ethical changes associated with AI integration.

Research that engages with the value of freedom primarily does so to justify measures necessary to uphold the integrity of individuals as human beings, thereby linking this value closely with the concept of human rights.

One study investigates the impact of AI on medical services, particularly in the allocation of medical resources and professionals' time in treating mental health conditions (Chavan et al., 2025). This context raises ethical dilemmas, such as whether the presence of a human being in post-intervention follow-ups for mental health patients is necessary. On the one hand, automation may lead to more efficient task distribution among professionals; on the other, given the sensitive nature of mental health care, such automation may pose risks to patient well-being. The authors emphasize that deploying AI in this domain necessitates a stable and robust understanding of the principle of human freedom. Another study invokes the concept of freedom – specifically, freedom of thought – in the context of online manipulation (Teo, 2024). The use of AI on online platforms may infringe upon this freedom by employing choice architectures that present users with content inferred purely by AI.

The discussions of workplace transformations analyzed in our study frequently invoke the concept of freedom, particularly in addressing the challenges posed by AI and the resulting shifts in the fundamental nature of certain professional roles. A systematic literature review examines how AI ethics – where freedom is considered a core value – serves as a foundation for ethical audits aimed at system developers, deployers, and researchers. Ethical considerations related to AI in the workplace may inspire new conceptions of professionalism. One study explores the integration of key AI ethical values – fairness, nonmaleficence, responsibility, freedom, and trust – into the organizational cultures of developers and operators (Klarin et al., 2024). From a more philosophical perspective, Sison (2024) raises the question of whether digitally transformed work can be considered virtuous. In this context, freedom is contrasted with dependency and is posited as a necessary condition for work to be subject to moral evaluation.

The value of dignity has been invoked to propose solutions to specific challenges arising in the business context due to the use of AI. Within the broader theme of human rights, the concept of data dignity has been introduced, positing that any data pertaining to a user should be treated as an extension of this person (Saura et al., 2024). This notion responds to the development of AI-based digital marketing, which presents issues such as the misalignment between personalized advertisements or social media content and established privacy standards. Another case concerns so-called deathbots (or griefbots) – chatbots designed to simulate the speech, appearance, and behavioral patterns of deceased individuals. As start-ups have successfully launched such technologies and commercial interest continues to grow, ethical scrutiny becomes increasingly urgent. The most commonly addressed ethical concern is whether these technologies violate the dignity of the deceased, particularly through commodifying their likeness for business purposes. However, scholars also highlight the need to consider the potential impact of these technologies on the dignity of other stakeholders, particularly grieving users (Lindemann, 2022). The value of dignity is also central in arguments for preserving inherently human aspects of work, especially human creativity, which is seen as needing protection amid increasing automation (Fioravante & Vaccaro, 2024).

The axiological dimension of justice plays a central role in shaping foundational discourse on the implications and consequences of AI deployment by specific groups, particularly concerning essential services that affect everyday life. One prominent issue involves the concept of vulnerable consumers – individuals who, due to temporary or permanent limitations, lack adequate access to information (Malgieri & Niklas, 2020). Research has explored the potential of AI technologies to identify such vulnerable consumers (Hermann et al., 2024), with the goal of enhancing service accessibility and supporting more equitable consumer decision-making – efforts explicitly guided by considerations of social justice. A comparable approach is evident in studies addressing financial inclusivity (Yang & Lee, 2024). In workplace contexts, critical perspectives have emerged regarding the use of AI to monitor and analyze employee behavior, particularly within human resources management (Hu & Zhao, 2021). The primary concern is that the inherent complexity of human resource decision-making may be compromised by algorithmic processes, resulting in outcomes that lack fairness or disregard essential human factors.

Ethical challenges related to AI and the value of safety primarily concern data usage, transformations occurring within business entities due to AI implementation, and AI-supported business education. The principle of beneficence was referenced mainly in relation to the deployment of AI in business contexts. At the organizational level, challenges have been identified regarding algorithmic bias and safety, particularly in conjunction with data privacy concerns (Shankar, 2024), including the use of biometric data (De Keyser et al., 2021). Sahlo (2024) also raises concerns about brand safety and personalization in the era of generative AI (GenAI) transformation in marketing. Kulkarni et al. (2024) demonstrated that AI readiness in micro, small, and medium enterprises, and its impact on skill development, work conditions, environment, and safety, directly influences social sustainability and the social and ethical behavior of employees. Therefore, it is crucial for business entities to develop and adopt AI regulatory frameworks (McLaughlin, 2023), including the principle of beneficence (Kriebitz & Lütge, 2020). At the application user level, debates mainly focus on the relationship between customer safety perception and trust in system reliability. As AI applications become increasingly accessible, users tend to trust them for their convenience and usefulness, often overlooking critical issues such as safety, privacy, and ethics (Kafali et al., 2024). The safety concerns emerging from the rapid and large-scale deployment of this technology are highly relevant given the unpredictability of both consumer and chatbot responses (De Freitas et al., 2024). Discussions on the use of Gen AI in business education (Gerlich, 2024) are also framed in terms of safety. Elbanna and Armstrong (2024) highlight the advantages of integrating new generative AI technologies in education but also point to ChatGPT's limitations, including factual inaccuracies, the potential reinforcement of bias, lack of deep understanding, and safety concerns.

The findings presented in this chapter highlight the importance of axiological underpinnings in contemporary scholarly debates on AI ethics. Through deeper analysis of the patterns and trends that emerge in these discussions, it is possible to identify key axiological shifts taking place within academic discourse across disciplines.

Regarding the value of freedom, two main interpretations emerged in AI ethics debates within the medical, social, and economic sciences: negative freedom, understood as the absence of external coercion and the freedom to act, and positive freedom, defined as self-realization and the ability to live in alignment with one's authentic self. The latter interpretation proved dominant. It is worth noting that axiological justifications grounded in the idea of freedom frequently invoked another fundamental value – human dignity. In studies foundational to AI ethics (i.e., those proposing ethical principles as the basis for medical, economic, or broader social practice), dignity was often understood in the Kantian sense as an inherent quality of the human being. In contrast, in discussions on the implementation of ethical principles, Taylor's interpretation of dignity as a socially constructed concept prevailed.

As for justice, the analysis of interrelations within the debates across the three academic disciplines revealed a predominant understanding of justice as the proportional distribution of goods in an egalitarian framework (as exemplified by Rawls). This axiological positioning often carried with it a socially grounded understanding of beneficence. Ethical challenges in AI were, therefore, primarily discussed in terms of beneficence as a systemic obligation rather than an individual moral duty to care for others.

Among all the values referenced, the most prominent one across the analyzed debates was security. It served as the axiological backdrop for virtually all discussions concerning the collection, acquisition, processing, and use of data by AI in each of the identified subdomains of social practice explored in the medical, social, and economic sciences. Two overarching trends could be observed, each grounded in a distinct understanding of security: freedom from threats (mainly economic) and existential security. The latter, which includes concerns such as identity stability, sense of meaning, social belonging, and life predictability, emerged as a recurring axiological context in discussions conducted within the examined disciplines.

In conclusion, our research not only demonstrated the significance of incorporating cultural (axiological) conditions into scientific discourse on AI ethics but also identified dominant axiological "shifts" taking place within ongoing debates. The limitations of our study – namely the selected value areas, the focus on only three disciplines, the time frame, the use of a single database (Scopus), and the chosen model of literature review – also mark directions for future research. Studies on the axiological foundations of academic discourse on AI ethics could be further expanded through qualitative research, such as interviews with representatives of specific disciplines. Such an approach would allow for a reconstruction of scholars' underlying beliefs regarding ethics and ethical practices in the context of AI.

Reference List

Adarkwah, M. A. (2024). *GenAI-ALE: A framework for generative AI in adult learning ecology*. Adult Learning. https://doi.org/10.1177/10451595241271161

Ahmad, M. (2020). Algorithmic humanitarianism: Data, dignity, and the refugee crisis. *Information, Communication & Society*, *23*(4), 538–554. https://doi.org/10.1080/1369118X.2018.1477967

Ashraf, M. A., & Islam, M. R. (2023). AI and the future of human rights in Bangladesh: A call for robust legal and ethical frameworks. *International Journal of Law and Information Technology*, *31*(4), 331–348. https://doi.org/10.1093/ijlit/eaae002

Baker, B., Mills, K. A., McDonald, P., & Wang, L. (2023). AI, Concepts of intelligence, and Chatbots: The "figure of man," the rise of emotion, and future visions of education. *Teachers College Record*, *125*(6), 60–84. https://doi.org/10.1177/01614681231191291

Bauer, W. A., & Dubljević, V. (2020). AI assistants and the paradox of internal automaticity. *Neuroethics*, *13*(3), 303–310. https://doi.org/10.1007/s12152-019-09423-6

Burris, S., & Leander, K. M. (2024). Critical posthumanist literacy: Building theory for reading, writing, and living ethically with everyday artificial intelligence. *Reading Research Quarterly*, *59*(4), 560–569. https://doi.org/10.1002/rrq.565

Cave, S., Whittlestone, J., Nyrup, R., Heigeartaigh, S. O., & Calvo, R. A. (2021). Using AI ethically to tackle covid-19. *The BMJ*, 37215. https://doi.org/10.1136/bmj.n364

Chavan, S., Sahiti, V., Gurpur, S., & Shelke, A. (2025). Critical insights into the impact of artificial intelligence on mental health, patient rights, and human rights. *Australasian Accounting, Business and Finance Journal*, *19*(1), 244–261. https://doi.org/10.14453/aabfj.v19i1.13.

Coeckelbergh, M. (2025). LLMs, truth, and democracy: An overview of risks. *Science and Engineering Ethics*, *31*(1). https://doi.org/10.1007/s11948-025-00529-0

Coghlan, S., Gyngell, Ch., & Vears, D. F. (2024). Ethics of artificial intelligence in prenatal and pediatric genomic medicine. *Journal of Community Genetics*, *15*(1), 13–24. https://doi.org/10.1007/s12687-023-00678-4

De Freitas, J., Uğuralp, A. K., Oğuz-Uğuralp, Z., & Puntoni, S. (2024). Chatbots and mental health: Insights into the safety of generative AI. *Journal of Consumer Psychology*, *34*(3), 481–491. https://doi.org/10.1002/jcpy.1393

De Keyser, A., Bart, A., Gu, X., Liu, S. Q., Robinson, S. G., & Kannan, P. K. (2021). Opportunities and challenges of using biometrics for business: Developing a research agenda. *Journal of Business Research*, *136*, 52–62. https://doi.org/10.1016/j.jbusres.2021.07.028

Dencik, L., & Sanchez-Monedero, J. (2022). Data justice. *Internet Policy Review*, *11*(1), 1–16. https://doi.org/10.14763/2022.1.1615

Elbanna, S., & Armstrong, L. (2024). Exploring the integration of ChatGPT in education: Adapting for the future. *Management and Sustainability*, *3*(1), 16–29. https://doi.org/10.1108/MSAR-03–2023–0016

Felber, N.A, Pageau, F., McLean, A., & Wangmo, T. (2022). The concept of social dignity as a yardstick to delimit ethical use of robotic assistance in the care of older persons. *Medicine, Health Care and Philosophy*, *25*(1), 99–110. https://doi.org/10.1007/s11019–021–10054-z

Fioravante, M., & Vaccaro, A. (2024, in press). Personalism in generative AI deployment: Deciding ethically when human creative expression is at stake. *Humanistic Management Journal*. https://doi.org/10.1007/s41463-024-00193-9.

Gerlich, M. (2024). The use of artificial intelligence in modern business education: The impact on students' cognitive and communication skills in the United Kingdom. *IEEE Engineering Management Review*, 1–10. https://doi.org/10.1109/EMR.2024.3441468

Grant, M. J., & Booth, A. (2009). A typology of reviews: An analysis of 14 review types and associated methodologies. *Health Information and Libraries Journal*, *26*, 91–108. https://doi.org/10.1002/wps.21230

Hermann, L., Williams, G. Y., & Puntoni, S. (2024). Deploying artificial intelligence in services to AID vulnerable consumers. *Journal of the Academy of Marketing Science*, *52*(5), 1431–1451. https://doi.org/10.1007/s11747-023-00986-8

Hertz, N. (2023). Neurorights – Do we need new human rights? A reconsideration of the right to freedom of thought. *Neuroethics*, *16*(1). https://doi.org/10.1007/s12152-022-09511-0

Hu, W., & Zhao, S. (2021). Study of employee behaviour based on artificial intelligence linguistic and speech analysis. *International Journal of Technology Management*, *86*(2–4), 183–195. https://doi.org/10.1504/IJTM.2021.118318

Jecker, N. S., Sparrow, R., Lederman, Z., & Ho, A. (2024). Digital humans to combat loneliness and social isolation: Ethics Concerns and policy recommendations. *Hastings Center Report*, *54*(1), 7–12. https://doi.org/10.1002/hast.1562

Kafali, E., Preuveneers, D., Semertzidis, T., & Daras, P. (2024). Defending against AI threats with a user-centric trustworthiness assessment framework. *Big Data and Cognitive Computing*, *8*(11). https://doi.org/10.3390/bdcc8110142

Kamalov, F., Santandreu Calonge, D., & Gurrib, I. (2023). New era of artificial intelligence in education: Towards a sustainable multifaceted revolution. *Sustainability*, *15*(16), 12451. https://doi.org/10.3390/su151612451

Katirai, A. (2024). The environmental costs of artificial intelligence for healthcare. *Asian Bioethics Review*, *16*(3), 527–538. https://doi.org/10.1007/s41649-024-00295-4

Kellmeyer, Ph. (2021). Big brain data: On the responsible use of brain data from clinical and consumer-directed neurotechnological Devices. *Neuroethics*, *14*(1), 83–98. https://doi.org/10.1007/s12152-018-9371-x

Kerasidou, A. (2021). Ethics of artificial intelligence in global health: Explainability, algorithmic bias and trust. *Journal of Oral Biology and Craniofacial Research*, *11*(4), 612–614. https://doi.org/10.1016/j.jobcr.2021.09.004

Klarin, A., Ali Abadi, H., & Sharmelly, R. (2024). Professionalism in artificial intelligence: The link between technology and ethics. *Systems Research and Behavioral*, *41*(4), 557–580. https://doi.org/10.1002/sres.2994.

Kneer, M., & Christen, M. (2024). responsibility gaps and retributive dispositions: Evidence from the US, Japan and Germany. *Science and Engineering Ethics*, *30*(6). https://doi.org/10.1007/s11948–024–00509-w

Kreutzer, T., Orbinski, J., Appel, L., An, A., Marston, J., Boone, E., & Vinck, P. (2025). Ethical implications related to processing of personal data and artificial intelligence in humanitarian crises: A scoping review. *BMC Medical Ethics*, *26*(1). https://doi.org/10.1186/s12910-025-01189-2

Kriebitz, A., & Lütge, Ch. (2020). Artificial intelligence and human rights: A business ethical assessment. *Business and Human Rights Journal*, *5*(1), 84–104. https://doi.org/10.1017/bhj.2019.28

Kulkarni, A. V., Joseph, S., & Patil, K. P. (2024). Artificial intelligence technology readiness for social sustainability and business ethics: Evidence from MSMEs in developing nations. *International Journal of Information Management Data Insights*, *4*(2). https://doi.org/10.1016/j.jjimei.2024.100250

Lazaridis, Ch. (2025). Palliative general anesthesia at terminal extubation: "Go gentle into that good night". *Neurocritical Care*. https://doi.org/10.1007/s12028–025–02228-x

Lindemann, N. (2022). The ethics of 'deathbots'. *Science and Engineering Ethics*, *28*(6). https://doi.org/10.1007/s11948-022-00417-x

Malgieri, G., & Niklas, J. (2020). Vulnerable data subjects. *Computer Law & Security Review*, *36*, 105377. https://doi.org/10.1016/j.clsr.2019.105377

Marshall, R., Pardo, A., Smith, D., & Watson, T. (2022). Implementing next generation privacy and ethics research in education technology. *British Journal of Educational Technology*, *53*(4), 737–755. https://doi.org/10.1111/bjet.13224
McLaughlin, M. (2023). Regulating artificial intelligence in international investment law. *Journal of World Investment and Trade*, *24*(2), 256–300. https://doi.org/10.1163/22119000-12340288
Murdoch, B., Jandura, A., & Caulfield, T. (2022). Privacy considerations in the Canadian regulation of commercially-operated healthcare artificial intelligence. *Canadian Journal of Bioethics*, *5*(4), 44–52. https://doi.org/10.7202/1094696ar
Natorski, M. (2024). Compromise in multilateral negotiations and the global regulation of artificial intelligence. *Democratization*, *31*(5), 1091–1116. https://doi.org/10.1080/13510347.2024.2351583
Picasso, F., Atenas, J., Havemann, L., & Serbati, A. (2024). Advancing critical data and AI literacies through authentic and real-world assessment design using a data justice approach. *Open Praxis*, *16*(3), 291–310. https://doi.org/10.55982/openpraxis.16.3.667
Sahlool, N. (2024). Navigating the artificial intelligence frontier: Strategic imperatives for safeguarding brand integrity. *Journal of Brand Strategy*, *13*(2), 123–130. https://doi.org/10.69554/UUXA3701
Saura, J. R., Škare, V., & Dosen, D. O. (2024). Is AI-based digital marketing ethical? Assessing a new data privacy paradox. *Journal of Innovation and Knowledge*, *9*(4), 100597. https://doi.org/10.1016/j.jik.2024.100597
Shankar, V. (2024). Managing the twin faces of AI: A commentary on "Is AI changing the world for better or worse?" *Journal of Macromarketing*, *44*(4), 892–899. https://doi.org/10.1177/02761467241286483
Sison, A. J. G. (2024). Can digitally transformed work be virtuous? *Business Ethics Quarterly*, *34*(1), 163–191. https://doi.org/10.1017/beq.2023.33
Staunton, C., Biasotto, R., Tschigg, K., & Mascalzoni, D. (2024). Artificial intelligence needs data: Challenges accessing italian databases to train AI. *Asian Bioethics Review*, *16*(3), 423–435. https://doi.org/10.1007/s41649-024-00282-9
Teo, S. (2022). How artificial intelligence systems challenge the conceptual foundations of the human rights legal framework. *Nordic Journal of Human Rights*, *40*(1), 216–234. https://doi.org/10.1080/18918131.2022.2073078
Teo, S. (2024). How to think about freedom of thought (and opinion) in the age of AI. *Computer Law and Security Review*, 53. https://doi.org/10.1016/j.clsr.2024.105969
Tortora, L. (2024). Beyond discrimination: Generative AI applications and ethical challenges in forensic psychiatry. *Frontiers in Psychiatry*, 152024. https://doi.org/10.3389/fpsyt.2024.1346059
Vilaza, G. N., & MaCashin, D. (2021). Is the automation of digital mental health ethical? Applying an ethical framework to chatbots for cognitive behaviour Therapy. *Frontiers in Digital Health*, 36. https://doi.org/10.3389/fdgth.2021.689736
Wang, Ch., Zhang, J., Lassi, N., & Zhang, X. (2022). Privacy protection in using artificial intelligence for healthcare: Chinese regulation in comparative perspective. *Healthcare (Switzerland)*, *10*(10). https://doi.org/10.3390/healthcare10101878
Westerstrand, S. (2024). Reconstructing AI ethics principles: Rawlsian ethics of artificial intelligence. *Science and Engineering Ethics*, *30*(5). https://doi.org/10.1007/s11948-024-00507-y
Yang, Y., & Lee, K. (2024). Ethical AI in financial inclusion: The role of algorithmic fairness on user satisfaction and recommendation. *Big Data and Cognitive Computing*, *8*(9). https://doi.org/10.3390/bdcc8090105
Zhui, L., Fenghe, L., Xuehu, W., Qining, F., & Wei, R. (2024). Ethical considerations and fundamental principles of large language models in medical education: Viewpoint. *Journal of Medical Internet Research*, *26*. https://doi.org/10.2196/60083

23 Empowering Adults in AI

A Framework for Enhancing Critical Skills

Tibor Vörös, Anna Wach, and Joanna Furmańczyk

Introduction: Why AI Literacy Matters for Adult Learners

In an era increasingly driven by artificial intelligence (AI), digital literacy is no longer a specialized skill – it has become a core competency. AI technologies are now embedded in everyday tools, ranging from workplace platforms to financial services and customer support applications. The ability to critically engage with AI – understanding how it works, where it can be applied, and what limitations it may have – has become essential not only for IT professionals but also for a wider audience (Holmes et al., 2019; Long & Magerko, 2020).

However, many adult learners – especially those with no background in information technology – remain uncertain about how AI works or how to evaluate its outputs. This knowledge gap is a major barrier not only to digital participation but also to responsible decision-making in AI-mediated environments (Zweig, 2022). Traditional education models, which often emphasize technical depth or theoretical abstraction, may fail to meet the learning needs of adults who require practical, relevant, and immediately applicable insights (Knowles et al., 2014).

This chapter presents arguments in favor of a different approach to AI education for adult learners: one rooted in experiential learning and oriented toward the development of critical skills. These include not just technical understanding but also critical thinking, adaptability, ethical reasoning, and communication. Such skills are essential for navigating complex and rapidly changing environments shaped by AI (Vuorikari et al., 2022). For business students and professionals, understanding how AI works, what its capabilities are, and how it might affect their field is becoming a core component of future-ready education.

The approach is especially relevant for business schools and professional training environments, where the goal is to empower diverse professionals with the skills to use AI critically and responsibly in their respective domains. As AI becomes a foundational element in decision-making, operations, and strategy, informed and reflective engagement becomes a core competency (Luckin & Holmes, 2016).

DOI: 10.4324/9781003659143-29

By focusing on experiential methods and critical competencies, this chapter contributes to the emerging field of AI literacy and offers practical guidance for educators designing inclusive and effective AI learning experiences for adult non-technical audiences.

AI and Education: Opportunities and Gaps

AI is increasingly being used to enhance teaching and learning processes. Intelligent tutoring systems, personalized learning platforms, and automated feedback tools allow educators to deliver differentiated instructions (Luckin & Holmes, 2016). AI-driven platforms can track learner performance in real time, adapt content dynamically, and support assessment through analytics. Tools like GPT-based writing assistants or image classifiers further extend the classroom by providing learners with instant feedback, additional resources, and cognitive support (Holmes et al., 2019). AI also plays a critical role in educational management, supporting educational institutions in making data-driven decisions (Zawacki-Richter et al., 2019).

While AI as a tool supports traditional teaching, AI as a subject of learning has become equally important. A growing number of programs now introduce AI-related topics for students from a variety of disciplines. The list includes introductory courses on machine learning concepts and extends to ethics modules that examine algorithmic bias and decision-making (Zweig, 2022).

However, most AI curricula are still geared toward learners with technical backgrounds. The content often assumes familiarity with programming, data structures, or statistical modeling. As a result, adult learners without such foundations may find AI education intimidating, inaccessible, or too abstract to be meaningful (Long & Magerko, 2020). This issue is especially acute in professional fields – such as business, healthcare, or public administration – where AI is already being deployed but the majority of workers are non-technical users.

The challenge lies not just in curriculum content but also in pedagogy. Traditional AI education often prioritizes conceptual mastery and coding proficiency over experiential learning and critical reflection. However, adult learners typically value relevance, real-world application, and self-direction (Knowles et al., 2014). They seek learning experiences that help them understand the workings of AI without necessarily building the technology themselves. Moreover, non-specialists need guidance on how to question AI systems and integrate them into their professional practice in a thoughtful manner (Vuorikari et al., 2022).

There is also a gap in addressing transversal competencies, which are not AI-specific skills, but are vital for using AI wisely. These include:

- Critical thinking: evaluating algorithmic outputs and questioning their reliability.

- Ethical reasoning: considering bias, accountability, and social impact.
- Communication: explaining AI-informed decisions and interacting with stakeholders.
- Adaptability: navigating AI-driven changes in roles, workflows, and expectations.

Despite their central importance, these skills are rarely integrated into technical AI curricula, leaving adult learners with limited preparation to engage with AI meaningfully (OECD, 2021).

To close these gaps, educational institutions should adopt AI teaching models that empower rather than exclude non-technical adult learners. This means shifting the focus from technical mastery to critical AI literacy. The focus is on understanding how AI works, where it can be applied, and what implications it brings. It also means using pedagogies of experience that allow learners to experiment, reflect, and apply their knowledge of AI in authentic contexts.

Experiential Learning and Competency Development

Despite technological advancements and a growing body of research on adult learning, contemporary education still frequently relies on a transmission-based model of teaching. However, a content-centered approach should be replaced by a student-centered one, allowing learners to engage with real-world problems, immerse themselves in meaningful learning activities, and actively explore their learning environments. A major shift from a teaching-focused to a learning-centered paradigm has been advocated for over three decades (Barr & Tagg, 1995).

Furthermore, as early as the 1980s, Knowles articulated the core principles of adult learning that continue to hold significant relevance in contemporary educational practice. These principles include: (1) the drive to satisfy cognitive curiosity; (2) the value of learners' prior knowledge and life experience; (3) readiness to learn and the centrality of intrinsic motivation; (4) a problem-centered approach to learning; and (5) the capacity for self-directed learning (Knowles et al., 2014).

Contemporary educational theories are largely grounded in cognitive psychology, which highlights the importance of active engagement in the construction and reconstruction of individual knowledge structures (Illeris, 2004). These frameworks include experiential learning theory (Kolb & Kolb, 2022), problem-based learning (Barrows & Tamblyn, 1980), action learning, and the concept of the reflective practitioner (Schön, 1987). They promote students' active involvement in the learning process through cognitive, emotional, and behavioral engagement, fostering deeper understanding and the development of meaningful knowledge.

When designing such learning experiences, it is worth drawing on the principles of constructivism (Efgivia et al., 2021), which emphasize learning through experience, social interaction, reflection-in-action and reflection-on-action, as well as the practical application of knowledge. Constructivist class design and delivery promote not only the development of holistic and enduring knowledge but also the enhancement of higher-order cognitive competencies. Problem-oriented learning environments provide students with opportunities not merely to memorize information, but to critically and reflectively engage with it – through processes such as argumentation, identifying patterns and relationships, participating in discussions, explaining concepts, and applying knowledge in practical contexts (Biggs & Tang, 2007). Constructivist education also emphasizes the importance of collaboration and peer learning (Crouch & Mazur, 2001), which support the development of social competencies. In today's context, both cognitive and social competencies are widely recognized as transversal skills – versatile abilities that are and will remain crucial for individuals navigating an increasingly dynamic and unpredictable labor market, regardless of their professional domain (Mishra et al., 2025).

In a world increasingly shaped by AI, non-technical professionals are expected to make informed, ethical, and context-aware decisions in AI-mediated environments. There are different models that define core future competencies. DigComp 2.2 framework emphasizes essential digital skills for citizens, including information and data literacy, communication, and problem-solving, which are crucial for interacting with AI technologies (Haase, 2024). The 4Cs competency model is a concept that identifies four key competencies necessary for effective functioning in the 21st century. These include critical thinking, creativity, communication, and cooperation (Lamri, 2019). OECD (2021) suggests integration of transversal competencies such as critical thinking, ethical reasoning, communication, and adaptability into learning curricula. These core competencies are no longer optional – they are essential for inclusive digital participation and the responsible use of AI. Traditional lecture-based approaches often fall short in cultivating these complex skills, particularly for adult learners who require practical relevance and active engagement. ***Experiential learning*** has emerged as a robust pedagogical model that can foster these competencies by encouraging reflection, collaboration, and ethical deliberation.

Critical thinking is indispensable in evaluating information, particularly as AI-generated outputs become increasingly prevalent. Learners must be equipped to analyze and question AI decisions critically in order to discern the relevance and reliability of AI applications. This enables learners to review data sources, question AI outputs, and recognize algorithmic bias. Experiential learning shifts learners from passive recipients of information to active participants in the process of meaning-making. Research findings (Spector & Ma, 2019) indicate that integrating critical thinking into the educational framework supports learners in effectively interacting with AI technologies. Moreover, research also suggests that critical thinking skills can be significantly improved through structured educational practices that promote active engagement with content. An experiential approach, using methods such as simulations and workshops, encourages self-reflection and enables learners to revise prior beliefs and build stronger critical faculties. Chaparro-Banegas et al. (2024) demonstrated that such methods measurably improved critical thinking scores among students engaging with AI-related workshops and seminars.

Incorporating AI into educational practices necessitates effective communication and collaboration skills. As AI technologies reshape the landscape of teamwork, the ability to articulate insights about AI processes and outcomes is critical to successful collaboration. Communication skills are often strengthened through interactive learning environments where students share their findings, debate methodologies, and collaborate on projects (Wang et al., 2024). Student-centered learning naturally involves communication through group projects and real-time problem-solving. In such settings, learners must translate AI concepts to others, justify their decisions, and collaborate on ethical dilemmas or design tasks. A study by Matei and Bertino (2023) demonstrated a direct link between AI preparedness in the workforce and non-technical skills such as communication and critical thinking.

The integration of AI into society raises significant ethical considerations, which is why ethical reasoning is essential. Learners must critically assess the consequences of using AI, recognizing issues such as data privacy and algorithmic bias. Noor et al. (2020) emphasize that experiential learning can help develop a sense of ethical awareness by immersing learners in contextual ethical dilemmas related to AI (Stamer et al., 2023). Engaging in case studies that explore the societal impacts of AI technology fosters discussions on moral responsibility and ethical considerations, preparing learners to navigate these complex issues effectively. Ethical reasoning prepares students to assess both the immediate and long-term consequences of AI applications, enabling them to advocate for the responsible use of AI in various domains. Research findings (Zhang et al., 2022) indicate that ethical AI education increases awareness of bias, privacy, and societal impact, which are of paramount importance as AI systems evolve. Experiential learning can bridge this gap by engaging learners in discussions focused on ethical case studies involving AI, such as bias in algorithms or privacy concerns related to data use. By examining real-world dilemmas, learners can develop ethical reasoning skills that highlight the social responsibilities associated with technology (Pandit et al., 2024).

In an era where technological advances are rapidly drivingshifts in industry standards and operations, adaptability is crucial for professionals. The capacity to adjust to new information, tools, and challenges is essential for success in AI-driven environments. Incorporating adaptability training into educational curricula fosters resilience among learners (Hendry et al., 2016). This adaptability is further enhanced through experiential learning programs, which allow individuals to navigate real-world scenarios requiring quick thinking and flexible responses (Murray, 2018). Furthermore, adaptability involves ethical considerations regarding the impact of decisions made using AI technologies. It is therefore essential to develop adaptability skills alongside a strong ethical framework.

As AI reshapes industries and everyday life, non-technical learners must acquire not just technical exposure, but also critical, ethical, and adaptive capacities. Experiential learning stands out as an effective strategy to build these core competencies. By emphasizing active participation, real-world relevance, and reflective inquiry, it empowers learners to think critically, communicate clearly, reason ethically, and adapt confidently to technological change.

Case Study: Experiential AI Learning in Practice

To bridge the gap between AI technologies and adult learners with no technical background, we implemented a series of experiential learning activities as part of a postgraduate training program. The goal was to develop critical thinking, adaptability, ethical reasoning, and communication skills. The participants were professionals from a variety of fields. Most of them had no prior training in computer science, but all were increasingly exposed to AI systems in their professional environments.

The design of the learning sequence followed Kolb's (1984) experiential learning cycle: concrete experience, reflective observation, abstract conceptualization, and active experimentation. The activities progressed in complexity, starting with intuitive interactions and culminating in critical debates and application. This case study outlines the exercises used, the learning goals, participant feedback, and reflections on skill development.

Image Recognition with Teachable Machine: Demystifying AI Capabilities

Activity

Participants began by creating a basic image classification model using Google's Teachable Machine. The goal was to simulate an AI-based car assistant capable of recognizing different vehicle types: ambulances, buses, trucks, and vans. Learners were provided with a pre-organized training image set and test images. Participants were instructed to:

- Form groups and work in groups.
- Create and label four categories in the platform (ambulance, bus, truck, van).
- Upload training images and train the machine learning model using Teachable Machine interface.
- Test the model by uploading individual test images and observing the predictions.

- Save the model outputs in a spreadsheet that automatically calculated standard classification metrics (accuracy, precision, recall, F1 scores – macro, micro, and weighted).

In the final step, learners presented their results, including:

- Confusion matrices for model performance.
- Examples of well- and poorly classified images.
- Problematic test items and potential reasons for misclassification.
- Attempts to fool the model by introducing unusual objects, altered backgrounds, or ambiguous images.
- Reflections on where such a system might be used in their workplace or everyday life.

Learning Goals

- Introduce participants to core machine learning concepts: training, testing, classification, and model evaluation.
- Encourage curiosity and playfulness in a low-stakes environment.
- Reveal the gap between intuitive human reasoning and statistical model behavior.
- Lay the groundwork for critical reflection on algorithmic decision-making.

Results

This exercise was highly effective as a "concrete experience" in Kolb's (1984) experiential learning model. Most participants had never trained a machine learning model before and were surprised by both the ease of use and the variability in the model's performance. Some models performed reasonably well for ambulances and buses had difficulty distinguishing between vans and trucks, especially with varying lighting or angles.

Participants discovered how training image quality and diversity directly impacted classification accuracy. They were able to see how even a small data bias (e.g., overrepresentation of white ambulances) led to misclassification of red or blue vehicles. The use of confusion matrices helped introduce participants to the complexity of model evaluation, revealing that a high overall accuracy did not always mean reliable performance across all classes.

Attempts to "fool" the system with unexpected objects or internet images led to lively discussion about overfitting, default categories, and the brittleness of AI decision-making in real-world conditions. Learners began to appreciate the difference between human and machine perception, and how AI systems depend on curated data rather than contextual understanding (Holmes et al., 2019; Zweig, 2022).

Several participants connected the experience to their own professional domains, identifying both potential uses and ethical concerns. Others questioned whether such models should be deployed without robust oversight and real-world validation, foreshadowing later activities.

Ethical Profiling: Understanding Bias and Perspective in Generative AI

Activity

In this exercise, participants explored how generative AI (e.g., ChatGPT) constructs narratives based on prompts and data framing. Learners were asked to select a real, internationally known figure with a controversial background – such as a politician, corporate leader, or celebrity philanthropist. Using AI, they generated two contrasting 300-word profiles of this individual:

- A *positive profile* written from the perspective of a public relations firm, highlighting accomplishments.
- A *critical profile* written from the viewpoint of an international watchdog organization, focusing on controversies, legal disputes, or unethical behavior.

Next, learners repeated the task using themselves as the subject, again generating a flattering and a critical profile. Finally, they wrote a short essay reflecting on the differences between the AI-generated profiles, the sources used, and the implications for bias, reliability, and ethical use of AI in professional and institutional settings.

Learning Goals

- Develop ethical reasoning by examining how language, framing, and source availability shape AI outputs.
- Enhance digital literacy by uncovering how generative models synthesize and amplify certain narratives.
- Promote reflective observation through comparison of third-party and self-generated content.
- Encourage personal accountability and sensitivity in using AI for profiling, communication, and decision-making.

Outcomes

Participants quickly realized how differently an AI system could present the same person depending on the prompt. The positive memos emphasized awards, publications, and philanthropy, while the critical versions drew on scandals, lawsuits, and international criticisms. Many learners noted the lack of source citations in AI outputs and how this undermined transparency and trust.

Comparing personal profiles generated similar insights. Some participants were surprised to see how minimal or outdated information surfaced about themselves, while others encountered inaccurate narratives. These findings prompted a rich discussion about AI's role in reputation management, media framing, and potential misuse in professional settings.

The exercise culminated in a class discussion about whether the fictional university should accept the donor, revealing diverse perspectives on ethical thresholds, reputational risk, and due diligence. Several learners suggested hybrid governance approaches – for example, combining AI research tools with manual vetting – to avoid both over-reliance and under-utilization.

This activity built strong connections to the ethical dimension of AI literacy and reinforced that adult learners, even without technical expertise, are capable of interrogating powerful technologies critically and responsibly (Holmes et al., 2019).

AI as a Business Assistant: Communicating Churn Insights to Decision Makers

Activity

In this task, participants explored the practical use of ChatGPT as an AI assistant in interpreting technical research and producing a persuasive business presentation. The group was given a technical research paper titled "Entropy-Based Trees to Support Decision Making for Customer Churn Management" (Gajowniczek et al., 2016). The paper describes the use of various machine learning tools (decision trees, neural networks, support vector machines, and logistic regression) to predict customer churn in the telecom industry. It is a typical content-heavy research paper, with references, technical details and engineering knowledge.

Participants were asked to:

- Use ChatGPT to summarize the main findings of the paper in non-technical terms.
- Develop a 10–15 minute mock board presentation to persuade a mobile telecom company's leadership to adopt a predictive churn model.
- Include a brief explanation of churn prediction, and their business implications (retention targeting, ROI).
- Use ChatGPT to simulate a comparison between Polish data presented in the study and assumed data trends in the Hungarian telecom sector.
- Critically reflect on the usefulness and limitations of ChatGPT as a business assistant in this process.

Learning Goals

- Apply AI in synthesizing technical insights into strategic communication.
- Develop data-informed decision-making skills relevant to real-world business problems.

- Build AI fluency by using generative tools to support, rather than replace, human judgment.
- Reflect on the ethical and practical limits of using AI in high-stakes business contexts.

Outcomes

Participants produced executive-style board presentations that emphasized churn reduction as a strategic lever for profitability. They translated technical evaluation metrics such as lift (e.g. identifying high-risk customers 3.6 times more effectively than random selection) and AUC (as a measure of overall prediction quality) into business terms. The use of ChatGPT allowed groups to:

- Navigate jargon-heavy sections of the paper and extract meaningful insights.
- Compare churn behaviors and telecom practices across national contexts using assumed market data.
- Draft professional, persuasive business cases with clear ROI modeling based on retention interventions.

During the final debrief, participants discussed ChatGPT's strengths (fast content synthesis, accessible language, help with structuring arguments) and its limits (lack of source transparency, occasional overconfidence, superficial context adaptation). Some noted that while ChatGPT could simulate the work of a junior analyst or technical assistant, it still required human oversight for credibility and accuracy – especially in boardroom settings.

The exercise reinforced that generative AI is not a substitute for critical business judgment but a powerful tool to augment reasoning, accelerate preparation, and improve communication in data-driven contexts.

Conclusion and Recommendations

This chapter has explored how experiential learning approaches can empower adult learners without a technical background to develop critical skills in understanding and using artificial intelligence.

The case study demonstrated that even participants unfamiliar with computer science could grasp the implications of AI systems through carefully designed activities. From image classification tasks using Teachable Machine to interpreting churn prediction models with ChatGPT, learners moved beyond abstract knowledge to actionable insights. Each exercise progressively deepened their understanding of AI's functionality and its broader societal, organizational, and ethical impacts.

The findings from these interventions contribute to a broader discussion in education and workforce development: AI literacy must go beyond coding. As AI tools become embedded in decision-making across industries, there is an urgent need for educational models that equip professionals not to build

AI, but to question, interpret, and apply it meaningfully. This is particularly true in adult learning contexts, where participants must be prepared to work in environments shaped by its influence. Some practical recommendations for educators and institutions are presented in Table 23.1.

By integrating hands-on, reflective, and socially contextualized tasks, the proposed framework supports the development of key competencies such as critical thinking, ethical reasoning, adaptability, and communication. These are essential not only for interpreting AI outputs but for engaging responsibly in increasingly AI-mediated professional environments.

This framework serves as a practical foundation, but more empirical research is needed to evaluate long-term impacts on professional behavior, decision-making, and organizational AI adoption. Cross-sectoral collaboration will be essential to iteratively refine AI literacy programs. Future work should also explore how experiential AI learning can be scaled for diverse learners in online, hybrid, and lifelong learning contexts.

In sum, AI literacy for non-technical adult learners is essential. When grounded in experiential learning and framed around real-world use, AI education can equip professionals to think critically, act ethically, and lead confidently in a daily life increasingly shaped by these systems.

Table 23.1 Practical recommendations for educators and institutions

Target/Approach	*How*
Start with Intuition, Not Abstraction	Use intuitive, low-barrier tools (e.g., Teachable Machine, ChatGPT) to engage learners early. These tools reduce the intimidation factor and provide immediate, relatable experiences with AI.
Align Tasks with Real-World Roles	Design activities that mirror learners' professional contexts – such as board presentations, stakeholder analysis, or ethical decision-making. This fosters relevance and transfer of learning.
Emphasize Reflection and Debate	Build in structured moments for critical reflection and peer discussion. Encourage learners to compare AI performance, evaluate limitations, and reflect on trust, transparency, and accountability.
Use AI as a Teaching Partner	Allow learners to experiment with generative AI tools during their tasks but embed structured debriefs to examine bias, accuracy, and over-reliance. Position AI as an assistant – not an oracle.

(*Continued*)

Table 23.1 (Continued)

Target/Approach	*How*
Integrate Transversal Skills	Ensure that digital competence frameworks (e.g., DigComp 2.2) and professional soft skills are embedded in the curriculum alongside AI-specific knowledge. These include ethical reasoning, critical communication, and adaptability in the face of uncertainty.
Ethical and Pedagogical Considerations	Educators should model responsible AI use. This includes making transparent the limitations of generative models, emphasizing data ethics, and resisting deterministic narratives that overstate AI's capabilities. Careful facilitation is needed to ensure learners do not develop misplaced trust in AI systems or treat outputs as neutral. Adult learners, particularly in leadership or decision-making roles, must leave the classroom not only more confident, but more discerning.

Source: Authors' own work.

Reference List

Barr, R. B., & Tagg, J. (1995). From teaching to learning: A new paradigm for undergraduate education. *Change: The Magazine of Higher Learning*, *27*(6), 12–26. https://doi.org/10.1080/00091383.1995.10544672

Barrows, H. S., & Tamblyn, R. M. (1980). *Problem-based learning: An approach to medical education*. Springer Publishing Company.

Biggs, J., & Tang, C. (2007). *Teaching for quality learning at university*. McGraw Hill, Society for Research into Higher Education & Open University Press.

Chaparro-Banegas, N., Mas-Tur, A., & Roig-Tierno, N. (2024). Challenging critical thinking in education: New paradigms of artificial intelligence. *Cogent Education*, *11*(1). https://doi.org/10.1080/2331186x.2024.2437899

Crouch, C. H., & Mazur, E. (2001). Peer Instruction: Ten years of experience and results. *American Journal of Physics*, *69*(9), 970–977. https://doi.org/10.1119/1.1374249

Efgivia, M. G., Adora Rinanda, R. Y., Suriyani, Hidayat, A., Maulana, I., & Budiarjo, A. (2021). *Analysis of constructivism learning theory:* 1st UMGESHIC International Seminar on Health, Social Science and Humanities (UMGESHIC-ISHSSH 2020), Gresik, Indonesia. https://doi.org/10.2991/assehr.k.211020.032

Gajowniczek, K., Orłowski, A., & Ząbkowski, T. (2016). Entropy based trees to support decision making for customer churn management. *Acta Physica Polonica A*, *129*, 971–979. https://doi.org/10.12693/APhysPolA.129.971

Haase, S. (2024). Future skills and (generative) AI – New era, new competencies? *The Human Side of Service Engineering*, *143*, 178–184. https://doi.org/10.54941/ahfe1005096

Hendry, G., Winn, P., Wiggins, S., & Turner, C. J. (2016). Qualitative evaluation of a practice-based experience pilot program for master of pharmacy students in Scotland. *American Journal of Pharmaceutical Education*, *80*(10), 165. https://doi.org/10.5688/ajpe8010165

Holmes, W., Bialik, M., & Fadel, C. (2019). *Artificial intelligence in education. Promise and implications for teaching and learning*. Independently published.

Illeris, K. (2004). *The three dimensions of learning*. Krieger Pub Co.

Knowles, M. S., Holton III, E. F., & Swanson, R. A. (2014). *The adult learner*. Routledge.

Kolb, D. A. (1984). *Experiential learning: Experience as the source of learning and development*. Englewood Cliffs, NJ: Prentice Hall. http://academic.regis.edu/ed205/Kolb.pdf

Kolb, A. Y., & Kolb, D. A. (2022). *Uczenie na podstawie doświadczania*. Dialogi i Zmysły.

Lamri, J. (2019). *21st century skills*. The Next Society Editions.

Long, D., & Magerko, B. (2020). What is AI literacy? Competencies and design considerations. In *CHI '20: Proceedings of the 2020 CHI conference on human factors in computing systems* (pp. 1–16). https://doi.org/10.1145/3313831.3376727

Luckin, R., & Holmes, W. (2016). *Intelligence unleashed: An argument for AI in education*. Open Ideas at Pearson.

Matei, S. A., & Bertino, E. (2023). Educating for AI cybersecurity work and research: Ethics. *Systems Thinking, and Communication Requirements*. https://doi.org/10.48550/arxiv.2311.04326 https://arxiv.org/abs/2311.04326

Mishra, C. E. B., Walters, D., Fraser, E. D. G., Gillis, D., & Jacobs, S. (2025). Higher education fields of study and the use of transferable skills at work: An analysis using data from the programme for the international assessment of adult competencies (PIAAC) in Canada. *Trends in Higher Education*, *4*(2), 19.

Murray, R. (2018). An overview of experiential learning in nursing education. *Advances in Social Sciences Research Journal*, *5*(1). https://doi.org/10.14738/assrj.51.4102

Noor, N. A. M., Ariffin, K., Darus, N. A., & Alias, A. (2020). The perceptions of students' experiential learning in relation to theoretical concept with real practice. *International Journal of Academic Research in Progressive Education and Development*, *9*(4). https://doi.org/10.6007/ijarped/v9-i4/8176

OECD. (2021). *AI and the future of skills, Volume 1*. OECD.

Pandit, S., Sarkar, S. K., Barik, S., & Sahu, S. K. (2024). AI in skill development, critical thinking, digital literacy, and AI-driven job preparation. In *Advances in educational technologies and instructional design book series* (pp. 23–76). https://doi.org/10.4018/979-8-3693-8191-5.ch002

Schön, D. A. (1987). *Educating the reflective practitioner: Toward a new design for teaching and learning in the professions*. Jossey-Bass.

Spector, J. M., & Ma, S. (2019). Inquiry and critical thinking skills for the next generation: From artificial intelligence back to human intelligence. *Smart Learning Environments*, *6*(1). https://doi.org/10.1186/s40561-019-0088-z

Stamer, T., Steinhäuser, J., & Flägel, K. (2023). Artificial intelligence supporting the training of communication skills in the education of health care professions: Scoping review. *Journal of Medical Internet Research*, *25*, e43311. https://doi.org/10.2196/43311

Vuorikari, R., Kluzer, S., & Punie, Y. (2022). *DigComp 2.2: The digital competence framework for citizens – With new examples of knowledge, skills and attitudes*. Publications Office of the European Union.

Wang, X., Huang, R., Sommer, M., Pei, B., Shidfar, P., Rehman, M. S., Ritzhaupt, A. D., & Martin, F. (2024). The efficacy of artificial intelligence-enabled adaptive learning systems from 2010 to 2022 on learner outcomes: A meta-analysis. *Journal of Educational Computing Research*, *62*(6), 1348–1383. https://doi.org/10.1177/07356331241240459

Zawacki-Richter, O., Marín, V. I., Bond, M., & Gouverneur, F. (2019). Systematic review of research on artificial intelligence applications in higher education – Where are the educators? *International Journal of Educational Technology in Higher Education*, *16*(1), 39. https://doi.org/10.1186/s41239-019-0171-0

Zhang, H., Lee, I., Ali, S., DiPaola, D., Cheng, Y., & Breazeal, C. (2022). Integrating ethics and career futures with technical learning to promote ai literacy for middle school students: An exploratory study. *International Journal of Artificial Intelligence in Education*, *33*(2), 290–324. https://doi.org/10.1007/s40593-022-00293-3

Zweig, K. (2022). *Awkward intelligence: Where AI goes wrong, why it matters, and what we can do about it.* MIT Press. https://doi.org/10.7551/mitpress/13915.001.0001

Index

Note: Page numbers in *italic* indicate a figure and page numbers in **bold** indicate a table on the corresponding page.